On Our Own Ground

On Our Own Ground

The Complete Writings

of William Apess,

a Pequot

Edited and with an Introduction

by Barry O'Connell

The University of Massachusetts Press

Amherst

A volume in the series:

Native Americans of the Northeast: Culture, History, and the Contemporary,

edited by Colin G. Calloway and Barry O'Connell

Frontispiece: Portrait of William Apess. Courtesy, American Antiquarian Society.

LC 91–27750

ISBN 0–87023–766–7 (cloth); 770–5 (paper)

Designed by Mary Mendell

Printed and bound by Thomson-Shore, Inc.

Library of Congress Cataloging-in-Publication Data

Apes, William, b. 1798.

[Works. 1992]

On our own ground : the complete writings of William Apess, a Pequot / edited and with an introduction by Barry O'Connell.

p. cm. — (Native Americans of the Northeast)

Includes bibliographical references (p.) and index.

ISBN 0–87023–766–7 (cloth : alk. paper). — ISBN 0–87023–770–5 (paper : alk. paper)

1. Indians of North America—New England. 2. Pequot Indians. 3. Indians, Treatment of—New England. 4. Apes, William, b. 1798. I. O'Connell, Barry, 1943– . II. Title. III. Series.

E78.N5A64 1992

974'.00497—dc20 91–27750 CIP

British Library Cataloguing in Publication data are available.

For Kristin,
who believed and gave
and loved so that this
might come into
being

Contents

Acknowledg-

ments

▲

Completion and celebration belong together. There are many people to be celebrated for all each has done to make this book a reality. In writing there are many hands: voices that feed the mind; good and mistaken books and articles without which one could not have learned; particular teachers and students who led one on. It has always seemed to me one of the strangest of contradictions to have but a single name on a title page for this, one of the most genuinely collaborative acts I know. So, imagine all the following, and those I do not know enough to name, crowding across the spaces in and around my own name. To them should belong whatever credit is due, and to me, conventionally and fairly, the responsibility for what falls short.

Books like this one especially depend upon libraries. But libraries are given life by those who everyday re-create them. I have had the happy privilege for this project of being able to work at the American Antiquarian Society, the kind of library scholars dream about. Without its collection, but more importantly without the constant generosity, knowledge, and interest of its staff, this book could not have been accomplished. As always, I am thankful to John Hench for his hospitality. Nancy Burkett, Associate Librarian, not only gave every assistance but treated the project almost as her own. Joanne Chaison, head of Readers' Services, taught me how to use the many resources of the collection and introduced me to scholars in the reading room who proved, at several key points, of indispensable assistance, most especially Michael Winship, who took time away from his own research to spend an afternoon leading me through the intricacies of nineteenth-century American book publishing. Georgia Barnhill, Curator of Graphic Arts, responded to my requests with grace and efficiency. The librarians at Robert Frost Library at Amherst College were the first to show me how much a scholar depends upon these, his true colleagues. With this, as with all my other projects over the last twenty years, I could not have done without the hours, the education, and the ideas so freely given to me. Michael Kasper and Leeta Bailey of the Reference Department deserve particular mention for their help this time around, but Margaret Adams Groesbeck is to blame for being the first to get me into the habit of believing that reference librarians can either answer every question or find the means to do so, a belief that has held up to tests of reality better than most.

I am grateful to Ronald C. Rosbottom, Dean of the Faculty at Amherst College, for coming through several times with modest grants, each of which funded student research assistants who contributed substantially to the book and without whom it would have taken months and years longer to complete. Each deserves credit by name: Stephanie Reents and I virtually began reading Apess together. For a year she combed every reference, census schedules, and any lead I provided to track Apess down. Libbie Rifkin took on the project for one summer and achieved a number of breakthroughs, the most tangible being Apess's enlistment record from the National Archives. At the very last stages Jo Park, Terri Webb, and Shawn Sullivan typed, proofread, and searched for references. I could not have gotten the book to press without them. And it was Shawn who discovered the full extent of Apess's indebtedness to Elias Boudinot's *A Star in the West*. Ben Steinberg carried out original research for me at the Connecticut State Library, double-checked census data, and continued the so far fruitless pursuit of Apess after 1837–38 and of his place and date of death—and, at the very last minute, voluntarily rescued me so that I could make a critical deadline. Michael Elliott read, typed, converted disks, and did the hard work of gathering the information for the footnotes to the *Eulogy on King Philip*. All of them, along with my students in English 62 with whom I first explored Apess, illustrate how much difference can be made by superb, independent, and interested students. Their presence at Amherst has been the most dependable of its several resources.

A semester as a Rockefeller Fellow at the Center for the Humanities at Wesleyan University provided the space, time, and collegiality to allow me finally to bring to fruition several projects while also helping me to generate many new ones, of which this is the first to be published. Richard Ohmann, Henry Abelove, Khachig Tololyan, and Karen Bock deserve special mention for the friendship they gave me and all they did to help me renew myself.

My own teachers have had to wait too long a time to be acknowledged. They have given me too much to be sufficiently characterized or thanked in this short space. Alan Heimert was my mentor. His passion, crankiness, brilliance, and his rejection of the "merely academic" enabled me to believe a fellow like me could find a place in the academy, despite many doubts about its purposes and practices. His example is before me every day. David Riesman began answering now countless requests from me when I was in graduate school. I doubt I have known another who enacts so finely the gifts of mind, of disinterest, and of collegiality that represent the most admirable ideals of a university. Robin Feild dedicated his life, his art, and his teaching to the possibility of a world in which justice and nonviolence would be the norms. For almost fifteen wonderful years I had the chance to be taught and inspired by him. It would require a long and prodigiously productive life as a teacher and a scholar to begin to return a portion of what these teachers have so amply and freely given me.

To my colleagues at Amherst in American Studies I am grateful for a number of years of promising and valuable collaborative efforts and for finally making me see that it was time to cast my voice elsewhere and in other media. In the English Department I have benefited from an always challenging group of colleagues. I want most to thank Kim Townsend and Jack Cameron for, each in his own way, supporting me and providing an example. Among my other colleagues at Amherst George Kateb has given me friendship, advice, intellectual provocation and criticism, and patiently believed in me, especially when I was unable to do so. David Wills has been so precious a friend, from that now long ago time when we arrived at Amherst nearly together, that I can only hope we will stay for the duration or have the good luck to share the next adventure, wherever it may take us.

I am grateful to my three readers, Kevin McBride, Arnold Krupat, and Neal Salisbury, for the time they devoted to my Introduction and their many attentive comments. And to Clark Dougan—could one ask for a better editor than a friend who is also demanding and witty, and likes one's prose?

Neal Salisbury has been a part of this project from its inception. Through him I learned much of what I can pretend to know about Native Americans in New England. And his quietly offering the hand of friendship and believing in me as a colleague rescued me from despair during a bad time. David Russell, dear friend and former student, loved me enough to refuse to accept my evasions. He, along with Jeff Titon, Laura Vogel, Olivia Dreier, and Kristin worked beautifully to teach me that I can realize in practice a substantial portion of what I imagine.

To all these, and to the most special people in my life, Kristin, Jamie, and Katharine, I owe more words and more than words can ever speak.

Introduction

Now let me ask you, white man, if it is a disgrace for to eat, drink,
and sleep with the image of God, or sit, or walk and talk with
them. Or have you the folly to think that the white man, being one in fifteen or sixteen, are the only
beloved images of God? Assemble all nations together in your imagination, and then let the whites
be seated among them. . . . Now suppose these skins were put together, and each skin had its
national crimes written upon it—which skin do you think would have the greatest? I will ask one
question more. Can you charge the Indians with robbing a nation almost of their whole continent,
and murdering their women and children, and then depriving the remainder of their lawful
rights, that nature and God require them to have? And to cap the climax, rob another nation to till
their grounds and welter out their days under the lash with hunger and fatigue. . . . I should look
at all the skins, and I know that when I cast my eye upon that white skin, and if I saw those crimes
written upon it, I should enter my protest against it immediately and cleave to that which is more
honorable.—William Apess, a Pequot, 1833

Nod!

This voice, and the consciousness of the nature of Euro-American racism it expresses, could have been heard in the 1960s or 1970s, possibly in the 1990s, but it would surprise many people, historians as well as lay people, to discover that it spoke in the first third of the nineteenth century and in New England.[1]

1. The only other and earlier text I know that expresses a comparable consciousness, Olaudah Equiano, *The Interesting Narrative of the Life* (London: By the author, 1789), could have come to Apess's attention since it was reprinted in the United States in 1829. Like Apess, Equiano uses direct address to interrogate the presumed white reader and to tax him or her with the hypocrisy of professing Christianity while cooperating in the subjugation of a people, and in its justification, because of the color of their skin. Equiano speaks only, however, to the treatment of enslaved Africans and African Americans. David Walker, *Appeal to the Coloured Citizens of the World* (1829; New York: Hill and Wang, 1965), might seem to offer a nearer analogue, but it does not read with the same immediacy as the Apess, nor is it, more importantly, addressed to whites. Its appeal is explicitly to African Americans, to the daughters and "sons of Africa," as a people who have suffered a form of subjugation different and worse than any other group in history. Apess, unlike either Equiano or Walker, does not separate one group from another. Native Americans, African

William Apess included his brief essay, "An Indian's Looking-Glass for the White Man," from which this quotation is taken, at the end of his collection of conversion narratives called *The Experiences of Five Christian Indians of the Pequot Tribe*, first published in 1833.[2] It was the third of his five books, all of which were published between 1829 and 1836, the short seven-year period in which he was a public figure. Historians know something about these years in Apess's life but almost nothing beyond what appears in *A Son of the Forest*, his autobiography, which was first published in 1829 (rev. ed., 1831), or in the short account of his life included in *The Experiences*. Because of his involvement in the Mashpee Revolt in 1833, he achieved sufficient, though brief, notoriety to receive notice in the New England press, although even here his skills as a writer and publicist were crucial to the moment and in the creation of the documents that have enabled interested historians to gain knowledge

---

Americans, and all other groups whites categorized as "nonwhite," including the Jewish people, are treated by Apess under the single rubric, people of color.

2. My spelling of Apess's name is unusual. Generally, when any notice has been paid him it has been with the spelling "Apes." The spelling of his name cannot itself be definitively given. I use "Apess" because the evidence is reasonably clear that this was his own preference. Although "Apes" is the spelling he used in both editions of *A Son of the Forest* (1829 and 1831), in the first edition of *The Experiences of Five Christian Indians* (1833), in *Indian Nullification of the Unconstitutional Laws of Massachusetts* (1835), and in the first edition of the *Eulogy on King Philip* (1836), the name is carefully and obviously deliberately changed in the second edition of the *Eulogy* (1837) and in the second edition of *The Experiences*, which itself has a slightly revised title: *Experience of Five Christian Indians* (1837). In *Experience* the change in spelling seems to have been important enough so that Apess corrected it not only on the new title page but in the copyright notice as well as throughout the text. These two publications represent, for now at least, Apess's last words. "Apess" appears as the spelling in another and intriguing context. A number of debt actions were brought against Apess in the last two years he was in Mashpee. In the first of these his name is entered in the plea as "Apess" (Barnstable Court of Common Pleas, April and September terms, 1836), as it also is in the second (Barnstable Court of Common Pleas, April term, 1837). In the last of these actions in 1838 the spelling is once again "Apes." He was, by this time, a well-known figure, and so the shifts in spelling appear deliberate. Does the spelling revert to "Apes" because he has changed his mind about it, because he couldn't correct it since he failed to appear in court for this action, or for some other reason? Why did he go to the trouble of changing the spelling to begin with? Speculation is all I have available. Perhaps it was to emphasize the Indianness of the name—or, simply, to make more difficult people's mispronouncing and being witty at the expense of "Apes," possibly an almost irresistible racial slur for Euro-Americans in their developing lexicon of anti-Indian and antiblack racism. Or he may have discovered, historian that he was of his own and his people's lives, that the second *s* had been lost in the translation from Pequot to English, from the oral to the written.

On another spelling matter: Either "Pequod" or "Pequot" is a correct spelling. Apess generally, though not always, uses "Pequod," but I have chosen to use "Pequot" throughout this edition. Contemporary members of the culture use "Pequot," as do virtually all scholars; see, for example, Laurence M. Hauptman and James D. Wherry, eds., *The Pequots in Southern New England: The Fall and Rise of an American Indian Nation* (Norman: University of Oklahoma Press, 1990).

of the event.[3] After 1836, when he delivered his *Eulogy on King Philip* twice in Boston, known records locate him only until 1838. After that, no trace has yet ✓ been found of his movements, of his life, or of his death.

Apess's militant consciousness is not only surprising in its modern ring but puzzling both to the common assumption that most Indians had disappeared from southern New England by the nineteenth century and to knowledgeable scholars who know something, though still much too little, about the scattered and impoverished New England Indians in this period. From what sources or experiences might Apess's consciousness have come, a consciousness which anticipates so strikingly pan-Indianism and the political sensibility signified in the 1980s and 1990s by the term "people of color"?

With the exception of the Mashpee Revolt, which Apess initiated and helped to lead, historians record no expressions of Indian rights or significant organizations, cultural, political, or otherwise, among Native Americans in New England in the nineteenth century. Are there records and events, inside histories of native communities in these years, continuities in oral traditions that historians have failed to uncover? Were these peoples following a familiar strategy among the oppressed, one many native cultures adopted in the face of encounters with Europeans and Euro-Americans, of withdrawal and silence so as to keep intact whatever could be hidden of their own existence and culture? Were they there and lost because, for the most part, historians did not bother to look? Or were the continuities, the keeping of stories and histories in the oral cultures of New England natives, broken sometime between the late eighteenth century and the first two decades of the twentieth, when Frank G. Speck did his important anthropological investigations of Native Americans in New England?[4]

3. William Apess, *Indian Nullification of the Unconstitutional Laws of Massachusetts Relative to the Marshpee Tribe; or, The Pretended Riot Explained* (Boston: Jonathan Howe, 1835). "Marshpee" was the common spelling in the first half of the nineteenth century, "Mashpee" the one used in the twentieth both by the town and by those Native Americans who designate themselves as "Mashpee." Discussion of the Mashpee Revolt can be found in several reasonably current accounts: Donald M. Nielsen, "The Mashpee Indian Revolt of 1833," *New England Quarterly* 58 (1985): 400–20, provides the basic historical account and is careful and reliable; see also Paul Brodeur, *Restitution: The Land Claims of the Mashpee, Passamaquoddy, and Penobscot Indians of New England* (Boston: Northeastern University Press, 1985), 16–20; James Clifford, "Identity in Mashpee," in *The Predicament of Culture: Twentieth-Century Ethnography, Literature, and Art* (Cambridge, MA: Harvard University Press, 1988), 277–346; Francis G. Hutchins, *Mashpee: The Story of Cape Cod's Indian Town* (West Franklin, NH: Amarta Press, 1979); and Russell M. Peters, *The Wampanoags of Mashpee: An Indian Perspective on American History* (n.p., n.d.), 30–37.

4. His publications were many. Among those most pertinent for this study are: *Territorial Subdivisions and Boundaries of the Wampanoag, Massachusett, and Nauset Indians,* Indian Notes and Monographs 44 (New York: Museum of the American Indian, Heye Foundation, 1928); "Native Tribes and Dialects of Connecticut: A Mohegan–Pequot Diary," in *Forty-third Annual Report of the Bureau of*

These questions will, I hope, provoke curiosity—and move others to begin to mine the field of New England Native American history and culture in the eighteenth, nineteenth, and twentieth centuries. A few have.[5] But they indicate something more than an odd corner of regional and national history that has yet to be investigated. The scarcity of books and articles about Native Americans in New England is not matched by a similar paucity of writing about Native Americans in much of the West. Regardless of region, however, Native Americans have been kept, and remain, largely outside the written histories of the United States.[6] If one turns to critical writings, histories and anthologies of American literature, the situation differs only in manner, but not substantially.[7] When Native Americans appear, either in the histories or in

American Ethnology, 1925–1926 (Washington, DC: Government Printing Office, 1928), 199–287; and "A Note on the Hassanamisico Band of Nipmuc," *Bulletin of the Massachusetts Archaeological Society* 4, no. 4 (1943): 49–56.

5. The earliest of importance for southern New England was Samuel G. Drake, who extensively collected documents and published several different historical accounts. The most notable, which went through many editions and had several titles, is his *Biography and History of the Indians of North America*, first published in 1832. Like Drake's works, John W. De Forest's *History of the Indians of Connecticut* (1851; Hamden, CT: Archon Press, 1964) remains valuable, though both frame their histories as accounts of a doomed people. From modern scholars, the two indispensable books are Neal Salisbury, *The Indians of New England: A Critical Bibliography* (Bloomington: Indiana University Press, 1982), and William S. Simmons, *Spirit of the New England Tribes: Indian History and Folklore, 1620–1984* (Hanover, NH: University Press of New England, 1986). And for the period before the eighteenth century, see Neal Salisbury, *Manitou and Providence: Indians, Europeans, and the Making of New England, 1500–1643* (New York: Oxford University Press, 1982).

6. This despite the efforts, now for almost a generation, of ethnohistorians, and a few colonial historians, who have produced superb works of scholarship: Gary Nash, *Red, White, and Black: The Peoples of Early America* (Englewood Cliffs, NJ: Prentice-Hall, 1974; 3rd ed., 1992); Francis Jennings, *The Invasion of America: Indians, Colonialism, and the Cant of Conquest* (Chapel Hill: University of North Carolina Press, 1975); James Axtell, *The European and the Indian: Essays in the Ethnohistory of Colonial North America* (New York: Oxford University Press, 1981), and *The Invasion Within: The Contest of Cultures in Colonial North America* (New York: Oxford University Press, 1985); Peter H. Wood, *Black Majority: Negroes in Colonial South Carolina from 1670 through the Stono Rebellion* (New York: Norton, 1974), and Wood, Gregory Waselkov, and M. Thomas Hatley, eds., *Powhatan's Mantle: Indians in the Colonial Southeast* (Lincoln: University of Nebraska Press, 1989); J. Leitch Wright, Jr., *The Only Land They Knew* (New York: Free Press, 1981); and James H. Merrell, *The Indian's New World: Catawbas and Their Neighbors from European Contact through the Era of Removal* (Chapel Hill: University of North Carolina Press, 1989), are prominent among them.

7. For a brief period in the nineteenth century this was not so, due almost entirely to the research and writing of Daniel C. Brinton. His collections and studies are many, but one might well begin with *Aboriginal Authors and Their Productions* (Philadelphia, 1883). A few isolated voices appeared in the twentieth century: Roy Harvey Pearce, *Savagism and Civilization: A Study of the Indian and the American Mind* (1953; rev. ed., Berkeley: University of California Press, 1988), an invaluable book; and Leslie Fiedler, *The Return of the Vanishing American* (New York: Stein and Day, 1968). Only very recently has this begun to change at all. For the first time an anthology of American literature has

literature, they do so in predictable and restricted guises as "remnants," "a doomed race," obstacles to the conquest and settlement of the "wilderness," as barbaric scalping savages or, alternately, as the "noble savage," too pure and Edenic to survive other than in white people's nostalgia and regret for a lost world of human and natural harmony. They are always, in effect, defined as √ outside the shaping forces in what becomes "America."

Indians cannot be accommodated in the available ideological frame- √ works—whether in the language of Manifest Destiny, which received its first full articulation in Apess's lifetime, justifying the removal of the Indians west *AMERICAN* of the Mississippi and legitimating a war of conquest against Mexico, or in the *IDEOLOGIES* Puritans' earlier "errand into the wilderness," or in all the countless renovations of the idea of Euro-Americans as God's chosen people with an exceptional and virtuous mission in the world. Euro-Americans' aggressions against Indians are seen as significant only as illustrations of the inevitable triumph of a superior civilization. Neither the indigenous histories and concerns of native peoples nor the complex relations between them and the Euro-Americans can be comprehended by the providential history that has generally passed for the actual history of the United States. To include these would undermine the construction of the particular ideological history that has shaped "America" as a virgin land settled by God's chosen people, mostly Anglo-Americans, who settled the eastern shores of North America in the name of freedom and opportunity. (If one doubts the continuing power of this ideology, simply notice the common rhetoric used by the current and previous presidential administrations to justify any action taken by the United States abroad.) The overt contradictions manifest in the dispossession of √ Native Americans would fracture the language of exceptionalism, dependent as it is on the idea of a missionary nation chosen to do God's work.

Apess's voice, his writing, and his history refuse these exclusions and sentimentalities. Though he will often play ironically with them, as in his title for his autobiography, *A Son of the Forest,* more often he directly attacks them

---

been published that includes Native Americans in more than a token or sentimental fashion: *The Heath Anthology of American Literature,* ed. Paul Lauter et al. (Lexington, MA: Heath, 1990). Its inclusiveness in turn depends on a body of critical, theoretical, and textual work, done mostly by anthropologists and folklorists over the last twenty years, which is just beginning to come to the attention of a few scholars in American literature. Arnold Krupat, in critical essays and several books, most directly in *The Voice in the Margin: Native American Literature and the Canon* (Berkeley: University of California Press, 1989), has sought to bridge these several disciplines. His introduction to the reissue of Pearce's book provides a good succinct history for the twentieth century of the exclusion of Native Americans from the world of American literature studies. The large and impressive body of contemporary Native American literature produced in the last twenty years has also been a stimulus to change. But it would be optimistic to predict that the full inclusion of Native Americans in the study of "American" literature is at hand.

and the unashamedly ideological constructions that have framed, and continue to frame, most historical and literary writing about the United States. Beginning with *A Son of the Forest,* his first published work, Apess manifested a remarkable consciousness that to express himself he must also take on the powerful and obliterating assumption in Euro-American culture that the Indians were nothing more than an inconvenience or a footnote in the shaping of the "American experiment." Thus Apess includes, at the end of *A Son of the Forest,* an appendix almost as long as his own history, which attempts to assemble a history of North American natives. He had it bound separately and frequently handed it out after his sermons, a sign of its importance to his sense of his mission.[8]

To seek, then, as this new edition of Apess's complete writings does, a revival of attention to this one man engages a project far beyond the fascinating and extraordinary individual William Apess was. If I begin to read Apess at all well, then he would have us, in attending him, inquire first about his immediate people, the Pequots, then about all New England Native Americans, and ultimately about all people of color in the history of North America. Retrieval of these histories would be, for him, only the beginning. Justice would yet be lacking, but, just as importantly, so would historical accounts that included Native Americans, African Americans, Euro-Americans, and, eventually, Asian Americans as full subjects in the history of the United States and in the shaping of its culture. Though one might naively argue that such a history would be "truer," its difference, its own ideological ground, would have the consequence that all Americans would understand themselves, their histories, and thus the present very differently. "Our" history and culture would no longer in its pronouns simultaneously make invisible the history and culture of Native Americans and disguise its own exclusivity. The advantages of such a new history, as Apess wonderfully grasped, are that contradictions could not be hidden and no single narrative could suffice.

More quotation from Apess may give a sharper sense of the relation, for him, of historical and personal memory and the construction of a less exclusionary American culture. His *Eulogy on King Philip* (1836) was his last and most pointed exploration of these issues:

> and as the immortal Washington lives endeared and engraven on the hearts of every white in America, never to be forgotten in time—even such is the immortal Philip honored, as held in memory by the degraded but yet grateful descendants who appreciate his character; so will ev-

---

8. I believe this is the "small pamphlet that contained a sketch of the history of the Indians of New England" to which he refers in *Indian Nullification,* although it is possible that he had put together earlier what would eventually become the historical section of his *Eulogy on King Philip.*

ery patriot, especially in this enlightened age, respect the rude yet all-accomplished son of the forest, that died a martyr to his cause, though unsuccessful, yet as glorious as the *American* Revolution. Where, then, shall we place the hero of the wilderness?

This eulogy, like all eulogies, is a call to remember. What or whom, though, does Apess want remembered? And by whom? Every *white* person remembers George Washington. Would it be possible to find anyone living in the United States who did not know who he was, no matter the extent, otherwise, of his or her historical ignorance? Nor is King Philip forgotten by "his descendants." Each of the two figures in the eulogy has his cause. The American Revolution is as well known as is Washington's name. Philip's cause is unnamed, as though either everyone would know it or it would be so obscure as to require more than a simple name. A double history and a double audience are being addressed: Native Americans know Euro-Americans and their history as well as knowing themselves and their own history, whereas they, in person and historically, are at best only partially known to white Americans.

Reading Apess's words can induce historical vertigo. Who, after all, is this obscure person who is speaking, and who is the almost equally as obscure figure he places alongside George Washington, first in the American pantheon of founders? Few Americans in 1990 would know who King Philip was. Speaking in Boston in 1836, Apess might reasonably have expected at least some members of the audience to know the name of an Indian leader once as hated and as feared in New England as Martin Luther King once was in the white South. For them the shock of Apess's juxtaposition of Washington and Philip might have been severe, an impiety, an inversion of a devil into a hero, or of the known hero into a devil. For those who did not know that Philip had, in the seventeenth century, led an alliance of New England Native Americans against the English colonists in a bitterly destructive war, Apess's pairing of the two men would still be disorienting. How could "patriots" pay equal respect to Washington and to someone they had never heard of, or to someone who had tried to drive the English colonists back into the sea?[9]

9. Apess had several immediate literary precedents upon which he could depend and from which he may have drawn some of his material. Washington Irving has an essay, "Philip of Pokanoket," in *The Sketch Book* (1819). J. W. Eastburn and R. C. Sands, *Yamoyden* (1820), a long narrative poem, depicts King Philip's War. Both works' sympathies are entirely with the Indians and critical of the Puritans. James D. Hart, *The Oxford Companion to American Literature,* 3rd ed. (New York: Oxford University Press, 1956), 855, comments that *Yamoyden* "was extremely popular, and inaugurated a new literary subject." John Augustus Stone's *Metamora; or, The Last of the Wampanoags,* a play about King Philip, was first produced in 1829. Pearce, in *Savagism and Civilization* (176), describes it as the "most popular of the Indian plays," one which spawned some thirty-five imitations in the next two

Apess does more than disquiet a comfortably exclusive Euro-American version of the North American past in this passage and throughout the *Eulogy*. He reminds his auditors and his readers that the United States came into being through two complex events: the aggression against Indian cultures and the theft of their land, which long predated and continued past the other founding activity, the *"American* Revolution," a discrete and limited moment. His use of italics is meaningful, too, perhaps simply emphasizing that the Revolution liberated only those so denominated.

Writing in the first age of the canonization of the "Founding Fathers," Apess cannily manipulates the rhetoric of patriotism. He especially echoes and responds to Daniel Webster, who in a series of important speeches between 1820 and 1826 consolidated the developing ideology of national patriotism.[10] Celebrated and repeated all over New England, they elevated the "Fathers" to a form of republican sainthood. His speeches forged a coherent story which began with a tableau of Pilgrims fleeing the oppression of the Old World and connected it to images of stalwart bravery and genius associated with leaders of the Revolution like Washington, Jefferson, and Adams. Webster's "First Settlement of New England," delivered on December 22, 1820, at Plymouth in commemoration of the "first landing" rings all the changes that have since become the staple stereotypes of innumerable primers and textbooks. His portrayal of the lowly, heroic, freedom-loving Pilgrims entirely

decades. It seems unlikely Apess would not at least have known of it. Revised in 1836 for Edwin Forrest by Robert Montgomery Bird, the play would undoubtedly have played in Providence, Boston, Hartford, and the other major New England cities in its second if not in its first version. Bird's role deserves note. He was himself a well-known playwright who, after revising *Metamora* turned, in some disillusionment, to writing novels, the most popular and successful of which was *Nick of the Woods* (1837), one of the most fiercely Indian-hating novels in the history of American literature.

The *Eulogy on King Philip* departs from these, and from the more fully and imaginatively articulated vision in Cooper's *The Pioneers* (1823), *The Last of the Mohicans* (1826), and *The Prairie* (1827), in refusing to see the conflict between Europeans and Native Americans as that between two tragically irreconcilable races and ways of life. Apess's Indians are not doomed to fade away. His Philip and his Indians suffer and are diminished, but in the *Eulogy* he insists upon connecting the past to the current treatment of Native Americans and calls for their full citizenship in a republic of equals.

10. I am grateful to Arnold Krupat for reminding me that the Cherokees attempted a similar expropriation of patriotic rhetoric throughout the controversy between 1830 and 1835 over the Indian Removal Act, which legislated their being dispossessed of their ancestral lands. Apess may have been no more successful in reaching his audience, though many of them might well have been among those Bostonians who took the side of the Cherokee against Jackson, a president Whig New Englanders particularly hated. I think they would have recognized and been affronted by his virtually explicit opposition to Daniel Webster's reverential and mythmaking accounts. Webster was, in 1836, as much a hero of respectable and reform-minded Bostonians as Jackson was a villain.

displaces the Indians, who are barely mentioned. The Pilgrims are the people who introduced civilization to "a new continent to be inhabited and culti-vated." Thus does Webster erase the Indians without even a verbal tic to suggest how utter was the repression of historical actuality. His speech at the laying of the cornerstone for the Bunker Hill Monument (June 17, 1825) and his elegy for Adams and Jefferson (August 2, 1826), whose deaths on July 4, 1826, provided an irresistible symbolism, extended and elaborated the themes of his Plymouth speech. Apess's elegy, knowingly I think, borrows the form most associated with a commemoration of the Fathers' unqualified virtues and inserts Philip among them. And, in recontextualizing the story of the Pilgrims, Apess seeks to expose Webster's ideologically seductive elisions. Who, he in effect asks, knowing what the Pilgrims actually did, would wish to claim them as the fathers of their country? Though he does not directly challenge the hagiography of the Revolutionary Fathers, Apess can be read as suggesting, for any ears that might be able to detect it, that if, after examina-tion, the Pilgrim Fathers prove poor models for an idealistic democracy, then its Revolutionary Fathers might have similarly dubious credentials.

Throughout the *Eulogy* and much of the rest of his writing, he subjects the whole complex of Euro-American ideological language to similar manip-ulation. The rhetoric of evangelical Christianity and of republican rights and liberty he makes the ground for granting Native Americans equality, subvert-ing their conventional function of defining natives as pagans and savages who, at best, might be convertible to minor status. His rhetorical strategy in the *Eulogy* effectively seeks to disable white Americans' ready assumption of a seamlessly glorious and singular American story. It tries, then, to shift per-spective so that what appears from one focal point to be the triumphant progress of Western civilization with its clear gallery of heroic figures becomes from another a series of crimes and a tragedy. This double perspective, in turn, by its irony implies the inadequacy of both.

I find most interesting Apess's fluency in the Euro-American consensual-ist language, which normally achieves its effects by forgetting the existence of Native and African Americans, and his use, at the same time, of irreconcilably conflicting understandings of the American genesis. He employs, for exam-ple, the concept of "patriot" to set Indian Philip and Euro-American George side by side. The term seems to conflate while it also stresses the incongruity of the two. The reference to Philip as "the hero of the wilderness" functions similarly in alluding both to a quality of "Indianness" and to his being like a "pioneer." Something beyond irony is at play. The very terminologies of an Americanist discourse, which value Euro-Americans precisely through im-plied contrast to their Indian opposites, are expropriated, inverted, or used as though they could characterize Indians as aptly as Euro-Americans. This

"Rev. William Apess, an Indian,"[11] confounds savage and civilized, pagan and Christian, devil and saint, villain and hero, the polarities upon which Euro-American culture has built its sense of legitimacy, of its superiority to Native and African Americans. The binary logic of "us/them" is riddled by Apess's words.

One could read Apess as engaging in a Native American version of what Henry Louis Gates, Jr., calls "signifyin(g)" in the African American tradition, an act of doubling and redoubling the assumed meanings of words and concepts in a dominant discourse. The term, and the language acts it indicates, speaks to the wiliness necessary to members of any group who are despised and subjugated. For such persons, to speak and to write involve always a consciousness of two audiences, one of which shares one's own experience in substantial part, the other of which belongs to the culture of domination. Straightforwardness is impossible for it risks retaliation from the powerful but to echo faithfully their language and understandings is to participate in one's own suppression. Mimicry, parody, the pretense of stupidity, exaggerated irony, all become essential devices for the inescapable duplicity required to speak "truly" in such situations. Maya Angelou in *I Know Why the Caged Bird Sings* provides an especially rich example in describing her grandmother's use of language:

> Knowing Momma, I knew that I never knew Momma. Her African-bush secretiveness and suspiciousness had been compounded by slavery and confirmed by centuries of promises made and promises broken. We have a saying among Black Americans which describes Momma's caution. "If you ask a Negro where he's been, he'll tell you where he's going." To understand this important information, it is necessary to know who uses the tactic and on whom it works. If an unaware person is told a part of the truth (it is imperative that the answer embody truth), he is satisfied that his query has been answered. If an aware person (one who himself uses the stratagem) is given an answer which is truthful but bears only slightly if at all on the question, he knows that the information he seeks is of a private nature and will not be handed to him willingly. Thus direct denial, lying and the revelation of personal affairs are avoided.

Angelou's example both describes "signifyin(g)" and is itself an instance of it, for it alerts the "aware person" that Angelou herself is controlling her autobiographical revelations which will always "embody truth" but never in ways that can be taken as complete, self-evident, or straightforward.[12] Doubling, or

11. This is how he signs himself on the title page of the *Eulogy on King Philip*.

12. The passage is quoted in Françoise Lionnet, *Autobiographical Voices: Race, Gender, Self-Portraiture*

signifyin(g), is thus the use of two or more codes of language, or of several √ voices, but as though only one was being employed.

Other kinds of mirroring and reversals may also be observed in the *Eulogy*. Just as most twentieth-century readers might well first wonder "Who is this King Philip?"—a question that itself locates them in a homogenized version of American history, regardless of their ethnic, racial, gender, or sexual identity—so, too, might well come the question "Who is this William Apess?" The question was asked in his own time, sometimes in straightforward curiosity but most often to deny that he had any business speaking at all. When he first began to exhort and preach in and around Colrain, Massachusetts, "the sons of the devil began to show their front—and I was treated not with the greatest loving kindness, as one of them threw an old hat in my face, and . . . others . . . threw sticks at me" (*A Son*). An Indian preaching the Christian Gospel, especially to largely Euro-American gatherings, was a curiosity at best, often perceived as a transgression against proper order. Later, when Apess catalyzed the discontent among the Mashpees and led them to assert their rights under the Constitution, he was excoriated as an agitator, and every effort was made by the established powers in church and state in Massachusetts to discredit and silence him.

His question about King Philip intends, I think, to recall such white New Englanders' righteous indignation against the presumption of an "inferior" speaking and acting as though equal and autonomous. It also expresses the historical veiling, the deliberate forgetting in the dominant culture, of individuals and events that might encourage and legitimate a revival of defiance and rebellion at another time. Apess's own obscurity and status as "a poor ignorant Indian" mirror and are mirrored by King Philip's. His invocation of Philip as a forgotten "father of his country," as someone both present in and absent from American history, evokes the figures of all Native Americans, including his own, shapers of this history and yet nearly as invisible to Euro-Americans, as almost completely erased in their collective memory as are "the remaining few" Apess hopes to assist by resurrecting Philip. This is to suggest that Apess recognizes himself in recalling Philip, leaders and defenders of their people both, while also attempting to signify the whole collectivity of Native Americans. Philip is, thus, a "son of the forest," as Apess is, not simply generically but through his chosen title for his autobiography, his first publication of himself to American society. By such acts of naming he inserts himself, Philip, and their people as subjects in a history that has regarded them, when at all, merely as objects "vanishing" before a superior civilization or as obstacles to it.

(Ithaca, NY: Cornell University Press, 1989), 131. I am indebted to this superb book not only for this passage but also for the use and the reading I make of it.

This eulogy, then, true to its genre, is a call to remember. Such remembrances imply and proclaim that one person's death is not the end, that others survive to mourn, kin in blood or spirit. The *Eulogy* asserts not only Apess's survival as a Pequot but also that of his people.

I have turned to this close reading to establish early in this introduction how complex and intriguing a thinker and writer William Apess was. This is not a "Native" who has "lost his voice," or who wishes "to be the licensed speaker of a dominant voice," or who is simply faithful to the "'sacral view of America,'" but one who struggles to find language with which to play out the elements of several cultural heritages: Pequot, Native American, Anglo-American, and, very possibly, African-American.[13]

MAKING A LIFE

Before turning directly to Apess's autobiographical writings, I want to offer a somewhat old-fashioned literal answer to the question "Who was William Apess?" Few documents exist (or they have yet to be uncovered) that record his life independent of his own autobiographical writings. Without these, one might rightly say that Apess would never have existed in written, or kept, history. The Mashpee Revolt did make its way into the major regional urban newspapers as well as into the local Cape Cod papers, into the legislative documents of the Massachusetts Great and General Court, and partly into local court records. All of these number among the relatively well-preserved documents on which historians depend and which tempt them to believe they can recapture all "that actually happened" and "mattered." His name does not appear in the federal census schedules for Connecticut and Massachusetts between 1810 and 1870, though it may yet turn up in those for New York or Rhode Island. Documentary evidence about his mother's and father's origins is scantier. Most of his female relatives cannot be reliably named, let alone traced. His own birth and death are not documented. Only because he announces it in his autobiography do we know when and where he was born.

13. My quotations are all from Arnold Krupat's discussion of Apess in *The Voice in the Margin: Native American Literature and the Canon* (Berkeley: University of California Press, 1989), 147, 148, 144. Their implication is somewhat unfair to Krupat's, as always, perceptive and theoretically informed reading. These comments are directed at Apess's autobiography, *A Son of the Forest*, and Krupat himself questions their adequacy when he turns to "An Indian's Looking-Glass for the White Man." Apess's writing needs to be read as a whole—as this essay seeks to demonstrate—so as to understand better the difficulties for an Indian in writing to a predominantly Euro-American readership without losing himself or his people. I also think—but this belongs to another discussion—that critics, especially those as sensitive as Krupat, need to remember that theoretical categories, in this case ones drawn from Bakhtin and Foucault, which help us to understand the discourses of power, can also reenact the very subordinations they mean to uncover.

We are, then, in the presence of the kinds of people who rarely appear in written history except, and occasionally, as statistics. Set aside, for the moment, that Apess was an Indian and thus even less likely to be noticed, counted, or set down in most historical records or seen as "significant" of any historical meaning if he were. Only a few pages into *A Son of the Forest* and it becomes evident that Apess's people were poor laborers. By class, if not by their identity as Native Americans, these were not the people of whom the stuff of written American history has been made. Because of their economic station they moved often, to find jobs, to improve however modestly their living situation, to relieve the unending monotony of bare survival, or to escape minor troubles with local authorities or quarrels with one's relatives, the result of the antagonisms among people with very little who must constantly depend on each other.

Add to all these facts that most of Apess's people were not only "Indians" in nineteenth-century New England, a people pitied or despised if they were noticed at all, but also Pequots. To be remembered is to be valued. As with individuals, so with cultures. They keep what they value and lose and forget what they do not. The Pequots were more than lost or forgotten. Memory of them was deliberately suppressed. In 1637 they were the objects of the first deliberately genocidal war conducted by the English in North America. The combined forces of the Plymouth, Connecticut, and Massachusetts Bay colonies surprised the main settlement of the Pequots on the Mystic River, surrounded and set fire to it, and then slaughtered every man, woman, and child they could catch who had escaped the flames. Some Pequots survived but were compelled to sign a treaty that declared them extinct as a people and forbade the use of their name forever. Some survivors were sold into slavery in the Caribbean, the others were divided between the Mohegans and the Narragansetts who had allied with the English during the Pequot War. An anonymous Puritan historian put the matter unabashedly:

> And in the war, which we made against them, God's hand from heaven was so manifested that a very few of our men in a short time pursued through the wilderness, slew, and took prisoners about 1,400 of them, even all they could find, to the great terror and amazement of all the Indians to this day; so that the name of the Pequots (as of Amalech) is blotted out from under heaven, there being not one that is, or (at least) dare call himself a Pequot.[14]

14. "God's Favors to New England," from *New England's First Fruits* (1643) quoted in Hauptman, "The Pequot War and Its Legacies," in Hauptman and Wherry, *The Pequots*, 76. Salisbury, *Manitou and Providence*, has the most extensive and reliable account of the war.

The Pequots were to be erased in history and name even if they could not be completely extinguished in life. And so they essentially disappeared from written history. When they are mentioned in history texts, it is usually only to note that after the war of 1637 they ceased to exist. Scholars in American history continue to be taught this and to teach it to others as a truth. To join in this forgetfulness, to fail to record their survival, is to continue to engage in a form of cultural genocide. The Pequots did not cease to exist, either as individuals or as a culture. Their survival was precarious, more so initially than that of other New England Native Americans. Cheating them of land, moralizing about the shame of their alcoholism and poverty, or lamenting the passage of a once noble people served only to increase the pressure on a people scattered and despised. All these acts also could be seen as forwarding the inevitable extinction that had long since been decreed for the Pequots.

By the time William Apess was born, the Pequots maintained two small reservations in southeastern Connecticut, one in North Stonington, the other in Ledyard. A steadily shrinking population inhabited each, disproportionately female because—surely in one of the most cruel of historical ironies—so many of the men had fought and died on the colonists' side in the French and Indian Wars and in the Revolution. The small number of remaining Pequot men typically left the reservation in order to find paying work to help their families. Whaling and other seagoing occupations were common; so, too, was working out as laborers on others' farms.[15] By the early nineteenth century the two reservations may have held, altogether, no more than a hundred people.

The Pequots were not themselves dwindling, though they were disappearing from official sight. From my research on Apess it is clear that throughout the region there were substantial small communities of Pequots off the reservation. Many, possibly most, had intermarried with non-Indians, some with African Americans, others, a smaller number I believe, with Euro-Americans. Given the available population records and the unreliable identifications of people by race and by ethnicity in them, it may never be possible to fix dependably how many Pequots, or Native Americans, there were in the first half of the nineteenth century in New England. And intermarriage with African Americans reinforced white New Englanders' already tenacious investment in believing the Indians were a declining and degenerate people.[16]

15. For this and other information about the Pequots after the war of 1637 and into the early nineteenth century, see Kevin A. McBride, "The Historical Archaeology of the Mashantucket Pequots, 1637–1900," esp. 104–8, and Jack Campisi, "The Emergence of the Mashantucket Pequot Tribe, 1637–1975," esp. 120–33, both in Hauptman and Wherry, *The Pequots*.
16. Carter G. Woodson, "The Relation of Negroes and Indians in Massachusetts," *Journal of Negro History* 5 (1920): 45–57, is an early and perhaps the first sympathetic investigation; Barbara W.

The motives and the routines that made Indian, African American, and poor people's lives marginal were well established among Euro-Americans by William Apess's time. These help explain how dependent on his autobiographical writings we are for the details of his life. They also indicate why Apess's writing is invaluable as a historical document for the study of Pequots, other Native Americans, African Americans, and at least the lower strata of the laboring classes in this period of New England history. Read for these ends, his books and pamphlets are as tantalizing as they are promising. Every insight and fact in them generate innumerable questions and possibilities for the writing of these histories.

These begin with his birth. Only the date seems certain, for we cannot even be sure of his mother's first name. He was born January 31, 1798, "where [my father] pitched his tent in the woods" (*A Son*), in Colrain, Massachusetts, the first child of William and Candace Apes.[17] What moved Wil-

---

Brown and James M. Rose, *Black Roots in Southeastern Connecticut, 1650–1900*, Gale Genealogy and Local History Series, vol. 8 (Detroit: Gale, 1980), offers extensive and invaluable documentation of the interconnections between these two peoples. More volumes like it are needed for the rest of the Northeast.

17. Since his parents' last name appears as "Apes" in all the documents I have found, I will risk the confusion of spelling their name differently from his. I have also left this spelling unchanged in all quotations from contemporary documents. He never gives his mother's first name and his father's only appears in supplementary material near the end of *Indian Nullification*. A William Apes appears in the 1820 federal census schedules for Colrain, married to an unnamed woman in the same age cohort as the woman I believe was Apess's mother would have been in 1820. William Apes is there listed as engaged in manufacture, which also fits, since we know from his son that he was a shoemaker. A William Apes purchased land in Colchester, Connecticut, in 1811 and resided there as late as 1814, almost precisely the years, according to *A Son of the Forest*, that Apess's father was in the Colchester area. Establishing who Apess's mother was is more uncertain. She was, according to her son, from southeastern Connecticut, a full-blooded Pequot whose family had settled, like many other Pequots, in and around Colchester. I believe that the Candace Apes who was owned as a slave and listed as a "Negro" woman by Captain Joseph Taylor of Colchester until he freed her in 1805 at age twenty-eight was probably Apess's mother. There are, however, several problems. Although the adult woman listed in the 1820 federal census schedule for Colrain as co-head of the household with William Apes is assigned to the age range that would allow for her having been born in 1777, Candace's birth year, she is identified as a "free white woman." The racial assignments in the federal census are rightly notorious for their inaccuracy and arbitrariness, and so one cannot make too much of this. William Apes is himself identified in this schedule as a "free white man," though he could, given common census practice, as easily have been identified as "colored" or "mulatto." Apess's insistence in the autobiography that his mother was a full-blooded Pequot princess cannot be altogether trusted either. He may have thought her so, but by the late eighteenth century in southern New England Native Americans and African Americans had commonly enough intermarried so that such clarity about racial identity was rarely possible, apart from the problems with these categories under any circumstances. Apess could also have been aware of his mother's mixed racial background and, knowing the power of contemporary whites' ideas about racial hierarchies and about the degeneracy of

liam Apes to bring his wife to begin their family to this remote small town in northwestern Massachusetts? It was far away from each parent's homeplace with their Pequot relatives in the New London/Groton area of southeastern Connecticut. Both had apparently lived in and around Colchester, Connecticut, all of their lives.[18] All Apess himself tells us is that, "not long after his marriage, [my father] removed to what was then called the back settlements, directing his course first to the west, and afterward to the northeast" (*A Son*). If the family moved to find work, why go so far away as Colrain? And why

---

racial mixing between Indians and blacks, have contented himself with the proud but, in these terms, nicely ambiguous assertion that his mother was one "in whose veins a single drop of the white man's blood never flowed" (*A Son*). The other problem for which one would like some explanation is that Apess was born in 1798, and yet Candace Apes was not freed by her master until 1805. It is possible, given the system of slavery in Connecticut, that Captain Taylor had allowed William Apes to marry his servant sometime in 1796 or 1797. Since we also know from Apess and from other sources how frequently Native Americans, like many of the poorest Americans, moved about seeking any kind of work and marginally more tolerable material circumstances, the newlyweds may have been in Colchester from the time of their marriage, with Candace working in the Taylor household and given permission to accompany her husband while he looked for work.

My research into the family history is heavily dependent on Brown and Rose, *Black Roots*, esp. 9–11. This is an indispensable source for the social history of Connecticut African and Native Americans. Brown and Rose have combed through and organized virtually every kind of local and state archival record. Most of the information in this note either comes directly from them or derives from their work. They list Candace as William Apess's mother.

18. The available evidence has many gaps and requires some surmise. "Apes" was not a common name. Using Brown and Rose, *Black Roots*, I can locate only a few before William Apess's generation. There is a William who served in the French and Indian Wars in a Connecticut regiment and was discharged in December 1757. It may be the same William whom the town of Stonington paid for "damage in small pox 6 April 1772" and who moved from Stonington to Groton between 1785 and 1789 but who was back in Stonington by 1791. The sources note that he had at least one son. Was he the father of William Apes? Apess's own autobiography says about his paternal grandfather only that he was "white," although his paternal grandmother was "an Indian," in fact a Pequot. Yet Apes itself seems clearly to have been a Pequot name. Brown and Rose note "the estate of Samuel Apes, Indian Man of Stonington was probated 1 May 1792" (11). North Stonington was the location of one of the two Pequot reservations, the home of the "eastern" or Paucatuck Pequots; the "western" or Mashantucket reservation was in Ledyard, town of Groton. This raises the possibility that the Apes family were eastern Pequots originally, though by the first half of the nineteenth century one risks making too much of a distinction between two closely related groups of Native Americans who lived only miles apart. In 1800 and 1810 the federal census schedules for Massachusetts show no Apes, which, of course, does not mean there were none in Massachusetts. *A Son of the Forest* makes it unambiguous that by the end of the eighteenth century a number of Pequots were settled, off the two reservations, throughout southeastern Connecticut and western Rhode Island and that, on both Apess's maternal and paternal sides, the families were located in and near Colchester and at least a few in and near Groton.

there, of all places? There may have been small factories in this hill town west of Greenfield, itself a substantial small trading and manufacturing city. Perhaps William Apes had found someone in the town willing to take him on as an apprentice shoemaker. One also should wonder if Apes had family there, though his son never suggests the possibility. Were there Native Americans there? This, again, is a possibility neither raised in *A Son of the Forest* nor likely, if one relies upon available printed sources and the assumptions common among scholars of New England Native Americans about where the surviving peoples were located. Or is it possible that William and Candace Apes, married sometime in 1796 or 1797, were running away from her master, thus needing to head toward the "back settlements" and as far from Colchester as possible?

Shortly after the birth of their first son, the couple moved back to Colchester and lived there in what Apess describes as "comparative comfort" for about three years. Then troubles began. The couple began to quarrel, separated, and then moved away, leaving Apess and his brothers and sisters with his maternal grandmother and grandfather.[19] Apess tells us no more about either of his parents' lives, except that he did not see his mother again for twenty years. If the birth records for his siblings are correct, then his parents must have reconciled and separated a number of times—since his mother was never with his father in the times between 1808 and 1813 when Apess visited him. It would tell us much about the lives of the poorest Americans in these years and about the Pequots if more could be found out about Apess's parents, especially about where his mother went and how she lived when she was apart from her husband.[20]

19. The documentary record and Apess's clear statements do not easily reconcile on the matter of his siblings. And there are some problems in the chronology and/or the biological logic in *A Son of the Forest*. His parents' separation would have occurred sometime in late 1801 or 1802. He says in the autobiography that he was left with his grandparents along with his two brothers and two sisters. If he was the eldest, as his recollections and what records exist indicate, then only an almost uninterrupted sequence of births and pregnancies could have resulted in four more children being born between February 1798 and late 1802. Brown and Rose assign six children to William and Candace Apes: "i. William—b. ca. 1798, ii. child—d. 12 Apr. 1802, iii. Elias—b. ca. 1804, iv. Mary Ann—b. ca. 1805, v. Gilbert—b. ca. 1809, vi. Griswold—b. ca. 1812 [1815/16 would be the correct birth date according to the federal census schedules for Connecticut for 1840 and 1850]" (*Black Roots,* 9–11). Their dates are more plausible but are irreconcilable with Apess's own statement, one I am inclined to trust since he has proved accurate in remembering dates and events in *A Son of the Forest* in every instance I have so far been able to confirm independently. Perhaps this is one example of confused recall almost thirty years later.

20. Brown and Rose, *Black Roots,* reproduce this intriguing and brief item: "William, Indian man, and Lucy Suncimon [sp.?], Indian woman, were accused of stealing a horse in Preston, 1814; case

Apess was, in effect, orphaned along with his brothers and sisters. What follows could be seen as a kind of case study, suitably horrible, illustrating the fate of impoverished and demoralized families—poor white, Native American, or African American—in nineteenth-century New England.[21] Apess's own words seem almost to invite readers of a better class to feel confirmed in their prejudices about the ignorance and pathology of the poor:

> Now my grandparents were not the best people in the world—like all others who are wedded to the beastly vice of intemperance, they would drink to excess whenever they could procure rum, and as usual in such cases, when under the influence of liquor, they would not only quarrel and fight with each other but would at times turn upon their unoffending grandchildren and beat them in a most cruel manner. [*A Son*]

The children often went hungry, they were so poorly clothed they suffered in the cold weather, and they depended on the kind offices of a near neighbor who took pity upon them, from time to time, and brought milk. One day, within weeks or a few months from the time his parents left, Apess was nearly beaten to death by his grandmother. He was saved only by the forcible intervention of an uncle who was also living in the house. So badly beaten and his arm broken in three places, it took him nearly a year to recover. His uncle, through the good offices of the kind and white neighbor, petitioned the selectmen of the town of Colchester for medical assistance. With this petition William Apess became the ward of the town which, when he recovered, bound him out to Mr. Furman, the friendly neighbor.

At the age of four or five the young child was removed from his family, and he never again, during his childhood, lived with his parents, or either set of his grandparents, or any of his relatives. The Furmans, in his own account, were good people, not too far removed in their class position from his own family's, for Mr. Furman "was a poor man, a cooper by trade, and obtained his living by the labor of his hands" (*A Son*). They allowed him to go to school for six winters, the whole extent of his formal education. They were Baptists,

---

dismissed (New London Co. Ct., June 1815)." So far, however, I have been unable to turn up any specific mention of Candace Apes between 1802 and 1820, when it is she, I am convinced, who is with William Apes in Colrain in time for the federal census taker to count them. Given the birth date of Griswold, Apess's youngest sibling, it seems possible that his parents were reconciled sometime in 1814 or 1815. This leaves thirteen years during which Candace Apes had to support herself by some means.

21. Harriet E. Wilson, *Our Nig; or, Sketches from the Life of a Free Black* (New York: Vintage, 1983), is an exemplary text for making such cross-cultural comparisons. Although a novel, Wilson's book is also evidently autobiographical and at many points parallels Apess's autobiographical writings.

another sign of their class, and while with them the young boy became interested in Christianity and began to be anxious about the state of his soul.

His relative security and happiness with the Furmans came to an end when they discovered that, following the lead of the oldest boy on the farm, he had made plans to run away. His indenture was sold to Judge William Hillhouse of Montville, a member of one of Connecticut's elite families and himself one of the most powerful men in the state.[22] The arrangement lasted less than a year. Apess very soon incurred the displeasure of the family, and as a consequence they ceased to clothe him decently, fed him poor fare, worked him very hard, forbade him to go to Methodist meetings, and kept him from continuing in school. He responded by running away several times and so had his indenture sold once again and to another and equally elite Connecticut family, the William Williamses of New London.[23] He was eleven and a half years old. Here, at first, he was well treated, lightly worked, clothed and fed properly. And he liked living in a bustling city for the first time: "The finery and show caught my eye and captivated my heart" (*A Son*). For about two or three years his life in the household went well.

Religion and class ruptured the tenuous bonds of good feeling that apparently softened the fundamentally economic nature of Apess's indenture. The spiritual strivings that had begun at the Furmans were stirred into a deep Christian conviction while he was at the Williamses. Methodists began holding meetings in the neighborhood, and Apess went. Their efforts stirred up a religious revival, and Apess experienced his religious conversion on March 15, 1813, a date he marks as exactly and carefully as he does his birth

[handwritten margin note: INTEREST IN METHODIST RELIGION.]

22. This is Judge William Hillhouse of the North Parish of New London, born in Montville, August 25, 1728, died at Montville, January 12, 1816. In 1767 he became the chief judge of the Court of New London County, a position he held for forty years. In 1785 he became a member of the Connecticut Governor's Council, a position he held until 1808. He was called the "patriarch of Montville." See Margaret P. Hillhouse, *Historical and Genealogical Collections Relating to the Descendants of Rev. James Hillhouse* (New York: Wright, 1924), 43 ff. He was also a major during the Revolution, a member of the Continental Congress from New London, 1783–86, and simultaneously a member of the Connecticut legislature. See also Frances Manwaring Caulkins, *History of New London, Connecticut* (New London: Utley, 1895), 667–68. (*The Index to . . .*, prepared by Cecelia Griswold [New London: Trustees of the Public Library, 1950], is a crucial tool in using this important local history).

23. William Williamses abound in this area and all up and down the Connecticut River valley from the seventeenth century on. This William Williams, sometimes known as William Williams III (his father was Captain William Williams and his grandfather was probably William Williams, Jr.), was born October 13, 1780/81, and died February 24, 1853. He was appointed judge of the probate court in 1819 for the District of Stonington (Ledyard, Stonington, Groton). He is also, I believe, the William Williams who was the appointed overseer of the Mashantucket Pequots from about 1813 to 1819. See J. Oliver Williams, *A Genealogy of Williams Families* (Brookline, MA, 1938).

date. The Williamses were Congregationalists, an inevitability given their elite position, and they objected to the Methodist practices and the indiscriminate mixing at their meetings of different racial and class groups. Methodism was, at this date in New England, significantly antiestablishment, especially in its successful appeal to the disenfranchised. Apess was forbidden to continue to attend meetings and began to be beaten often for disobeying and other offenses.

His solution was again to run away, in late March or April 1813, this time with another boy, John Miner, himself also perhaps in service in the Williams household and the son of a local poor white family.[24] Afraid of being caught and brought back, the two made their way to New York and found lodgings and jobs. Hearing that his master had offered a fifteen-dollar reward for his return, Apess panicked. He then met up with a recruiter of militiamen for the War of 1812 and enlisted as a drummer boy. On the march north to Plattsburgh he was forcibly converted into an infantryman. Believing that this relieved his obligation and feeling homesick for his father, he again attempted to run away. Caught but not punished, he was involved in several of the abortive efforts to capture Montreal and fought in the far more glorious (for the Americans) Battle of Lake Champlain on September 11, 1814. Sometime around the middle of March 1815, it seems from his account, he obtained his release from the army.[25]

Rum provided his most dependable companionship from the time he left the Williamses throughout his time in the army. After the army, he spent the

---

24. From Brown and Rose, *Black Roots*, 9–11: "Indian boy William Apes, ae. 15, ran away from William Williams of New London, 1813 (*Connecticut Gazette*, April 21, 1813)."

25. Apess's enlistment and service record provides the only physical description that exists. There is also one portrait, a full-face one, which appears as the engraved frontispiece in the 1831 edition of *A Son of the Forest*. For the most part, the official records corroborate Apess's own. The desertion he describes is not noted in the record, which makes sense since he mentions no formal procedures being initiated to punish him. The notation that he deserted on September 14, 1815, suggests that he "obtained his release" by letting himself out, impatient with the delays in demobilizing the soldiers and the efforts of the president to persuade Congress to support a larger standing army after the peace treaty with Great Britain had been signed. From the internal evidence in *A Son of the Forest*, I think he actually left the army considerably earlier in 1815 than September.

Enlistment and service record: "No. 2030. (Organization) *Name:* William Apes. *Rank:* Private. *Regiment:* US Army. *Co.:*———. *Regimental Commander:*———. (Description) *Height:* 5′ 2″. *Eyes:* hazel. *Hair:* black. *Complexion:* dark. *Age:* 17. *Occupation:* laborer. (Where from) *Town or county:*———. *State:* Connecticut. (Enlistment) *When:* April 19 1813. *Where:* New York. *By Whom:* Capt. McKeon. *Period:* April 19 1818. Military Roll: MR [Militia regiment] Capt. J. McKeon 3rd Arty Aug 31 1813 to Dec 31 1813 present. DR [Delaware regiment] Capt AS Brooks Co. Feb 16 R Plattsburgh Feb 28 R. Capt. Ed. Allen's Co. April 30, June 30 JR Captain Brook's Co. Aug. 31 1815 Present JR Capt. Churchill's Co. Plattsburgh, Oct. 31 1815. Deserted Sept 14, 1815" (from *Registers of Enlistments in the US Army, 1798–1914*, vols. 1 and 2 (A, B), 1798 May on, (A, B) p. 203).

next year, possibly two, in Canada, part of it with "my brethren, who ornamented the wood with their camps and chanted the wild beasts of prey with
their songs" (*Exps.*). Some of the Canadian Indians with whom he stayed were
apparently in Quebec, and others were the Mohawks and the Mississauga
Ojibwas around the Bay of Quinte in eastern Ontario. Both communities
were especially plagued with alcoholism in these years, but Apess implies,
without ever recounting, that while he was among these "brethren" he gained
some positive sense of himself as an Indian.[26]

Much of this time, however, he was "addicted to drinking rum" (*A Son*)
and moved from job to job, working as a baker in Montreal, a farm laborer, a
servant, a cook on a lake sloop, for a merchant, and finally, apparently far
gone into alcoholism, he obtained work on a month-long hunting and fishing
expedition in order to dry out. His comment suggests the shape he was in:
"We had very little rum, and that little we found abundantly sufficient. By
degrees I recovered my appetite" (*A Son*).

After several false starts Apess began, on foot, sometime around April
1816 to return "home," to southeastern Connecticut. Having little money, he
had repeatedly to stop along the way and take whatever jobs he could find.
The process took the better part of the year until he got as far as Hartford
where, instead of going on home, he began to drink again. In the spring of
1817, again apparently recovered from his latest bouts of drinking and with
enough money to buy himself "good clothes," he at last reached the Colchester area and reunited with his relatives, though not with any of his immediate
family. He had been gone so long without word that they thought him dead.
For the next year and a half he stayed in the area, working as a hired hand on
one or another farm. His spiritual commitments were renewed after a lapse of
almost five years. He resumed regular attendance at Methodist meetings and
became attached enough so that he accepted baptism by immersion at Bozrah, Connecticut, in December 1818.

With his baptism his life stabilizes. In the spring of 1819 he journeys by
foot to Colrain where his father has again located and decides to stay with him

26. At the same time that Apess was in this part of Canada, Peter Jones (Kahkewaquonaby), only
four years his junior, was growing up in another Mississauga community farther to the west along
the shores of Lake Ontario. Both became Methodist preachers, promoters and leaders of their
peoples, and important writers. Peter Jones's writing was as extensive as Apess's. Both authored
autobiographies and histories. One wishes it were possible to document that they met, but it does
not seem that Apess ever got quite that far west in Ontario, and Jones apparently made his first
visit to the Mississauga settlement on the Bay of Quinte in 1826, long after Apess had returned to
New England. Jones, *Life and Journals of Kah-ke-wa-quo-na-by* (Toronto: Green, 1860) and *History of
the Ojebway Indians* (London: Bennett, 1861), should be read along with Donald B. Smith's excellent biography, *Sacred Feathers: The Reverend Peter Jones (Kahkewaquonaby) & the Mississauga Indians*
(Lincoln: University of Nebraska Press, 1987).

a while and learn how to make shoes. It is probably on this occasion that he sees his mother again for the first time in twenty years. While in Colrain he feels God's call to exhort and preach and begins to do so. From this turn onward his life seems to achieve a new steadiness, although there are many troubles. He gets married to Mary Wood, a devout Methodist whom he had met at meetings in Connecticut, "a woman of nearly the same color as myself" (*A Son*), on December 16, 1821, in Salem, Connecticut.[27] And eventually, in April 1829, before he completes the manuscript for the first edition of *A Son of the Forest*, he is formally ordained a minister in the Protestant Methodist church.

Virtually nothing is known about Apess's life in the four years between his completion of the autobiography and his arrival in Mashpee, the old Indian town on Cape Cod, in May of 1833. He preached and, like all Methodist ministers, did so on a circuit, which would have meant that he was often apart from his wife. They had children, but only three are known of. In *A Son of the Forest*, he refers to "my little ones" and, in the 1829 edition, to a son. Two daughters married brothers named Chummuck in Mashpee, according to local memory, but for the rest, if there were others, and for the names of any of his children, no record has yet been found.[28]

Many Methodist circuit riders had to support themselves independently of their preaching. The faithful were often—almost certainly so with those Apess would have served—themselves at best of the middling sorts, and their greatest generosity would only rarely be sufficient to support a minister and his family. It would be useful to know what other occupations Apess pursued, how and where he housed himself and the family. In 1831 he was sent by the New York Annual Conference of Protestant Methodists to preach to the Pequots. His sermon, *The Increase of the Kingdom of Christ*, was also published that year in New York City, so there is some reason to think he may have been in the city a good deal, especially since his revised edition of *A Son of the Forest* was also published there the same year. The publication in 1833 of *The Experiences of Five Christian Indians of the Pequot Tribe* presents some of the fruits

27. "*APIS*, William of Cold Rain, Mass., m. Mary Wood, of Salem, December 16 1821, by Rev. John Whittlesey" (*Lucian Barbour Index to Connecticut Public Records*, from the Salem Vital Records, 9). Mary Apess says of herself in *Experiences:* "I was born in Lyme, Conn., A.D. 1788, on the third day of January. My father was a descendant of one of the Spanish islands, or a native of Spain. My mother was an English woman, a descendant of the Woods family of Lyme. My father died when I was small." After his death the family was so poor that Mary had to be bound out. It seems unambiguous that Mary was also illegitimate. Her account of her father's origins and William's characterization of her color also suggest that he was part Native American and Spanish or, more likely by this late date when most Native Americans in the Caribbean had long since been wiped out, African American with some mixture of Spanish and possibly Native American heritage.

28. The daughters' marriages and their husbands' names are in Speck, *Territorial Subdivisions*, 90.

of his mission to his people. These several publications, all in all, suggest that he was devoting a substantial amount of time in the four years to reading and writing.

His ministry to his people, his "brethren," as he always refers to them in his writing, continued. He tells us that when he first heard about Mashpee he was on tour among them preaching in Kingston, Rhode Island, and in Scituate and Plymouth, Massachusetts. His publications and his own accounts of his preaching in *Indian Nullification of the Unconstitutional Laws of Massachusetts* suggest that his sermons generally focused on the long history of Native Americans being denied their rights by Euro-Americans and on Christ's Gospel as meant for men and women of every race, making the point that it was thoroughly egalitarian in ways that neither American society nor most of its Christian churches were.

It was initially in his role as a preacher that Apess came to Mashpee, the only surviving Indian town in Massachusetts, and stirred up enough trouble to grant him an occasional modest place in conventional historical annals. He came there in May 1833 simply out of curiosity, it seems. He had heard mixed reports. Some told him that the Mashpees were well served by a good minister who also protected them and their lands against those whites who would defraud them. "Others asserted that they were much abused" (*I.N.*). Whether he also expected to find only another impoverished and degraded reservation, like the two Pequot ones in Connecticut, or hoped to find a more vital Native American community can only be guessed. Or perhaps he came already with some knowledge of the history of the Mashpees' efforts to gain the right to govern themselves.

Whatever his knowledge, he became immediately involved in the long-standing discontent and struggle within Mashpee against the overseers imposed on the community by the Commonwealth of Massachusetts. The three men had the power, which they seem to have exercised freely, to lease out grazing and haying lands to neighboring whites, to grant woodlot rights, to bind out in employment any man, woman, or child in the community, and to control who entered and who could stay in the township. This last power they commonly employed to keep out free blacks so as to prevent any further racial mixing.[29]

Equally galling to the Mashpees was the daily irritant of having a non-Indian minister whom they did not choose, the Reverend Phineas Fish, a Congregationalist, settled upon them by Harvard College, paid out of money left in trust to Harvard for the benefit of Native Americans, and occupying

29. During a brief period of independence in the eighteenth century, Mashpee had grown and prospered, in part because the townspeople controlled who could settle there. A number of black men were adopted into the community and the culture.

house and lands he claimed as his own. His orthodox theology and his flat preaching style (he read his sermons as well) would not have drawn the Mashpees to him.[30] But he seems, in addition, to have been remarkably lazy and dismissive of the needs of the Mashpees. His assumption of their racial inferiority capped his several unattractive qualities. As it was, when Apess arrived only a few Native Americans attended Fish's services, the rest of the congregation being made up of a small number of whites from neighboring Cape Cod towns. They occupied the pews of privilege. Christian residents of Mashpee attended services conducted, probably in Wampanoag, their own language, by one of their own, Blind Joe Amos, a Baptist preacher. Making matters worse was Phineas Fish's refusal to permit Amos's congregation to meet in the Old Indian Meeting House, his unapologetic indifference to the Mashpees' needs, and his unconcealed conviction that they were no more able than children.

The arrival of a newcomer, and one such as Apess who was ready to assume a leadership role, catalyzed the discontent among them. They adopted him into the community and pledged to provide him with a house, to grant him farming, fishing, and wood rights, while he organized a small Methodist meeting and joined with Blind Joe Amos in establishing a temperance organization. At the same time, at Apess's urging and probably with his authorship, the community agreed to two petitions: one to the governor of Massachusetts and his Council, the second to the Corporation of Harvard College. The first, "the Indian Declaration of Independence," proclaimed that after July 1, 1833, "we, as a tribe, will rule ourselves, and have the right to do so; for all men are born free and equal, says the Constitution of the country." Included was a declaration that no white man would be permitted to take wood or cut hay at Mashpee after July 1, without the Indians' explicit permission. The second petition, requesting the discharge of Phineas Fish, contained a list of grievances, among them the fact that the Mashpees had never been consulted about his selection. It added that they had chosen Apess for their minister and that they intended to take control of *their* meetinghouse.

Events moved quickly and dramatically. By the end of June, Governor Levi Lincoln was threatening to call out the troops to put down what he saw as

---

30. Apess, Daniel and Israel Amos, Isaac Coombs, and other leaders of the Mashpee Revolt charged that in twenty-five years Fish had added almost no members to his church and that no more than eight or ten Indians ever attended his services. Their obviously interested account (which need not mean it was any less true) gains pointed collaboration, at least on the qualities of Fish's preaching, in a sympathetic account of Fish by a contemporary and friend: "He possessed a strong mind, was a good scholar, and one of the best ethical writers in this country, but was a feeble speaker in the pulpit"; quoted in Donald G. Trayser, *Barnstable: Three Centuries of a Cape Cod Town* (Hyannis, MA: Goss, 1939), 91.

an insurrection. Less hysterical men prevailed, and the troops were never called out, but the governor's response communicates the intensity and excitement of the moment—and how unaccustomed white New Englanders were to Indians asserting their rights. On July 1 Apess and several of the Mashpees confronted a group of whites who had come to take wood. They were forbidden to do so, and when they ignored the order Apess and the others began to unload the wood from their carts. Some evidence suggests that the white men had been deliberately sent to test the Indians' determination. Apess was arrested on July 4 and charged with "riot, assault, and trespass," for which he served thirty days in jail, paid a hundred-dollar fine, an enormous sum in 1833, and had to post bond for another hundred in a promise "to keep the peace for six months."[31]

His talents as an organizer and publicist were not to be suppressed. His presence seems to have emboldened his brethren as well. Their agitation for their rights continued. "An Indian's Appeal to the White Men of Massachusetts" was composed, probably by Apess, and published in several newspapers in the state. Following it, a petition from the Mashpees was formally presented to the Massachusetts House for the abolition of the overseership, for the incorporation of the town, and for the repeal of all existing laws affecting the Mashpees "with the exception of the law preventing their selling their lands" (*I.N.*). Apess, along with Isaac Coombs and Daniel Amos, then addressed the House. Coombs and Amos spoke briefly. Apess's speech was "fearless, comprehensive and eloquent" and sought "to prove that, under such laws and such Overseers, no people could rise from their degradation" (*I.N.*).

In March 1834 the state legislature granted the citizens of Mashpee, in effect, the same rights of township self-governance as all other citizens in Massachusetts. Phineas Fish proved a more stubborn presence and Harvard College, as always, more resistant to the claims of right and democracy. Not until 1840, and then only when he was forcibly ejected from a parish meeting, did Fish give up. By that time Apess, too, had departed—whence and for what reasons are unknown.

Throughout the Indians' attempt to nullify the laws of the Commonwealth, most of the press and the local and state political establishment wished to believe that Apess was the sole cause of the difficulty. Portrayed as an

31. Barnstable Court of Common Pleas, September term, 1833 (p. 489): "The Commonwealth of Massachusetts vs. Wm Apes, Joseph Pocknett, Labourer, Jacob Pocknett, Labourer, Nicholas Pocknett, Labourer, Aaron Keater, Labourer, Charles De Grasse, Labourer, & Abraham Jackson, Labourer." Only Apess, De Grasse, and Jacob Pocknett were sentenced. Apess was unmistakably singled out as the ringleader, to be silenced under threat of forfeiting his expensive bond. De Grasse and Jacob Pocknett were sentenced to ten days in jail, and no fines or bonds were required of them.

outside agitator and manipulator, he was the target of a number of efforts to divide the community. Apess's role was pivotal, but he did not create what he helped organize and express. His importance, then and now, in these events is due to his militancy and his brilliant expropriation of the Anglo-American language of constitutionalism, rights, and citizenship. His choice of the word "nullification," in clear echo of South Carolina's assertion of states' rights against the federal government only a year earlier, during the Nullification Crisis, indicates his wit and his political astuteness. So, too, his repeated reminders of the indignation expressed by many Massachusetts citizens on behalf of the Cherokees: "Perhaps you have heard of the oppression of the Cherokees and lamented over them much, and thought the Georgians were hard and cruel creatures; but did you ever hear of the poor, oppressed and degraded Marshpee Indians in Massachusetts, and lament over them?" (*I.N.*).

Mashpee remained home for Apess and his family for some time after the revolt had succeeded in most of its aims. Within the next eighteen months he seems to have lost his position of leadership. One unsympathetic white observer commented, "Apes was popular among the Indians for a while but is now understood to be rapidly losing their confidence & not without good reason." To which Benjamin Franklin Hallett, the young Cape Cod Democratic politician and attorney who had voluntarily represented the Mashpees, responded in agreement.[32] Neither man provides the slightest hint of the possible causes. The three debt actions brought against Apess in the Barnstable court, one in each of the years from 1836 to 1838, would seem evidence that his economic state was precarious as well. His two presentations of the *Eulogy on King Philip* in Boston in January 1836, and his publication of a second edition of *The Experiences of Five Christian Indians* in 1837 are the only other public records of his existence in these years. He seems to have left Mashpee in 1838. Had he gone to another ministry, some record should have survived. It is only speculation that he may have turned to rum, in bitterness or for consolation, after his great success in Mashpee and thus begun a brief or long slide into anonymity. Such silence surrounding the final act of this man of passion and eloquence seems eerie.[33]

---

32. The quotation is from James Walker, "Facts in Regard to the Difficulties at Marshpee," October 17, 1835, quoted in Nielsen, "Mashpee Indian Revolt," 418. Nielsen also provides the paraphrase of Hallett's response. Hallett was important to the Mashpees' cause in several capacities. As editor of the *Boston Daily Advocate*, an important reform paper, he gave them dependable and positive press coverage in the state's capital and major city. He also, on several occasions, defended Apess and his role against the many whites and newspaper editorialists who sought to discredit him.

33. Elemire Zolla, in *The Writer and the Shaman: A Morphology of the American Indian,* trans. Raymond Rosenthal (New York: Harcourt Brace, 1969), discusses Apess and is one of the first critics in the

TELLING A LIFE
"Nothing but a poor ignorant Indian" (A Son)

From such beginnings as Apess's, what outcomes could have been expected? Born to a nation despised and outcast and perhaps, to add to the stigma, not only part white, a "mulatto" or "mixed breed," but also part African American, a child with William Apess's history who simply made it to adulthood would be doing well. The life course for such a man was already scripted and the variations in it finite and predictable. The common story would be a short, economically miserable life at the mercy of every circumstance and prejudice, relieved by occasional bouts of Christian repentance in alternation with longer dependence on the pleasures of alcohol. A few, born into such circumstances, might succeed in achieving a decent family life, a modest economic stability, and might raise their own children to adulthood. Who would dare doubt the inner strength required simply to go forward in life by these scripts, having endured what Apess, and countless others of his people, did? One must wonder, too, about the scars inflicted and how, and if, these were overcome.

For the most part we, in fact, do not know how Apess made his life, how he survived the cruelties and separations his autobiographical accounts narrate quite matter-of-factly. All we know reliably is how he shaped his life in writing. He marked his passage, identified himself, by acting through writing and by speaking so passionately and astutely that an unwilling society briefly read and listened.

His writing and publication were the most considerable by any Native American before the 1840s. Much of it is directly autobiographical, although *Indian Nullification* (1835) provides, along with "An Indian's Looking-Glass for the White Man" (1833) and the *Eulogy on King Philip* (1836), the primary exposition of his political thought and action. *A Son of the Forest* (1829) is the first published autobiography by a Native American. In length and narrative sophistication it moves substantially beyond earlier manuscript autobiographical sketches by Native Americans.[34] *The Experiences of Five Christian*

---

twentieth century to do so. He believes Apess was murdered, although he offers no evidence for the assertion. I assume Zolla found this plausible, given that David Walker, the African American militant who was Apess's near contemporary, was apparently poisoned in his Boston shop and not even a suspect was ever found. Although such an end for Apess cannot be disproved, I find it unlikely. His leadership of the Mashpees had passed, and his constituency was too scattered and weak to be a political threat. The abolitionist movement had, by 1837, come to consume the energies of the reform-minded Euro-Americans who would have been the most probable allies for an Indian rights movement.

34. There were Native Americans before Apess who wrote autobiographical statements or sketches, most notably Samson Occom and, in his letters to Eleazar Wheelock, Occom's fellow

Indians (1833) includes a briefer autobiography significantly different in rhetoric and tone from *A Son of the Forest*. All the writing records his development and articulation of an identity as a "native," the term he preferred over the alien and, in the 1820s, denigrating one of "Indian." From 1831 onward, expressions of his own sense of identity are subordinated to his exploration of Native American history and rights.

Wonder as we might about how Apess psychically survived the circumstances of his life, it is more mysterious how he might have conceived these autobiographical acts and acquired the practical skills to enact them. His status as one of the earliest of Native American writers may be taken to mark what an exceptional person he was; it should, more importantly, signify one of the great divides between Euro-American and Native American cultures. Natives created and lived their cultures through an extensive body of oral and communal traditions. The new society Euro-Americans sought to create in the United States depended upon the written word. Natives, from this perspective, were simply illiterates and primitives who lacked all but the rudiments of written languages. For a Native American to command literacy required reaching across a great body of cultural difference; it also required access to all the institutions of literacy: schools, libraries and books, newspapers, editors, and publishers. In the early nineteenth century Euro-America did not yet grant universal access even to the first stages of this

Mohegan, Joseph Johnson. Neither, however, was published until the twentieth century, although other writings by these and other Native American writers were. More significantly, no Native American before Apess, at least any so far known, wrote and published a book-length account of his or her life. The only other possible candidate is Catharine Brown whose *Memoir of . . . a Christian Indian of the Cherokee Nation* (1824) had gone through three editions by the time *A Son of the Forest* appeared. However, her memoirs were "authored" by Rufus Anderson. Anderson was more than a white editor/amanuensis who simply took down and organized Brown's reflections, considerable intervention though that would be. Brown's memoirs are consistently in the third person, and the narrative voice is unmistakably that of a Euro-American self-consciously presenting the life of an "Indian." Apess begins a long and complex practice of Native American "autobiographies" and does so in apparently complete control of his own narrative. Unlike most later Native American autobiographers, his is not a story told to another, most typically an anthropologist, whose own ends may primarily move the collecting of the life story and as editor controls the structure of the narrative. His autobiography also appeared with no editor of any kind noted, unlike Sarah Winnemucca's *Life among the Paiutes* (1883) and many other autobiographies by literate Native Americans. George Copway (Ojibwa), *The Life, History, and Travels of Kah-Ge-Ga-Gah-Bowh* (1847), and Peter Jones (Ojibwa), *Life and Journals of Kah-ke-wa-quo-na-by* (1860), Apess's immediate successors in written autobiography were, like him, ministers of the Christian Gospel.

Indian autobiographies have received considerable and sophisticated critical attention in the last decade, arguably more than any other form of Native American expressive traditions. Just why this should be deserves exploration on its own, but since this edition and editor participate in the fascination, it may not be appropriate here and, in any case, may deflect the primary subject. See the Bibliographic Essay herein for a review of this scholarship.

process to those it recognized as its own. The lower orders might usefully be taught enough to read the Bible. So, too, but less frequently, might freed and enslaved black people be taught, especially in the North. "Indians" inhabited another and more ambivalent category in Euro-Americans' consciousnesses. As "savages," that is, as uncivilized, untutored nomads, they had no place in the rising republican empire. In some part of the Euro-American sensibility this meant urging Native Americans to convert to "American" ways, to be- √ come individual property-holding farmers and educated, that is, literate, citizens. Once converted they would, of course, no longer be distinguishable culturally as "Indians." In another, the need was to believe that Indians could never be anything but "savages." Contact with civilization would only mean the loss of whatever virtues belonged to the savage state and the acquisition of the vices of the civilized. For Apess, or any other Native American, to become literate, then, in this ideological script, entailed being represented as in an intermediate state, a location where one was neither Native nor Euro-American but someone, at best, on the edge of either degeneracy or complete assimilation. To write as a Native American could only be an unspeakable contradiction.

With only six winters of primary education between the ages of five and eleven, Apess had achieved little proficiency as a reader (and, presumably, even less as a writer), a fact he wittily remarks on at the expense of Judge Hillhouse, his second "owner": "this good man did not care much about the Indian boy. He wished to hear me read: I could make out to spell a few words, and the judge said, 'You are a good reader.'—I hope he was a better judge at law" (*Exps.*). His first book, though it has its awkwardnesses, does not seem the writing of a precariously literate or uneducated man but the work of someone of fairly wide reading and some experience as a writer. When, in the course of the fifteen years after Judge Hillhouse's patronizing compliment, and how did he learn to write with the facility, canniness, and self-consciousness so abundantly evident in his books? Not when he was indentured to the Williamses, and surely not during the years in the army or the drunken times that followed. Apess was always, by necessity and perhaps by wish, on the move even after his life settled down somewhat in the 1820s. Yet by 1829 *A Son of the Forest* has been completed. He is altogether silent on what support and patronage he must have received simply to have the time, the advice, and the freedom from material cares to write his longest and first work, to say nothing of the subsequent ones.[35]

35. Thanks to the careful work of my research assistant, Shawn Sullivan, there is an answer for how Apess could have prepared the Appendix to *A Son of the Forest*, a task which would have required exceptional research and editorial skills as well as access to extensive library resources. It is essentially reworked, paraphrased, and outright lifted from Elias Boudinot's *A Star in the West; or, A*

These questions may tempt some to surmise that Apess is only in name the author of these writings. Hidden editorial hands and full-fledged ghost writing were common enough in the rapidly developing commercial publishing and writing institutions of the United States in the 1820s and 1830s. The precedent of the *Memoir of Catharine Brown* (1824) might easily have been seen as justification for someone in the New York or Boston publishing scene to take down and edit Apess's reminiscences.[36] The abolitionist movement would, a few short years ahead, make such practices commonplace in the emerging genre of the slave narrative. Like African Americans, most Native Americans were not literate and were very often assumed to be incapable of much literacy. A Native American in command of all the resources of the written language threatened images dear to Euro-American ideas about Indians in this period. A noble savage would be versed in the ways of nature and free of the corruptions of the cultivated whereas the tomahawk-wielding, murdering savage would be unreachable by the civilizing instrument of literacy. And yet there were Native Americans who had written, and some had published: Samson Occom, Joseph Johnson, and Hendrick Aupaumut from the eighteenth century; Elias Boudinot, the Cherokee editor, probably the best known, perhaps with David Cusick, the Tuscaroran historian of the Six Nations, of the few who published before Apess in the nineteenth century.[37]

With the exception of *Indian Nullification,* there are no evident signs of an editorial presence that might have done some, or all, of the writing. None of his books is prefaced, or authorized, by anyone else, unlike the nearly mandatory testimonials by whites in books by African Americans. Each book appears as though no one would, or should, find it remarkable that an "Indian" could write a book, especially one that purported to be his autobiography. Apess's uncompromising militancy in his later books and his unhesitant provision in *A Son of the Forest* of the real names of those who dealt badly with him seem further evidence that he controlled the shaping and the content.

Humble Attempt to Discover the Long Lost Ten Tribes of Israel . . . (Trenton, NJ: Fenton, Hutchinson, and Dunham, 1816). Boudinot (1740–1821) was a congressman from New Jersey, a founder of the American Bible Society, and the patron of the Cherokee editor, Elias Boudinot, who took his benefactor's name as his own. "Borrowings," such as Apess's, were more commonly and unabashedly done before the midcentury when copyright law, notions of the singularity of authorship and originality, and the possibility of writers making a living from their work helped to generate stricter ideas about individual ownership.

36. I have been unable thus far to find any evidence about Apess's relationship with his New York publishers or to how and from whom he raised the money to pay for his several publications. Because *A Son of the Forest* is copyrighted in New York City I am tempted to believe he wrote it there, but this is evidence too slender to count.

37. Aupaumut was not actually published until 1827, and Samson Occom, an important figure in New England Native American history and culture, had only a few short pieces published in the eighteenth century. Most of his writing has never been published.

There perhaps cannot be conclusive proof, in the absence of any of the manuscripts, that Apess was the primary or the sole author of the books published under his name. The fact of his several publications, the existence of two autobiographies and his substantial revisions of the first edition of *A Son of the Forest,* his indisputably having delivered the address which is then published as the *Eulogy on King Philip,* and the number of independent testimonies during the Mashpee Revolt to his eloquence as a speaker, however, make his authorship more than probable. There is, as well, I believe, a consistency of voice and sensibility in, and from, each of the five books that argues for a single author. Had it been someone other than Apess, I believe there would be some evidence for that person's identity. If there had been a ghost writer, it would have had to have been a Euro-American. The two likeliest candidates, Lydia Maria Child and William Joseph Snelling, wrote out of a consciousness about Native Americans, in their work prior to Apess's, which, though sympathetic, was unmistakably "other." Neither manifested, in these or later writings, the capacity to mimic persuasively a voice speaking as though from within a Native American world.[38]

38. Lydia Maria Child is just beginning to receive the critical attention she deserves—for the quality and interest of her writing and as one of the most courageous figures in American literary history. Her novel, *Hobomok* (1824), appeared when American writers had been experimenting for two decades with "the Indian" as a major theme in the development of a nationalist literature. Her treatment differs from her fellows (they were all men) in having a remarkably independent woman as her central figure who also chooses to marry an Indian. *The First Settlers of New-England* (1828) is explicitly critical of the Puritans' treatment of Native Americans and was substantially motivated by Child's opposition to current United States policies toward them. She also wrote a number of newspaper articles and stories about Native Americans. I am indebted to Carolyn Karcher's brilliant introduction to her edition of *Hobomok & Other Writings on Indians* (New Brunswick, NJ: Rutgers University Press, 1986), which is invaluable for those interested in Child, in the representation of Native Americans in literature, and in American writing of the period.

William Joseph Snelling's *Tales of the Northwest* (1830) is considered by some critics to be one of the few straightforward and unideological portraits of Native Americans written in the first half of the nineteenth century. Snelling, a native Bostonian like Child, returned to Boston in 1828 after a seven-year sojourn in the upper Midwest. It is conceivable he and Apess might have met then. Snelling attempted to make his living as a professional writer and journalist. He took on, as one means of earning income, compiling and editing books. He has been directly associated with Apess through the recurrent attribution in some bibliographies of the authorship of *Indian Nullification* to him. Snelling did not, I believe, write the book, although he may have provided some of the narrative sections connecting the selections from newspapers and public documents. A good deal of the book is directly in Apess's voice, so much so that, at most, Snelling may have taken down dictation from Apess. What seems probable is that he helped by assembling the wide variety of documents in the volume and then edited these together with Apess's direct contributions. Samuel Gardner Drake is the source of the attribution to Snelling, having written in his copy (which is now in the Mashpee Historical Society): "This work was written by William J. Snelling, who often consulted me during the progress of it. It was done at the request of Wm. Apes, whose name appears in the Title." The entry under Snelling, no. 18425, in the *Bibliography of American Literature,*

Autobiography, like all writing, cannot escape being collaborative. Language and convention implicate it in a broad culture of other voices, other writers and readers. But to a special extent the genre requires and constructs the illusion of an individual in command of his life by his ability to give it an apparent coherence in its telling. The sense of authenticity, of sincerity, always implied by the convention of autobiography assumes that the writer and the subject are one, each witness to and test of the other; so the reader may feel confident that the author is the "I" saying "I was there, I am the man." Gender and authority, in the historical practice of autobiography, do not accidentally modify each other. For most of Western history the claim of autonomy complicit with the autobiographical "I" was reserved to a special few, by class and by gender. And this "I" thus was freed from any necessary bonds to others and could be apprehended as a distinguishable self.[39]

Other questions about Apess's development as a writer seem to me more intriguing and important and to the point than establishing that he was the sole author. Assume, or accept, that his hand moved the pen that made the sentences in the books with his name on the title pages. What moved and shaped his writing remains a critical question, which may be inseparable from how he became practically able to write a book like *A Son of the Forest*. What could have emboldened or enabled him to presume that the story of his life might interest American readers? Indentured servants from gentry houses, whatever their race or culture, had no encouragement then, any more than their counterparts do now, to believe their lives had value. A yet larger, or different, sense of self would be required to believe that the representation of such a life in autobiography had worth. Writing an autobiography was an

---

comp. Jacob Blanck, vol. 7, edited and completed by Virginia L. Smyers and Michael Winship (New Haven: Yale University Press, 1983), comes to a similar conclusion: "William Apes was the author of several other books, and was certainly capable of writing this one. It is, however, sometimes ascribed to Snelling. The source of the Snelling attribution is probably the *Catalogue of the Private Library of Samuel G. Drake . . .* , Boston, 1845, No. 544, where Drake . . . assigns authorship to Snelling. It was possibly edited or put into final shape by Snelling. The copyright is in Apes's name."

39. I can only simplify here one of the most extended debates and explorations in literary theory and in intellectual history. The history of the constitution and construction of the Western concept of the self has become the arena through which move most of the important issues in political, psychological, feminist, and literary theory over the last several decades. Most pertinent for my concerns here is that, as rich and complex as this large literature is, very little of it as yet speaks to the history and construction of ideas of self, consciousness, and individuality in non-Western cultures. Arnold Krupat's "Native American Autobiography and the Synecdochic Self," in Paul John Eakin, ed., *American Autobiography: Retrospect and Prospect* (Madison: University of Wisconsin Press, 1991), very nicely sets out some of the major issues as they bear on Native American writing. He takes his primary examples from Apess's writing.

astonishing act for a native in these years. Apess should have been trebly disqualified—by class, by culture, and by his "race."

Nowhere within Native American cultures could he have found examples or practices to justify or to assist his venture. Though an individual might tell stories in which he or she figured, the concept of constructing an entire life story simply did not exist among Native Americans. Autobiography was a Euro-American genre, already by 1820 a developed repertoire of particular literary gestures.[40]

One could read *A Son of the Forest*—though not, I think, Apess's other texts—as simply constructed on the model of an exemplary life. "Here is a man," we might parse the structure of the story he tells, "who by the dint of his own extraordinariness, his hard work and determination, overcame the handicaps with which he was born and made something of himself." Franklin's *Autobiography*, first published in the United States in 1818, may have been known to Apess. Even if it were not, Franklin's mode of autobiographical representation, the narrative of the man who succeeds on his own by his very ability at representing himself, had begun to become part of American vernacular culture. In the scant formal education Apess did have he would probably have encountered, read or heard, stories about exemplary lives—George Washington's certainly, possibly Daniel Boone's, maybe a few others.

Puritan notions of social order and hierarchy maintained their hold sufficiently into the 1820s, especially in the Connecticut society in which Apess grew up, so that upward social mobility did not have the unambiguous value it came to have by the Civil War. Being any version of a "self-made" man was still a dubious status in New England, one that suggested slippery rather than admirable doings. It took some time, and considerable propaganda, before the model Franklin so persuasively articulated could become a wholly affirmed part of the culture of his native region. A man of lowly origins did not, in the 1820s, thus have a cultural norm available to legitimate constituting his life experiences as a progressive march up the economic or status ladder. An Indian's life might, in nineteenth-century Euro-American culture, be an exemplum, but only of what was already believed about all Indians. One might thus have the life of a noble savage, necessarily "told to" a white editor/amanuensis. The *Life of Ma-Ka-Tai-Me-She-Kia-Kiak, or Black Hawk . . .* (1833) is among the first and a good example. Or one might have the story of an Indian destroyed by too close acquaintance with white ways, a negative exemplar. "The Experience of Anne Wampy," in Apess's *The Experiences of Five*

---

40. The first two chapters of H. David Brumble III, *American Indian Autobiography* (Berkeley: University of California Press, 1988), provide a useful exposition of what he calls "preliterate traditions of American Indian autobiography."

Christian Indians (1833), could be so read. And finally there could be the autobiography of an Indian fully converted to the ways of civilization and Christianity, as in *Memoir of Catharine Brown* (1824). Such accounts of Indians converted to Christianity have the longest history, dating back to John Eliot's, the Mayhews', and Daniel Gookin's missionary activity in the seventeenth century.

The single autobiographical model readily available to Apess was also the oldest form of Western autobiography. From his early experiences of evangelical Protestantism he would have become familiar with the tradition of testifying to one's sense of sin and to the conviction of one's belief in Christ's saving grace. His first encounter with this form of narrating one's life story would have been oral. It was also common practice, when one presented oneself for membership in a church, for baptism, for a license—in the Methodist churches—to exhort, and for ordination, to account for oneself, for how one came to Christ and persisted in His ways. Often, written accounts were also required.

The conventions for organizing a conversion narrative were well established and almost indefinitely replicable for any length of life story. The writer or teller would first describe his or her life before coming into an awareness of the promise of the Christian way. Then came a detailed account of the important steps in a journey toward this awareness. The first climax in the narrative involved the struggle to believe that Christ had the power and would actually save such a sinner as oneself. This was, in the language Apess knew, the moment of conviction. Commonly, it was followed by a time of peace and serenity, of the assurance of Christ's presence in one's life. The story rarely came to an end with this first stage of assurance. Disruption almost inevitably had to follow, a time of testing and of temptation, often a falling away, not from one's belief in Christ but from faith in one's own salvation. One got lost or wandered away. In time, and with much struggle and discouragement, one returned to Christ's saving presence a second time and achieved reassurance. Its depth was measured by one's constancy in the Christian life. This pattern of assurance, decline, and reassurance permitted any number of repetitions.

A Son of the Forest and "The Experience of the Missionary," in *The Experiences,* can be seen as readily fitting this model. The end of both accounts is Apess's triumphantly becoming a fully ordained Methodist minister. He represents himself in the early pages as a being without home or parents, ignorant of any awareness of heaven or hell, and then as someone who comes slowly to believe that Christ's Word may be for him. While at the Williamses he begins regularly to attend Methodist meetings, struggles in agony to overcome his despair of Christ's caring to redeem someone of his humble nature,

achieves conviction finally, and with it a wonderful sense of relief and affirmation. This is quickly disrupted, and Apess begins his life as a runaway, an
enlisted man in the army, and a drunk. Roughly five years later, near the
bottom of the social ladder and the exhaustion of his own psychic resources,
he rehearses the first journey, discovers that Christ has called him to preach,
and thus knows his vocation: He marries and settles down, and is ordained
after his perseverance is several times tested. The End!

Thus converted, the Indian identity should be resolved into the Christian, important only as evidence of the possibility that Christ can overcome
any disability. That Apess, instead, employed his Christian identity so as to
assert, more forcibly and coherently, his identity as a Native American makes
clear that he had in mind more, or other, ambitions and models than a plain
conversion narrative. A Son of the Forest and "The Experience of the Missionary" justify his conversion and present his credentials as a Methodist
preacher; they also—and as much—explore being a Pequot, a Native American, in New England. The Appendix to A Son, "on the origin and character of
the Indians, as a nation," itself almost as long as the autobiography, demonstrates his deliberate intention. Lest we overlook it, Apess points out that to
include the Appendix he has "somewhat abridged 'his life.'" But were the
Appendix not there, the rhetoric and the design of his spiritual autobiography identify his struggles in becoming an Indian with those entailed in
becoming a Methodist.

A Son of the Forest indicates, and in some measure narrates, a lengthy
process of reflection and agony on Apess's part to name himself, his history,
and the identities and histories of his people. The process is partially evident
through his canny manipulations of white American's expectations of how an
Indian must be represented. The drunken and degenerate Indian, broken by
close contact with Euro-American civilization, is perhaps the most vividly
figured. The figure of his grandmother in a drunken rage beating him almost
to death nearly opens the book. The prelude to it is an image of Indians, of his
parents, incapable of settling down, inveterate wanderers unable to make a
living in this modern world or to create a proper, that is, an American, family
owning property or working together to acquire it.

Apess does not conceal his difficulties in identifying with his people
during much of his childhood. Little wonder if we think only of his parents'
abandoning him, the treatment by his grandparents, and his being separated
from the age of four or five from daily contact with his family or, presumably,
with other Pequots in the area.[41] He did not, in effect could not, think of

41. I wish it were possible to know more about the nature and extent of Apess's contacts with other
Pequots from the time he was placed with the Furmans until he ran away from the Williamses in

himself as a Pequot, and he resisted white people's identifying him as an "Indian." He states this plainly—"so completely was I weaned from the interests and affections of my brethren"—and then gives it full imaginative force by recalling an experience from his boyhood. He was living with the Furmans, the first white family who took on his indenture and the only one with whom there seemed to have been genuine affectional ties. Nine or ten, perhaps younger, when the encounter happened, he was out in the woods gathering berries with several members of the Furman family when they met a group of women also gathering berries. They were of a complexion, as Apess remembered it, "to say the least, as *dark* as that of the natives." Just the sight of them was enough to frighten the young boy and, terror-stricken, he runs all the way home because "my imagination had pictured out a tale of blood." He explains "that the great fear I entertained of my brethren was occasioned by the many stories I had heard of their cruelty toward the whites—how they were in the habit of killing and scalping men, women, and children" (*A Son*).

Although the writer means to communicate to his readers his virtual alienation from any affirmative identity in his childhood as a Pequot, or as a native, his shaping of the account carefully explicates the power of dominant white representations in his understanding, as a child, of his experience. Any capacity he might have had to imagine Indians other than as they were constructed by Euro-Americans was checked by the brutalities he had suffered. He speaks it simply: "I had received a lesson in the unnatural treatment of my own relations, which could not be effaced" (*A Son*). His inner sense of himself at age nine or ten could not have been securely that he was "white," but he clearly thought of himself as "not Indian." His stark terror of a few dark-skinned women gathering berries, though he was in the company of familiar adults, manifests how pervasive remained the tales of savage Indians,

---

1813 and ended up in the army. The six years with the Furmans may not have separated him, even daily, from contact with his family and other Pequots if one remembers that it was the Furmans who were the helpful neighbors who brought milk to Apess and his siblings when he lived with his grandparents. Apess might well have seen his uncle and other relatives, perhaps his brothers and sisters also, very regularly. (Apess says that after his beating the selectmen of Colchester decided "that we should be severally taken and bound out" [*A Son*], but I have yet to locate any record or other mention of any of his siblings' indentures. It seems probable that, like Apess, they were placed in households in the locality.) At the homes of both the Hillhouses and the Williamses, gentry establishments with a substantial number of household servants, there may well have been other natives in service, although Apess never mentions any. He tells us, a number of times, that he did see his father, the person to whose house he first went each time he ran away, which suggests the possibility that he may have seen his father quite often. His strong wish to return "home," after his time in Canada, and the apparent warmth of his reunion with his family and "brethren" also imply stronger ties to family and nation than *A Son of the Forest* gives felt reality to.

killers and scalpers, in New England households. Apess attributes his great fear to having been told *many* such stories. Mr. Furman is presented as moved by the boy's terror but not as having the slightest anxiety that there were any scalping and killing savages marauding among the berry bushes. Such hostilities were in the past, safely enough to be made the stuff of stories to thrill and to haunt children. The storied Indians were invisible. New Englanders' fantasies embodied the blend of vulnerability and power out of which convictions of racial superiority come. The women in the woods could have been actual Native Americans engaged in a traditional subsistence activity. Apess saw them as savages. The ironies of the story are only heightened by his adult assurance that the berry gatherers were, after all, "white" women. If his white companions particularly noticed them at all, they would have seen them as of no special significance, quiet evidence for the inevitable succession of the civilized—for they could unhesitatingly distinguish between simple stories and the reality of their own cultural power, between truly alien complexions and merely dark ones.

Several times Apess speaks gratefully of the Furmans' kindness and affection as exceptional among the whites whom he served. A servant girl in the house lies one day to Mr. Furman by accusing the boy of having threatened her with a knife. Apess denies the allegation, but Furman does not believe him and flogs him with the justification: "I will learn you, you Indian dog, how to chase people with a knife" (*A Son*).

The placement of these two stories in close relation indicates Apess's intentions as a writer. The kindest whites carry a deep conviction not only of Indians' inferiority but of their irredeemable savagery. A dog may be trained, may become a better dog, but a dog he or she will always be and, in any moment of irritation, the animal may bite, just as Indians may resort to the knife, with all its associations with scalping. Any sensible person would run from such people and suppress whatever identity he might feel or have with them. Separated from his own immediate and extended family, his labor and all his needs in the power of white people, how could this child feel any sense of being a part of any Native American community or tradition? He knew with certainty only his dependence on whites for a modicum of affection, perhaps a small bit of respect, expressions of which he also knew but thinly veiled their suspicions of him and all he represented.

The adult writer insists upon the partiality of Euro-Americans' ideology while communicating the conditions that gave it such power. Throughout the first part of *A Son of the Forest* Apess reminds his readers of the full history of Indian–white relations. His strategy is both shocking and subtle. The reader's empathy is elicited by relating experience almost as though from within a child's consciousness and in a mode that assumes and does not disturb his or her beliefs about Indians—only to have Apess turn back on the assumptions. The most evident example involves his vivid re-creation of being beaten by his grandmother, itself prefaced by descriptions of the children's utter misery and her apparently callous cruelty. He concludes by assuming the reader's voice, which he hears exclaiming, "What savages your grandparents were to treat . . . helpless children in this cruel manner," exactly the conclusion he has, in effect, promoted. The echo of the reader's voice generates Apess's responding in his adult voice with a sharp indictment of whites for dispossessing natives of their lands and then corrupting them. Rum is both a direct injury by whites and a consolation to which natives have been driven because all else has been taken from them. He emphasizes that he was treated badly only when his relatives were drunk. The sympathetic Euro-American reader is thus told that part of the blame belongs to him and his people. The turnabout in the narrative gains power by one's having been lulled toward a patronizing sympathy and then shocked by the complete disruption of the very expectations the narrative, and the ideology it so knowingly parodies, sets up.

The berry-picking incident is brought to a similar conclusion by revising the history that portrays whites as innocents enduring bloody and unmotivated Indian attacks. Apess does more, however, for by performing the revision at the end of the story he shows how the Euro-American ideology works through suppressing part of, and so inverting, the actual history:

> But the whites did not tell me that they were in a great majority of instances the aggressors—that they had imbrued their hands in the lifeblood of my brethren, driven them from their once peaceful and happy homes—that they introduced among them the fatal and exterminating diseases of civilized life. If the whites had told me how cruel they had been to the "poor Indian," I should have apprehended as much harm from them. [*A Son*]

With Mr. Furman the process is strikingly individualized. This otherwise good man is driven by an ideology which, precisely because it is unconscious, disables any doubt. He assumes that the story of the knife-wielding Apess has to be true because that is how "Indians" are: "But the poor man soon found out his error, as *after* he had flogged me he undertook to investigate the matter, when to his amazement he discovered it was nothing but fiction."

Literary fictions seem also to be in Apess's consciousness. The title of his first autobiography is one of its most intriguing qualities. "A son of the forest" has an especially literary and almost genteel ring to it. It immediately places Apess's book in the context of the emerging nationalist literature in the United States. As early in poetry as Philip Freneau, whose "Indian Burying

Ground" refers to "the children of the forest," and in fiction with Charles
Brockden Brown's *Edgar Huntly* (1799), American writers had begun to exploit Indian themes and characters to foreclose "American" literature's being
seen as only a provincial aping of the European, but it is in the 1820s that an
exploration of "the Indian" becomes almost the compulsory means of liter-
arily expressing "the American." Cooper is the best known of the writers, but
there were many others: Washington Irving, John Neal, Lydia Maria Child,
and Catharine Maria Sedgwick among them. These writers made the concept
of Indians as children of the forest a commonplace. (It would make a useful
chapter in the history of European images of Native Americans to have an
exact account of the origin and diffusion of the phrase and of the concept of
Indians as children of the forest.) Apess may have simply picked up his title
because it was in the cultural air or possibly directly from James Lawson's
popular verse narrative, *Ontwa, the Son of the Forest* (1822).

The title asserts a peculiarly self-conscious claim to Indianness, which is
reiterated on the title page with "A Native of the Forest" immediately modify-
ing "William Apes." For him to choose these representations seems, at first,
somewhat odd. In Euro-American usage these phrases were patronizing in
their association with a primitive, natural, and childlike state. These were
names native peoples were even less likely to give themselves than other
European-imposed names like "Indian." By choosing them, Apess signifies
that he can only express himself and his experience in the media of the
dominant culture through its representational codes. Having the title page
additionally inform the reader that the book was "Written by Himself" acknowledges the presumption that "sons of the forest" are generally illiterate.

His text somewhat complicates any assurance of all this being fully self-
possessed and deliberately ironic. He can be playful and unmistakably witty
when, for example, he interjects these comments in the middle of an explanation of his objection to being called "Indian": "I could not find [Indian] in the
Bible and therefore concluded that it was a word imported for the special
purpose of degrading us. At other times I thought it was derived from the
term *in-gen-uity*" (*A Son*). But is the irony unintentional in this story, which
occurs quite late in *A Son of the Forest*? Shortly after his baptism in Connecticut
in December 1818 Apess decides to visit his father in Colrain, several days'
journey away. On one of these days, despite having walked a long time, he
continues on after dark, thinking he can soon reach his father's house:

> Unfortunately, I took the wrong road and was led into a swamp. I
> thought I was not far from the main road . . . and not being aware of the
> dangerous situation in which I was placed, I penetrated into the labyrinth
> of darkness with the hope of gaining the main road. At every step I

became more and more entangled—the thickness of the branches above me shut out the little light afforded by the stars, and to my horror I found that the further I went, the deeper the mire; at last, I was brought to a dead stand.

Lost in the woods and swamp on his way to his own father's house, a route he presumably had traveled often before, how can this figure be taken as an Indian? Indians do not get lost in the woods—at least not in American literature and stereotype. They are, after all, attuned to the movements and signs and sounds of nature beyond the capacities of all but the most exceptional whites. Is Apess in this passage teasing these assumptions? Might he be responding to well-known literary representations of the Indian's "true nature" like those in Cooper's *The Pioneers* (1823), *The Last of the Mohicans* (1826), and *The Prairie* (1827), which had almost at once consolidated for Euro-American culture a whole ideological complex about Indians and their nature? Cooper's novels gained cultural power through their elegiac tone about a time safely in the distant past when Indians, the French, and the English contended for survival and dominance in the Northeast and Old Northwest. The Indian as noble and doomed could elicit sympathy and regret while his passage legitimated the poignant but inevitable fact of the superiority of Euro-American civilization. These, and other novels, depended upon and shaped an idea of a people fully, or virtually, extinct in the lands of the original thirteen colonies.[42]

We might read Apess's "getting lost" not only as a metaphor for his spiritual struggle for his Christian vocation but also as a commentary on all that had happened to actual Native Americans in the East who were lost from the sight of the dominant culture, lost from cultural consciousness, and also lost in terms of much of their ancestral heritage. They were, at best, wards of state governments which presumed that they would soon disappear either by assimilation or by simply dying out. It may overread this intriguing episode in *A Son of the Forest* also to point out that Apess represents himself as lost on his way to his father's house, the father who is part white and part Indian and who

42. These ideas were so pervasive as to have the status of facts. Two almost randomly chosen examples can illustrate how reflexive they were. The first is from the *Boston Daily Advocate*, October 30, 1837, the reform newspaper that fiercely supported the cause of the Mashpees and the Cherokees. The editors are commenting on the tour by "chiefs" of some of the western Indian nations of the cities of the East: "how vain it is for their feeble tribes . . . to contend with this mighty nation"; "these noble relics of a once powerful race"; "these sons of the forest." Or this, from De Forest's *History*, 446: "Nothing is left but a little and miserable remnant, hanging around the seats where their ancestors once reigned supreme, as a few half-withered leaves may sometimes be seen clinging to the upper branches of a blighted and dying tree."

chooses, at least from time to time, to live far away from any Native American community (at least any known to historians of the period).

This suggestion may provoke other questions about the significance of the title Apess chose for this first book. To be a son of the forest is to be literally without human parents, a child of nature. Though one might read Apess's self-presentation in the autobiography as following Euro-American conventions in stressing his lonely and individual struggle toward success or, in this case, conversion, its religious equivalent, the title expresses both his own experience of isolation from his human parents and his affirmative affiliation with all that whites associated with being Indian. If it represents any denial of his father, it also refuses to confirm the overt patriarchalism of his Connecticut gentry guardians. Judge Hillhouse may be the "patriarch of Montville," but neither he nor William Williams is, in Apess's version, anything but a hypocritical father pretending benevolence while stealing Indian lands, the Indians' patrimony: "They had possession of the red man's inheritance and had deprived me of liberty; with this they were satisfied and could do as they pleased" (*A Son*).[43] He would not have them as fathers, regardless of their pretension, just as later, in the *Eulogy on King Philip*, he rejects George Washington as the sole father of *his* country.

Are mothers to be found here even allusively? Need the phrase "a son of the forest" reflexively invoke patriarchy?[44] Sons, after all, have a father and a mother. Nature, in the European cosmology, was seen as feminine, and so one might read the title as showing both how Apess regathers himself figuratively into a community of Native Americans and how he recovers for himself some kind of mother in substitution for the one who abandoned him (for longer than did his father) and whose own mother beat him. Women are marked ambivalently throughout the autobiography. One need only recall the berry

43. To speak of the Indians' "patrimony" risks reinforcing a recurrent European mistake about Native American cultures and societies. European observers and commentators insisted that native women were oppressed by the men, mere drudges with fewer rights and less power than European women freely enjoyed. No single generalization covers these many and diverse cultures. However, in most, women in fact exercised power and authority far beyond what any European woman of almost any class possessed in the nineteenth century. Many native cultures were matrilineal, some matrifocal, and most honored women without enshrining them. Descent and inheritance, then, often followed the women's line among Native Americans. Apess himself takes care to point out that among the Pequots one belonged to the nation if one's mother was a Pequot. James Axtell, *The Indian Peoples of Eastern America: A Documentary History of the Sexes* (New York: Oxford University Press, 1981), is a beautifully edited anthology of documents by Europeans about their perceptions of gender relations among Native Americans. It provides the beginnings of a cultural history of the European need to portray native societies as male-dominated.

44. The repeated refrain in his conversion narrative in *The Experiences* is "children of nature" or, when referring to himself, "the little Indian boy."

pickers from whom Apess flees to Mr. Furman, a male protector, like his own uncle, from ferocious Indian women—or the servant girl in the Furman household who lies about Apess wielding a knife. She has a successor in the Williams household whom he portrays as constantly persecuting him, telling stories so that he will get flogged, and pushing him down the stairs so forcibly as to injure him seriously. And later in the 1829 version of *A Son of the Forest*, Apess focuses on a Methodist woman with whom he and his family board who treats his wife and child cruelly and spreads rumors about him to the Methodist Conference so that he is denied a license to preach.

What these figures of women all have in common, beginning with his mother and including the Methodist boardinghouse keeper, is that they alienate him from the community of his brethren or that they punish him for being Indian, reminding him of his isolation from any supportive or legitimating community—or, as with the berry pickers, they represent his estrangement. Two women, Mrs. Furman and Aunt Sally George, stand apart. Not only do they seem to be the only nurturant presences in Apess's telling of his life, they also suggest how one might link the apparently discordant forms Apess depends upon to structure his account. I will return to them a bit later.

I have not provided a single or simple answer to the question of what models Apess could have drawn on to write his life. My readings should suggest how much he had to work with the discursive practices through which Euro-Americans maintained Native Americans' inferiority. I have also indicated how much, in text and life, he had to struggle with his estrangement from his own people, his "brethren." His experience with his grandparents and his education while at the Furmans would have given Euro-American ideologies about Indians an enhanced power, a nearly impenetrable illusion of truth. I doubt we can dependably recover imaginatively how much he must have suffered. We can and should try. His autobiographical texts give many of the exterior marks of his pain but with a detachment or an impersonality that might remind us that the novel has not yet gained dominion over most literary practices. Like Franklin, Apess writes about his inner life more in notation than in a re-creative mode designed to elicit a reader's empathetic identification with the protagonist. This can be off-putting, can seem boring or unfeeling or flat, in this postromantic age, which expects of all its narrative forms—news or film, talk shows or novels—a quickened sense of a personal and feeling presence. Passion and conflict figure largely, nonetheless, in his autobiographical texts. They are most evident in his more obviously rhetorical gestures. More subtly and importantly, they are present in his struggle to negotiate among the forms of representation available to him so as to speak simultaneously personally and as a Native American.

The conversion narrative is the most overt of these and, for most twentieth-century readers, the most resistant. Many assume a Christianized ✓ Indian is no more than a convert to Euro-American ways. The language of evangelical Protestantism that Apess employs often strikes contemporary ears as formulaic and monotonous. This violates expectations of how an "Indian" writer should talk, as though it could only be inauthentic for a Native American to speak through any medium originating in European culture. In truth, neither Euro-Americans nor Native Americans have available some culturally unmixed terrain on which to move or any pure medium free from the effects of the other. Well before the early nineteenth century, Indians in New England had had taken from them a land base sufficient to maintain cultures largely segregated from European influences. Native cultures did not, however, thus disappear or become assimilated into Anglo- or Euro-American culture. Cultural adaptation, we may need reminding, never stops and cannot reflexively be taken as a sign of one culture's absorption into another. Apess and any Native American who wished to move Euro-Americans had no choice but to employ comprehensible expressive forms. But before Apess could have conceived this adult vocation he had to break out of his isolation from his fellow Pequots. Locating himself in sympathetic relationship to them required resisting the daily power whites had over him and undermining the power of their ideas, which justified the subordination of Indians. It also meant overcoming, or compensating for, the psychic scarring he endured from his parents' abandonment and, most brutally, from his Pequot grandparents.

Evangelical Christianity, specifically the Methodists, gave him the means. This can seem paradoxical unless we remember that although Protestant Christianity dominated every aspect of American culture in the first half of the nineteenth century it was neither homogeneous nor undivided. The sectarian and denominational quarrels were not simply narrowly theological. Every political struggle in the society, every matter of race, reform, gender, and class, found expression in religious life. Apess may possibly have been a less knowing narrator of his conversion to Methodism than he is in the passages I have examined, but the structure of his conversion narrative—far less conventional than it first appears—demonstrates how Christianity be- ✓ came a means for him to develop a powerful identification with his fellow Pequots and, eventually, with all people of color.[45]

Apess's time with the Furmans is decisive in the formation of his association of dissenting Christianity with being an outcast. His time with them, from age five to eleven, seems to have been the only period in his entire childhood when he had a genuine home. Their role in rescuing him from his grand-

---

45. "The Experience of the Missionary," in *The Experiences*, makes the connection between his form of Christianity and his developing Indian nationalism considerably more explicit than his narrative in *A Son of the Forest*.

parents, their previous kindness to him and his siblings, and the fact that they were near neighbors, farming people close in status and manner to what he already knew, could only have drawn him—in his need—toward them. Several details in his autobiography indicate that, as a child, he felt a powerful attachment to them, especially to Mrs. Furman. He always characterizes her fondly, remembering her gentleness, her caring conversations with him, and that she never raises voice or whip to him, unlike his grandparents, her husband, any of Apess's subsequent masters, and most of his first employers. Her mother also lived with the family. She died when Apess was about eight. His remembrance reinforces a sense of how much he had once felt himself a part of the family: "She had always been so kind to me that I missed her quite as much as her children, and I had been allowed to call her mother" (*A Son*).

Mrs. Furman introduces Apess to religious anxiety and to evangelical Christianity. His account suggests how deliberately she did so and how much the boy may have heard in her concern the tones of someone he could accept as a mother. When he is six she asks him if he has ever thought about what will happen to him when he dies. He responds that only old people die, so she shows him the graves of children younger than himself: "I felt an indescribable sensation pass through my frame; I trembled and was sore afraid and for some time endeavored to hide myself from the destroying monster" (*A Son*). Shortly thereafter he is taken to his first religious meeting, a Baptist one, for the Furmans were Baptists. He describes himself as taking pleasure in these gatherings, in hearing the word of God. And he begins to struggle to become a Christian. The movement of the narrative unmistakably associates going to Baptist meeting with securely belonging to the family. Emotional and religious shelters become one.[46]

Five years later the Furmans expel him from the family. *A Son of the Forest*, written twenty years after, mutes the betrayal and trauma I believe he felt.[47]

---

46. This association is more fully drawn in "The Experience of the Missionary," as are his hopes: "They, being Baptist people and having no children of their own, became more fond of me than is usual for people to be of adopted children." After he has worshiped with them for a while and describes the sweetness of it, he concludes: "And so it caught my youthful heart. . . . And my mind became more knitted together with them" (*Exps.*).

47. Again, the account in "The Experience of the Missionary" is more direct, one of the elements in it that makes me think that, though it was not published until 1833, Apess may have written all but its last pages before he began *A Son of the Forest*: "I was alone in the world, fatherless, motherless, and helpless, as it were, and none to speak for the poor little Indian boy. Had my skin been white, with the same abilities and the same parentage, there could not have been found a place good enough for me. But such is the case with depraved nature, that their judgment for fancy only sets upon the eye, skin, nose, lips, cheeks, chin, or teeth and, sometimes, the forehead and hair; without further examination, the mind is made up and the price set" (*Exps.*). While Apess may generalize "depraved nature" to all white people in these words, they are most immediately in reference to the Furmans.

His exile is ostensibly caused by his agreeing to the plan of one of the older children to run away as a kind of adventure. When he is discovered, the Furmans decide it is time for him to have another master. Apess's brief comment speaks the enormity of his loss: "I had the world and everything my little heart could desire on a string."

The retrospective narration he creates about these years shapes another tale, however, one that reflects what must have been his struggle for much of his life. Consider his experience: Abandoned by his natal parents and nearly beaten to death by his grandmother, he comes to believe he has a home with a kind white family, unlike his own Indian family in every important way. Then they cast him out—in fact, they trick him into leaving by suggesting he can come back, and then when he does he discovers he has actually been "sold" to his new master. What identity remains for him? Being an Indian might at least provide an explanation for this treatment. The chapters (II, III, and IV) devoted to the three white families with whom he grew up between 1802 and 1813 enact a recurrent pattern in which his identity as an outcast child, an Indian no one wants, is connected to his attraction to evangelical sects, which antagonizes his guardians. These sects become a middle ground between the white world that denies and oppresses him and his own family and people, with whom there seems no immediate way to affiliate.

This pattern is manifested in his first account of his happiness in attending Baptist meetings with the Furmans. But then "the enemy of my soul . . . would strive to lead me away." This "enemy" conventionally is the devil, the tempter, of course. Apess continues in the same passage, however, in a way to suggest that the enemy, devil though he may be, is inseparable from white prejudice against Indians:

> I remember that nothing scarcely grieved me so much, when my mind had been thus petted [by hearing the Word of God], than to be called by a nickname. . . . I know nothing so trying to a child as to be repeatedly called by an improper name. I thought it disgraceful to be called an Indian; it was considered as a slur upon an oppressed and scattered nation. [*A Son*]

What begins as a description of being attended by Mrs. Furman and of his attendance at church gets turned, by being called an Indian, to his attending to being a native and his relationship to other Native Americans. His story about his terrifying meeting with the berry pickers he took to be Indians follows immediately, and he notes that he feared "Indians" more than any physical punishment. Almost immediately following this, Mr. Furman displaces Mrs. Furman in the narration, and Apess reports his being badly beaten several times by him. One of these times is when Furman calls him an

"Indian dog." Perhaps the most decisive beating occurs when the boy is in the middle of a frightening spiritual crisis, which Mr. Furman decides to solve by "beating the devil" out of him. He lapses from the Furmans' church and from obedience to them. And he loses his place as his mistress's "favorite."

His experience in this household leads him toward Christianity while also imposing on him its prejudices against Native Americans. It is as though Mrs. Furman communicates to him that he can be petted and loved, can become a Baptist, only by forgetting that he is a native. When he remembers, or they do, he loses his relation to them and to their church. By casting him out they unforgettably tell him he will always be a dispensable alien, or so it seems he understood it. His association of them with the Baptists may explain why he turns to the Methodists. He never again mentions the Baptists in his autobiographies, although they shared with the Methodists a powerful evangelical appeal, because of their egalitarian practices, to the lower classes, to African Americans, and to Native Americans. They also were scorned by proper New England gentry for indiscriminately mixing members of the social order and for their enthusiastic preaching and worship—all the qualities Apess specifically mentions as explanation for his feeling at home with the Methodists.

The rendition of his time with Judge Hillhouse and the Williamses carries no hint of any emotional bond, in memory or in historical fact. It also seems significant that Apess brings his father back at this point as an active presence in the narrative. (In his actual life, given that the Furmans lived in Colchester, as did his father, Apess may have seen him before this, but he makes no mention of it.) Each time he runs away from the Hillhouses and the Williamses he goes to his father. He also announces himself in an independent voice, as though he were already an adult. And his language approximates the contractual in its objective assessment of their treatment of him and of his behavior in return. Whatever the gestures these two gentry families might have made to the boy, the adult narrator speaks with no illusion that there could ever be intimate ties. He is a bound boy, an Indian, and a servant. What matters is how well he is treated, fed, clothed, housed, and whether he is given the opportunity for schooling and to attend the worship services he chooses. With both households he describes himself from the beginning as ready to assert his rights and to oppose any undue exercise of authority. Religious difference is the primary means by which he inscribes his distance from both.

The conflicts that lead to his leaving both families are presented as primarily over his being forbidden to attend Methodist meetings. His being flogged for his disobedience—and the point he makes throughout these chapters about a pattern of beatings from his white masters—echoes against the brutal beating that opens the book, as though to confirm his words to his readers that such violence finally has its origins in what white people do to Native Americans, that whites are the ones to fear.

Both the Hillhouses' and the Williamses' Congregational ways are focused upon as inadequate to the needs of the spirit. Apess, in these passages, repeats the complaints revivalists had been bringing against settled and formal churches since the Great Awakening. But he chooses those that emphasize the emptiness and pretension of these pillars of the settled order. Their prayers are rote and unfelt, their preachers rely too much on learning for its own sake and read their texts, and the definitive sign of their spiritual deadness is recognizable by all evangelicals: "It [the minister's preaching] did not arouse me to a sense of my danger—and I am of the opinion that it had no better effect on the people of his charge" (*A Son*).

Apess's presentation of his turn to the Methodists makes plain, I think, how he made, or found, in them a place to join being Christian and Native American. Methodist meeting became a means to resist the scorn and the cultural superiority, the class and the racial domination, of all that the Hillhouses and Williamses represented. In meetings he could also engage a form of worship that equally honored the oral and the written, even favored oral expressivity over a command of the written word. His doing so was not idiosyncratic, for there is considerable evidence that evangelicals reached and converted Native Americans where the older and more formal denominations routinely failed. Through the Methodists one could see the falsities of the claims the powerful made about their own moral superiority. The Methodists' egalitarian practices indicted all the existing hierarchies, and their preaching stressed that Christ's message was for the poor and the oppressed. The reaction of the wellborn and established to the Methodists confirmed Apess's sense of belonging:

> About this time the Methodists began to hold meetings in the neighborhood, and . . . a storm of persecution gathered; the pharisee and the worldling united heartily in abusing them. The gall and wormwood of sectarian malice were emitted, and every evil report . . . was freely circulated. And it was openly said that the character of a respectable man would receive a stain, and a deep one, too, by attending one of their meetings. [*A Son*]

The stories, Apess tells us, that people spread about the Methodists were so bad as to keep people of "character" from risking their reputations by coming to the meetings except, that is, to scoff and disrupt, a behavior he then reads as a sign that these people's moral conduct is even beneath "the heathen." Apess turns the social, racial, and moral hierarchy on its head through his exposition of Methodism. He makes explicit that, for him, joining the

Methodists affirms his being a native and his rejection of the codes of the dominant order:

> I thought I had no character to lose in the estimation of those who were accounted great. For what cared they for me? They had possession of the red man's inheritance and had deprived me of liberty; with this they were satisfied and could do as they pleased; therefore, I thought I could do as I pleased, measurably. I therefore went to hear the *noisy Methodists*. [*A Son*]

The first time that he comes close to the conviction that Christ is his Savior, his words convey what he remembered as essential: "I felt convinced that Christ died for all mankind—that age, sect, color, country, or situation made no difference. I felt an assurance that I was included in the plan of redemption with all my brethren" (*A Son*).

When the Williamses try to prevent his attendance at Methodist meetings he runs away for the last time. His long bout with rum and his declension from Christian practice follow. About seven years pass before he returns to the Methodist fold and finds his vocation as a preacher. I cannot, without making this extended introduction too full, examine the several ways in which these years seem to have brought him still closer to his identification with Native Americans. His autobiographical rendering becomes, I think, more episodic in its account of the later years and lacks the intensity of feeling that so evidently gives design to the earliest parts of the narrative.

One substantial development should be mentioned. When he decides to return to Connecticut after his postwar sojourn in Canada, it is to go "home." And he speaks of missing his brethren. The only other time he has named a home for himself in the narrative it was with the Furmans. Home now becomes seeing and being with his fellow Pequots.

Aunt Sally George is the most notable of these. A relative on his father's side, possibly his sister or an aunt, Sally George plays a role in the two autobiographies; hers is one of the lives in *The Experiences of Five Christian Indians,* and she seems to have been, from other sources, one of several Pequot women who led the nation, keeping it and its precariously held land base together. Apess pays her extended tribute in *A Son of the Forest* and in *The Experiences* as a holy woman revered by whites and Native Americans alike. He mentions living with her one winter (probably 1817/18).

Every four weeks, he says, they had a meeting which drew people from "Rhode Island, Stonington, and other places," and Aunt Sally would, it appears, preach. The specification of where "people" came from makes it probable that they were all Native Americans, possibly only Pequots but they could also have been Narragansetts. This ostensibly Methodist and informal congregation may have been thoroughly unorthodox. Aunt Sally George was illiterate and probably spoke only broken English. Pequot was unquestionably her first language, and she exhorted, I suspect from Apess's account, in her native tongue. Some of the details he gives are blurred, perhaps deliberately, so as to avoid discipline or censure from the Methodist Conference. Enough is told to suggest that these meetings joined elements of Pequot spiritual traditions with evangelical Methodism. None of the participants may have consciously married the two, but the setting of the meetings and their being presided over by a woman preacher who was also an elder of the nation known for her capacity to cure people's physical and spiritual ills are wonderfully suggestive. Perhaps here, in the woods of the small remnant of the once extensive Pequot lands, Apess fully brought his two heritages together:

> These seasons were glorious. We observed particular forms, although we knew nothing about the dead languages, except that the knowledge thereof was not necessary for us to serve God. We had no house of divine worship, and believing "that the groves were God's first temples," thither we would repair when the weather permitted. The Lord often met with us, and we were happy in spite of the devil. Whenever we separated it was in perfect love and friendship. [*A Son*]

THE PEQUOT LEGACY

William Apess's family were New Englanders—and Indians, Pequots, unmistakably. They may, the evidence also suggests, have been part African American. Were they invisible to Euro-Americans in the region as Pequots or as Indians? And to themselves as well? What might it have meant in nineteenth-century New England to be "Indian," in one's consciousness and in one's daily life? I have sketched some of the ways they were represented by Euro-American culture. How did they represent themselves? Apess's writing can be understood as a constant endeavor to articulate the presence and being of Native Americans as an active part of American society. Because Euro-Americans controlled all the representational codes and, through them, named Indians either as being a pitiable race corrupted by its contact with civilization or as noble savages doomed to extinction, Apess had to exploit implicit contradictions between Euro-American ideas and their practice. An evangelical and egalitarian Christian rhetoric gave him one means, republican theory and ideals another. A historical discourse seems to me another, for it could enable him to question the version of history that enshrined the inevitability of the Indian's extinction. It might also make possible, in time, a very different understanding of Native Americans and thus of the relations between them and Euro-Americans.

This may explain why so much of his writing seeks to recover existences and experiences that have been lost. These include his own sense of identity and the presence in New England of surviving native populations. An awareness of one is necessary to an awareness of the other in his writing, as it has been for Native Americans in New England from the eighteenth century to the present. Asserting one's cultural identity as a "native" requires the recognition, or the invocation, of a community of Native Americans.

By 1829, when Apess first wrote, the surviving Native Americans in New England had been reduced materially to the margins of the economic and occupational world. A few lived on reservation lands scattered through Connecticut, Rhode Island, Vermont, Maine, and Massachusetts, but most seem to have chosen to leave the utter impoverishment of these uneconomic sites. Apess characterized reservation dwellers as "the most mean, abject, miserable race of beings in the world—a complete place of prodigality and prostitution" (*Exps.*). Life off the reservations could not have been dramatically better if the evidence I have so far gathered proves to be a reliable sample of the whole. Day labor was the common lot of the employed, and these laborers were, at least sometimes, cheated of their pay by employers who could depend on the Indians having no recourse. For many the situation was yet closer to the edge. Unable to obtain dependable employment and without sufficient land on their own to maintain their traditional economy, Indians made and sold baskets and brooms. The stress was great enough so that it appears there were many broken marriages and instances of men leaving their families simply because they could not tolerate their own helplessness in providing the basic means of survival for a wife and children. This, for example, seems to be what happened with Apess's parents. Indian children were commonly taken from families and "put out" to labor for white families in return for their upbringing, and Indian women worked on the lowliest rungs of the economic ladder in service to wealthy white people. To this extent, at least, and perhaps in most of the other details of his life, we might be justified in seeing Apess as "typical."

Indians, then, were out of whites' daily sight, because they either worked outside the main flow of the New England economy or lived "behind the stairs" in gentry houses, the lowest and predictably the most despised servants, possibly ostracized by other servants, if Apess's several anecdotes represent others' experience as well as his own. They seemed to have lived in places as out of the way as were their occupations. Apess himself, remember, was born in a tent, which his father had pitched somewhere in the woods near Colrain. Many lived at the far edge of settlements in poor housing; others joined with free blacks, their partners as the most despised group in New England. Marriages across the two cultural lines were common and further united these two stigmatized peoples. Exact numbers and statistics cannot be cited and, were they to be found, they would, I believe, substantially undercount the number of Indians in New England throughout the nineteenth century. Men were at sea or, as was often the case for the poorest Americans of whatever group, on the road looking for whatever employment could be found. Migration was an inescapable fact of life then, as it so often is today, for those whom society refuses to value or to acknowledge except as members of a pool from which to draw workers to be paid the lowest wages in the worst of conditions. Censuses notoriously miss such people. Those people who might be found and who might have identified themselves as "Indian," or by the name of a cultural group such as "Mohegan" or "Pequot," could not have been registered in most federal censuses in the nineteenth century because there was no category for them. One could only be "white," "colored," or "mulatto."

Economic marginality generated cultural marginality. If all Indians were "dogs," and many appeared to whites to live little better than animals, or if they had to disappear—at least by the reductive and arbitrary racial categories assumed by whites—"upward" into a white racial order that would eventually erase the marks of their "Indianness" or "degenerate" into communities of black Americans, their keeping alive a sense of their personal and cultural identity as Pequots or Mohegans, Narragansetts or Wampanoags, would have required extraordinary gifts—gifts which some must have possessed or we would know nothing about these people; and there would be no descendants.

The making of baskets and brooms, an apparently old and traditional "Indian" craft, could be seen as one such form of cultural pride and persistence. The process of gathering the materials for the baskets could be the means for one generation to pass on to another not only skills but a body of traditional values about the presence of the Spirit in all of nature. The shapes and the designs might themselves both represent continuities in the cultures and function as adaptations to the pressures on native communities in New England. For many native peoples in New England basket and broom making became, in the nineteenth century, a necessary means to economic survival. Making these traditional items for market required difficult changes, among them standardization in production. Making them to be valued and used apart from the values and ends of their makers involved some of the most complex alterations in native cultures. Yet, as this account from a twentieth-century Schaghticoke woman makes evident, the whole process could function as a form of survival and resistance:

> I spoke to a Mohawk basket-maker not long ago and asked her how she felt about weaving sweet grass into her baskets. Sweet grass is used by her

people in their ceremonies and like tobacco is believed to have a great power. It was used long ago in ceremonial baskets. . . .

She told me . . . that was why she always talked to the sweet grass and to her baskets as she made them. She said that she asked forgiveness for having to sell the baskets, but that she needed the money to survive. Using the sweet grass would keep the baskets strong and alive, and she hoped that the people who bought them would appreciate their signifi-cance. The basket weaver explained that she never picked the grass without making a tobacco offering. Her people believe that you have to give something for everything you take. . . . That is the old way, our way.

It helps me to remember another thing my grandmother used to say: "Sometimes it is better to bend like the willow than to be strong and break like the oak."[48]

Basket and broom making, like other aspects of Native American history and expression, could also become the occasion for recurrent and terrible humiliations because of Euro-Americans' responses. Recall the example Thoreau chooses to exemplify how the market works in a capitalist society:

Not long since, a strolling Indian went to sell baskets at the house of a well-known lawyer in my neighborhood. "Do you wish to buy any baskets?" he asked. "No, we do not want any," was the reply. "What!" exclaimed the Indian as he went out the gate, "do you mean to starve us?" Having seen his industrious white neighbors so well off,—that the lawyer had only to weave arguments, and by some magic wealth and standing followed, he had said to himself; I will go into business; I will weave baskets; it is a thing which I can do. Thinking that when he had made the baskets he would have done his part, and then it would be the white man's to buy them. He had not discovered that it was necessary for him to make it worth the other's while to buy them, or at least make him think that it was so, or make something else which it would be worth his while to buy.[49]

In such a society a person is only as valuable as the worth of his or her product on the market. Although the presence in many New England households and museums of Indian baskets from this period manifests that they

48. Trudie Lamb Richmond, "Spirituality and Survival in Schaghticoke Basket-Making," in Ann McMullen and Russell G. Handsman, eds., *A Key into the Language of Woodsplint Baskets* (Washington, CT: American Indian Archaeological Institute, 1987), 129. This whole book is one of the best single studies I know of the process of cultural maintenance and change among New England Native Americans. I have depended entirely on it for this all too summary paragraph on a fascinating, rich, and complex subject.

49. *The Illustrated Walden* (Princeton, NJ: Princeton University Press, 1973), 19.

had some value, Thoreau's anecdote reminds the historian both of the persistence of Indians in the region and of the precarious dignity of anyone who had to make a living by going from door to door persuading people of the economic value of her product, one which embodied sacred traditions and values.

Apess knew, directly and painfully, about basket making and peddling and their degradation of native peoples' dignity and their material decency. His grandmother supported the family, at least in part, by peddling brooms and baskets. As he remembered it:

> Sometimes we had something to eat, and at other times nothing. Many are the times we have gone to bed supperless, to rest our little weary limbs, stretched upon a bundle of straw, and how thankful we were for this comfort; and in the morning we were thankful to get a cold potato for our breakfasts. We thought it good fare. There was a white man who lived about a mile off, and he would, at times, bring us some frozen milk, which for a time supplied the calls of nature. We suffered thus from the cold; the calls of nature, as with almost nakedness; and calumny heaped upon us by the whites to an intense degree. [*Exps.*]

This was not the worst of it. The mixture of apparently kind acts from some white people and abusiveness from others must have borne down on his grandmother to a degree we can only dimly grasp by seeing what it drove her to:

> my grandmother had been out among the whites, with her baskets and brooms, and had fomented herself with the fiery waters of the earth, so that she had lost her reason and judgment and, in this fit of intoxication, raged most bitterly and in the meantime fell to beating me most cruelly; calling for whips, at the same time, of unnatural size, to beat me with; and asking me, at the same time, question after question, if I hated her. And I would say yes at every question; and the reason why was because I knew no other form of words. Thus I was beaten, until my poor little body was mangled and my little arm broken into three pieces, and in this horrible situation left for a while. And had it not been for an uncle of mine, who lived in the other part of the old hut, I think that she would have finished my days; but through the goodness of God, I was snatched from an untimely grave. [*Exps.*]

"Question after question, if I hated her": The phrase offers a route back into the finally unimaginable inner life of Apess's grandmother. Is it possible at this distance in time and in our own states of being to acknowledge how much hatred and humiliation this woman must have suffered day after day, trying to survive and having to make herself and her goods pleasing to whites—for a pittance? Anne Wampy, another Pequot basket maker, and one of Apess's converts to Christianity, was remembered years later by John Avery in his *History of the Town of Ledyard,* leaving her house each spring covered from head to foot by all the baskets she had made over the winter. She returned, always, as he recalled, having sold all her baskets and having spent all the money to drink herself into a stupor. Through Apess we can almost hear her words: "When Christian come to talk with me, me no like 'em; me no want to see 'em; me love nobody; I want no religion. . . . by me, by me come trouble very much, me very much troubled. Me no like Christians, me hate 'em; hate every body" (*Exps.*).

When Apess went in 1831 with a formal charge "to preach to my native tribe," he "found them a poor, miserable company" (*Exps.*). Anne Wampy, "an old veteran of the woods," seems to have been the worst of them. His own personal history might have haunted him in this journey, but he says nothing about it. As readers we are asked to attend Anne Wampy, to hear her words as closely as possible to the way she spoke them. What kind of recovery might this be? The text does not provide any straightforward response. Unlike the proud claim to be the child of Indian royalty with which he opens *A Son of the Forest,* or the assertive nationalism of the *Eulogy on King Philip,* or the calmly stern reproach of whites in "An Indian's Looking-Glass," these Indians, these Pequots, are uncomfortably close—as he portrays them—to the common images of Indians as degenerate wretches. It is interesting that Apess attempts to give us an approximation of Anne Wampy's own speech. Is it a translation of her Pequot, or a rendering of a kind of Pidgin English? Her conversion, in the account, is as pleasing as it is unexpected. But it, too, can be read as a conversion from the woods and all that they represent, a shedding of an Indian identity to assume the white robes of Christianity.

If one reads *The Experiences of Five Christian Indians* as a whole, these ambivalences about, or in, Apess's writing can be resolved.[50] His own account is consistently sharper in blaming whites for the conditions of contemporary Indians than he is in *A Son of the Forest.* His grandmother is entirely exonerated of any responsibility for what she does because of what white people have done to her. In Mary Apess who writes her own experience, in Hannah Caleb who dictates hers and whose speech Apess also seems to try to catch precisely, and in Aunt Sally George, also a dictated account in direct discourse, one has

50. Some editions of *The Experiences of Five Christian Indians of the Pequot Tribe,* though not the one I have worked with, include as part of the title *or, An Indian's Looking-Glass for the White Man.* This fuller title reinforces my reading here that Apess meant the book to function as a whole so as to subvert any reading that might accommodate these conversion stories to a justification of Euro-American culture and its primacy.

women who almost explicitly conjoin identities as Native Americans with being Christian. And Apess follows Anne Wampy's story with "An Indian's Looking-Glass." No ambiguity governs its sentences. There Apess insists that whites look upon their treatment of Indians and accept that their actions are the cause of Indians' degradation, not some inborn incapacity or any other inevitability. In effect he is, as through the example of Anne Wampy, saying, "Look at what you have wrought, our poverty and exclusion, and at the images you then manipulate to justify doing nothing." But hear his own words:

> Having a desire to place a few things before my fellow creatures who are traveling with me to the grave, and to that God who is the maker and preserver both of the white man and the Indian, whose abilities are the same and who are to be judged by one God, who will show no favor to outward appearances but will judge righteousness—now I ask if degradation has not been heaped long enough upon the Indians? And if so, can there not be a compromise? Is it right to hold and promote prejudices? If not, why not put them all away? I mean here, among those who are civilized. [*Exps.*]

For a Pequot to convert to Christianity is not, in this understanding, to take on white ways but only to claim one of her rights as a human being. Nor need she hide anything of her history, be it as painful and modest as Anne Wampy's, for it is a sign of her survival and of what she has endured at the hands of white people. Apess seems clearly to have understood that his people had to be made visible to whites, that their marginalities should not be disguised. White people had to see that they were responsible for the history Indians were living. Christianity was a faith that could be offered to Indians because it affirmed their equality with all other humans. Those who employed Christianity otherwise, who patronized or humiliated Indians, could only be false prophets.

BEYOND AUTOBIOGRAPHY

William Apess's life existed apart from his autobiographical acts, and it continued after he finished writing his primary one. What we know of the aftermath depends on his pen as much as does what we know of the preface. When the pen is silent he dies into that silence. Some documents may yet surface which can provide the sparest of facts, but it is unlikely there will be anything beyond what he has already left to give us the turns of his consciousness between 1831 and 1837. His mission involved conversion, and Christianity was, as I have shown, implicated in it. He sought salvation for a whole people. To that end his need was not to convert Native Americans to Christianity but to controvert Euro-Americans' historical exclusion of his people from the making of America. His preaching, at least from 1831 forward, concentrated on the civil and religious rights of the Indians. His comments in *Indian Nullification* indicate that he deliberately aimed to reach and to shame whites but that he also saw himself preaching to Indians to encourage them to demand their rights. He meant, I think, to locate himself and his people, all ✓ people of color, in the present and the future of the United States. His only instrument was language.

It may not be correct to say that his thought develops or changes after the second edition of *A Son of the Forest* in 1831. Enough is simply not known about him, and the evidence is mixed, but there are substantial differences in the books that follow the first autobiography and the sermon published also in 1831, *The Increase of the Kingdom of Christ*, with its important appendix, *The Indians: The Ten Lost Tribes*.[51] The autobiographical mode gives way almost entirely to more explicitly historical and political concerns. He also takes confident possession of Christian rhetoric and biblical examples as a primary means to rebuke the pretensions and practices of white society. The pietistic language that can be found in *A Son of the Forest* never recurs. Scripture is quoted to make irrefutable his claims about Indians' equality, not to elucidate a doctrinal point, or to examine the state of his own soul, or to urge his readers to a conventional repentance for their sins.

Christianity itself becomes an object of explicit critique—at least as it has been used by Euro-Americans to justify their conquest and destruction of Native Americans. So strong is his language on occasion that it sometimes feels as though he has come to doubt that any form of Christian religion can be an instrument of good for his people. His condemnation of the Pilgrims and the Puritans for their hypocrisies is matched in vehemence by his comments on the missionaries of his own day who were sent to "convert the poor heathen":

> But must I say, and shall I say it, that missionaries have injured us more than they have done us good, by degrading us as a people, in breaking up

51. Some of my argument about his thinking after 1831 is qualified by my attribution of the writing of the larger part of "The Experience of the Missionary" to a time before he wrote *A Son of the Forest*. Much in it indicates the kind of consciousness I will be sketching. Then there is the matter of his revisions both of *A Son of the Forest* for the 1831 edition and of *The Experiences of Five Christian Indians* for the edition of 1837. He removes from the autobiography his strong attack on the Methodist Episcopal church for its treatment of him. In the second edition of *The Experiences*, "An Indian's Looking-Glass" has been excised to be replaced by a banal paragraph. These are not the editorial decisions of an increasingly militant man. On the other hand, the revisions in 1831 reinforce my sense of a later development in his thought, and those in 1837 may reflect his feelings of defeat after losing the leadership at Mashpee.

our governments and leaving us without any suffrages whatever, or a legal right among men? Oh, what cursed doctrine is this! It most certainly is not fit to civilize men with, much more to save their souls; and we poor Indians want no such missionaries around us. But I would suggest one thing . . . let the ministers and people use the colored people they have already around them like human beings, before they go to convert any more; and let them show it in their churches; and let them proclaim it upon the housetops. [*Eulogy*]

The *Eulogy on King Philip* can be read as a sustained documentation of the evils repeatedly committed in the name of Christianity. Though much of it reviews closely the encounters between the English and Native Americans in the seventeenth century, Apess powerfully and often indicts current practices.

Apess, however, seeks most to expose to whites the way they have melded Christian language and ideas into an ideology of righteous subjugation and outright racial extinction. He most commonly targets the notion that Euro-Americans have been sent and blessed by God to supplant the Indians, that the taking of their lands and their lives belongs to a divinely blessed mission. So pervasive among Euro-Americans was this assumption that Apess needed to attempt the subversion of each of the historical and religious pieties that constituted the whole ideological complex. The "sons of the Pilgrims" should "blush" instead of celebrating December 22, by tradition the day the Pilgrims landed at Plymouth Rock, a tradition reinstated and affirmed since 1820 when the day began to be marked by increased publicity and the services of distinguished public orators. Blushing instead of celebrating meant that Anglo-Americans must recognize that, "although the Gospel is said to be glad tidings to all people, yet we poor Indians never have found those who brought it as messengers of mercy, but contrawise," so that not only must December 22 but also July 4 be "days of mourning and not of joy" (*Eulogy*). The Revolution, the supreme icon in Euro-American mythology, marks Native American history as well. With it began the unrelieved deprivation of natives' liberty and the deliberate destruction of their cultural and physical beings.[52]

He develops after 1831 most dramatically in his articulation of issues of

52. My emphasis here follows Apess, but also, I think, the shape of the history. Before the American Revolution native cultures were of course attacked and besieged by Europeans, but the royal powers in Europe, including the king of England, maintained for their own ends an idea of themselves as protectors to the Indians. This meant that these powers across the sea could, at times, be appealed to by Native Americans and used as counterbalances against the immediate aims of the colonists. The rivalries among the European colonial powers also provided Indians with possibilities for pursuing their own ends by manipulating the competition. After the Revolution these recourses diminish or altogether disappear, and from Washington's presidency onward there is an unwavering commitment on the part of the federal government to the removal of the

race. First, his own perception of African Americans appears to have shifted. At several points in the earlier autobiographical writings he distinguishes himself from African Americans. However low his status, it remains higher than theirs: "I never cried out like the poor African, 'Massa, Massa—Mister, Mister,' but called them by their regular names" (*Exps.*). The comment is not vicious; it functions simply to mark the distance between his station and that of African Americans. Four or five years later, when he wrote "An Indian's Looking-Glass," his rhetoric joins the experiences of Native Americans and African Americans. Not only do they belong together as people of color, their exploitation at the hands of white people, one group by having its lands taken, the other by having its labor stolen, has been the means by which Euro-Americans gained riches and power. And both have had their subjection rationalized in the name of religion: "I do not hesitate to say that through the prayers, preaching, and examples of these pretended pious has been the foundation of all the slavery and degradation in the American colonies, toward colored people" (*Eulogy*).

Whites are named and addressed as such more frequently—if not as a race, at least as a people who have insisted on constituting themselves as a superior creation. Earlier in his writing career he, like African American writers both before and after him, became fascinated with the literature about the Ten Lost Tribes of Israel. Indians, black people, and their white supporters found it strategic to claim an identity as one of the Lost Tribes at a time when racism was becoming fully articulated in Christian societies. The claim countered the school in Euro-American racism that explained the differences in human beings by arguing that God had separately created races, placing the (white) children of Adam over all the others. Belief in the survival of the Lost Tribes, and of the Indians' descent from them, affirmed a single parentage for all human beings and thus their equality before God. It also placed Indians, or African Americans, as kin to the progenitors of the culture that now sought to condemn them as inferior.

This element in his thought does not disappear after 1831, but he gives it less prominence as he more confidently and fully attacks white racism. Occasionally in *A Son of the Forest* and, most explicitly, in *The Indians: The Ten Lost Tribes* Apess appears to have accepted one of the most powerful instruments in Euro-Americans' belief systems about Indians: that these were a people,

---

Indians and to confining them to the smallest possible land base. This policy is moved and justified by an equally unqualified belief in the inevitability of the extinction of native cultures, so that, when natives did not "cooperate" and assimilate as quickly as Euro-Americans expected, laws could be passed and policies enacted that attempted to outlaw, or otherwise destroy, their languages and their distinctive cultural and sacred rituals.

however regrettably, who were doomed to disappear before the progressive √
march of civilization. His conclusion to *The Indians* rehearses the theme
exactly in its blend of elegiac sadness and almost glad inevitability:

> Suffice it to say, what is already known, that the white man came upon our
> shores—he grew taller and taller until his shadow was cast over all the
> land—in its shade the mighty tribes of olden time wilted away. A few, the
> remnant of multitudes long since gathered to their fathers, are all that
> remain; and they are on their march to eternity.

The two ideas were, in their way, linked. Subscription to the idea that Indians
were one of the Ten Lost Tribes left unchallenged the progressive historicism
that assumed the superiority of later over earlier cultures. And, as proto-Jews,
Indians were no less objects of conversion to the "superior" religion of Christianity than they were as unmodified savages.

Separatism, not assimilation or conversion to a superior culture, becomes
Apess's emphasis. His experience in Mashpee might have been decisive in this
shift. Throughout that conflict, his writing, and the writing he seems to have
penned in the name of the Mashpees, insists upon the distance between
natives and whites. In recalling his eager anticipation of meeting many happily converted Christian Indians on his first visit to Mashpee he makes broad
but still pointed comedy of the matter. Waiting outside the Old Indian Meeting House just before the first service he attends,

> I turned to meet my Indian brethren and give them the hand of friend-
> ship; but I was greatly disappointed in the appearance of those who
> advanced. All the Indians I had ever seen were of a reddish color,
> sometimes approaching a yellow, but now, look to what quarter I would,
> most of those who were coming were pale faces, and, in my disappoint-
> ment, it seemed to me that the hue of death sat upon their countenances.
> It seemed very strange to me that my brethren should have changed their
> natural color and become in every respect like white men. [*I.N.*]

The first point, of course, is that they *are* all white men coming to the Old
Indian Meeting House, which has been usurped by the false minister, Phineas
Fish, himself one of those missionaries who regards Native Americans as
permanently inferior. Apess's mischief goes further as he mocks and inverts a
number of the usual associations in American culture between hue and value,
doing so beyond, I suspect, the capacity of many of his contemporary readers
to detect. Here whites are in danger of extinction, not triumphant "pale faces"
but ones full of death. And who, in this play of color, would choose to
be white? Not his brethren certainly! They have already suffered and lost

enough to the degree they have become in any manner "like white men." Racial or cultural assimilation is not something any sensible Native American would desire.

At other places in the later writing Apess does not risk his point being missed. His indictment of whites takes many forms, but this, from the *Eulogy*, may be the most unsparing. It follows an emphatic characterization of Euro-Americans as "our visitors":

> And although I can say that I have some dear, good friends among white people, yet I eye them with a jealous eye, for fear they will betray me. Having been deceived so much by them, how can I help it? Being brought up to look upon white people as being enemies and not friends, and by the whites treated as such, who can wonder? Yes, in vain have I looked for the Christian to take me by the hand and bid me welcome to his cabin, as my fathers did them, before we were born; and if they did, it was only to satisfy curiosity and not to look upon me as a man and a Christian. And so all of my people have been treated, whether Christians or not.

This reads as though the Furmans had never existed. And if his Pequot grandparents are in this passage it is now as complete victims without any responsibility for their treatment of their grandson. No concessions are given to any aspect of white culture. Its practitioners are, at their best, betrayers of their own stated ideals.

Already by 1833, it seems, Apess had despaired of reaching Euro-Americans through an appeal to their Christian beliefs. His experience at Mashpee could only have reinforced his expectation that whites would never accept natives as their peers, their brothers and sisters in Christ. The response among whites to his role in inciting the Mashpees to agitate for their rights was nearly uniform. Benjamin Franklin Hallett's testimony to the Joint Committee of the Massachusetts legislature details, in taking time to defend Apess, how constantly Apess was attacked, how his character was impugned, and how he was seen as the problem to be dealt with. His opponents were not only the ordinary white citizens in the towns surrounding Mashpee who benefited from ready access to its resources; they ranged from the local courts and town officers to the governor himself. Josiah Fiske, the governor's appointed mediator and investigator for the whole affair, clearly saw Apess as the sole problem and plotted to have him arrested in front of the whole community so as to demoralize the people. His account confirms Apess's determination to employ an American tradition and rhetoric in addition to, or other than, the evangelical to win protection for his people:

Perceiving that it was the settled purpose of Apes to establish in the minds of the natives a belief that each generation had a right to act for itself, and that guardianship laws which had been imposed by the consent of one generation, could not be enforced against the will of another; and fearing that his ascendancy over the minds of these uninformed persons had become so great as to lead them into greater difficulties, if not . . . to involve them in bloodshed, [I ordered the sheriff to execute the warrant already issued for his arrest].[53]

The echoes from Jefferson are unmistakable. These are the ideas of the most radical strand of democratic republicanism. Each generation must make its own laws and, if need be, its own revolution. The hand of the past is always a heavy one and cannot be permitted to lie on a new generation. If one could not persuade people to behave as true Christians toward the original inhabitants of these lands, then one's energy needed to be devoted to winning for Indians full rights as citizens. Apess speaks it succinctly near the end of his last known public address: "I say, then, a different course must be pursued, and different laws must be enacted, and all men must operate under one general law" (*Eulogy*).

In all the documents from Mashpee and in the *Eulogy*, no hint appears that Apess any longer subscribes to any aspect of the belief in the inevitable disappearance of Native Americans. When he refers to the ancient Israelites it is for another kind of image than of an ancient people who will be replaced in God's favor by a new chosen race: "We regarded ourselves, in some sort, as a tribe of Israelites suffering under the rod of the despotic pharaohs; for thus far, our cries and remonstrances had been of no avail" (*I.N.*). The language of rights, of oppression by an unjust people, of equality—racial and political—becomes increasingly central.

This language could not, however, simply be taken up by Apess. He understood that the Revolution, which enshrined republican principles in the American commonwealth, also excluded African Americans and Native Americans from their reach. His writing suggests that he may have understood that there was no paradox in these exclusions, that the very forms of American republicanism might require not only a body of people who were defined as incapable of equality but also the possession of an apparently inexhaustible bounty of "open" land. The bounty depended in turn, of course, on the elimination of the Indians. How, then, could Native Americans appeal

---

53. Massachusetts General Court, Senate, . . . no. 14, *Documents Relative to the Marshpee Indians,* Josiah Fiske's Report to Governor Levi Lincoln, 25.

for inclusion as citizens to the very forms that substantially constituted themselves by excluding them?

Claiming Philip as "the greatest man that was ever in America" (*Eulogy*), as a father to "his country," was one means. With it Apess could attempt to get Americans to recognize the inescapable doubleness of all of their history. By taking over the patriotic language of the dominant culture and switching its referents he could disrupt the almost seamless ideology of a racist republicanism that cloaked itself in universalistic language. He might also, by the very outrageousness of his deliberate undercutting of Euro-Americans' expectations, provoke them to think again about their history. The following, from the Bill of Complaints the Mashpees presented to the Massachusetts Great and General Court, offers a fine example of his agility at reclaiming and rewriting American history so that Indians were fully, even primarily, present:

> And we do not know why the people of this Commonwealth want to cruelize us any longer, for we are sure that our fathers *fought, bled, and died for the liberties* of their now weeping and suffering children. . . . *Oh, white man! white man!* The blood of our fathers, spilt in the Revolutionary War, cries from the ground of our native soil, to break the chains of oppression, and let our children *go free!*[54]

Indian fathers fought, and were still fighting, against Euro-Americans for all of the same liberties as those claimed in the great founding documents of the United States. The use of "our fathers" echoed the reflexive invocation in patriotic speeches and blurred the clarity of whose fathers were whose. The passage extends its conflation of red and white fathers of independence, makers of *the* Revolution, by quickly eliding Indian fathers who fought against white American fathers to preserve the liberty of their children with those Indian fathers from Mashpee who fought and died on the American side in the Revolution. Such language makes an almost irrefutably double claim against the legitimacy of Euro-Americans' monopoly of democratic rights and freedom. Indians were as devoted defenders of liberty as their Euro-American fellows, and they also fought and died to help establish American independence.

√ Apess's writings reveal an extraordinary evolution of political consciousness and personal identity from when he wrote the first version of his autobiography sometime in 1828/29 to his valedictory performance in the *Eulogy on King Philip*. The contents of this consciousness are disparate, but perhaps this is

54. Massachusetts General Court, House, . . . no. 11, "Memorial of the Marshpee Indians: A Voice from the Marshpee Indians," January 1834, 13–14.

always and necessarily the case. What makes Apess especially remarkable are the elements he chose to express his place in American society. Evangelical Christianity is the most prominent of these, but always modified by his half-taunting, half-ironic "Indian Preacher." This qualifier acknowledges his status in white eyes as an exotic curiosity and as illegitimate. His identity as a Pequot, a "son of the forest," becomes established and elaborated in his recurrence to the history of European and Native American relations. His appeal to republicanism, common enough in the history of American dissent, asserts the rights of Native Americans as Americans, as full participants in a democratic polity. This assertion also challenges Euro-Americans' self-definition as the exclusive originators of the ideas of liberty, individuality, and republican government.

His unapologetic descriptions of the experience of being at the bottom of ✓ American society undermine the pieties about the United States as a classless society. He is irreverent about the powerful and their pretensions to moral superiority. And he has the eyes of the vulnerable for seeing the connections among economic, religious, and political institutions in the maintenance of privilege. His childhood experience gave him intimate knowledge of the undersides of the big houses of the powerful and respectable. The emptiness of their religious observances seemed only fit to this born-again Pequot who knew that much of the Hillhouse and Williams fortunes rested on the theft of his people's lands. The recollection of the hypocrisy of Connecticut respectables shapes some of his sharpest observations, like the memorable "Connecticut . . . where they are so pious that they kill the cats for killing rats, and whip the beer barrels for working upon the Sabbath" (*Eulogy*). And, through his attacks on white racism, he begins to articulate the common suffering and interests of "people of color," against a culture that grounded its conviction of its superiority by subordinating them.

These come together in a struggle for a moral and political stance independent of the Euro-American, which yet can condemn any denial of constitutional rights and Christian love to those, Native and African Americans specifically, subjugated by Euro-Americans. These dispossessed peoples are to be equal citizens in a republic established on their displacement and enslavement. Apess's insistence, finally, on rewriting the history of Native Americans and Europeans shapes a rhetorical ground through which he and his people can be both "un-American" and the "first Americans." In text, and in lived history, these identities resist reconciliation. So it must be that Apess's writing moves in tension and struggle against the pieties of Americanism while requiring its language and assumptions.

Apess's near complete absence from written histories and from American literature invites many explanations. A voice such as his would have been

√ intolerable to all but a few in a culture just beginning its formative imperial adventures. Native Americans were no economic or physical threat to the majority culture in New England, but in the 1820s and the 1830s they remained a military threat east of the Mississippi. Those who were not militarily threatening held lands Euro-Americans hungered for. And all Indians, to the extent that they maintained their cultures, represented an ideological challenge to "American" ways. The intellectuals of the society—ministers, academics, writers and journalists, politicians, and what passed for scientists in that time—not only defended slavery and Indian removal but were busily spawning articulations of racial and cultural superiority in every form and forum. Dissenters there were, but because we have come to honor their names we may forget how few they were and how marginal. Apess was something other than a dissenter. He sought to speak in the voice of a people the majority culture meant to suppress, in the name of an idea of American history which, had it been accepted, would have denied to Euro-Americans the conviction of superiority and of divine mission they needed to conduct their conquests. Indians and black people had, in different ways, to be rendered culturally and morally negligible if the white settlement of the West and the full operation of the slave system were to proceed.

In 1923 the Indian Council of New England was formed. It marked the end of a long public silence among the native peoples of the region and a determination to become visible. Their organization manifested the cultural revivalism stirring Native Americans throughout the country. For its emblem the council chose the words "I still live."[55] Almost seventy years later, after three generations in oral tradition, these words have become "We are still here," the slogan current among many contemporary Native Americans in New England. The persistence speaks admirably of the stamina of Native Americans. It also speaks eloquently of the powerful commitment in Euro-American culture to a denial of the actual histories and peoples who shaped the society. Euro-America's very conception of itself cannot survive such a recognition.

The words carry other resonances—of voices, first of all, insisting on recognition, of pride in survival, of measured defiance, and of witty word players' quiet reminder that failing to notice the existence of others does not mean they have ceased to exist.

"We are still here" testifies to qualities in Native American cultures to which little attention or appreciation has been given. These cultures have withstood every kind of assault that a numerically much larger and deter-

55. I am indebted to Frank G. Speck, "Reflections upon the Past and Present of the Massachusetts Indians," *Bulletin of the Massachusetts Archaeological Society* 4 (1943): esp. 34. His essay is admirably impatient, at moments passionately so, with American historians' narrowness and ignorance.

mined culture could muster for almost 500 years. The devastations and the losses are uncountable—to Native Americans and to Euro-Americans and to the culture that has been developed out of their interactions. But Native Americans have survived and grown despite everything, including near biological extinction. They have not simply survived in terms of some reductive genetic genealogy; they have also re-formed and maintained distinctive cultural practices and repertoires. To do so, Native Americans have had to be endlessly inventive, patient, resistant to despair, and to have a faith and a vision to furnish the strength to continue.

William Apess's writing, his presence in our history and our literature, ✓ does much to demonstrate these capacities. It also reminds us of the terrible costs exacted in people's lives when any group assumes the right, and has the power, to name another's being and prospects. All of us, Americans with whatever modifier, should be haunted by the voice of his grandmother, asking "question after question, if I hated her," so as to remember into our own day what human beings do to their fellows once they have found the means of defining them as inferior or other. The language and practice of democratic republicanism were built, in part, on the bodies of Native Americans and African Americans who provided the land and the labor out of which the conditions of a democratic settlement were created for Euro-Americans. This past can be redeemed, but only through a ceaseless struggle to make a fully democratic society, one in which all peoples truly share power, in which people of different cultures and languages celebrate the presence of others by seeking to understand them, a society of many tongues, a colloquy of difference, a true cosmopolis instead of merely another imperial capital. Apess would not, I think, have wished to be called a pioneer; the word is an honorific in the imperial lexicon that condemned his people. He was an inventive survivor, a man who refused to be extinguished and who understood that he could not live on unless his people also did. So they have. The Pequots are still with us, not one of the Ten Lost Tribes of Israel, not a saving remnant, not ✓ noble or bloody savages, but Americans of a mixed and proud history.

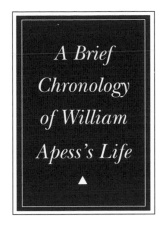

1798   Born Colrain, Massachusetts, January 31, the first child of William and Candace Apes.

1801   Parents separate; William placed with his maternal grandparents in Colchester, Connecticut.

1802   Apess's grandmother beats him badly. The town of Colchester binds the boy out to near neighbors, a childless couple, Mr. and Mrs. Furman.

1802–9 From his sixth birthday until his twelfth he attends school during the winter term.

1809   Indenture sold by Mr. Furman to Judge William Hillhouse of New London. Runs away several times. After about six months his indenture again sold—to William Williams in the city of New London.

1809–13 Begins seriously attending Methodist meetings. On March 13, 1813, he has a conversion experience. Runs away to New York City, enlists as drummer boy in a militia unit and goes to the Canadian front, most of the time around Plattsburgh.

1813–15 Involved in several abortive expeditions against Montreal and in the Battle of Lake Champlain, September 11, 1814, when the American forces achieve one of their few victories in the War of 1812. Musters himself out of the army around April or May 1815.

1815–16 Travels to Montreal, upper Canada, Fort Niagara, the Bay of Quinte, and Kingston, holding a variety of temporary jobs, spending some time with his fellow Native Americans in eastern Ontario.

1816–17 In the fall or early winter, starts to return to Connecticut on foot. Reaches the Colchester or Groton, Connecticut, area probably in late April or May 1817.

1818 Baptized by immersion by the Reverend Mr. Barnes.

1819–20 Decides he wishes to see his father again; mother and father have reunited and are living in Colrain. Apess begins to exhort in Methodist class meetings and eventually to preach, though without a license.

1821–24 Returns to Connecticut. Meets and, on December 21, 1821, marries Mary Wood of Salem, Connecticut. The chronology for these years is unclear. The couple live in southeastern Connecticut for a time, and Apess travels to wherever he can find work. At least one child is born in these years, a son, and possibly two daughters.

1825–27 Goes to Providence, Rhode Island, to find work and moves the family there. Becomes a class leader in a local Methodist society. Again begins to exhort and, after some months, is licensed by the Methodists to do so. Decides to become a missionary.

1827–29 Travels around Long Island, the Hudson River valley, Boston, New Bedford, Martha's Vineyard and Nantucket, and north of Boston as an itinerant Methodist exhorter, working much of the time, it seems, with mixed groups of African and Native Americans.

1829 At the April quarterly conference in Utica of the Methodist Episcopal church his request to become a licensed preacher is denied. Joins the more "republican" Protestant Methodists and is ordained by them. Writes *A Son of the Forest* sometime between late 1828 and July 25, 1829, when he deposits copyright title in New York City.

1830 No record of his whereabouts or activities.

1831 Appointed by the New York Annual Conference of the Protestant Methodists to preach to his people, the Pequots. Publishes *The Increase of the Kingdom of Christ.*

1831–33 Little is known about his activities in these years, though he apparently continues to preach to communities of Native Americans and African Americans and also, at least on occasion, to Euro-Americans about the injustices committed against Indians.

1833 Goes to Mashpee for the first time. Mashpee Revolt. Arrested for disturbing the peace, sentenced to jail for thirty days and to pay a hefty fine. *The Experiences of Five Christian Indians; or, An Indian's Looking-Glass for the White Man* published in Boston.

1834 Mashpees granted the right to elect their own selectmen.

1835 *Indian Nullification of the Unconstitutional Laws of Massachusetts* published in Boston.

1836   On January 8 delivers the *Eulogy on King Philip;* repeats it by request on January 26; published in Boston later that same year. In September in a debt action in the Barnstable Court of Common Pleas his name is entered as "Apess."

1837   Second editions of the *Eulogy* and *Experience of Five Christian Indians* published in Boston, by William *Apess.*

1838   Household goods and estate attached by the Barnstable Court of Common Pleas for debt; an inventory of these survives. No other record of Apess has yet been uncovered for after this date.

On Our Own Ground

PART 1

*A Son
of the Forest:
The Experience
of William Apess,
a Native of
the Forest*

Written by Himself

A Son of the Forest, published in 1829, was Apess's first book. Internal evidence, however, indicates that it was not his first venture in autobiographical writing. Much of "The Experience of the Missionary" in *The Experiences of Five Christian Indians* (1833) appears to have been composed six months or a year earlier than the longer autobiography. Possibly Apess wrote the first account for a Methodist Conference as part of his request for ordination. A second edition of *A Son of the Forest* was issued in 1831, considerably revised and somewhat rearranged. It is from this edition that the following text has been printed. Because there are, in effect, three different autobiographical accounts from Apess, close comparison of the three can tell us something of importance about his compositional practice and changes in his thinking. Although the 1829 edition of *A Son of the Forest* is not included in this collection, "The Experience of the Missionary" and the 1831 edition of *A Son of the Forest* can be directly and fully compared, and the Textual Afterword documents the most substantial alterations from the 1829 to the 1831 editions.

When Apess wrote, autobiography was not yet the common literary form it has since become. Accounts of conversion experiences however, were familiar to almost everyone in the early nineteenth-century United States. Oral or written testimony about one's spiritual experience had been mandatory for generations in most Protestant churches. The invention and popularity of revivals from the Great Awakening onward made the practice, along with hymn singing, a generative form in American vernacular cultures. Literary models, especially John Bunyan's *Grace Abounding* (1666) and *Pilgrim's Progress* (1678 and 1684), also played an important role in shaping conventional patterns for such testimony. Bunyan's books were widely distributed in the United States and, along with the Bible, could be found even in those households with few books. Those who could not read would still have known these writings because they were, again like the Bible, often read aloud. A twentieth-century reader approaching these kinds of autobiographies might remember that the language of spiritual concern and regeneration, though it can be formulaic, also can express much of the range of a person's life experience and sensibilities.

A Son of the Forest deserves attention as one of the earliest—if not *the* earliest—autobiographies written and published by a Native American. This means not only that Apess had few, if any, models for his endeavor but also that one may well see in his book the articulation of issues of identity and the formulation of modes of representation characteristic of later Native American autobiographies.

A
Son
of the
Forest

▲

PREFACE

In offering to the public a second edition of this work, the Author cannot but testify his gratitude for the liberal patronage bestowed upon the first edition—notwithstanding the many disadvantages under which it appeared. The present edition is greatly improved, as well in the printing as in the arrangement of the work and the style in which it is written. The first edition was hurried through the press, in consequence of which many inaccuracies occurred.

It has been carefully revised; those parts which some persons deemed objectionable have been stricken out;[1] and in its improved form it is now submitted to the public, with the earnest prayer of the author that it may be rendered a lasting blessing to everyone who may give it even a cursory perusal.

1. The objectionable parts appear to be entirely his account of his being rejected as a candidate for ordination in the Methodist Episcopal church and his decision to join the Protestant Methodists, who did ordain him. In the 1829 edition he provides quite lengthy documentation for his conviction that this rejection came because he was an Indian (see Textual Afterword). In this edition, because all of this is excised, the reader does not know that he leaves the Methodist Episcopal church or that he is finally ordained.

CHAPTER I

William Apess, the author of the following narrative, was born in the town of Colrain, Massachusetts, on the thirty-first of January, in the year of our Lord √ seventeen hundred and ninety-eight.[1] My grandfather was a white man and married a female attached to the royal family of Philip, king of the Pequot tribe of Indians, so well known in that part of American history which relates

1. January 30 is the date he gives in *The Experiences of Five Christian Indians* (1833).

to the wars between the whites and the natives.[2] My grandmother was, if I am not misinformed, the king's granddaughter and a fair and beautiful woman. This statement is given not with a view of appearing great in the estimation of others—what, I would ask, is *royal* blood?—the blood of a king is no better than that of the subject. We are in fact but one family; we are all the descendants of one great progenitor—Adam. I would not boast of my extraction, as I consider myself nothing more than a worm of the earth.

I have given the above account of my origin with the simple view of narrating the truth as I have received it, and under the settled conviction that I must render an account at the last day, to the sovereign Judge of all men, for every word contained in this little book.

As the story of King Philip is perhaps generally known, and consequently the history of the Pequot tribe, over whom he reigned, it will suffice to say that he was overcome by treachery, and the goodly heritage occupied by this once happy, powerful, yet peaceful people was possessed in the process of time by their avowed enemies, the whites, who had been welcomed to their land in that spirit of kindness so peculiar to the red men of the woods. But the violation of their inherent rights, by those to whom they had extended the hand of friendship, was not the only act of injustice which this oppressed and afflicted nation was called to suffer at the hands of their white neighbors— alas! They were subject to a more intense and heart-corroding affliction, that of having their daughters claimed by the conquerors, and however much subsequent efforts were made to soothe their sorrows, in this particular, they considered the glory of their nation as having departed. (*See Appendix.*)

From what I have already stated, it will appear that my father was of mixed blood, his father being a white man and his mother a native or, in other words, a red woman. On attaining a sufficient age to act for himself, he joined the Pequot tribe, to which he was maternally connected. He was well received, and in a short time afterward married a female of the tribe, in whose veins a single drop of the white man's blood never flowed. Not long after his marriage, he removed to what was then called the back settlements, directing his course first to the west and afterward to the northeast, where he pitched his tent in the woods of a town called Colrain, near the Connecticut River, in the state of Massachusetts. In this, the place of my birth, he continued some time and afterward removed to Colchester, New London County, Connecticut. At

2. Apess may be deliberately eliding the two great Indian–English wars in seventeenth-century New England: the Pequot War of 1637 and King Philip's War of 1675–76. But I suspect he has just confused them. Philip was not king of the Pequots, a culture located in the southeastern part of what is now Connecticut, but the sachem of the Pokanokets located in and around Mount Hope in Rhode Island.

the latter place, our little family lived for nearly three years in comparative comfort.

Circumstances, however, changed with us, as with many other people, in consequence of which I was taken together with my two brothers and sisters into my grandfather's family. One of my uncles dwelt in the same hut. Now my grandparents were not the best people in the world—like all others who are wedded to the beastly vice of intemperance, they would drink to excess whenever they could procure rum, and as usual in such cases, when under the influence of liquor, they would not only quarrel and fight with each other but would at times turn upon their unoffending grandchildren and beat them in a most cruel manner. It makes me shudder, even at this time, to think how frequent and how great have been our sufferings in consequence of the introduction of this "cursed stuff" into our family—and I could wish, in the sincerity of my soul, that it were banished from our land.

Our fare was of the poorest kind, and even of this we had not enough. Our clothing also was of the worst description: Literally speaking, we were clothed with rags, so far only as rags would suffice to cover our nakedness. We were always contented and happy to get a cold potato for our dinners—of this at times we were denied, and many a night have we gone supperless to rest, if stretching our limbs on a bundle of straw, without any covering against the weather, may be called rest. Truly, we were in a most deplorable condition—too young to obtain subsistence for ourselves, by the labor of our hands, and our wants almost totally disregarded by those who should have made every exertion to supply them. Some of our white neighbors, however, took pity on us and measurably administered to our wants, by bringing us frozen milk, with which we were glad to satisfy the calls of hunger. We lived in this way for some time, suffering both from cold and hunger. Once in particular, I remember that when it rained very hard my grandmother put us all down cellar, and when we complained of cold and hunger, she unfeelingly bid us dance and thereby warm ourselves—but we had no food of any kind; and one of my sisters almost died of hunger. Poor dear girl, she was quite overcome. Young as I was, my very heart bled for her. I merely relate this circumstance, without any embellishment or exaggeration, to show the reader how we were treated. The intensity of our sufferings I cannot tell. Happily, we did not continue in this very deplorable condition for a great length of time. Providence smiled on us, but in a particular manner.

Our parents quarreled, parted, and went off to a great distance, leaving their helpless children to the care of their grandparents. We lived at this time in an old house, divided into two apartments—one of which was occupied by my uncle. Shortly after my father left us, my grandmother, who had been out among the whites, returned in a state of intoxication and, without any provocation whatever on my part, began to belabor me most unmercifully with a club; she asked me if I hated her, and I very innocently answered in the affirmative as I did not then know what the word meant and thought all the while that I was answering aright; and so she continued asking me the same question, and I as often answered her in the same way, whereupon she continued beating me, by which means one of my arms was broken in three different places. I was then only four years of age and consequently could not take care of or defend myself—and I was equally unable to seek safety in flight. But my uncle who lived in the other part of the house, being alarmed for my safety, came down to take me away, when my grandfather made toward him with a firebrand, but very fortunately he succeeded in rescuing me and thus saved my life, for had he not come at the time he did, I would most certainly have been killed. My grandparents who acted in this unfeeling and cruel manner were by my mother's side—those by my father's side were Christians, lived and died happy in the love of God; and if I continue faithful in improving that measure of grace with which God hath blessed me, I expect to meet them in a world of unmingled and ceaseless joys. But to return:—

The next morning, when it was discovered that I had been most dangerously injured, my uncle determined to make the whites acquainted with my condition. He accordingly went to a Mr. Furman, the person who had occasionally furnished us with milk, and the good man came immediately to see me. He found me dreadfully beaten, and the other children in a state of absolute suffering; and as he was extremely anxious that something should be done for our relief, he applied to the selectmen of the town in our behalf, who after duly considering the application adjudged that we should be severally taken and bound out. Being entirely disabled in consequence of the wounds I had received, I was supported at the expense of the town for about twelve months.

When the selectmen were called in, they ordered me to be carried to Mr. Furman's—where I received the attention of two surgeons. Some considerable time elapsed before my arm was set, which was consequently very sore, and during this painful operation I scarcely murmured. Now this dear man and family were sad on my account. Mrs. Furman was a kind, benevolent, and tenderhearted lady—from her I received the best possible care: Had it been otherwise I believe that I could not have lived. It pleased God, however, to support me. The great patience that I manifested I attribute mainly to my improved situation. Before, I was almost always naked, or cold, or hungry—now, I was comfortable, with the exception of my wounds.

In view of this treatment, I presume that the reader will exclaim, "What savages your grandparents were to treat unoffending, helpless children in this cruel manner." But this cruel and unnatural conduct was the effect of some cause. I attribute it in a great measure to the whites, inasmuch as they introduced among my countrymen that bane of comfort and happiness, ardent spirits—seduced them into a love of it and, when under its unhappy influence, wronged them out of their lawful possessions—that land, where reposed the ashes of their sires; and not only so, but they committed violence of the most revolting kind upon the persons of the female portion of the tribe who, previous to the introduction among them of the arts, and vices, and debaucheries of the whites, were as unoffending and happy as they roamed over their goodly possessions as any people on whom the sun of heaven ever shone. The consequence was that they were scattered abroad. Now many of them were seen reeling about intoxicated with liquor, neglecting to provide for themselves and families, who before were assiduously engaged in supplying the necessities of those depending on them for support. I do not make this statement in order to justify those who had treated me so unkindly, but simply to show that, inasmuch as I was thus treated only when they were under the influence of spirituous liquor, that the whites were justly chargeable with at least some portion of my sufferings.

After I had been nursed for about twelve months, I had so far recovered that it was deemed expedient to bind me out, until I should attain the age of twenty-one years.[3] Mr. Furman, the person with whom the selectmen had placed me was a poor man, a cooper by trade, and obtained his living by the labor of his hands. As I was only five years old, he at first thought that his circumstances would not justify him in keeping me, as it would be some considerable time before I could render him much service. But such was the attachment of the family toward me that he came to the conclusion to keep me until I was of age, and he further agreed to give me so much instruction as would enable me to read and write. Accordingly, when I attained my sixth year, I was sent to school, and continued for six successive winters. During this time I learned to read and write, though not so well as I could have wished. This was all the instruction of the kind I ever received. Small and imperfect as was the amount of the knowledge I obtained, yet in view of the advantages I have thus derived, I bless God for it.

3. Being "bound out" was a common practice in New England in the nineteenth century in dealing with people who were indigent, with orphans without relatives willing to take them in, and with those, like Apess, who had been abused. Native Americans, women and children especially, were often bound out—the adults usually for shorter periods, the children often until they reached adulthood. In return for the right to the labor of the indentured, the bondholders undertook to provide food, lodging, and clothing and sometimes other things like education.

CHAPTER II

I believe that it is assumed as a fact among divines that the Spirit of Divine Truth, in the boundless diversity of its operations, visits the mind of every intelligent being born into the world—but the time when is only fully known to the Almighty and the soul which is the object of the Holy Spirit's enlightening influence. It is also conceded on all hands that the Spirit of Truth operates on different minds in a variety of ways—but always with the design of convincing man of sin and of a judgment to come. And, oh, that men would regard their real interests and yield to the illuminating influences of the Spirit of God—then wretchedness and misery would abound no longer, but everything of the kind give place to the pure principles of peace, godliness, brotherly kindness, meekness, charity, and love. These graces are spontaneously produced in the human heart and are exemplified in the Christian deportment of every soul under the mellowing and sanctifying influences of the Spirit of God. They are the peaceable fruits of a meek and quiet spirit.

The perverseness of man in this respect is one of the great and conclusive proofs of his apostasy, and of the rebellious inclination of his unsanctified heart to the will and wisdom of his Creator and his Judge.

I have heard a great deal said respecting infants feeling, as it were, the operations of the Holy Spirit on their minds, impressing them with a sense of their wickedness and the necessity of a preparation for a future state. Children at a very early age manifest in a strong degree two of the evil passions of our nature—*anger* and *pride*. We need not wonder, therefore, that persons in early life feel good impressions; indeed, it is a fact, too well established to admit of doubt or controversy, that many children have manifested a strength of intellect far above their years and have given ample evidence of a good work of grace manifest by the influence of the Spirit of God in their young and tender minds. But this is perhaps attributable to the care and attention bestowed upon them.

If constant and judicious means are used to impress upon their young and susceptible minds sentiments of truth, virtue, morality, and religion, and these efforts are sustained by a corresponding practice on the part of parents or those who strive to make these early impressions, we may rationally trust that as their young minds expand they will be led to act upon the wholesome principles they have received—and that at a very early period these good impressions will be more indelibly engraved on their hearts by the cooperating influences of that Spirit, who in the days of his glorious incarnation said, "Suffer little children to come unto me, and forbid them not, for of such is the kingdom of heaven."

But to my experience—and the reader knows full well that experience is the best schoolmaster, for what we have experienced, that we know, and all the world cannot possibly beat it out of us. I well remember the conversation that took place between Mrs. Furman and myself when I was about six years of age; she was attached to the Baptist church and was esteemed as a very pious woman. Of this I have not the shadow of a doubt, as her whole course of conduct was upright and exemplary. On this occasion, she spoke to me respecting a future state of existence and told me that I might die and enter upon it, to which I replied that I was too young—that old people only died. But she assured me that I was not too young, and in order to convince me of the truth of the observation, she referred me to the graveyard, where many younger and smaller persons than myself were laid to molder in the earth. I had of course nothing to say—but, notwithstanding, I could not fully comprehend the nature of death and the meaning of a future state. Yet I felt an indescribable sensation pass through my frame; I trembled and was sore afraid and for some time endeavored to hide myself from the destroying monster, but I could find no place of refuge. The conversation and pious admonitions of this good lady made a lasting impression upon my mind. At times, however, this impression appeared to be wearing away—then again I would become thoughtful, make serious inquiries, and seem anxious to know something more certain respecting myself and that state of existence beyond the grave, in which I was instructed to believe. About this time I was taken to meeting in order to hear the word of God and receive instruction in divine things. This was the first time I had ever entered a house of worship, and instead of attending to what the minister said, I was employed in gazing about the house or playing with the unruly boys with whom I was seated in the gallery. On my return home, Mr. Furman, who had been apprised of my conduct, told me that I had acted very wrong. He did not, however, stop here. He went on to tell me how I ought to behave in church, and to this very day I bless God for such wholesome and timely instruction. In this particular I was not slow to learn, as I do not remember that I have from that day to this misbehaved in the house of God.

It may not be improper to remark, in this place, that a vast proportion of the misconduct of young people in church is chargeable to their parents and guardians. It is to be feared that there are too many professing Christians who feel satisfied if their children or those under their care enter on a Sabbath day within the walls of the sanctuary, without reference to their conduct while there. I would have such persons seriously ask themselves whether they think they discharge the duties obligatory on them by the relation in which they stand to their Maker, as well as those committed to their care, by so much negligence on their part. The Christian feels it a duty imposed on him to conduct his children to the house of God. But he rests not here. He must have an eye over them and, if they act well, approve and encourage them; if otherwise, point out to them their error and persuade them to observe a discreet and exemplary course of conduct while in church.

After a while I became very fond of attending on the word of God—then again I would meet the enemy of my soul, who would strive to lead me away, and in many instances he was but too successful, and to this day I remember that nothing scarcely grieved me so much, when my mind has been thus petted, than to be called by a nickname. If I was spoken to in the spirit of kindness, I would be instantly disarmed of my stubbornness and ready to perform anything required of me. I know of nothing so trying to a child as to be repeatedly called by an improper name. I thought it disgraceful to be called an Indian; it was considered as a slur upon an oppressed and scattered nation, and I have often been led to inquire where the whites received this word, which they so often threw as an opprobrious epithet at the sons of the forest. I could not find it in the Bible and therefore concluded that it was a word imported for the special purpose of degrading us. At other times I thought it was derived from the term *in-gen-uity*. But the proper term which ought to be applied to our nation, to distinguish it from the rest of the human family, is that of "*Natives*"—and I humbly conceive that the natives of this country are the only people under heaven who have a just title to the name, inasmuch as we are the only people who retain the original complexion of our father Adam.[4] Notwithstanding my thoughts on this matter, so completely was I weaned from the interests and affections of my brethren that a mere threat of being sent away among the Indians into the dreary woods had a much better effect in making me obedient to the commands of my superiors than any corporal punishment that they ever inflicted. I had received a lesson in the unnatural treatment of my own relations, which could not be effaced, and I thought that, if those who should have loved and protected me treated me with such unkindness, surely I had not reason to expect mercy or favor at the hands of those who knew me in no other relation than that of a cast-off member of the tribe. A threat, of the kind alluded to, invariably produced obedience on my part, so far as I understood the nature of the command.

I cannot perhaps give a better idea of the dread which pervaded my mind on seeing any of my brethren of the forest than by relating the following occurrence. One day several of the family went into the woods to gather berries, taking me with them. We had not been out long before we fell in with a company of white females, on the same errand—their complexion was, to say the least, as *dark* as that of the natives. This circumstance filled my mind with terror, and I broke from the party with my utmost speed, and I could not

4. This somewhat inscrutable assertion depends upon Apess's belief that Native Americans were one of the Ten Lost Tribes of Israel. As such, they were "Semites," and thus their complexions were more like Adam's than those of Gentile Euro-Americans.

muster courage enough to look behind until I had reached home. By this time my imagination had pictured out a tale of blood, and as soon as I regained breath sufficient to answer the questions which my master asked, I informed him that we had met a body of the natives in the woods, but what had become of the party I could not tell. Notwithstanding the manifest incredibility of my tale of terror, Mr. Furman was agitated; my very appearance was sufficient to convince him that I had been terrified by something, and summoning the remainder of the family, he sallied out in quest of the absent party, whom he found searching for me among the bushes. The whole mystery was soon unraveled. It may be proper for me here to remark that the great fear I entertained of my brethren was occasioned by the many stories I had heard of their cruelty toward the whites—how they were in the habit of killing and scalping men, women, and children. But the whites did not tell me that they were in a great majority of instances the aggressors—that they had imbrued their hands in the lifeblood of my brethren, driven them from their once peaceful and happy homes—that they introduced among them the fatal and exterminating diseases of civilized life. If the whites had told me how cruel they had been to the "poor Indian," I should have apprehended as much harm from them.

Shortly after this occurrence I relapsed into my former bad habits—was fond of the company of boys—and in a short time lost in a great measure that spirit of obedience which had made me the favorite of my mistress. I was easily led astray, and, once in particular, I was induced by a boy (my senior by five or six years) to assist him in his depredations on a watermelon patch belonging to one of the neighbors. But we were found out, and my companion in wickedness led me deeper in sin by persuading me to deny the crime laid to our charge. I obeyed him to the very letter and, when accused, flatly denied knowing anything of the matter. The boasted courage of the boy, however, began to fail as soon as he saw danger thicken, and he confessed it as strongly as he had denied it. The man from whom we had pillaged the melons threatened to send us to Newgate, but he relented.[5] The story shortly afterward reached the ears of the good Mrs. Furman, who talked seriously to me about it. She told me that I could be sent to prison for it, that I had done wrong, and gave me a great deal of wholesome advice. This had a much better effect than forty floggings—it sunk so deep into my mind that the impression can never be effaced.

I now went on without difficulty for a few months, when I was assailed by fresh and unexpected troubles. One of the girls belonging to the house had taken some offense at me and declared she would be revenged. The better to

5. The nearest Connecticut state prison, named after the famous English prison.

effect this end, she told Mr. Furman that I had not only threatened to kill her but had actually pursued her with a knife, whereupon he came to the place where I was working and began to whip me severely. I could not tell for what. I told him I had done no harm, to which he replied, "I will learn you, you Indian dog, how to chase people with a knife." I told him I had not, but he would not believe me and continued to whip me for a long while. But the poor man soon found out his error, as *after* he had flogged me he undertook to investigate the matter, when to his amazement he discovered it was nothing but fiction, as all the children assured him that I did no such thing. He regretted being so hasty—but I saw wherein the great difficulty consisted; if I had not denied the melon affair he would have believed me, but as I had uttered an untruth about that it was natural for him to think that the person who will tell one lie will not scruple at two. For a long while after this circumstance transpired, I did not associate with my companions.

CHAPTER III

About the time that I had attained my eighth year a sect called the Christians visited our neighborhood.[6] Their hearts were warm in the cause of God— they were earnest and fervent in prayer, and I took great delight in hearing them sing the songs of Zion. Whenever I attended their meetings, which I did as often as possible, I listened to the word of God with the greatest degree of attention. It was not long before I resolved to mend my ways and become a better boy. By my strict attendance on divine worship and my orderly behavior, I attracted the notice of some of the people, who, when they discovered that I was seriously impressed, took me by the hand and strove by every possible means to cheer and encourage me. The notice thus taken of me had a very happy influence on my mind. I now determined to set about the work of repentance. On one occasion the minister addressed the people from a text touching the future state of mankind.

He spoke much on the *eternal happiness* of the righteous and the *everlasting misery* of the ungodly, and his observations sunk with awful weight upon my mind, and I was led to make many serious inquiries about the way of

6. This was probably the group of dissenting Methodists led by James O'Kelly and others who had seceded from the main body in 1793 in a dispute over the power of bishops. They named themselves the Christian Church. They might also have been followers of either Barton Stone or Alexander Campbell, Presbyterians by original training and leaders of the Second Great Awakening marked by the great outdoor camp meetings in the West, at the most famous of which, Cane Ridge, Kentucky, in 1801, Stone preached. Both men separated from the Presbyterians to found the "Christian government," which became formally known as the Christian Church about 1832 (eventually the Disciples of Christ).

salvation. In these days of young desires and youthful aspirations, I found Mrs. Furman ever ready to give me good advice. My mind was intent upon learning the lesson of righteousness, in order that I might walk in the good way and cease to do evil. My mind for one so young was greatly drawn out to seek the Lord. This spirit was manifested in my daily walk; and the friends of Christ noticed my afflictions; they knew that I was sincere because my spirits were depressed. When I was in church I could not at times avoid giving vent to my feelings, and often have I wept sorely before the Lord and his people. They, of course, observed this change in my conduct—they knew I had been a rude child and that efforts were made to bring me up in a proper manner, but the change in my deportment they did not ascribe to the influence of divine grace, inasmuch as they all considered me *too young* to be impressed with a sense of divine things. They were filled with unbelief. I need not describe the peculiar feelings of my soul.

I became very fond of attending meetings, so much so that Mr. Furman forbid me. He supposed that I only went for the purpose of seeing the boys and playing with them. This thing caused me a great deal of grief; I went for many days with my head and heart bowed down. No one had any idea of the mental agony I suffered, and perhaps the mind of no untutored child of my age was ever more seriously exercised. Sometimes I was tried and tempted— then I would be overcome by the fear of death. By day and by night I was in a continual ferment. To add to my fears about this time, death entered the family of Mr. Furman and removed his mother-in-law. I was much affected, as the old lady was the first corpse I had ever seen. She had always been so kind to me that I missed her quite as much as her children, and I had been allowed to call her mother.

Shortly after this occurrence I was taken ill. I then thought that I should surely die. The distress of body and the anxiety of mind wore me down. Now I think that the disease with which I was afflicted was a very curious one. The physician could not account for it, and how should I be able to do it? Neither had those who were about me ever witnessed any disorder of the kind. I felt continually as if I was about being suffocated and was consequently a great deal of trouble to the family, as someone had to be with me. One day Mr. Furman thought he would frighten the disease out of me. Accordingly, he told me that all that ailed me was this: that the devil had taken complete possession of me, and that he was determined to flog him out. This threat had not the desired effect. One night, however, I got up and went out, although I was afraid to be alone, and continued out by the door until after the family had retired to bed. After a while Mr. F. got up and gave me a dreadful whipping. He really thought, I believe, that the devil was in me and supposed that the birch was the best mode of ejecting him. But the flogging was as fruitless as the preceding threat in the accomplishment of his object, and he, poor man, found out his mistake, like many others who act without discretion.

One morning after this I went out in the yard to assist Mrs. Furman milk the cows. We had not been out long before I felt very singular and began to make a strange noise. I believed that I was going to die and ran up to the house; she followed me immediately, expecting me to breathe my last. Every effort to breathe was accompanied by this strange noise, which was so loud as to be heard a considerable distance. However, contrary to all expectation I began to revive, and from that very day my disorder began to abate, and I gradually regained my former health.

Soon after I recovered from my sickness, I went astray, associating again with my old schoolfellows and on some occasions profaning the Sabbath day. I did not do thus without warning, as conscience would speak to me when I did wrong. Nothing very extraordinary occurred until I had attained my eleventh year. At this time it was fashionable for boys to run away, and the wicked one put it into the head of the oldest boy on the farm to persuade me to follow the fashion. He told me that I could take care of myself and get my own living. I thought it was a very pretty notion to be a man—to *do business for myself and become rich.* Like a fool, I concluded to make the experiment and accordingly began to pack up my clothes as deliberately as could be, and in which my adviser assisted. I had been once or twice at New London, where I saw, as I thought, everything wonderful: Thither I determined to bend my course, as I expected that on reaching the town I should be metamorphosed into a person of consequence; I had the world and everything my little heart could desire on a string, when behold, my companion, who had persuaded me to act thus, informed my master that I was going to run off. At first he would not believe the boy, but my clothing already packed up was ample evidence of my intention. On being questioned I acknowledged the fact. I did not wish to leave them—told Mr. Furman so; he believed me but thought best that for a while I should have another master. He accordingly agreed to transfer my indentures to Judge Hillhouse for the sum of twenty dollars.[7] Of course, after the bargain was made, my consent was to be obtained, but I was as unwilling to go now as I had been anxious to run away before. After some persuasion, I agreed to try it for a fortnight, on condition that I should take my dog with me, and my request being granted I was soon under the old man's roof, as he only lived about six miles off. Here everything was done to make me contented, because they thought to promote their own interests by securing my services. They fed

7. Judge William Hillhouse of New London County, chief judge of the county court. He was one of the most prominent and powerful of the old gentry of Connecticut. He had fought in the Revolution and had sat in the Continental Congress. Twenty dollars would have been in 1804, when the transfer occurred, about two months' salary for a common laborer.

me with knickknacks, and soon after I went among them I had a jackknife presented to me, which was the first one I had ever seen. Like other boys, I spent my time either in whittling or playing with my dog and was withal very happy. But I was homesick at heart, and as soon as my fortnight had expired I went home without ceremony. Mr. Furman's family were surprised to see me, but that surprise was mutual satisfaction in which my faithful dog appeared to participate.

The joy I felt on returning home, as I hoped, was turned to sorrow on being informed that I had been *sold* to the judge and must instantly return. This I was compelled to do. And, reader, all this sorrow was in consequence of being led away by a bad boy: If I had not listened to him I should not have lost my home. Such treatment I conceive to be the best means to accomplish the ruin of a child, as the reader will see in the sequel. I was sold to the judge at a time when age had rendered him totally unfit to manage an unruly lad. If he undertook to correct me, which he did at times, I did not regard it as I knew that I could run off from him if he was too severe, and besides I could do what I pleased in defiance of his authority. Now the old gentleman was a member of the Presbyterian church and withal a very strict one. He never neglected family prayer, and he always insisted on my being present. I did not believe or, rather, had no faith in his prayer, because it was the same thing from day to day, and I had heard it repeated so often that I knew it as well as he. Although I was so young, I did not think that Christians ought to learn their prayers, and knowing that he repeated the same thing from day to day is, I have no doubt, the very reason why his petitions did me no good. I could fix no value on his prayers.[8]

After a little while the conduct of my new guardians was changed toward me. Once secured, I was no longer the favorite. The few clothes I had were not taken care of, by which I mean no pains were taken to keep them clean and whole, and the consequence was that in a little time they were all "tattered and torn" and I was not fit to be seen in decent company. I had not the opportunity of attending meeting as before. Yet, as the divine and reclaiming impression had not been entirely defaced, I would frequently retire behind the barn and attempt to pray in my weak manner. I now became quite anxious to attend evening meetings a few miles off: I asked the judge if I should go and take one of the horses, to which he consented. This promise greatly delighted me—but when it was time for me to go, all my hopes were dashed at once, as the judge had changed his mind. I was not to be foiled so easily; I watched the first opportunity and slipped off with one of the horses, reached

8. The issue here is rote prayers, "learned," as opposed to the spontaneous prayer favored by the evangelical Protestants at whose services Apess felt most moved and at home.

✓ the meeting, and returned in safety. Here I was to blame; if he acted wrong, it did not justify me in doing so; but being successful in one grand act of disobedience, I was encouraged to make another similar attempt, whenever my unsanctified dispositions prompted; for the very next time I wished to go to meeting, I thought I would take the horse again, and in the same manner too, without the knowledge of my master. As he was by some means apprised of my intention, he prevented my doing so and had the horses locked up in the stable. He then commanded me to give him the bridle; I was obstinate for a time, then threw it at the old gentleman and run off. I did not return until the next day, when I received a flogging for my bad conduct, which determined me to run away. Now, the judge was partly to blame for all this. He had in the first place treated me with the utmost kindness until he had made sure of me. Then the whole course of his conduct changed, and I believed he fulfilled only one item of the transferred indentures, and that was work. Of this there was no lack. To be sure I had enough to eat, such as it was, but he did not send me to school as he had promised.

A few days found me on my way to New London, where I stayed a while. I then pushed on to Waterford, and as my father lived about twenty miles off, I concluded to go and see him. I got there safely and told him I had come on a visit and that I should stay one week. At the expiration of the week he bid me go home, and I obeyed him. On my return I was treated rather coolly, and this not suiting my disposition, I run off again but returned in a few days. Now, as the judge found he could not control me, he got heartily tired of me and wished to hand me over to someone else, so he obtained a place for me in New

✓ London. I knew nothing of it, and I was greatly mortified to think that I was sold in this way. If my consent had been solicited as a matter of form, I should not have felt so bad. But to be sold to and treated unkindly by those who had got our fathers' lands for nothing was too much to bear. When all things were ready, the judge told me that he wanted me to go to New London with a neighbor, to purchase salt. I was delighted and went with the man, expecting to return that night. When I reached the place I found my mistake. The name of the person to whom I was transferred this time was Gen. William Williams, and as my treatment at the judge's was none of the best, I went home with him contentedly.[9] Indeed, I felt glad that I had changed masters and more especially that I was to reside in the city. The finery and show caught my eye and captivated my heart. I can truly say that my situation was better now than it had been previous to my residence in New London. In a little time I was

9. The Williamses were perhaps the most powerful and extensive family in the Connecticut River valley. This William Williams was also a judge, and a bit later than this date, 1809/10, he became an appointed overseer of the Mashantucket Pequots.

furnished with good new clothes. I had enough to eat, both as it respects quality and quantity, and my work was light. The whole family treated me kindly, and the only difficulty of moment was that they all wished to be masters. But I would not obey all of them. There was a French boy in the family, who one day told Mr. Williams a willful lie about me, which he believed and gave me a horsewhipping, without asking me a single question about it. Now, I do not suppose that he whipped so much on account of what the boy told him as he did from the influence of the judge's directions. He used the falsehood as a pretext for flogging me, as from what he said he was determined to make a good boy of me at once—as if stripes were calculated to ✓ effect that which love, kindness, and instruction can only successfully accomplish. He told me that if I ever run away from him he would follow me to the uttermost parts of the earth. I knew from this observation that the judge had told him that I was a runaway. However cruel this treatment appeared, for the accusation was false, yet it did me much good, as I was ready to obey the general and his lady at all times. But I could not and would not obey any but my superiors. In short, I got on very smoothly for a season.

The general attended the Presbyterian church and was exact in having all his family with him in the house of God. I of course formed one of the number. Though I did not profess religion, I observed and felt that their ways were not like the ways of the Christians. It appeared inconsistent to me for a minister to read his sermon—to turn over leaf after leaf, and at the conclusion say "Amen," seemed to me like an "empty sound and a tinkling cymbal." I was not benefited by his reading. It did not arouse me to a sense of my danger— and I am of the opinion that it had no better effect on the people of his charge. I liked to attend church, as I had been taught in my younger years to venerate the Sabbath day; and although young I could plainly perceive the difference between the preachers I had formerly heard and the minister at whose church I attended. I thought, as near as I can remember, that the Christian depended on the Holy Spirit's influence entirely, while this minister depended as much upon his learning. I would not be understood as saying anything against knowledge; in its place it is good, and highly necessary to a faithful preacher of righteousness. What I object to is placing too much reliance in it, making a god of it, etc.[10]

10. This is an extended comparison of the practices in a revivalist church like the Christians, mentioned earlier, with the more formal rituals of the long-established Presbyterian and Congregational, or "Old Light," congregations. Among the chief differences were the style and manner of preaching—for the revivalist, the written and read text was anathema, representing an overdependence on learning and a lack of faith in the Holy Spirit. The reference to an "empty sound and a tinkling cymbal," echoing the famous passage from 1 Cor. 13:1, is to Isaac Watts's hymn, "Love": "Had I the tongues of Greeks and Jews, / And nobler speech than Angels use, / If

Everything went on smoothly for two or three years. About this time the Methodists began to hold meetings in the neighborhood, and consequently a storm of persecution gathered; the pharisee and the worldling united heartily in abusing them. The gall and wormwood of sectarian malice were emitted, and every evil report prejudicial to this pious people was freely circulated. And it was openly said that the character of a respectable man would receive a stain, and a deep one, too, by attending one of their meetings. Indeed, the stories circulated about them were bad enough to deter people of "character!" from attending the Methodist ministry. But it had no effect on me. I thought I had no character to lose in the estimation of those who were accounted great. For what cared they for me? They had possession of the red man's inheritance and had deprived me of liberty; with this they were satisfied and could do as they pleased; therefore, I thought I could do as I pleased, measurably. I therefore went to hear the *noisy Methodists*. When I reached the house I found a clever company. They did not appear to differ much from "respectable" people. They were neatly and decently clothed, and I could not see that they differed from other people except in their behavior, which was more kind and gentlemanly. Their countenance was heavenly, their songs were like sweetest music—in their manners they were plain. Their language was not fashioned after the wisdom of men. When the minister preached he spoke as one having authority. The exercises were accompanied by the power of God. His people shouted for joy—while sinners wept. This being the first time I had ever attended a meeting of this kind, all things of course appeared new to me. I was very far from forming the opinion that most of the neighborhood entertained about them. From this time I became more serious and soon went to hear the Methodists again, and I was constrained to believe that they were the true people of God. One person asked me how I knew it. I replied that I was convinced in my own mind that they possessed something more than the power of the devil.

I now attended these meetings constantly, and although I was a sinner before God, yet I felt no disposition to laugh or scoff. I make this observation because so many people went to these meetings to make fun. This was a common thing, and I often wondered how persons who professed to be considered great, i.e., "ladies and gentlemen," would so far disgrace themselves as to scoff in the house of God and at his holy services. Such persons let themselves down below the heathen, in point of moral conduct—below the heathen, yes, and below the level of the brute creation, who answer the end for which they were made.

---

love be absent I am found / Like tinkling brass, an empty sound." Watts's great hymns were mainstays of evangelical Protestantism.

But notwithstanding the people were so wicked, the Lord had respect unto the labors of his servants; his ear was open to their daily supplications, and in answer to prayer he was pleased to revive his work. The power of the Holy Ghost moved forth among the people—the spirit's influence was felt at every meeting—the people of God were built up in their faith—their confidence in the Lord of hosts gathered strength, while many sinners were alarmed and began to cry aloud for mercy. In a little time the work rolled onward like an overwhelming flood. Now the Methodists and all who attended their meetings were greatly persecuted. All denominations were up in arms against them, because the Lord was blessing their labors and making them (a poor, despised people) his instruments in the conversion of sinners. But all opposition had no other effect than of cementing the brethren more closely together; the work went on, as the Lord was with them of a truth and signally owned and blessed their labors. At one of these meetings I was induced to laugh; I believe it must have been to smother my conviction, as it did not come from my heart. My heart was troubled on account of sin, and when conviction pressed upon me, I endeavored not only to be cheerful but to laugh, and thus drive away all appearance of being wrought upon. Shortly after this I was affected even unto tears. This the people of the world observed and immediately inquired if I was one of the Lamb's children. Brother Hill was then speaking from this passage of Scripture—*Behold the Lamb of God, that taketh away the sins of the world* [John 1:29]. He spoke feelingly of his sufferings upon the cross—of the precious blood that flowed like a purifying river from his side—of his sustaining the accumulated weight of the sins of the whole world and dying to satisfy the demands of that justice which could only be appeased by an infinite atonement. I felt convinced that Christ died for all mankind—that age, sect, color, country, or situation made no difference. I felt an assurance that I was included in the plan of redemption with all my brethren. No one can conceive with what joy I hailed this *new* doctrine, as it was called. It removed every excuse, and I freely believed that all I had to do was to look in faith upon the Lamb of God that made himself a free-will offering for my unregenerate and wicked soul upon the cross. My spirits were depressed—my crimes were arrayed before me, and no tongue can tell the anguish I felt.

After meeting I returned home with a heavy heart, determined to seek the salvation of my soul. This night I slept but little—at times I would be melted down to tenderness and tears, and then again my heart would seem as hard as adamant. I was greatly tempted. The evil one would try to persuade me that I was not in the pale of mercy. I fancied that evil spirits stood around my bed—my condition was deplorably awful—and I longed for the day to break, as much as the tempest-tossed mariner who expects every moment to be washed from the wreck to which he fondly clings. So it was with me upon the wreck of the world—buffeted by temptations, assailed by the devil, sometimes in despair, then believing against hope. My heart seemed at times almost ready to break, while the tears of contrition coursed rapidly down my cheeks. But sin was the cause of this, and no wonder I groaned and wept. I had often sinned, and my accumulated transgressions had piled themselves as a rocky mountain on my heart, and how could I endure it? The weight thereof seemed to crush me down. In the night season I had frightful visions and would often start from my sleep and gaze round the room, as I was ever in dread of seeing the evil one ready to carry me off. I continued in this frame of mind for more than seven weeks.

My distress finally became so acute that the family took notice of it. Some of them persecuted me because I was serious and fond of attending meeting. Now, persecution raged on every hand, within and without, and I had none to take me by the hand and say, "Go with us and we will do thee good." But, in the midst of difficulties so great to one only fifteen years of age, I ceased not to pray for the salvation of my soul. Very often my exercises were so great that sleep departed from me—I was fearful that I should wake up in hell. And one night when I was in bed, mourning like the dove for her absent mate, I fell into a doze. I thought I saw the world of fire—it resembled a large solid bed of coals—red and glowing with heat. I shall never forget the impression it made upon my mind. No tongue can possibly describe the agony of my soul, for now I was greatly in fear of dropping into that awful place, the smoke of the torment of which ascendeth up forever and ever. I cried earnestly for mercy. Then I was carried to another place, where perfect happiness appeared to pervade every part and the inhabitants thereof. Oh, how I longed to be among that happy company. I sighed to be free from misery and pain. I knew that nothing but the attenuated thread of life kept me from falling into the awful lake I beheld. I cannot think that it is in the power of human language to describe the feelings that rushed upon my mind or thrilled through my veins. Everything appeared to bear the signet of reality; when I awoke, I heartily rejoiced to find it nothing but a dream.

I went on from day to day with my head and heart bowed down, seeking the Savior of sinners, but without success. The heavens appeared to be brass; my prayers wanted the wings of faith to waft them to the skies; the disease of my heart increased; the heavenly physician had not stretched forth his hand and poured upon my soul the panacea of the Gospel; the scales had not fallen from my eyes, and no ray of celestial light had dispelled the darkness that gathered around my soul. The cheering sound of sincere friendship fell not upon my ear. It seemed as if I were friendless, unpitied, and unknown, and at times I wished to become a dweller in the wilderness. No wonder, then, that I was almost desponding. Surrounded by difficulties and apparent dangers, I was resolved to seek the salvation of my soul with all my heart—to trust entirely to the Lord and, if I failed, to perish pleading for mercy at the foot of the throne. I now hung all my hope on the Redeemer and clung with indescribable tenacity to the cross on which he purchased salvation for the *"vilest of the vile."* The result was such as is always to be expected when a lost and ruined sinner throws himself entirely on the Lord—*perfect freedom.* On the fifteenth day of March, in the year of our Lord, eighteen hundred and thirteen, I heard a voice in soft and soothing accents saying unto me, *Arise, thy sins which were many are all forgiven thee, go in peace and sin no more!*

There was nothing very singular (save the fact that the Lord stooped to lift me up) in my conversion. I had been sent into the garden to work, and while there I lifted up my heart to God, when all at once my burden and fears left me—my heart melted into tenderness—my soul was filled with love— love to God, and love to all mankind. Oh, how my poor heart swelled with joy—and I could cry from my very soul, Glory to God in the highest!!! There was not only a change in my heart but in everything around me. The scene was entirely altered. The works of God praised him, and I saw him in everything that he had made. My love now embraced the whole human family. The children of God I loved most affectionately. Oh, how I longed to be with them, and when any of them passed by me, I would gaze at them until they were lost in the distance. I could have pressed them to my bosom, as they were more precious to me than gold, and I was always loath to part with them whenever we met together. The change, too, was visible in my very countenance.

I enjoyed great peace of mind, and that peace was like a river, full, deep, and wide, and flowing continually; my mind was employed in contemplating the wonderful works of God and in praising his holy name, dwelt so continually upon his mercy and goodness that I could praise him aloud even in my sleep. I continued in this happy frame of mind for some months. It was very pleasant to live in the enjoyment of pure and undefiled religion.

CHAPTER IV

The calm and sunshine did not, however, continue uninterrupted for any length of time; my peace of mind, which flowed as a river, was disturbed. While the adversary tempted me, the fire of persecution was rekindled. It was considered by some members of the family that I was too young to be religiously inclined and consequently that I was under a strong delusion. After a time, Mr. Williams came to the conclusion that it was advisable for me to absent myself entirely from the Methodist meetings.

This restriction was the more galling, as I had joined the class and was extremely fond of this means of grace. I generally attended once in each week, so when the time came round I went off to the meeting, without permission. When I returned, Mrs. Williams prepared to correct me for acting contrary to my orders; in the first place, however, she asked me where I had been; I frankly told her that I had been to meeting to worship God. This reply completely disarmed her and saved me a flogging for the time. But this was not the end of my persecution or my troubles.

The chambermaid was in truth a treacherous woman; her heart appeared to me to be filled with deceit and guile, and she persecuted me with as much bitterness as Paul did the disciples of old. She had a great dislike toward me and would not hesitate to tell a falsehood in order to have me whipped. But my mind was stayed upon God, and I had much comfort in reading the holy Scriptures. One day after she had procured me a flogging, and no very mild one either, she pushed me down a long flight of stairs. In the fall I was greatly injured, especially my head. In a consequence of this I was disabled and laid up for a long time. When I told Mr. Williams that the maid had pushed me down stairs, she denied it, but I succeeded in making them believe it. In all this trouble the Lord was with me, of a truth. I was happy in the enjoyment of his love. The abuse heaped on me was in consequence of my being a Methodist.

Sometimes I would get permission to attend meetings in the evening, and once or twice on the Sabbath. And oh, how thankful I felt for these opportunities for hearing the word of God. But the waves of persecution and affliction and sorrow rolled on, and gathered strength in their progress, and for a season overwhelmed my dispirited soul. I was flogged several times very unjustly for what the maid said respecting me. My treatment in this respect was so bad that I could not brook it, and in an evil hour I listened to the suggestions of the devil, who was not slow in prompting me to pursue a course directly at variance with the Gospel. He put it into my head to abscond from my master, and I made arrangements with a boy of my acquaintance to accompany me.[11] So one day Mr. Williams had gone to Stonington, I left his house, notwithstanding he had previously threatened, if I did so, to follow me to the ends of the earth. While my companion was getting ready I hid my clothes in a barn and went to buy some bread and cheese, and while at the store, although I had about four dollars in my pocket, I so far forgot myself as to buy a pair of shoes on my master's account. Then it was that I began to lose sight of religion and of God. We now set out; it being a rainy night, we bought

11. John Miner, perhaps another indentured servant in the household. He was, in any case, evidently from a poor white family in the vicinity. The two boys would have run away no later than the end of March in 1813.

a bottle of rum, of which poisonous stuff I drank heartily. Now the shadows of spiritual death began to gather around my soul. It was half-past nine o'clock at night when we started, and to keep up our courage we took another drink of the liquor. As soon as we left the city, that is, as we descended the hill, it became very dark, and my companion, who was always fierce enough by daylight, began to hang back. I saw that his courage was failing and endeavored to cheer him up. Sometimes I would take a drink of rum to drown my sorrows—but in vain; it appears to me now as if my sorrows neutralized the effects of the liquor.

This night we traveled about seven miles, and being weary and wet with the rain, we crept into a barn by the wayside, and for fear of being detected in the morning, if we should happen to sleep too long, we burrowed into the hay a considerable depth. We were aroused in the morning by the people feeding their cattle; we laid still, and they did not discover us. After they had left the barn we crawled out, made our breakfast on rum, bread, and cheese, and set off for Colchester, about fourteen miles distant, which we reached that night. Here we ventured to put up at a tavern. The next morning we started for my father's, about four miles off. I told him that we had come to stay only one week, and when that week had expired he wished me to redeem my promise and return home. So I had seemingly to comply, and when we had packed up our clothes, he said he would accompany us part of the way; and when we parted I thought he had some suspicions of my intention to take another direction, as he begged me to go straight home. He then sat down on the wayside and looked after us as long as we were to be seen. At last we descended a hill, and as soon as we lost sight of him, we struck into the woods. I did not see my father again for eight years. At this time, I felt very much disturbed. I was just going to step out on the broad theater of the world, as it were, without father, mother, or friends.

After traveling some distance in the woods, we shaped our course toward Hartford. We were fearful of being taken up, and my companion coined a story, which he thought would answer very well. It was to represent ourselves, whenever questioned, as having belonged to a privateer, which was captured by the British, who kindly sent us on shore near New London; that our parents lived in the city of New York and that we were traveling thither to see them.

Now, John was a great liar. He was brought up by dissipated parents and accustomed in the way of the world to all kinds of company. He had a good memory, and having been where he heard war songs and tales of blood and carnage, he treasured them up. He therefore agreed to be spokesman, and I assure my dear reader that I was perfectly willing, for abandoned as I was I could not lie without feeling my conscience smite me. This part of the business being arranged, it was agreed that I should sell part of my clothing to defray our expenses. Our heads were full of schemes, and we journeyed on until night overtook us. We then went into a farmhouse to test our plan. The people soon began to ask us questions, and John as readily answered them. He gave them a great account of our having been captured by the enemy, and so straight that they believed the whole of it. After supper we went to bed, and in the morning they gave us a good breakfast, and some bread and cheese, and we went on our way, satisfied with our exploits. John now studied to make his story appear as correct as possible. The people pitied us, and sometimes we had a few shillings put into our hands. We did not suffer for the want of food. At Hartford we stayed some time, and we here agreed to work our passage down to New York on board of a brig—but learning that the British fleet was on the coast, the captain declined going. We then set out to reach New York by land. We thought it a good way to walk. We went by way of New Haven, expecting to reach the city from that place by water. Again we were disappointed. We fell in company with some sailors who had been exchanged, and we listened to their story—it was an affecting one, and John concluded to incorporate a part of it with his own. So shortly afterward he told some people that while we were prisoners we had to eat bread mixed with pounded glass. The people were foolish enough to believe us. At Kingsbridge an old lady gave us several articles of clothing. Here we agreed with the captain of a vessel to work our way to New York. When we got under way, John undertook to relate our sufferings to the crew. They appeared to believe it all, until he came to the incredible story of the "glass bread." This convinced the captain that all he said was false. He told us that he knew that we were runaways and pressed us to tell him, but we declined. At length he told us that we were very near to Hellgate (Hurl-gate).—that when we reached it the devil would come on board in a stone canoe, with an iron paddle, and make a terrible noise, and that he intended to give us to him. I thought all he said was so. I therefore confessed that we were runaways—where and with whom we had lived. He said he would take me back to New London, as my master was rich and would pay him a good price. Here the devil prompted me to tell a lie, and I replied that the general had advertised me one-cent reward. He then said that he would do nothing with me further than to keep my clothes until we paid him. When the vessel reached the dock, John slipped off, and I was not slow to follow. In a few days we got money to redeem our clothing; we took board in Cherry Street, at two dollars per week; we soon obtained work and received sixty-two and a half cents per day. While this continued, we had no difficulty in paying our board. My mind now became tolerably calm, but in the midst of this I was greatly alarmed, as I was informed that my master had offered fifteen dollars reward for me and that the captain of one of the packets was looking for me.[12] I dared not go back and therefore determined to go to Philadelphia; to this John objected and advised me to go to sea, but I could find no vessel. He entered on board a privateer, and I was thus left entirely alone in a strange city. Wandering about, I fell in company with a sergeant and a file of men who were enlisting soldiers for the United States Army. They thought I would answer their purpose, but how to get me was the thing. Now they began to talk to me, then treated me to some spirits, and when that began to operate they told me all about the war and what a fine thing it was to be a soldier. I was pleased with the idea of being a soldier, took some more liquor and some money, had a cockade fastened on my hat, and was off in high spirits for my uniform. Now, my enlistment was against the law, but I did not know it; I could not think why I should risk my life and limbs in fighting for the white man, who had cheated my forefathers out of their land.[13] By this time I had acquired many bad practices. I was sent over to Governor's Island, opposite the city, and here I remained some time. Too much liquor was dealt out to the soldiers, who got drunk very often. Indeed, the island was like a hell upon earth, in consequence of the wickedness of the soldiers. I have known sober men to enlist, who afterward became confirmed drunkards, and appear like fools upon the earth. So it was among the soldiers, and what should a child do, who was entangled in their net? Now, although I made no profession of religion, yet I could not bear to hear sacred things spoken of lightly, or the sacred name of God blasphemed; and I often spoke to the soldiers about it, and in general they listened attentively to what I had to say. I did not tell them that I had ever made a profession of religion. In a little time I became almost as bad as any of them, could drink rum, play cards, and act as wickedly as any. I was at times tormented with the thoughts of death, but God had mercy on me and spared my life, and for this I feel thankful to the present day. Some people are of opinion that if a person is once born of the Spirit of God he can never fall away entirely, and because I acted thus, they may pretend to say that I had not been converted to the faith. I believe firmly that, if ever Paul was born again, I was; if not, from whence did I derive all the light and happiness I had heretofore experienced? To be sure it was not to be compared to Paul's— but the change I felt in my very soul.

I felt anxious to obtain forgiveness from every person I had injured in any manner whatever. Sometimes I thought I would write to my old friends and request forgiveness—then I thought I had done right. I could not bear to

12. William Williams began advertising for the return of his runaway indentured servant around the end of April 1813 (*Connecticut Gazette*, April 21, 1813).

13. Against the law because he was actually only fifteen; thus, his enlistment records were falsified to list him as seventeen.

hear any order of Christians ridiculed, especially the Methodists—it grieved me to the heart.

CHAPTER V

It appeared that I had been enlisted for a musician, as I was instructed while on the island in beating a drum. In this I took much delight. While on the island I witnessed the execution of a soldier who was shot according to the decision of a court martial. Two men had been condemned for mutiny or desertion. It is impossible for me to describe the feelings of my heart when I saw the soldiers parade and the condemned, clothed in white, with Bibles in their hands, come forward. The band then struck up the dead march, and the procession moved with a mournful and measured tread to the place of execution, where the poor creatures were compelled to kneel on the coffins, which were alongside two newly dug graves. While in this position the chaplain went forward and conversed with them—after he had retired, a soldier went up and drew the caps over their faces; thus blindfolded, he led one of them some distance from the other. An officer then advanced and raised his handkerchief as a signal to the platoon to prepare to fire—he then made another for them to aim at the wretch who had been left kneeling on his coffin, and at a third signal the platoon fired and the immortal essence of the offender in an instant was in the spirit land. To me this was an awful day—my heart seemed to leap into my throat. Death never appeared so awful. But what must have been the feelings of the unhappy man who had so narrowly escaped the grave? He was completely overcome and wept like a child, and it was found necessary to help him back to his quarters. This spectacle made me serious; but it wore off in a few days.

Shortly after this we were ordered to Staten Island, where we remained about two months. Then we were ordered to join the army destined to conquer Canada. As the soldiers were tired of the island, this news animated them very much. They thought it a great thing to march through the country and assist in taking the enemy's land. As soon as our things were ready we embarked on board a sloop for Albany and then went on to Greenbush, where we were quartered. In the meantime I had been transferred to the ranks. This I did not like; to carry a musket was too fatiguing, and I had a positive objection to being placed on the guard, especially at night.[14] As I had only enlisted for a drummer, I thought that this change by the officer was contrary to law and, as the bond was broken, liberty was granted me; there-

14. Though this may sound like unjustified complaining, it may not when one remembers that Apess was only fifteen, stood five feet, two inches tall, and was slight of build.

fore, being heartily tired of a soldier's life, and having a desire to see my father once more, I went off very deliberately; I had no idea that they had a lawful claim on me and was greatly surprised as well as alarmed when arrested as a deserter from the army. Well, I was taken up and carried back to the camp, where the officers put me under guard. We shortly after marched for Canada, and during this dreary march the officers tormented me by telling me that it √ was their intention to make a fire in the woods, stick my skin full of pine splinters, and after having an Indian powwow over me, burn me to death. Thus they tormented me day after day.[15]

We halted for some time at Burlington but resumed our march and went into winter quarters at Plattsburgh. All this time God was very good to me, as I had not a sick day. I had by this time become very bad. I had previously learned to drink rum, play cards, and commit other acts of wickedness, but it was here that I first took the name of the Lord in vain, and oh, what a sting it left behind. We continued here until the ensuing fall, when we received orders to join the main army under Gen. Hampton.[16] Another change now took place: We had several pieces of heavy artillery with us, and of course horses were necessary to drag them, and I was taken from the ranks and ordered to take charge of one team. This made my situation rather better. I now had the privilege of riding. The soldiers were badly off, as the officers were very cruel to them, and for every little offense they would have them flogged. One day the officer of our company got angry at me and pricked my ear with the point of his sword.

We soon joined the main army and pitched our tents with them. It was now very cold, and we had nothing but straw to lay on. There was also a scarcity of provisions, and we were not allowed to draw our full rations. Money would not procure food—and when anything was to be obtained the officers always had the preference, and they, poor souls, always wanted the whole for themselves. The people generally have no idea of the extreme sufferings of the soldiers on the frontiers during the last war; they were indescribable; the soldiers ate with the utmost greediness raw corn and everything eatable that fell in their way. In the midst of our afflictions, our valiant general ordered us to march forward to subdue the country in a trice. The pioneers had great difficulty in clearing the way—the enemy retreated, burning everything as they fled. They destroyed everything, so that we could not find forage for the horses. We were now cutting our way through a wilderness

15. All this would have occurred in late summer and fall of 1813.
16. General Wade Hampton was placed at the head of the American troops stationed at Lake Champlain in July 1813. He led one wing of the second of several almost comically inept attempts by the Americans to take Montreal. Hampton resign from the army in March 1814.

and were very often benumbed with the cold. Our sufferings now for the want of food were extreme—the officers, too, began to feel it, and one of them offered me two dollars for a little flour, but I did not take this money, and he did not get my flour; I would not have given it to *him* for fifty dollars. The soldiers united their flour and baked unleavened bread; of this we made a *delicious* repast.

After we had proceeded about thirty miles, we fell in with a body of Canadians and Indians—the woods fairly resounded with their yells. Our "brave and chivalrous" general ordered a picked troop to disperse them; we fired but one cannon, and a retreat was sounded to the great mortification of the soldiers, who were ready and willing to fight. But as our general did not fancy the smell of gunpowder, he thought it best to close the campaign by retreating with seven thousand men, before a "host" of seven hundred. Thus were many a poor fellow's hopes of conquest and glory blasted by the timidity of one man. This little brush with an enemy that we could have crushed in a single moment cost us several men in killed and wounded. The army now fell back on Plattsburgh, where we remained during the winter; we suffered greatly for the want of barracks, having to encamp in the open fields a good part of the time.[17] My health, through the goodness of God, was preserved notwithstanding many of the poor soldiers sickened and died. So fast did they go off that it appeared to me as if the plague was raging among them.

When the spring opened, we were employed in building forts. We erected three in a very short time. We soon received orders to march and joined the army under General Wilkinson, to reduce Montreal. We marched to Odletown in great splendor, "heads up and eyes right," with a noble commander at our head and the splendid city of Montreal in our view. The city, no doubt, presented a scene of the wildest uproar and confusion; the people were greatly alarmed as we moved on with all the pomp and glory of an army flushed with many victories. But when we reached Odletown, John Bull met us with a picked troop. They soon retreated, and some took refuge in an old fortified mill, which we pelted with a goodly number of cannonballs. It appeared as if we were determined to sweep everything before us. It was really amusing to see our feminine general with his nightcap on his head and a dishcloth tied round his precious body, crying out to his men, "Come on, my brave boys, we will give John Bull a bloody nose." We did not succeed in taking the mill, and the British kept up an incessant cannonade from the fort. Some of the balls cut down the trees, so that we had frequently to spring out of their way when falling. I thought it was a hard time, and I had reason too, as I was in the front of the battle, assisting in working a twelve-pounder, and the British aimed directly at us. Their balls whistled around us and hurried a good many of the soldiers into the eternal world, while others were most horribly mangled. Indeed, they were so hot upon us that we had not time to remove the dead as they fell. The horribly disfigured bodies of the dead—the piercing groans of the wounded and the dying—the cries for help and succor from those who could not help themselves—were most appalling. I can never forget it. We continued fighting till near sundown, when a retreat was sounded along our line, and instead of marching forward to Montreal we wheeled about, and, having once set our faces toward Plattsburgh and turned our backs ingloriously on the enemy, we hurried off with all possible speed. We carried our dead and wounded with us. Oh, it was a dreadful sight to behold so many brave men sacrificed in this manner. In this way our campaign closed. During the whole of this time the Lord was merciful to me, as I was not suffered to be hurt. We once more reached Plattsburgh and pitched our tents in the neighborhood. While here, intelligence of the capture of Washington was received. Now, says the orderly sergeant, the British have burnt up all the papers at Washington, and our enlistment for the war among them; we had better give in our names as having enlisted for five years.[18]

We were again under marching orders, as the enemy, it was thought, contemplated an attack on Plattsburgh. Thither we moved without delay and were posted in one of the forts. By the time we were ready for them, the enemy made his appearance on Lake Champlain, with his vessels of war. It was a fine thing to see their noble vessels moving like things of life upon this mimic sea, with their streamers floating in the wind. This armament was intended to cooperate with the army, which numbered fourteen thousand men, under the command of the captain general of Canada, and at that very time in view of our troops.[19] They presented a very imposing aspect. Their red uniform, and the instruments of death which they bore in their hands, glittered in the sunbeams of heaven, like so many sparkling diamonds. Very fortunately for us and for the country, a brave and noble commander was placed at the head of the army.[20] It was not an easy task to frighten him. For notwithstanding his men were inferior in point of number to those of the enemy, say as one to seven, yet relying on the bravery of his men, he deter-

17. This is General James Wilkinson, who replaced General Henry Dearborn as commander of the American forces on the north shore of Lake Ontario and along the St. Lawrence. This encounter occurred in the fall of 1813 before Wilkinson was relieved of his command in late March. Our "brave and chivalrous general" could have been either Wilkinson or Hampton, though given Wilkinson's reputation it was probably he. Apess's account sounds very much like a description of a skirmish in November 1813, ninety miles from Montreal when a British force of 800 nearly routed Wilkinson's army of some 8,000.
18. Washington was captured and burned on August 24 and 25, 1814.
19. General Sir George Prevost.
20. General Alexander Macomb, who in late August had taken command of the troops at Plattsburgh. His troops were indeed heavily outnumbered by the British.

mined to fight to the last extremity. The enemy, in all the pomp and pride of war, had sat down before the town and its slender fortifications and commenced a cannonade, which we returned without much ceremony. Congreve rockets,[21] bombshells, and cannonballs poured upon us like a hailstorm. There was scarcely any intermission, and for six days and nights we did not leave our guns, and during that time the work of death paused not, as every day some shot took effect. During the engagement, I had charge of a small magazine. All this time our fleet, under the command of the gallant M'Donough, was lying on the peaceful waters of Champlain.[22] But this little fleet was to be taken, or destroyed: It was necessary, in the accomplishment of their plans. Accordingly, the British commander bore down on our vessels in gallant style. As soon as the enemy showed fight, our men flew to their guns. Then the work of death and carnage commenced. The adjacent shores resounded with the alternate shouts of the sons of liberty and the groans of their parting spirits. A cloud of smoke mantled the heavens, shutting out the light of day—while the continual roar of artillery added to the sublime horrors of the scene. At length, the boasted valor of the haughty Britons failed them— they quailed before the incessant and well-directed fire of our brave and hardy tars and, after a hard-fought battle, surrendered to that foe they had been sent to crush. On land the battle raged pretty fiercely. On our side the Green Mountain boys behaved with the greatest bravery. As soon as the British commander had seen the fleet fall into the hands of the Americans, his boasted courage forsook him, and he ordered his army of heroes, fourteen thousand strong, to retreat before a handful of militia.

This was indeed a proud day for our country. We had met a superior force on the lake, and "they were ours." On land we had compelled the enemy to seek safety in flight. Our army did not lose many men, but on the lake many a brave man fell—fell in the defense of his country's rights. The British moved off about sundown.

We remained in Plattsburgh until the peace. As soon as it was known that the war had terminated, and the army disbanded, the soldiers were clamorous for their discharge, but it was concluded to retain our company in the service—I, however, obtained my release. Now, according to the act of enlistment, I was entitled to forty dollars bounty money and one hundred and sixty acres of land. The government also owed me for fifteen months' pay. I have

21. Named after Sir William Congreve (1772–1828), a British artillery specialist. His rocket, invented in 1805, was an important advance in rocket technology. These had a range of up to 9,000 feet and could weigh between eight and forty-two pounds.

22. Captain Thomas Macdonough, thirty years old at the time, a naval officer who led his fleet brilliantly. His victory gave the United States unequivocal control of Lake Champlain and led to the retreat to Canada of the invading British army.

not seen anything of bounty money, land, or arrearages, from that day to this. √
I am not, however, alone in this—hundreds were served in the same manner.
But I could never think that the government acted right toward the "*Natives*,"
not merely in refusing to pay us but in claiming our services in cases of
perilous emergency, and still deny us the right of citizenship; and as long as
our nation is debarred the privilege of voting for civil officers, I shall believe
that the government has no claim on our services.[23]

CHAPTER VI

No doubt there are many good people in the United States who would not
trample upon the rights of the poor, but there are many others who are
willing to roll in their coaches upon the tears and blood of the poor and
unoffending natives—those who are ready at all times to speculate on the
Indians and defraud them out of their rightful possessions. Let the poor
Indian attempt to resist the encroachments of his white neighbors, what a hue
and cry is instantly raised against him. It has been considered as a trifling
thing for the whites to make war on the Indians for the purpose of driving
them from their country and taking possession thereof. This was, in their
estimation, all right, as it helped to extend the territory and enriched some
individuals. But let the thing be changed. Suppose an overwhelming army
should march into the United States for the purpose of subduing it and
enslaving the citizens; how quick would they fly to arms, gather in multitudes
around the tree of liberty, and contend for their rights with the last drop of
their blood. And should the enemy succeed, would they not eventually rise
and endeavor to regain liberty? And who would blame them for it?

When I left the army, I had not a shilling in my pocket. I depended upon
the precarious bounty of the inhabitants, until I reached the place where
some of my brethren dwelt.[24] I tarried with them but a short time and then set
off for Montreal. I was anxious, in some degree, to become steady and went to √
learn the business of a baker. My bad habits now overcome my good intentions. I was addicted to drinking rum and would sometimes get quite intoxi-

23. The Treaty of Ghent was signed the day before Christmas, 1814, but news of it did not reach
the United States until early February 1815. President Madison sought to maintain a larger
peacetime standing army—probably the reason Apess's company was retained in service. He, in
fact, mustered himself out no later than September 14, 1815, when his enlistment record notes
him as having deserted. Although this may well be the reason he never received pay, bounty, or the
land grant, many veterans of the War of 1812 were cheated of these.
24. It seems most likely that these would have been some branch of the Mohawks since Apess was
traveling between Plattsburgh and Montreal. However, it is also possible that these were Sokoki,
Western Abenakis. Unlike the Mohawk they were Algonquians and, though their language differed from Pequot, Apess and they might still have been able to converse.

cated. As it was my place to carry out the bread, I frequently fell in company, and one day, being in liquor, I met one of the king's soldiers, and after abusing him with my tongue, I gave him a sound flogging. In the course of the affair I broke a pitcher which the soldier had, and as I had to pay for it, I was wicked enough to take my master's money, without his knowledge, for that purpose. My master liked me, but he thought, if I acted so once, I would a second time, and he very properly discharged me. I was now placed in a bad situation—by my misconduct, I had lost a good home! I went and hired myself to a farmer, for four dollars per month. After serving him two months, he paid me, and with the money I bought some decent clothes. By spells, I was hired as a servant, but this kind of life did not suit me, and I wished to return to my brethren. My mind changed, and I went up the St. Lawrence to Kingston, where I obtained a situation on board of a sloop, in the capacity of a cook, at twelve dollars per month. I was on board the vessel some time, and when we settled the captain cheated me out of twelve dollars. My next move was in the country; I agreed to serve a merchant faithfully, and he promised to give me twelve dollars a month. Everything went on smooth for a season; at last I became negligent and careless, in consequence of his giving me a pint of rum every day, which was the allowance he made for each person in his employment.

While at this place, I attended a Methodist meeting—at the time I felt very much affected, as it brought up before my mind the great and indescribable enjoyments I had found in the house of prayer, when I was endeavoring to serve the Lord. It soon wore off, and I relapsed into my former bad habits.[25]

I now went again into the country and stayed with a farmer for one month; he paid me five dollars. Then I shifted my quarters to another place and agreed with a Dutch farmer to stay with him all winter at five dollars a month. With this situation I was much pleased. My work was light—I had very little to do except procuring firewood. I often went with them on hunting excursions; besides, my brethren were all around me, and it therefore seemed like home. I was now in the Bay of Quinte; the scenery was diversified. There were also some natural curiosities. On the very top of a high mountain in the neighborhood there was a large pond of water, to which there was no visible outlet—this pond was unfathomable. It was very surprising to me that so great a body of water should be found so far above the common level of the earth. There was also in the neighborhood a rock that had the appearance of being hollowed out by the hand of a skillful artificer; through this rock wound

25. The chronology is not dependably clear here. Apess probably left the army in Plattsburgh in March or April 1815, by his own account. All these experiences probably occurred between spring 1815 and late summer 1815.

a narrow stream of water: It had a most beautiful and romantic appearance, √ and I could not but admire the wisdom of God in the order, regularity, and beauty of creation; I then turned my eyes to the forest, and it seemed alive with its sons and daughters. There appeared to be the utmost order and regularity in their encampment.[26]

Oh, what a pity that this state of things should change. How much better would it be if the whites would act like a civilized people and, instead of giving my brethren of the woods "rum!" in exchange for their furs, give them food and clothing for themselves and children. If this course were pursued, I believe that God would bless both the whites and natives threefold. I am bold to aver that the minds of the natives were turned against the Gospel and soured toward the whites because *some* of the missionaries have joined the unholy brethren in speculations to the advantage of themselves, regardless of the rights, feelings, and interests of the untutored sons of the forest. If a good missionary goes among them, and preaches the pure doctrine of the Gospel, he must necessarily tell them that they must "love God and their neighbor as themselves—to love men, deal justly, and walk humbly." They would naturally reply, "Your doctrine is very good, but the whole course of your conduct is decidedly at variance with your profession—we think the whites need fully as much religious instruction as we do." In this way many a good man's path is hedged up, and he is prevented from being useful among the natives, in consequence of the bad conduct of those who are, properly speaking, only "wolves in sheep's clothing." However, the natives are on the whole willing to receive the Gospel, and of late, through the instrumentality of *pious missionaries,* much good has been done—many of them have been reclaimed from the most abandoned and degrading practices and brought to a knowledge of the truth as it is in Jesus!

Chapter VII

By many persons great objections have been raised against efforts to civilize the natives—they allege that they have tried the experiment and failed. But how did they make the experiment, and why did they fail? We may with √ perfect safety say that these persons were prompted to the efforts they made by sinister motives, and they failed because they undertook that in their own strength which nothing short of the power of God could effect. A most

26. Apess's idyll at the Bay of Quinte seems to have occurred in the winter of 1815 and the early spring of 1816. "Brethren," here as elsewhere in his writing, always refers to Native Americans. These "brethren" would have been Mohawks, if Apess was on the northeast side of the bay. There had been a reservation there since 1784. These could have been, were he on the southwest shore, the Mississauga who had a village there.

sweeping charge has been brought against the natives—a charge which has no foundation in truth. It is this, that they are not susceptible of improvement; now, subsequent facts have proved that this assertion is false. Let us look around us, and what do we behold? The forests of Canada and the West are vocal with the praises of God, as they ascend from the happy wigwams of the natives. We see them flocking to the standard of Emmanuel. Many of them have been converted to God and have died in the triumphs of faith. Our religious papers have, from time to time, recorded the blessed effects of the divine spirit—of the strong faith of the expiring Indian. The hopes of the Christian have been elevated, and there is everything to cheer and encourage the followers of the Lamb in so good and noble a cause.

Some people make this charge against the natives, who never knew anything about religion, and I fancy that it would be as difficult for any man who lives in a state of voluptuousness to get to heaven by his own strength as it would be for a native. The Methodists have perhaps done more toward enlightening the poor Indians and bringing them to a knowledge of the truth than all other societies together. I do not say that they did it of their own strength, but that they were the happy instruments in the hands of the Lord Jesus, in accomplishing that which others have failed in performing, as they (the Methodists) relied altogether on the blessing of God. They preached not themselves, but Christ Jesus—and him crucified: And while they were doing this, they sought not their own advancement. And no wonder that they succeeded—the natives were melted down into tenderness and love, and they became as kind and obliging as any people could be.

It is my opinion that our nation retains the original complexion of our common father, Adam. This is strongly impressed on my mind. I think it is very reasonable, and in this opinion I am not singular, as some of the best writers of the age, among whom we find a Clinton, a Boudinot, a West, and a Hinds, have expressed their sentiments in its favor.[27] But to return:

27. The context is Apess's belief that the Indians were descendants of the Ten Lost Tribes of Israel and thus due every respect as creatures as equally in God's favor as Euro-American Christians. This belief attempted to counter the conviction, used by many Euro-Americans to justify their depredations on the Indians, that these were an inferior people incapable of civilization and Christianity. The references are to De Witt Clinton (1769–1828), senator from New York, mayor of New York City, and the governor of the state (1817–23), responsible for the building of the Erie Canal. One of the most important and innovative politicians in the early republic, he was much interested in Native Americans and their origins and wrote about them; see esp. *The Life and Writings* (New York: Baker and Scribner, 1849). Elias Boudinot (1740–1821) was a member of the Continental Congress from New Jersey and the first president of the American Bible Society. The Cherokee editor, Elias Boudinot, was his protégé. The Euro-American Boudinot wrote one of the major texts on this issue, from which Apess took most of the Appendix to *A Son of the Forest*. See Boudinot, *A Star in the West; or, A Humble Attempt to Discover the Long Lost Ten Tribes of Israel* (Trenton,

In the spring the old gentleman set us to making maple sugar. This took us into the woods, which were vocal with the songs of the birds; all nature seemed to smile and rejoice in the freshness and beauty of spring. My brethren appeared very cheerful on account of its return and enjoyed themselves in hunting, fishing, basket making, etc. After we had done making sugar, I told the old gentleman I wished to go and see my friends in the East, as I had been absent about three years: He consented, though he wished me to tarry longer with him. I then went to Kingston, where I fell into bad company, with drunkards. They were friends as long as my money held out, but when that failed, their friendship turned to enmity. Thus all my money was gone, and I was alone and destitute in a strange place. I went to live with a man for a while but had not been with him but a few days before I found much trouble in the wigwam. The lady of the house was a lady indeed; when she went to bed she could not get up without assistance, and very often her husband would mourn over her and say what a wretch he had been ever since he had married her. She was very intemperate, and here I saw the evil of ardent spirits. They soon after broke up housekeeping, and I of course lost my place. I had not refrained from my evil practices, and some of my wicked companions advised me to steal for a living, but as I had no inclination to rob anyone, I had prudence and firmness to resist the temptation. Those who advised me to do so were not my brethren but whites. My eyes were now opened to see my pretended friends in their true light. I concluded that such friends were not useful to me, and I was awakened to reflection and determined to leave their society.

One Sabbath, as I was passing by a chapel, I heard a good man of God giving good advice to his people. He earnestly exhorted them to faithfulness and prayer. I went in, and while listening to his fervent discourse, all my promises of reformation rose up before me. I was very much affected—my spirit was troubled, and I began to think seriously about my situation. The next day I sat down in the sun to sun myself and to consider as to my future course. As I found I was friendless, without money, and without work, the desire of my heart was to get home. While reflecting on this, to me, important subject, it appeared as if God was working for me, as four boatmen about going on a hunting and fishing excursion came to purchase stores. I asked them if I should go with them—they wished to know where I was going, and I

NJ: Fenton, Hutchinson, and Dunham, 1816). West and Hinds I have not been able to identify definitively. West is probably John West (177[?]–1845), who published in 1827 *Journal during a Residence at the Red River Colony British N.A. and Excursions Among the Northwest American Indians* (London: Seeley, 1827). Hinds may be Samuel Hinds, bishop of Norwich (England), whose *History of the Rise and Early Progress of Christianity* (London: Baldwin and Gadock, 1828) might have been available to Apess and which had material relevant to his point here.

told them I was willing to go anywhere. One of them hired me to fish, and I went with them; the time passed rapidly on, and I felt as happy as a king. We had very little rum, and that little we found abundantly sufficient. By degrees I recovered my appetite. I was with these good men upward of a month, part of which time we spent in fishing and part in hunting deer. They then returned to see their families, taking me with them. The one who had hired me to fish, when I told him that I wished to go home, acted like a gentleman and paid me my wages. After purchasing a pair of shoes, I had only one shilling left. I now started for home, a distance of more than three hundred miles.[28] This was a long journey to perform alone, and on foot. But, thank God, I found friends—many who were willing to supply me with food and render me assistance. I had no difficulty until I reached Utica, where I lost my shilling. I was now penniless. Fortunately, I agreed with the captain of a boat to work my passage down the Mohawk River. In this way I got along some distance. When I left the boat I had to beg or work, as answered my purpose best, as I was extremely anxious to get home; therefore, I preferred the shortest method. But nevertheless I refused not to work. But unfortunately the people in this part of the country, seeing I was an Indian, took but little notice of me. I was also exposed to some temptations, as I met often in the road the veriest wretches that defile the earth—such as would forget the dignity of human nature so far as to blackguard me because I was an Indian.[29] A son of the forest would never stoop so low as to offer such an insult to a stranger who happened to be among them. I was much mortified, and believing that they ought to be corrected for so flagrant a breach of good manners and "civilization," I thought seriously, in one or two instances, of inflicting summary punishment; but this feeling gave way to that of pity. It appeared to me as if they had not the sense and wisdom of the brute creation.

When I reached Albany, the bells were tolling. The solemn sound entered into the deepest recesses of my soul, pressed down as it were with a multitude of sorrows. It appeared to be a very solemn time. They were engaged in depositing the mortal remains of a man in the narrow and darksome grave, who had been killed the day before by a stroke of lightning. Oh, how thankful I felt that I had not been taken off instead of that man. I immediately went to Hoosick, passing through the pleasant town of Troy. I was now about one hundred miles from home, and not having clothes suitable for the season, I concluded to go to work in order to get such as would answer

---

28. Kingston, Ontario, to New London or Colchester, Connecticut, would in fact be considerably farther, more on the magnitude of five to six hundred miles.
29. "blackguard": i.e., to revile him.

to make my appearance in at home. So I began to make inquiries for work and come across one Esquire Haviland, who engaged me to help him the remainder of the season, at eight dollars per month. He treated me with the utmost kindness; he took me to church to hear the word of God, dressed me up in good clothes, and took the best care of me while I remained with them. When I left them, instead of going home, as I intended, I steered my course for Old Hartford, where I fell in with some of the rough people of the world, and made a halt. I again listened to the advice of the wicked and turned aside from the path of virtue. I soon agreed to go to sea with one of my new comrades, but we could not ship ourselves. I now got to drinking too much of the accursed liquor again. As we failed in our project at Hartford, we started for New Haven, where I abandoned the notion of going to sea and went to work, and all I got for two months' labor was a pair of pantaloons. I thought surely that these were hard times. Winter was now coming on apace, and as I had very little clothing, I had to do the best I could. I saw the impropriety of keeping bad company, and I must in this respect acknowledge that I was a √ very fool, and only a half-witted Indian—the Lord had often warned me of my danger, and I was advised of the evil consequences by those who I believe were concerned for my welfare here and hereafter.

In the spring I had good clothes, and withal looked very decent, so I thought that I would make another effort to reach my home. In my journey, being in the land of steady habits, I found the people very benevolent and kind. I experienced but very little difficulty on the way, and at last I arrived in safety at the home of my childhood. At first my people looked upon me as one risen from the dead. Not having heard from me since I left home, being more than four years, they thought I must certainly have died, and the days of mourning had almost passed. They were rejoiced to see me once more in the land of the living, and I was equally rejoiced to find all my folks alive. The whites with whom I had been acquainted were also very glad to see me. After I had spent some time with my relations in Groton and visited all my old friends, I concluded to go to work and be steady. Accordingly, I hired myself to a Mr. Geers, for a month or two. I served him faithfully, but when I wanted my pay he undertook to treat me as he would a degraded African slave. He took a cart stake in order to pay me, but he soon found out his mistake, as I made him put it down as quick as he had taken it up. I had been cheated so often that I determined to have my rights this time, and forever after.[30]

30. Apess probably reached Connecticut in the summer of 1816. This would place him in Old Hartford and New Haven in the fall and winter of 1816/17, so that his reunion with his family would have occurred in April 1817, a bit more than four years since he had run away from William Williams.

CHAPTER VIII

I was now about nineteen years of age and had become quite steady.[31] I
attended meetings again quite often, and my mind was powerfully wrought
upon. At this time my heart was susceptible of good impressions. I would
think upon the varied scenes of my life—how often the Lord had called me,
and how for a season I attended to that call—of the blessed and happy times I
had experienced in the house of God, and in secret devotion—and the days of
darkness and nights of sorrowful anguish since those days when the Spirit of
God breathed upon my soul. *Then,* I enjoyed happiness in a preeminent degree! *Now,* I was miserable, I had offended God—violated his laws—abused
his goodness—trampled his mercy underfoot and disregarded his admonitions. But still he called me back to the path of duty and of peace. I was
pressed down by a load of shame and a weight of guilt too intolerable to be
borne. Hour after hour, and day after day, did I endeavor to lift my heart to
God, to implore forgiveness of my sins and grace to enable me to lay hold of
the promise to the vilest of the vile, through Jesus Christ our Lord. But the
Holy Spirit flew not to my relief. I then thought that I must die and go to hell.

My convictions were so powerful that I could scarcely eat. I had no relish
for food. The anguish of my soul afflicted my body to such a degree that I was
almost too weak to perform my labor. Sleep seldom visited my eyelids. My
employer found out that the Lord was teaching me, but he made light of it
and said he was going to heaven across the lots. I thought he might go *that*
way, but for my part I must take another course.[32] May the Lord forgive him
and teach him the good and the right way. By this time my employer had
become good to me, and as I wished to engage elsewhere for six months, my
time being out with him, he gave me a recommendation.

One of the neighbors wished me to join with him six months, so we
agreed. They treated me as a brother. But my sins troubled me so much that I
had no comfort. My soul was weighed down on account of my many transgressions, and I was tempted by the enemy of souls to believe that I had
committed the unpardonable sin—but he was a liar, as the sequel proved, for
after many prayers, and groans, and tears, and sighs, I found some relief.
This, at the time, astonished me, as I was one of the vilest sinners on the face
of the earth.[33] Now I think the devil took advantage of me in this manner. I

31. Spring and summer 1817.
32. To go across lots is to take a shortcut. The common saying in vernacular speech is "to go to hell
across lots," precisely the implication of Apess's "I thought he might go *that* way."
33. The "unpardonable sin" is to despair of Christ's power to save one, which is, in effect, to believe
oneself greater than God, to be beyond this power. To find relief signified Christ's forgiving
presence and one's faith in it.

have heretofore stated that I associated with bad company, with such persons as often profaned the holy name of God. I always disliked to hear anyone swear, but one day when I was angry I swore a horrid oath, and the very instant that it passed my lips my heart beat like the pendulum of a clock, my conscience roared despair and horror like thunder, and I thought I was going to be damned right off. I gave utterance to the word without thinking what I was doing; it could not be recalled, and afterward I thought I would not have said it for all the world. This was the *first* and the *last* time that I ever used so awful an expression, and I thought this of itself sufficient to sink my soul to the shades of everlasting night. Now, the way in which the devil took the advantage of me was this: Whenever I became fervent in my supplications at the throne of mercy for pardon on my guilty soul, he would try to persuade me that I had in uttering the oath referred to forever closed the door of hope.

I still continued to pray and attend meetings, notwithstanding the work was very hard, and the meeting seven miles off; but I did not neglect attending it a single Sabbath during the summer. I generally returned, as I went, with a heavy heart. I now went to a camp meeting but did not experience that depth of enjoyment which I desired. Being determined to persevere in the way of well-doing, I united with the Methodist Society, that is, on trial, for six months. I had never been at a camp meeting and, of course, knew nothing about it. It far exceeded my expectations. I never witnessed so great a body of Christians assembled together before—I was also astonished with their proceedings, was affected by their prayers, charmed by their songs of praise, and stood gazing at them like a brainless clown. However, I soon solicited the prayers of this body of Christians, for my poor soul was greatly troubled. But behold, one of the brethren called on me to pray. I began to make excuse, but nothing would do; he said, pray, and I thought I must. I trembled through fear and began to wish myself at home; I soon got on my knees, and of all the prayers that man ever heard, this attempt must have exceeded—I feared man more than my creator God. While endeavoring to pray, it appeared as if my words would choke me—the cold chills run over my body—my feelings were indescribably awful. This, however, had a very good effect upon me, as it learned me not to please man so much as God. The camp meeting was a very happy one; I found some comfort and enjoyed myself tolerably well. The parting scene was very affecting—serious thoughts passed through my mind, as I gazed on this large number of respectable and happy people, who were about to separate and meet not together again till the blast of the archangel's trump shall bring them in a twinkling to the judgment seat of Christ. And so it was, for we have never met altogether again—some have taken their everlasting flight.

When I returned home, I began to tell the family all about the camp meeting, what a blessed time we had, etc., but they ridiculed me, saying we were only deluded. I attempted to exhort them to seek an interest in the sinner's friend, but to no purpose, as they only laughed at me.

When the time for which I engaged had expired, I went among my tribe at Groton. I lived this winter with my aunt, who was comfortably situated.[34] She was the handmaid of the Lord, and being a widow, she rented her lands to the whites, and it brought her in enough to live on. While here we had some very good times. Once in four weeks we had meeting, which was attended by people from Rhode Island, Stonington, and other places and generally lasted three days. These seasons were glorious. We observed particular forms, although we knew nothing about the dead languages, except that the knowledge thereof was not necessary for us to serve God. We had no house of divine worship, and believing "that the groves were God's first temples," thither we would repair when the weather permitted.[35] The Lord often met with us, and we were happy in spite of the devil. Whenever we separated it was in perfect love and friendship.

My aunt could not read, but she could almost preach and, in her feeble manner, endeavor to give me much instruction. Poor dear woman, her body slumbers in the grave, but her soul is in the paradise of God—she has escaped from a world of trouble. The whites were anxious to have the honor of burying her; she was interred very decently, the whites being as numerous as the natives. Indeed, all who knew her wished to show the veneration in which they held her by following her remains to their last earthly resting place. Her name was Sally George, and she was deservedly esteemed for her piety. In her sphere she was a very useful woman and greatly beloved by all who knew her. She was very attentive to the sick, kind to the unfortunate, good and benevolent to the poor and the fatherless. She would often pour into the ear of the sin-sick soul the graciously reviving promises of the Gospel. While she lay sick, she expressed a desire to go and see her brethren, who lived about eight miles off; she said the Lord would give her the strength, and so he did. She then visited her friends, and after enjoying some religious conversation, she returned home to die. The fear of death was now taken away, and she exhorted all around her to be faithful and serve the Lord. She died in the full triumphs of the faith, on the 6th of May, 1824, aged 45 years. In her death, happy as it was, the church had sustained an almost irreparable loss. But

> She bathes her weary soul,
> In seas of heavenly rest,

34. For more on Aunt Sally George, see "The Experience of Sally George" in *The Experiences of Five Christian Indians* and the introduction to this volume.
35. The line is from William Cullen Bryant's "Forest Hymn."

> Where not a wave of trouble rolls,
> Across her peaceful breast.[36]

The next season I engaged with a Mr. Wright in the same neighborhood and continued with him some time.[37] While there I did wrong, as I got angry at the mistress of the house, who, by the by, was an extremely passionate woman, and uttered some unguarded expressions. I found I had done wrong and instantly made my humble confession to Almighty God, and also to my brethren, and obtained forgiveness. I continued to attend meeting and had many blessed times. The spirit of the Lord moved upon my heart, and I thought it to be my duty to call sinners to repentance. It was determined to have another camp meeting this season, and Brother Hyde preached a preparatory sermon from this portion of divine truth: *By night, on my bed, I sought him whom my soul loveth: I sought him but I found him not. I will rise now, and go about the city; in the streets, and in the broad ways, I will seek him whom my soul loveth: I sought him but I found him not. The watchman that go about the city found me: to whom I said, saw ye him whom my soul loveth? It was but a little that I passed from them, but I found him whom my soul loveth: I held him and would not let him go, until I had brought him to my mother's house, and unto the chamber of her that had conceived me. I charge you, O ye daughters of Jerusalem, by the roes and by the hinds of the field, that ye stir not up, nor awake my love till he please* (Song of Solomon 3:1–5).

After Brother Hyde had concluded his sermon, I felt moved to rise and ✓ speak. I trembled at the thought; but believing it a duty required of me by my heavenly father, I could not disobey, and in rising to discharge this sacred obligation, I found all impediment of speech removed; my heart was enlarged, my soul glowed with holy fervor, and the blessing of the Almighty sanctified this, my first public attempt to warn sinners of their danger and invite them to the marriage supper of the Lamb. I was now in my proper element, just harnessed for the work, with the fire of divine love burning on my heart. In this frame of mind I went to camp meeting, and here the presence of the Lord was made manifest—his gracious spirit was poured out upon the people, and while he was present to cheer and bless his followers, his awakening power sought out the sinner and nailed conviction on his heart. Oh, it was a joyful scene. Here were the followers of the Lord praising him in strains of the liveliest joy—there the brokenhearted mourner shedding tears of penitential sorrow over the long black catalog of his offenses. Many a

36. This is from Isaac Watts's hymn, "When I Can Read My Title Clear."

37. Apess breaks his chronology by taking the story of Aunt Sally George through to her death. "The next season" is spring to fall 1818. He uses here, of course, the language of farming, in which a season can be planting time (spring to early summer) or harvest (late summer to midautumn) or the whole cycle of planting through harvest.

gracious shower of divine mercy fell on the encampment—many a hitherto drooping plant revived, and many a desolate and ruined heart was made the home of new, and happy, and heavenly feelings. I have reason to believe that at least one hundred sinners were reclaimed at this meeting, while many went away with their heads bowed down under a sense of their numerous trans- gressions. Shortly after this meeting, I felt it my duty to observe the ordinance of baptism by immersion, believing it as a scriptural doctrine. There were three other candidates for this ordinance, which was administered by Rev. Mr. Barnes, at a place called Bozrah, in the month of December 1818. It was a very solemn, affecting, and profitable time; the Lord in truth was present to bless.

Shortly after this I felt a desire to see my family connections again and therefore left this part of the country, after obtaining a certificate of my standing in society, etc., as is generally done by Methodists when they remove from one place to another. Nothing worthy of special notice occurred during my journey, except losing my way one night. It happened in this manner: Having reached the neighborhood of my father's residence about sundown, and being extremely anxious to complete my journey, I concluded to continue on, as I expected to reach his house by two o'clock in the morning. Unfortu- nately, I took the wrong road and was led into a swamp. I thought I was not far from the main road as I fancied that I heard teams passing on the other side of the swamp; and not being aware of the dangerous situation in which I was placed, I penetrated into the labyrinth of darkness with the hope of gaining the main road. At every step I became more and more entangled—the thickness of the branches above me shut out the little light afforded by the stars, and to my horror I found that the further I went, the deeper the mire; at last, I was brought to a dead stand. I had found it necessary to feel my way with a stick—now it failed in striking on solid ground; fortunately, in groping about I found a pole, which I suppose must have been twelve or fifteen feet long, and thrusting it in, met with no better success. I was now amazed; what to do I knew not; shut out from the light of heaven—surrounded by appalling darkness—standing on uncertain ground—and having proceeded so far that to return, if possible, were as "dangerous as to go over." This was the hour of peril—I could not call for assistance on my fellow creatures; there was no mortal ear to listen to my cry. I was shut out from the world and did not know but that I should perish there, and my fate forever remain a mystery to my friends. I raised my heart in humble prayer and supplication to the father of mercies, and behold he stretched forth his hand and delivered me from this place of danger. Shortly after I had prayed the Lord to set me free, I found a small piece of solid earth, and then another, so that after much difficulty I succeeded in once more placing my feet upon dry ground. I then fell upon my knees and thanked my blessed master for this singular interposition of his providence and mercy. As this circumstance occasioned so much delay, and withal fatigued me so much, I did not reach home until daylight. I found my father well, and all the family rejoiced to see me. On this occasion I had an opportunity of making some remarks to the friends who came to see me. My father, who was a member of the Baptist church, was much pleased, and what was far better, we had a time of refreshing from the presence of the Lord. I now agreed with my father to tarry with him all winter, and he agreed to learn me how to make shoes. In this new business I made some progress.[38]

CHAPTER IX

I was now very constant in attending meetings. In the neighborhood there was a small class of Methodists, firmly united to each other; I cast in my lot with this little band and had many precious seasons. They agreed in all points of doctrine but one, and that related to *perfect love*—some said it was inconsistent, and another said it was not.[39] I could not see wherein this inconsistency manifested itself, as we were commanded to *love God with all our hearts, and contend for that faith once delivered to the saints.*

While in Colrain the Lord moved upon my heart in a peculiarly powerful manner, and by it I was led to believe that I was called to preach the Gospel of our Lord and Savior Jesus Christ. In the present day, a great variety of opinion prevails respecting the holy work. We read in the Bible that in former days holy men spoke as they were moved by the Holy Ghost. I think this is right and believe more in the validity of such a call than in all the calls that ever issued from any body of men united.[40] My exercises were great—my soul was

38. He would have reached his father, then in Colrain, Massachusetts, sometime in the winter or early spring of 1819. A "time of refreshing" means a revival, a special outpouring of God's grace on his people. Apess did also, at this juncture, learn to be a shoemaker.

39. The argument involves the belief that Christ enjoins us to "perfect love," love like his and God the Father's, which knows no taint of self-regard and in which one is willing to lay down one's life for another. The "inconsistency" speaks to the fact that as creatures of the Fall, of original sin, we are by definition incapable of such love. Apess resolves the matter in his belief that God will make available to us what we need to meet his requirements, here signified as "*that faith once delivered to the saints.*"

40. Apess addresses here one of the issues that repeatedly led to new tensions within the evangelical community under the influence of revivalism. The emphasis on inspiration and evidence of the active presence of the Holy Ghost made it difficult to defend fixed rituals of worship or forms of settled authority. One of the critical forms of authority for any institutionalized church involves the selection and discipline of its ministers. Apess positions himself with those who stress the limitations of the ways of men and the greater reliability of God's. Therefore, feeling the call to preach from within had greater authority than any examination or licensing procedure such as that employed by the Methodist Conference to decide who was qualified to preach.

pained when the Lord placed before me the depravity of human nature. I commenced searching the Scriptures more diligently, and the more I read, the more they opened to my understanding; and something said to me, "Go now and warn the people to flee from the wrath to come!" And I began immediately to confer with flesh and blood, excusing myself, saying, Lord I cannot. I was nothing but a poor ignorant Indian and thought the people would not hear me. But my mind was the more distressed, and I began to pray more frequently to God to let this "cup pass from me." In this manner was I exercised day by day; but in the evening I would find myself in our little meetings exhorting sinners to repentance and striving to comfort the saints. On these occasions I had the greatest liberty. Now I did not acquaint my brethren with my feelings or exercises, for the devil tempted me to believe that they would take no notice of it. At length, the spell that bound me was broken. I dreamt one night that I was about taking a journey, that my road lay through a miry place in a dark and dreary way. It was with no little difficulty that I descended the steep. Then I beheld at some distance before me a large plain, on which the sun shone with perfect brightness, and when I succeeded in reaching this plain, all at once an angel of the blessed Lord stood in my way. After having addressed me, he read some extracts from St. John's Gospel, respecting the preaching of the word of life. This dream was the means of troubling me still more.

I now requested, if the Lord had called me to this holy work, that he would make it manifest by a sign. So one day, after prayer, I went to a friend and told him, if he was willing to give out an appointment for meeting at his house, I would try and exhort. He assented, and in giving out the appointment he made a mistake, as he informed the people that there would be a *sermon* instead of an exhortation, and when I attended, in place of finding a few persons at my friend's house, I found a large congregation assembled at the schoolhouse. I now thought I was in a sad predicament—I had never preached; but I called mightily upon God for assistance. When I went in, every eye was fixed on me, and when I was commencing the meeting, it appeared as if my confidence in God was gone; my lips quivered, my voice trembled, my knees smote together, and in short I quaked as it were with fear. But the Lord blessed me. Some of the people were pleased, and a few displeased. Soon after this, I received an invitation to hold a meeting in the same place again. I accordingly went, and I found a great concourse of people who had come out to hear the Indian preach, and as soon as I had commenced, the sons of the devil began to show their front—and I was treated not with the greatest loving kindness, as one of them threw an old hat in my face, and this example was followed by others, who threw sticks at me. But in the midst I went on with my sermon, and spoke from 2 Peter 2:9. *The Lord knoweth how to deliver the godly out of temptations, and to reserve the unjust until the day of judgment, to be punished.* The Lord laid too his helping hand; the sons of night were confused. Now I can truly say that a native of the forest cannot be found in all our country who would not blush at the bad conduct of many who enjoy in a preeminent degree the light of the Gospel. But so it is, that in the very center of Gospel light and influence thousands of immortal souls are sitting in darkness, or walking in the valley of the shadow of death! It is the truth, and a melancholy truth indeed![41]

I had an invitation to speak at another place about nine miles distant. Still, I was not satisfied; and I made it a subject of constant and serious prayer—I implored the Lord all the way, that if I was truly called to preach the everlasting Gospel I might have some token of his favor. I found the congregation large and respectful, and I spoke from Jeremiah 6:14.[42] We had a good time, but nothing special occurred. The congregation in the afternoon was much larger than in the morning, and it was impressed upon my mind to speak from this portion of the holy Scriptures: *The Lord knoweth how to deliver the godly out of temptation, and reserve the unjust to the day of judgment to be punished.* The Lord gave me strength, and we had a most gracious and glorious exhibition of his presiding presence, as many wept bitterly on account of their sins, while the saints of the most high rejoiced in the prospect of a complete and triumphant deliverance from the power of their sworn and cruel foe. Now I was assured that my call was of God, and I returned home praising him.

Shortly after this, my father began to oppose me—perhaps he thought, with some of the whites, that there were enough preachers in the land already. Be this as it may, I continued to exercise my gift and preached wherever a door was opened and, I trust, with some success.

It was now nearly time for the Conference to commence its session, and one of our circuit preachers very kindly told me that I had better desist until I should have obtained a license; if I did not, I would break the rules of the church—but I had already violated these.[43] Considering my youth and good intentions, he overlooked this conceived error and informed me that if I waited patiently I should have a license to exercise my gift by way of exhorta-

41. Apess was now in and around Colrain in northwestern Massachusetts. His discovery of his vocation and his first exhortations would have occurred between 1819 or 1820 and the spring or summer of 1821, when he returned to Connecticut.

42. "They have healed also the hurt *of the daughter* of my people slightly, saying, Peace, peace; when *there* is no peace."

43. Quarterly Methodist Conferences controlled for particular regions all matters of discipline within the Methodist Episcopal church. The most recurrent and important had to do with who was licensed to exhort and who to preach and on what circuit, since in this period most Methodist preachers did not serve a single settled parish.

tion, and that the preacher who was to succeed him would think it wrong if he found me holding meetings without authority from my brethren, and I partly consented. But the time was so long before the matter could be finally regulated that I could not sheathe my sword, and having on the armor, I took the field and preached till the new elder come among us; and when he found me preaching, what do you think he did? Why, he placed me under censure. Now, he wanted me to confess that I was in error; but I was such a blind Indian that I could not see how I was in error in preaching *Christ Jesus, and Him crucified,* and of course could not conscientiously confess as erroneous that which I believed to be right. He told me that if I *was* right, not to confess, but as I did *not* confess he cast me out of the church, showing plainly that he believed that no person is called of God to preach his word unless ordained of man! No comment is necessary on this fact.

This unkind treatment, as I regarded it, had nearly proved the ruin of my soul. The waters of affliction had well-nigh overwhelmed me—my hopes were drowned, and having been excluded from the pales of the church, I viewed myself as an *outcast from society.* Now the enemy sought to prevail against me, and for a season overcome me; I gave way for a little while but soon returned to my *first love.* I went then to my native tribe, where meetings were still kept up. I tarried here but a short time and then went to Old Saybrook; here I found a few Methodists, but they were too feeble to form a society, as persecution was at its height.[44] There were also a few colored people who met regularly for religious worship; with these I sometimes assembled.

About this time I met with a woman of nearly the same color as myself— she bore a pious and exemplary character.[45] After a short acquaintance, we were united in the sacred bonds of marriage; and now I was going on prosperously; but at last a calamity fell upon me, which nearly crushed me to the dust. A man exacted work of me, for a debt that I did not honestly owe, and while making his shoes, I concluded to pay myself, which I did. Immediately my conscience smote me, but I could not replace it in time, so I made ample restitution and a frank confession before all my brethren—and the Lord was good, for he wiped out the blot and restored me to his favor. I then went to Middletown and remained a short time, where I got out of business;

44. It appears he left the area around Colrain and returned to southeastern Connecticut sometime between late winter and spring 1820/21.
45. This would have occurred in the fall of 1821 since William Apess and Mary Wood of Salem, Connecticut, were married in that town on December 16, 1821, by the Reverend John Whittlesey. Mary Wood's mother, by her account, was an "English woman," and her father from one of the Spanish islands. He was, it would seem, of either mixed Native and Hispanic American ancestry or African and Hispanic or possibly all three.

crossed over the river and agreed to serve a tavern keeper for one month. I now sought every opportunity to be alone, and when my month was up I received my wages and sent it to my wife. I had now to seek another place, and as I went along, I prayed that my family might not suffer, as I knew that they were innocent, and my little ones too small to help themselves. After a little while, the Lord opened the way, and I obtained a situation with a Mr. Hail, in Gloucester, for two months, at twelve dollars a month. It being harvest time, my employer allowed each of his hands a half-pint of spirits every day. I told him I did not want my portion, so he agreed to pay me a little more. I *abstained entirely, and found that I could not only stand labor as well but perform more than those who drank the spirits.* All the hands exclaimed against me and said that I would soon give out; but I was determined that *touch not, taste not, handle not,* should be my motto; God supported me, and I can truly say that my health was better, my appetite improved, and my mind was calm. My general drink was molasses, or milk and water. Some persons say, that *they* cannot do without spirituous liquors, but I say it is a curse to individuals, to families, to communities, to the nation, and to the world at large. I could enlarge on this momentous subject—I could speak from experience, as I have too often felt its baneful effects, but as I intend, if the Lord spares me, to publish an essay on Intemperance, I leave it for the present. When my time was out, Mr. Hail paid me like a gentleman and also gave me three dollars and twenty-five cents, in lieu of the spirits—a sum sufficient to buy my poor dear children some clothes. The family were loath to part with me, as I had endeavored to live a godly life—I held a prayer meeting with them and departed with tears in my eyes.

I now bent my course for Hartford and engaged labor work at twenty dollars a month—then I went home and spent one week with my dear family and, according to my engagements, returned to Hartford, but my place was taken up, and I did not know what to do. While in this extremity, a thought struck me—I remembered that I had a sister living in Providence. Thither I went and soon found my sister, who was very kind to me. I had no difficulty in procuring work.[46] The Spirit of the Lord now fell afresh upon me, and I at once entered into the work without conferring with flesh and blood. I appointed meeting for exhortation and prayer—the Lord blessed my feeble efforts, and souls were converted and added to the church. I continued here

46. Apess's separation from his family and constant journeying in search of work characterized the necessities affecting not only most Native Americans in New England but many, if not most, propertyless Americans for much of the nineteenth century. He would have gone to Providence the first time sometime circa 1825/26, I think—given his reference to several children. The sister was probably Mary Ann (b. ca. 1805). She was married twice—first to a Peters and then to Anthony Tattoon.

five months and then, taking a letter of recommendation, returned to my family; and when I had concluded to remove to Providence, as the place of my future residence, the society gave me a certificate to the church in Providence—I there joined, and I was shortly appointed to the office of class leader, which office I filled for two years.[47] I now obtained a verbal permission to appoint meetings from Brother Webb, the preacher in charge. Brother Kent succeeded him. After this change I applied for a license to exhort—but I was opposed by two or three persons on account of not having lived long enough in the place. The rest of the class, about thirty in number, were anxious that I should have a license, and a division had like to have been the consequence of withholding it from me. In a month or two after, the affair was settled to mutual satisfaction, and it was agreed that I should have license to exhort. I went from place to place, improving my gift, and the Lord blessed my labors. I now felt it more strongly my duty, and an inward satisfaction in preaching the "word." Sometimes, however, the evil one would tempt me to give it up, but instantly my conscience would reprove me. Many a severe combat have I had with the enemy respecting my competency, and I come to the conclusion that if I could not give *"refined!"* instruction, and neglected to discharge my duty to God and my fellow men on that account, I could not enjoy his smiles. So I was determined in the strength of the Lord to go on in the way wherein I was called.

My mind was now exercised about entering the work as a missionary. I prayed to the Lord, if it was his will to open the way, as I was poor, and had a family to maintain, and did not wish to depend upon public charity. My desire was to do something at the same time that would enable me to keep my family. Now, a gentleman wished me to take out some religious books and sell them. I did so and went praying to God all the way to bless me—and so he did, and his blessing attended my labors wherever I went. I had also some success in selling my books and made enough to support my little family and defray my necessary traveling expenses. So I concluded to travel, and the Lord went with me. In one of these excursions, I went over on Long Island and from thence to New York, where my bodily strength was reduced by a fever. Here in the hour of sickness the Lord was with me—I experienced his comforting presence, the kindness of friends, and the quiet of a peaceful conscience. It was a sore trial for me to be absent, in such a situation, from my family, but it "was good to be afflicted"—and how beautiful was this passage of Scripture fulfilled which says, *Seek first the kingdom of heaven, and all things else shall be added.* How beautiful and numerous are his promises, and how strikingly fulfilled. I

47. The Methodists organized themselves locally into societies, which were in turn divided into smaller groups, "classes," for purposes of prayer and exhortation.

have seen all these promises verified. Blessings unnumbered and undeserved showered upon me.

From New York I went to Albany, stopping at the different villages and exhorting the people to repentance, and the Lord seconded my efforts. I was very sick for about one month, and my friends thought I would not recover; but although I was very much reduced, I did not think my sands had yet run their course—I believed that God would spare me to preach his Gospel; and according to my faith it was, for I speedily recovered and commenced again my labor of love. On Arbor Hill the Lord poured out his spirit in a powerful manner. Here a class of about thirty members was organized, and at a number of places where I labored several were added, but how many in the whole I cannot say precisely; let it suffice that through my instrumentality some souls were brought from a state of sin and darkness to the light and favor of God— to whom be all the glory ascribed.

After having been absent six months I returned home and found my dear family and friends in the enjoyment of their usual health. After remaining about a fortnight, I went to Boston. Here the Lord blessed my labors among the friends of the cross. While in Boston I met with a professed infidel, who wished to draw me into an argument by hooting at me for believing in Jesus Christ, the Savior of fallen men. I spoke to him about being a *good gentleman,* and he replied that I, in common with my brethren, believed that no man was a gentleman unless he was under the influence of priestcraft; and I told him that I considered every man a gentleman who acted in a becoming manner. He then asked by what authority I believed in Jesus Christ as my Savior; I answered, by an internal witness in my soul, and the enjoyment of *that* peace emanating from this Savior, which the "world can neither give nor take away." This stirred his passions, and he said, "I suppose you think I am an atheist," to which I replied in the negative and assured him that he was an infidel.[48] I then spoke to him of Jesus Christ and his Apostles; and he replied that they were all fools together and I was as great a one as any. He turned pale and looked as if he would have swallowed me up alive—and I gave him an exhortation and went on my way. After spending about two months in Boston, I returned home; then I visited New Bedford, Martha's Vineyard, and Nantucket, preaching the word wherever a door was opened—and the Lord was not unmindful of me, his presence accompanied me, and I believe that much good was done. Again I visited my family and then went to Salem, and I found many precious souls. We held several meetings, and the Lord came forth in the galleries of grace, and my labor of love proved very profit-

48. The distinction is a fine one. An atheist is anyone who denies the existence of God, or gods. An infidel is someone who specifically rejects Christianity and is actively hostile to it.

able to the dear people, and when I left them the parting scene was very affecting. I now visited the different towns, preaching as I went along, until I reached Newburyport, and having taken letters of recommendation from the various preachers, I was kindly received; and reporting myself to Brother Bartholomew Otheman, the preacher in charge, he provided lodgings for me. It so happened that Brother John Foster, his colleague, was sick, and they needed some help, and I thought the brethren were glad that I had come among them. At night I preached for Brother Otheman, and the next evening in the church where Brother Foster officiated, and an appointment was given out for me to preach in the course of the next Sunday at the same church, but having an intercourse in the meantime with Brother Foster, and finding him highly tinctured with Calvinism, I thought I would converse freely with him on the subject.[49] This course soured his mind against me, and he gave out my future appointments in such a way that I thought best to preach the word in the dwelling houses of the inhabitants; and I had as many hearers as I could have wished, and I bless the Lord that much good was done in his name. I made several attempts toward a reconciliation; he could hear no proposals, I could make no concessions, as I had not injured or given him any cause of offense; and he went on to persecute me, notwithstanding the remonstrances of his brethren. My motives were pure, and I bless the Lord that a day will come when the secrets of all hearts shall be revealed. I forgive the poor man for all the injury he attempted to do me, and I hope the righteous judge of all men will also forgive him.

From Newburyport I went to Portland, Maine, where I had some gracious times and labored with success, and then returned to my abiding place at Providence, R.I., with a recommendation. I reported myself to the preacher in charge and asked for a certificate; he said that my recommendation was "genuine," but he had heard evil reports respecting me and preferred inquiring into the matter before he granted my request. I felt glad that the brother had promised to make inquiry, as I knew that I should come out well. As this would take some time I crossed over to Long Island, preached at Sag Harbor and other places with success, and then went to New York, where I remained but a short time and then proceeded to Albany. Here I was known and was received in a friendly way and continued to preach wherever an opportunity offered; while here, a certificate of my membership was received from the church in Providence, and on the force of it I entered the church. I now applied for license to preach and was recommended to the quarterly

---

49. Brother Foster, this is to say, doubted the ability of people to come to Christ by their own efforts and will.

Conference as a suitable candidate, but the Conference thought differently; ✓ so after improving my gift three months I made another application.[50]

I had been advised by the preachers to improve on Watervliet circuit in order that they might have an opportunity to form an estimate of my talents and usefulness, and this was right. I accordingly went forward with fear and trembling, but the Lord enabled me to take up the cross and stood by me at this time. Several, I trust, through my instrumentality, passed from death unto life. I held meetings in Albany, and crowds flocked out, some to *hear* the truth and others to *see* the "Indian." The worth of souls lay near my heart, and the Lord was pleased to own the labors of his feeble servant. From Albany I went to Bath, where the power of the Almighty was felt in a wonderful manner; it appeared as though all the inhabitants were engaged in seeking the salvation of their souls—many wept bitterly and cried aloud for mercy, and seven or eight in the judgment of charity *passed from death unto life.* I then went on to my appointment at Watervliet, and here the Lord was present to awaken sinners and reclaim backsliders.

At Troy I found a number of good Christian friends, with whom I had several very good meetings, and the power of the Lord was made manifest. One evening as I was preaching to some colored people, in a schoolhouse, the power of the Lord moved on the congregation, both white and colored—hard hearts began to melt and inquire what they must do to be saved. We had a very *refreshing season from the presence of the Lord.*

I now went into all surrounding villages preaching the word of eternal life and exhorting sinners to repentance. Before the quarterly meeting, I took a tour to the west, as far as Utica, holding meetings by the way, and I found God as precious as ever; and being absent three weeks, I returned in order to attend the Conference, which was to be held on the 11th of April.[51]

I can truly say that the spirit of prejudice is no longer an inmate of my bosom; the sun of consolation has warmed my heart, and by the grace of God assisting me, I am determined to sound the trump of the Gospel—to call upon men to turn and live. Look, brethren, at the natives of the forest—they come, notwithstanding you call them "*savage,*" from the "east and from the west, the north and the south," and will occupy seats in the kingdom of heaven before you. Let us one and all "contend" valiantly "for that faith once

50. At this point Apess cut out nearly eight pages from the first edition. These narrate his conflict with the Conference of the Methodist Episcopal church over the right to preach and his conviction that he was being denied ordination because he was an Indian. He leaves the Methodist Episcopals and joins the newly forming antiepiscopal Protestant Methodist church, which ordains him in 1829/30. These passages are printed in their entirety in the Textual Afterword.

51. 1829.

delivered to the saints"; and if we are contented, and love God with all our hearts, and desire the enjoyment of his peaceful presence, we shall be able to say with the poet,

> Let others stretch their arms like seas,
> And grasp in all the shore;
> Grant me the visits of his grace,
> And I desire no more.[52]

Now, my dear reader, I have endeavored to give you a short but correct statement of the leading features of my life. When I think of what I am, and how wonderfully the Lord has led me, I am dumb before him. When I contrast my situation with that of the rest of my family, and many of my tribe, I am led to adore the goodness of God. When I reflect upon my many misdeeds and wanderings, and the dangers to which I was consequently exposed, I am lost in astonishment at the long forbearance and the unmerited mercy of God. I stand before you as a monument of his unfailing goodness. May that same mercy which has upheld me still be my portion—and may author and reader be preserved until the perfect day and dwell forever in the paradise of God.

William Apess

52. Another Isaac Watts hymn, "God, My Only Happiness."

Appendix

INTRODUCTION

Believing that some general observations on the origin and character of the Indians, as a nation, would be acceptable to the numerous and highly respectable persons who have lent their patronage to his work, the subscriber has somewhat abridged "his life" to make room for this Appendix. In the following pages the reader will find some "general observations" touching his brethren. He is conscious that they are thrown together without that order that an accomplished scholar would observe—and he takes this means of saying that he is indebted in a great measure to the works of the venerated Boudinot, late president of the American Bible Society, Brainerd, Colden, and several other gentlemen, as well as to the newspaper press and missionary journals, for many of the interesting facts, etc., which will be found in this department of his work.[1]

Wm. Apess

1. Apess's indebtedness to Elias Boudinot's *Star in the West* (1816) is almost entire. Unless otherwise noted, everything Apess puts within quotation marks he has taken from Boudinot, though with

Ever since the discovery of America by that celebrated navigator, Columbus, the "civilized" or enlightened natives of the Old World regarded its inhabitants as an extensive race of "savages!" Of course, they were treated as barbarians, and for nearly two centuries they suffered without intermission, as the Europeans acted on the principle that *might* makes *right*—and if they could succeed in defrauding the natives out of their lands and drive them from the seaboard, they were satisfied for a time. With this end in view, they sought to "engage them in war, destroy them by thousands with ardent spirits, and fatal disorders unknown to them before." Every European vice that had a tendency to debase and ruin both body and soul was introduced among them. Their avowed object was to obtain possession of the goodly inheritance of the Indian, and in their "enlightened" estimation, the "end justified the means." When I reflect upon the complicated ills to which my brethren have been subject, ever since history has recorded their existence—their wanderings, their perils, their privations, and their many sorrows, and the fierceness of that persecution which marked their dwellings and their persons for destruction—when I take into consideration the many ancient usages and customs observed religiously by them, and which have so near and close resemblance to the manners, etc., of the ancient Israelites, I am led to believe that they are √ none other than the descendants of Jacob and the long lost tribes of Israel. In view of this subject, the late Mr. Boudinot says that there is a possibility that these unhappy children of misfortune may yet be proved to be the descendants of Jacob; and if so that, though cast off for their heinous transgressions, they have not been altogether forsaken and will hereafter appear to have been, in all their dispersions and wanderings, the subjects of God's divine protection and gracious care.

The writer above referred to is of the opinion that if the natives had been favored with early instruction, and their cause had been faithfully and fully represented to posterity, "their character would have been considered in a very different point of light from what it now is." It is often said of the *"savages"* that their mode of carrying on war, and the method of treating their prisoners, is cruel and barbarous in the extreme—but did not the whites set them the brutal example? When they first visited these shores, they found the wilderness, as they called it, teeming with a healthy and happy population; here they found, after the first natural impulses of fear had subsided, fast and

---

much rearrangement. At several points he also simply paraphrases. The Brainerd is David Brainerd, Calvinist missionary to the Indians in the eighteenth century. His complete journals, edited by Jonathan Edwards, were published as *An Account of the Life of the Late Reverend Mr. David Brainerd*. See also Cadwallader Colden, *The History of the Five Indian Nations*, another well-known eighteenth-century account.

firm friends in the sons of the forest. And what return did they receive for all their friendship?[2]

The following extracts from the bishop of Chiapas, de Las Casas, who came over from Spain for the purpose of teaching the natives, is directly in point:

"I was one of the first who went to America. Neither curiosity nor interest prompted me to undertake so long and dangerous a voyage. The saving the souls of the heathen was my sole object. Why was I not permitted, even at the expense of my blood, to ransom so many thousands of souls, who fell unhappy victims to avarice and lust? It was said that barbarous executions were necessary to punish or check the rebellion of the Americans. But to whom was this owing? Did not this people receive the Spaniards who first came among them with gentleness and humanity? Did they not show more joy in proportion, in lavishing treasure upon them, than the Spaniards did greediness in receiving it? But our avarice was not yet satisfied. Though they gave up to us their lands and their riches, we would take from them their wives, their children, and their liberty. To blacken the characters of these unhappy people, their enemies assert that they are scarce human creatures. But it is *we* who ought to blush for having been less men, and more barbarous than they. They are represented as a stupid people, and addicted to vice. But have they not contracted most of their vices from the example of Christians? But it must be granted that the Indians still remain untainted with many vices usual among Europeans. Such as ambition, blasphemy, swearing, treachery, and many such monsters, which have not yet taken place among them. They have scarce an idea of them. All nations are equally free. One nation has no right to infringe on the freedom of another. Let us do to these people, as we would have them have done to us, on a change of circumstances. What a strange method is this of propagating the gospel; that holy law of grace, which, from being slaves to Satan, initiates us into the freedom of the children of God."

The abbé Clavijero, another Spanish writer, confirms this idea of the South Americans. "We have had intimate converse," says he, "with the Americans; have lived some years in a seminary destined for their instruction—attentively observed their character—their genius—their disposition and manner of thinking; and have, besides, examined with the utmost diligence their ancient history—their religion—their government—their laws and their customs. After such long experience and study of them, we declare that the mental qualities of the Americans are not in the least inferior to those of the Europeans."

2. These introductory passages seem to be Apess's own writing. The extracts from Boudinot begin with the next paragraph.

Who were the first aggressors, and who first imbrued their hands in blood? Not the Indian. No: He treated the stranger as a brother and a friend, until that stranger, whom he had received upon his fertile soil, endeavored to enslave him and resorted to brutal violence to accomplish his designs. And if they committed excesses, they only followed in the footsteps of the whites, who must blame themselves for provoking their independent and unyielding spirits, and by a long series of cruelty and bloodshed drove them to arms. This was the case in the colony of Virginia, where the natives rose upon the whites, who in their turn "waged a destructive war against the Indians, and murdered men, women, and children."[3]

Dr. Robertson, in his *History of America,* says that the English, like the Spaniards, regardless of those principles of faith, honor, and humanity, which regulate hostilities among civilized nations and set bounds to their rage, seemed to regard everything allowable that tended to accomplish their designs. They hunted the Indians like wild beasts, rather than enemies; and as the pursuit of them to their places of retreat in the woods was both difficult and dangerous, they endeavored to allure them from their inaccessible fastnesses, by offers of peace and promises of oblivion, made with such an artful appearance of sincerity as deceived the crafty Indian chief, and induced the Indians to return in the year 1623 to their former settlements and resume their usual peaceful occupations. The behavior of the two people seemed now to be perfectly reversed. The Indians, like men acquainted with the principles of integrity and good faith, on which the intercourse between nations is founded, confided in the reconciliation, and lived in absolute security, without suspicion of danger; while the English, with perfidious craft, were preparing to imitate savages in their revenge and cruelty.

"On the approach of harvest, when a hostile attack would be most formidable and fatal, the English fell suddenly on all the Indian plantations, and murdered every person on whom they could lay hold, and drove the rest to the woods, where so many perished with hunger that some of the tribes nearest to the English were totally extirpated."

Robertson, again speaking of the war in New England, between Connecticut and Providence, in their first attempt against the Pequot Indians, says "that the Indians had secured their town, which was on a rising ground in a swamp, with palisades. The New England troops, unperceived, reached the palisades. The barking of a dog alarmed the Indians. In a moment, however, they started to their arms, and raising the war-cry, prepared to repel the assailants. The English forced their way through into the fort, or town, and setting fire to the huts, which were covered with reeds, the confusion and

3. This paragraph is Apess's. It echoes several passages in his other writing. See esp. *A Son.*

terror quickly became general. Many of the women and children perished in the flames, and the warriors, endeavoring to escape, were either slain by the English, or falling into the hands of the Indian allies, who surrounded the fort at a distance, were reserved for a more cruel fate. The English resolved to pursue their victory, and hunting the Indians from one place of retreat to another, some subsequent encounters were hardly less fatal than the first action. In less than three months, the tribe of the Pequots was nearly extirpated.

"Thus the English stained their laurels by the use they made of victory. Instead of treating the Pequots as an independent people, who made a gallant effort to defend the property, the rights and freedom of their nation, they retaliated upon them all the barbarities of American war. Some they massacred in cold blood, others they gave up to be tortured by their Indian allies, a considerable number they sold as slaves in Bermuda, the rest were reduced to servitude among themselves."

Dr. Boudinot says that this tribe (the Pequots referred to above) "were a principal nation of the east, and very forcibly reminds one of the similarity of the same name in Jeremiah 50:21, where the inhabitants of Pekod are particularly mentioned; and also in Ezekiel 23:23. The difference in spelling one with a *k* and the other with a *q* is no uncommon thing; the Indian languages being very guttural, *k* is generally used where an Englishman would use the *q*.

"Columbus was as competent to form a proper estimate of the character of the natives as any other man. In his account to his patrons, he says:—'I swear to your majesties, that there is not a better people in the world than these; more affectionate, affable, or mild. They love their neighbors as themselves. Their language is the sweetest, softest, and most cheerful, for they always speak smiling.'"

That the whites were treated by the natives of New England with the utmost kindness there is no doubt. The Reverend Mr. Cushman, in a sermon preached at Plymouth in 1620, thus speaks of the treatment of the Indian to the whites: "The Indians are said to be the most cruel and treacherous people in all these parts, even like lions, *but to us* they have been like lambs, so kind, so submissive and trusty, as a man may truly say, many Christians are not so kind or sincere. Though when we came first into this country, we were few, and many of us very sick, and many died, by reason of the cold and wet, it being the depth of winter, and we having no houses or shelter, yet when there were not six able persons among us, and the Indians came daily to us by hundreds, with their sachems or kings, and might in one hour have made despatch of us; yet such fear was upon them, as that they never offered us the least injury in word or deed. And by reason of one *Tisquanto*, that lives among us, and can speak English, we have daily commerce with their kings, and can know what is done or intended toward us among the savages."

Governor Hutchinson bore unqualified testimony to the kindness and courtesy of the natives. The celebrated Wm. Penn represented them as being a "kind and benevolent people." Mr. Smith, in his history of New Jersey, says they manifested the greatest cordiality and friendship for the inhabitants.

The real character of the aborigines is thus noticed by Father Charlevoix, who had by extensive travel among the tribes scattered from Quebec to New Orleans a great opportunity of forming a proper estimate of Indian customs, manners, etc. In speaking of the real character of the nations, he says "that with a mien and appearance altogether savage; and with manners and customs which favor that greatest barbarity, they enjoy all the advantages of society. At first view one would imagine them without form of government, laws or subordination, and subject to the wildest caprice. Nevertheless, they rarely deviate from certain maxims and usages, founded on good sense alone, which holds the place of law, and supplies in short the want of legal authority. They manifest much stability in their engagements they have solemnly entered upon; patience and affliction, as well as submission to what they apprehend to be the appointment of Providence; in all this they manifest a nobleness of soul and constancy of mind, at which we rarely arrive with all our philosophy and religion. They are neither slaves to ambition nor interest, the two passions that have so much weakened in us the sentiments of humanity (which the kind author of nature has engraven on the human heart), and kindled those of covetousness which are yet generally unknown among them.

"The nearer view we take of our savages, the more we discover in them some valuable qualities. The chief part of the principles by which they regulate their conduct; the general maxims by which they govern themselves; and the bottom of their characters, have nothing which appear barbarous. The ideas, though now quite confused, which they have retained of a first Being; the traces, though almost effaced, of a religious worship, which they appear formerly to have rendered to the Supreme Deity, and the faint marks which we observe, even in their most indifferent actions, of the ancient belief, and the primitive religion, may bring them more easily than we think of into the way of truth, and make their conversion to Christianity more easily to be effected, than that of more civilized nations."

Mr. Boudinot, after speaking more particularly of the general character of the Indian nations—of their kindness to women and children who are taken prisoners, and of their great delicacy toward the former, of their haughty tempers, etc.—proceeds to give the following extract from Wynne's History of America; he says:

"But let us come nearer home. Who set them the example of barbarity, even to those whom they invaded and plundered of their property—deprived of their lands and rendered their whole country a scene of horror, confusion and distress? Wynne, in his history of America, tells us, 'that the New England people, in an early day, as we have already seen, made an attack upon the Pequot Indians, and drove eight hundred of them with about two hundred of their women and children, into a swamp—a fog arising, the men escaped, except a few, who were either killed or wounded. But the helpless women and children surrendered at discretion. The Sachem's wife, who some time before, had rescued the Weathersfield maidens, and returned them home, was among them. She made two requests, which arose from a tenderness and virtue not common among savages. 1st. That her chastity might remain unviolated. 2d. That her children might not be taken from her. The amiable sweetness of her countenance, and the modest dignity of her deportment, were worthy of the character she supported for innocence and justice, and were sufficient to show the Europeans, that even barbarous nations, sometimes produce instances of heroic virtue. It is not said by the historian, whether her requests were granted or not, but that the women and children were dispersed through the neighboring colonies, the male infants excepted, who were sent to the Bermudas,'—1 vol. 66. Indeed, had the Indians, on their part, been able to answer in writing, they might have formed a contrast between themselves and their mortal enemies, the civilized subjects of Great Britain. They might have recapitulated their conduct in the persecution of *Indians, witches,* and *Quakers* in New England.—*Indians* and *Negroes* in New York, and the cruelty with which the aborigines were treated in Virginia.

"These invaders of a country (in the peaceable possession of a free and happy people, entirely independent, as the deer of the forests) made war upon them with all the advantage of fire arms and the military knowledge of Europe, in the most barbarous manner—not observing any rules of nations, or the principles of modern warfare, much less the benign injunctions of the Gospel. They soon taught the Indians by their fatal examples, to retaliate with the most inveterate malice and diabolical cruelty. The civilized Europeans, though flying from the persecution of the old world, did not hesitate to deny their professed religion of peace and good will to men, by murdering, men, women and children—selling captives as slaves—cutting off the heads, and quartering the bodies of those who were killed, nobly fighting for their liberty and their country, in self-defense, and setting them up in various places, in ignoble triumph at their success. Philip, an independent sovereign of the Pequots, who disdained to submit, but died fighting at the head of his men, had his head cut off and carried on a pole with great rejoicings, to New Plymouth, where Wynne says, his skull is to be seen to this day.—Vide vol. 1, 106 to 108.

"This conduct produced greater violence and barbarity on the part of the other nations of Indians in the neighborhood, often joined by French Europeans who acted, at time, worse than the native Indians, and by this means, a total disregard of promises and pledged faith on both sides, became common.—Ibid. 124–6."

After reading the above, I presume that no person will doubt that great injustice has been done to the Indians, and I also think that no liberal mind will say that they are the *only* savages. It is a matter of sober fact that the natives, on their first acquaintance with the Europeans, manifested themselves generous, high-minded, kind, and hospitable, and these feelings marked all their intercourse with the whites, while they were treated with humanity; and it was not till after repeated aggressions on the part of the whites, not until they were overreached, and their friends and relatives carried into hopeless captivity, that they exhibited that deep and settled hatred to the whites, which may very properly be termed a hereditary animosity.[4]

The social kindness of the Indians has been referred to by many writers. Le Page Du Pratz says that they behaved toward each other with a kindness and regard not to be found among civilized nations. In his history of Louisiana, he says, "We are equally charmed with that natural and unaffected gravity, which reigns in all their behavior, in all their actions, and in the greatest part of their diversions. Also with the civility and deference they show to their equals, and the respect of young people to the aged. And lastly, never to see them quarrel among themselves, with those indecent expressions, oaths and curses, so common among us; all which are proofs of good sense and a great command of temper. ("I have studied with these Indians a considerable number of years, and I never could learn that there ever were any disputes or boxing matches among either the boys or men." 2nd vol. 156.) In short, to make a brief portrait of these people, with a savage appearance, manners, and customs, which are entirely barbarous there is observable among them a social kindness free from almost all imperfections which so often disturb the peace of society among us. They appear to be without passion; but they do that in cold blood, and sometimes through principle, which the most violent and unbridled passion produces in those who give no ear to reason. They seem to √ lead the most wretched life in the world; and yet they were, perhaps the only happy people on earth, before the knowledge of the objects which so work upon and seduce us, had excited in them, desires which ignorance kept in supineness; but which have not as yet (in 1730) made any great ravages among them. We discover in them a mixture of the fiercest and most gentle manners. The imperfections of wild beasts, and the virtues and qualities of the heart and mind which do the greatest honor to human nature."

4. This, and the following two paragraphs are from Boudinot, although they are in the first person and without quotation marks.

He further observes "that upon an acquaintance with the Indians, he was convinced that it was wrong to denominate them savages, as they are capable of making good use of their reason and their sentiments are just. That they have a degree of prudence, faithfulness, and generosity, exceeding that of nations who would be offended at being compared with them. No people, says he, are more hospitable and free than the Indians. Hence they may be esteemed a happy people, if that happiness was not impeded by their passionate fondness for spirituous liquors, and the foolish notion they hold in common with many professing Christians, of gaining reputation and esteem by their prowess in war. But to whom do they owe their uncommon attachment to both these evils? Is it not the white people who came to them with destruction in each hand, while we did but deceive ourselves with the vain notion, that we were bringing the glad tidings of salvation to them. Instead of this, we have possessed these unoffending people with so horrid an idea of our principles, that among themselves they call us the *accursed people;* and their great numbers, when first discovered, show that they had, comparatively, but few wars before we came among them."

The Indian character, I have observed before, has been greatly misrepresented. Justice has not and, I may add, justice cannot be fully done to them by the historian. My people have had no press to record their sufferings or to make known their grievances; on this account many a tale of blood and woe has never been known to the public. And during the wars between the natives and the whites, the latter could, through the medium of the newspaper press, circulate extensively every exaggerated account of "Indian cruelty," while the poor natives had no means of gaining the public ear. It therefore affords me much gratification to bear testimony of the philanthropy of some of the white men, and that his brethren had found compassion in the breasts of those who sought to do justice to the poor despised tribes of the wilderness; and I cannot refrain from presenting to my readers the following article, which originally appeared in the Analectic Magazine, during the time that the United States was engaged in a war with the Creek Indians.[5]

Traits of Indian Character

The rights of the savage have seldom been deeply appreciated by the white man—in peace he is the dupe of mercenary rapacity; in war he is regarded as a ferocious animal, whose death is a question of mere precaution and convenience. Man is cruelly wasteful of life when his own safety is endangered, and he is sheltered by impunity—and little mercy is

5. These may be Apess's own words.

to be expected from him who feels the sting of the reptile, and is conscious of the power to destroy.

It has been the lot of the unfortunate aborigines of this country, to be doubly wronged by the white man—first, driven from their native soil by the sword of the invader, and then darkly slandered by the pen of the historian. The former has treated them like beasts of the forest; the latter has written volumes to justify him in his outrages. The former found it easier to exterminate than to civilize; the latter to abuse than to discriminate. The hideous appellations of savage and pagan, were sufficient to sanction the deadly hostilities of both; and the poor wanderers of the forest were persecuted and dishonored, not because they were guilty, but because they were ignorant.

The same prejudices seem to exist, and are in common circulation, at the present day. We form our opinions of the Indian character from the miserable hordes that infest our frontiers. These, however, are degenerate beings, enfeebled by the vices of society, without being benefited by its arts of living. The independence of thought and action, that formed the main pillar of their character, has been completely prostrated, and the whole moral fabric lies in ruins. Their spirits are debased by conscious inferiority, and their native courage completely daunted by the superior knowledge and power of their enlightened neighbors. Society has advanced upon them like a many-headed monster, breathing every variety of misery. Before it, went forth pestilence, famine, and the sword; and in its train came the slow, but exterminating curse of trade. What the former did not sweep away, the latter has gradually blighted. It has increased their wants, without increasing the means of gratification. It has enervated their strength, multiplied their diseases, blasted the powers of their minds, and superinduced on their original barbarity the low vices of civilization. Poverty, repining, and hopeless poverty—a canker of the mind unknown to sylvan life—corrodes their very hearts.—They loiter like vagrants through the settlements, among spacious habitations replete with artificial comforts, which only render them sensible of the comparative wretchedness of their own condition. Luxury spreads its ample board before their eyes, but they are expelled from the banquet. The forest, which once furnished them with ample means of subsistence, has been leveled to the ground—waving fields of grain have sprung up in its place; but they have no participation in the harvest; plenty revels around them, but they are starving amidst its stores; the whole wilderness blossoms like a garden, but they feel like the reptiles that infest it.

How different was their case while yet the undisputed lord of the soil.

Their wants were few, and the means of gratifying them within their reach. They saw everyone around them sharing the same lot, enduring the same hardships, living in the same cabins, feeding on the same aliments, arrayed in the same rude garments. No roof then rose but what was open to the houseless stranger; no smoke curled among the trees, but he was welcome to sit down by its fire, and join the hunter in his repast. "For," says an old historian of New England, "their life is so void of care, and they are so loving also, that they make use of those things they enjoy as common goods, and are therein so compassionate that rather than one should starve through want, they would all starve: thus do they pass their time merrily, not regarding our pomp, but are better content with their own, which some men esteem so meanly of." Such were the Indians while in the pride and energy of primitive simplicity: they resemble those wild plants that thrive best in the shades of the forest, but which shrink from the hand of cultivation, and perish beneath the influence of the sun.

In the general mode of estimating the savage character, we may perceive a vast degree of vulgar prejudice, and passionate exaggeration, without any of the temperate discussion of true philosophy. No allowance is made for the difference of circumstances, and the operations of principles under which they have been educated. Virtue and vice, *though radically the same,* yet differ widely in their influence on human conduct, according to the habits and maxims of the society in which the individual is reared. No being acts more rigidly from rule than the Indian. His whole conduct is regulated according to some general maxims early *implanted in his mind.* The moral laws that govern him, to be sure, are but few, but then he conforms to them all. The white man abounds in laws of religion, morals, and manners; but how many does he violate?

A common cause of accusation against the Indians is, the faithlessness of their friendships, and their sudden provocations to hostility. But we do not make allowance for their peculiar modes of thinking and feeling, and the principles by which they are governed. Besides, the friendship of the whites toward the poor Indians was ever cold, distrustful, oppressive, and insulting. In the intercourse with our frontiers they are seldom treated with confidence, and are frequently subject to injury and encroachment. The solitary savage feels silently but acutely; his sensibilities are not diffused over so wide a surface as those of the white man, but they run in steadier and deeper channels. His pride, his affections, his superstitions, are all directed toward fewer objects, but the wounds inflicted on them are proportionably severe, and furnish motives of hostility which we cannot sufficiently appreciate. Where a community is also limited in number, and forms, as in an Indian tribe, one great patriarchal family, the injury of the individual, is the injury of the whole; and as their body politic, is small, the sentiment of vengeance is almost instantaneously diffused. One council fire is sufficient to decide the measure. Eloquence and superstition combine to inflame their minds. The orator awakens all their martial ardor, and they are wrought up to a kind of religious desperation by the visions of the prophet and the dreamer.

An instance of one of these sudden exasperations, arising from a motive peculiar to the Indian character, is extant in an old record of the early settlement of Massachusetts. The planters of Plymouth had defaced the monuments of the dead at Passonagessit, and had plundered the grave of the sachem's mother, of some skins with which it had been piously decorated. Everyone knows the hallowed reverence which the Indians entertain for the sepulchres of their kindred. Even now, tribes that have passed generations, exiled from the abode of their ancestors, when by chance they have been traveling, on some mission to our seat of government, have been known to turn aside from the highway for many miles distance, and guided by wonderful accurate tradition, have sought some tumulus, buried perhaps in the woods, where the bones of their tribe were anciently deposited; and there have passed some time in silent lamentation over the ashes of their forefathers. Influenced by this sublime and holy feeling, the sachem, whose mother's tomb had been violated, in the moment of indignation, gathered his men together, and addressed them in the following beautifully simple and pathetic harangue—an harangue which has remained unquoted for nearly two hundred years—a pure specimen of Indian eloquence, and an affecting monument of filial piety in a savage.

"When last the glorious light of all the sky was underneath this globe, and birds grew silent, I began to settle as my custom is, to take repose. Before mine eyes were fast closed, methought I saw a vision, at which my spirit was much troubled; and, trembling at that doleful sight, a spirit cried aloud—behold, my son whom I have cherished, see the breasts that gave thee suck, the hands that lapped thee warm and fed thee oft! canst thou forget to take revenge of those wild people, who have defaced my monument in a despiteful manner, disdaining our antiquities and honorable customs? See now, the sachem's grave lies like the common people, defaced by an ignoble race. Thy mother doth complain, and implores thy aid against this thievish people, who have newly intruded in our land. If this be suffered I shall not rest quiet in my everlasting habitation.—This said, the spirit vanished, and I, all in a sweat, not able scarce to speak, began to get some strength and recollect my spirits that were fled, and determined to demand your counsel, and solicit your assistance."

Another cause of violent outcry against the Indians, is their inhumanity to the vanquished. This originally arose partly from political and partly from superstitious motives. Where hostile tribes are scanty in numbers, the death of several warriors completely paralyzes their power; and many an instance occurs in Indian history, where a hostile tribe, that had long been formidable to its neighbor, has been broken up and driven away, by the capture of its principal fighting men. This is a strong temptation to the victor to be merciless, not so much as to gratify any cruelty of revenge, as to provide for future security. But they had other motives, originating in a superstitious idea, common to barbarous notions, and even prevalent among the Greeks and Romans—that the manes of their deceased friends slain in battle, were soothed by the blood of the captives. But those that are not thus sacrificed are adopted into their families, and treated with the confidence, and affection of relatives and friends; nay, so hospitable and tender is their entertainment, that they will often prefer to remain with their adopted brethren, rather than return to the home and the friends of their youth.

The inhumanity of the Indians towards their prisoners has been heightened since the intrusion of the whites. We have exasperated what was formerly a compliance with policy and superstition into a gratification of vengeance. They cannot but be sensible that we are the usurpers of their ancient dominion, the cause of their degradation, and the gradual destroyers of their race. They go forth to battle smarting with injuries and indignities which they have individually suffered from the injustice and the arrogance of white men, and they are driven to madness and despair, by the wide-spreading desolation and the overwhelming ruin of our warfare. We set them an example of violence, by burning their villages, and laying waste their slender means of subsistence; and then wonder that savages will not show moderation and magnanimity towards men, who have left them nothing but mere existence and wretchedness.

It is a common thing to exclaim against new forms of cruelty, while reconciled by custom, we wink at long-established atrocities. What right does the generosity of our conduct give us to rail exclusively at Indian warfare? With all the doctrines of Christianity, and the advantages of cultivated morals, to govern and direct us, what horrid crimes disgrace the victories of Christian armies. Towns laid in ashes; cities given up to the sword; enormities perpetrated, at which manhood blushes, and history drops the pen. Well may we exclaim at the outrages of the scalping knife; but where, in the records of Indian barbarity, can we point to a violated female?

We stigmatize the Indians also as cowardly and treacherous, because they use stratagem in warfare, in preference to open force; but in this they are fully authorized by their rude code of honor. They are early taught that stratagem is praiseworthy; the bravest warrior thinks it no disgrace to lurk in silence and take every advantage of his foe. He triumphs in the superior craft and sagacity by which he has been enabled to surprise and massacre an enemy. Indeed, man is naturally more prone to subtlety than open valor, owing to his physical weakness in comparison with other animals. They are endowed with natural weapons of defense; with horns, with tusks, with hoofs and talons; but man has to depend on his superior sagacity. In all his encounters, therefore, with these, his proper enemies, he has to resort to stratagem; and when he perversely turns his hostility against his fellow man, he continues the same subtle mode of warfare.

The natural principle of war is to do the most harm to our enemy, with the least harm to ourselves; and this of course is to be effected by cunning. That chivalric kind of courage which teaches us to despise the suggestions of prudence, and to rush in the face of certain danger, is the offspring of society, and produced by education. It is honorable, because in fact it is the triumph of lofty sentiment over an instinctive repugnance to pain, and over those selfish yearnings after personal ease and security which society has condemned as ignoble. It is an emotion kept up by pride, and the fear of shame; and thus the dread of real evils is overcome by the superior dread of an evil that exists but in the mind. This may be instanced in the case of a young British officer of great pride, but delicate nerves, who was going for the first time into battle. Being agitated by the novelty and awful peril of the scene, he was accosted by another officer, of a rough and boisterous character—"What, sir," cried he, "do you tremble?" "Yes sir," replied the other, "and if you were half as much afraid as I am, you would run away." This young officer signalized himself on many occasions by his gallantry, though had he been brought up in savage life, or even in a humbler and less responsible situation, it is more than probable he could never have ventured into open action.

Besides, we must consider how much the quality of open and desperate courage, is cherished and stimulated by society. It has been the theme of many a spirit-stirring song, and chivalric story. The minstrel has sung of it in the loftiest strain of his lyre—the poet has delighted to shed around it all the splendors of fiction—and even the historian has forgotten the sober gravity of narration, and burst forth into enthusiasm and rhapsody in its praise. Triumphs and gorgeous pageants have been its reward— monuments, where art has exhausted its skill, and opulence its treasures have been erected to perpetuate a nation's gratitude and admiration.

Thus artificially excited, courage has arisen to an extraordinary and factitious degree of heroism; and arrayed in all the glorious "pomp and circumstance" of war, this turbulent quality has ever been able to eclipse many of those quiet, but invaluable virtues, which silently ennoble the human character, and swell the tide of human happiness.

But if courage intrinsically consist in the defiance of hunger and pain, the life of the Indian is a continual exhibition of it. He lives in a perpetual state of hostility and risk.—Peril and adventure are congenial to his nature; or rather, seem necessary to existence. Surrounded by hostile tribes, he is always equipped for fight, with his weapons in his hands. He traverses vast wildernesses, exposed to the hazards of lonely sickness, or lurking enemies, or pining famine. Stormy lakes present no obstacle to his wanderings; in his light canoe of bark, he sports like a feather on their waves, and darts with the swiftness of an arrow down the roaring rapids of the river.—Trackless wastes of snow, rugged mountains, the glooms of swamps and morasses, where poisonous reptiles curl among the rank vegetation, are fearlessly encountered by this wanderer of the wilderness. He gains his food by the hardships and dangers of the chase; he wraps himself in the spoils of the bear, the panther, and the buffalo, and sleeps among the thunders of the cataract.

No hero of ancient or modern days can surpass the Indian in his lofty contempt of death, and the fortitude with which he sustains all the varied torments with which it is frequently inflicted. Indeed we here behold him rising superior to the white man, merely in consequence of his peculiar education. The latter rushes to glorious death at the cannon's mouth; the former coolly contemplates its approach, and triumphantly endures it, amid the torments of the knife and the protracted agonies of fire. He even takes a savage delight in taunting his persecutors, and provoking their ingenuity of torture; and as the devouring flames prey on his very vitals, and the flesh shrinks from the sinews, he raises his last song of triumph, breathing the defiance of an unconquered heart, and invoking the spirits of his fathers to witness that he dies without a groan.

Notwithstanding all the obloquy with which the early historians of the colonies have overshadowed the characters of the unfortunate natives, some bright gleams will occasionally break through, that throw a degree of melancholy luster on their memories. Facts are occasionally to be met with, in their rude annals, which, though recorded with all the coloring of prejudice and bigotry, yet speak for themselves; and will be dwelt on with applause and sympathy, when prejudice shall have passed away.

In one of the homely narratives of the Indian wars in New England, there is a touching account of the desolation carried into the tribe of the

Pequot Indians. Humanity shudders at the cold-blooded accounts given, of indiscriminate butchery on the part of the settlers. In one place we read of the surprisal of an Indian fort in the night, when the wigwams were wrapped in flames, and the miserable inhabitants were shot down and slain, in attempting to escape, "all being dispatched and ended in the course of an hour." After a series of similar transactions, "Our soldiers," as the historian piously observes, "being resolved by God's assistance to make a final destruction of them," the unhappy savages being hunted from their homes and fortresses, and pursued with fire and sword, a scanty but gallant band, the sad remnant of the Pequot warriors, with their wives and children, took refuge in a swamp.

Burning with indignation, and rendered sullen by despair—with hearts bursting with grief at the destruction of their tribe, and spirits galled and sore at the fancied ignominy of their defeat, they refused to ask their lives at the hands of an insulting foe, and preferred death to submission.

As the night drew on they were surrounded in their dismal retreat, in such manner as to render escape impracticable. Thus situated, their enemy "plied them with shot all the time, by which means many were killed and buried in the mire." In the darkness and fog that precedes the dawn of day, some few broke through the besiegers and escaped into the woods; "the rest were left to the conquerors, of which many were killed in the swamp, like sullen dogs who would rather, in their self-willedness and madness, sit still and be shot through, or cut to pieces," than implore for mercy. When the day broke upon this handful of forlorn, but dauntless spirits, the soldiers we are told, entered the swamp, "saw several heaps of them sitting close together, upon whom they discharged their pieces, laden with ten or twelve pistol bullets at a time; putting the muzzles of their pieces under the boughs, within a few yards of them; so as, besides those that were found dead, many more were killed and sunk into the mire, and never were minded more by friend or foe."

Can any one read this plain unvarnished tale, without admiring the √ stern resolution, the unbending pride, and loftiness of spirit, that seemed to nerve the hearts of these self-taught heroes, and raise them above the instinctive feelings of human nature? When the Gauls laid waste the city of Rome, they found the nobles clothed in their robes, and seated with stern tranquility in their curule chairs; in this manner they suffered death, without an attempt at supplication or resistance. Such conduct in them was applauded as noble and magnanimous; in the hapless Indian it was reviled as obstinate and sullen. How much are we the dupes of show and circumstance! How different is virtue arrayed in purple, and enthroned in state, from virtue destitute and naked, reduced to the last stage of wretchedness, and perishing obscurely in a wilderness.

Do these records of ancient excesses fill us with disgust and aversion? Let us take heed that we do not suffer ourselves to be hurried into the same iniquities. Posterity lifts up its hands with horror at past misdeeds; because the passions that urged to them, are not felt, and the arguments that persuaded to them are forgotten; but we are reconciled to the present perpetration of injustice by all the selfish motives with which interest chills the heart and silences the conscience. Even at the present advanced day, when we should suppose that enlightened philosophy had expanded our minds, and true religion had warmed our hearts into philanthropy—when we have been admonished by a sense of past transgressions, and instructed by the indignant censures of candid history—even now, we perceive a disposition breaking out to renew the persecutions of these hapless beings. Sober-thoughted men, far from the scenes of danger, in the security of cities and populous regions, can coolly talk of "exterminating measures," and discuss the *policy* of extirpating thousands. If such is the talk of the cities, what is the temper displayed on the borders? The sentence of desolation has gone forth—"the roar is up amidst the woods"; implacable wrath, goaded on by interest and prejudice, is ready to confound all rights, trample on all claims of justice and humanity, and to act over those scenes of sanguinary vengeance which have too often stained the pages of colonial history. These are not the idle suggestions of fancy; they are wrung forth by facts, which still haunt the public mind.

As yet our government has in some measure restrained the tide of vengeance, and inculcated lenity toward the hapless Indians. Such temper is worthy of an enlightened government—let it still be observed—let sharp rebuke and signal punishment be inflicted on those who abuse their delegated power, and disgrace their victories with massacre and conflagration. The enormities of the Indians form no excuse for the enormities of white men. It has pleased heaven to give them but limited powers of mind, and feeble lights to guide their judgments: it becomes us who are blessed with higher intellects to think for them, and set them an example of humanity. It is the nature of vengeance, if unrestrained, to be headlong in its actions, and to lay up, in a moment of passion, ample cause for an age's repentance. We may roll over these miserable beings with our chariot wheels, and crush them to the earth; but when passion has subsided, and it is too late to pity or to save—we shall look back with unavailing compunction at the mangled corpses of those whose cries were unheeded in the fury of our career.

In a little while, the remaining tribes will go the way that so many have gone before. The few hordes that still linger about the shores of Huron and Superior, and the tributary streams of the Mississippi, will share the fate of those tribes that once lorded it along the proud banks of the Hudson; of that gigantic race that are said to have existed on the borders of the Susquehanna, and of those various nations, that flourished about the Potomac and the Rappahannock, and that peopled the forests of the vast valley Shenandoah. They will vanish like a vapor from the face of the earth—their very history will be lost in forgetfulness—and "the places that now know them, will know them no more forever."

Or if perchance some dubious memorial of them should survive the lapse of time, it may be in the romantic dreams of the poet, to populate in imagination his glades and groves, like the fauns and satyrs, and sylvan deities of antiquity. But should he venture upon the dark story of their wrongs and wretchedness—should he tell how they were invaded, corrupted, despoiled—driven from their native abodes and the sepulchres of their fathers—hunted like wild beasts about the earth, and sent down in violence and butchery to the grave—posterity will either turn with horror and incredulity from the tale, or blush with indignation at the inhumanity of their forefathers.—"We are driven back," said an old warrior, "until we can retreat no further—our hatchets are broken—our bows are snapped—our fires are nearly extinguished—a little longer and the white men will cease to persecute us—for we will cease to exist!"

The warlike ability of the Indians has been very generally despised by European officers—and this opinion has cost many thousands of men their lives. The following brief account of their military conduct will not be uninteresting to the general reader, and it will show, from good authority, that the number of Indians engaged in every battle in which they proved victorious has always been exaggerated by their enemies—and European officers particularly, having often been beaten by a comparatively small number of untutored natives of the forests, have been led to give very false reports of the combats in which they have been engaged.[6]

"In Col. Boquet's last campaign of 1764, I saw (says Col. Smith) the official return made by the British officers, of the number of Indians that were in arms against us in that year, which amounted to thirty thousand. As I was then lieutenant in the British service, I told them I was of opinion, that there was not above one thousand in arms against us, as they were divided by Broadstreet's army, being then at Lake Erie. The British officers hooted at me, and said that they could not make England sensible of the difficulties they

---

6. This paragraph may be Apess's own.

labored under in fighting them; and it was expected that their troops could fight the undisciplined savages in America, five to one as they did the East Indians, and therefore my report would not answer their purpose, as they could not give an honorable account of the war but by augmenting their numbers.

"Smith's opinion was, that from Braddock's defeat, until the time of his writing, there never were more than three thousand Indians, at any time in arms against us, west of Fort Pitt, and frequently not more than half of that number."

Boudinot says that, "According to the Indians' own account, during the whole of Braddock's war, or from 1755 to 1758, they killed and took fifty of our people for one that they lost. In the war of 1763, they killed, comparatively, few of our people, and lost more of theirs, as the frontier inhabitants, especially the Virginians, had learned something of their method of war; yet even in this war, according to their account (which Smith believed to be true), they killed and took ten of our people for one they lost.

"The Indians, though few in number, put the government to immense expense of blood and treasure, in the war from 1756 to 1791. The following campaigns in the western country, will be a proof of this.

"General Braddock's in the year 1755—Col. Armstrong's against the Chataugau town, on the Allegheny, in 1757—General Forbes' in 1758—Gen. Stanwix's in 1759—Gen. Moncton's in 1760—Col. Boquet's in 1761—and again in 1763, when he fought the battle of Brushy Run, and lost above one hundred men; but by taking the advice and assistance of the Virginia volunteers, finally drove the Indians—Col. Armstrong's up the west branch of the Susquehanna in the same year—Gen. Broadstreet's up Lake Erie in 1764—Col. Boquet's at Muskingum at the same time—Lord Dunmore's in 1774, Gen. M'Intosh's in 1778, and again in 1780,—Col. Bowman's in 1779—Gen. Clark's in 1782—and against the Wabash Indians in 1776—Gen. Logan's against the Shawnee in the same year, and Col. Harmer's in 1790—Gen. Wilkinson's in 1791,—Gen. St. Clair's in 1791, and Gen. Wayne's in 1794, which in all are twenty-three campaigns, besides smaller expeditions, such as the French Creek expedition, Colonels Edward's, Loughrie's, etc. All these were exclusive of the numbers of men who were internally employed as scouting parties, in erecting forts, guarding stations, etc. etc.

"When we take the foregoing account into consideration, may we not reasonably conclude that the Indians are the best disciplined troops in the world, especially when we consider that the ammunition and arms that they are obliged to use are of the worst sort, without bayonets or cartouch boxes. No artificial means of carrying either baggage or provisions, while their enemies have every warlike implement, and other resources, to the utmost of their desire. Is not that the best discipline, that has the greatest tendency to annoy the enemy, and save their own men? It is apprehended that the Indian discipline is better calculated to answer their purpose in the woods of America than the British discipline in the plains of Flanders. British discipline in the woods is the way to have men slaughtered, with scarcely any chance to defend themselves.

"*Privates.*—The Indians sum up their art of war thus—'The business of the private warrior is to be under command, or punctually to obey orders—to learn to march a-breast in scattered order, so as to be in readiness to surround the enemy, or to prevent being surrounded—to be a good marksman, and active in the use of their musket or rifle—to practice running—to learn to endure hunger or hardships with patience and fortitude—to tell the truth at all times to their officers, more especially when sent out to spy the enemy.'

"*Concerning Officers.*—They say that 'it would be absurd to appoint a man to an office, whose skill and courage had never been tried—that all officers should be advanced only according to merit—that no single man should have the absolute command of an army—that the counsel of officers should determine when and how an attack is made—that it is the duty of officers to lay plans, and take every advantage of the enemy—to ambush and surprise them, and to prevent the like to themselves. It is the duty of officers to prepare and deliver speeches to the men in order to animate and encourage them, and on a march to prevent the men, at any time, getting into a huddle, because if the enemy should surround them in that position, they would be greatly exposed to the enemy's fire. It is likewise their business, at all times, to endeavor to annoy the enemy, and save their own men; and therefore ought never to bring on an attack without considerable advantage, or without what appeared to them to insure victory, and that with a loss of but few men. And if at any time they should be mistaken in this, and are likely to lose many men in gaining the victory, it is their duty to retreat, and wait for a better opportunity of defeating their enemy, without the danger of losing so many men.' Their conduct proves that they act on these principles.

"This is the statement given by those who are experimentally acquainted with them, and as long as the British officers despised both Indians and Americans who studied their art of war, and formed themselves on the same plan, they were constantly beaten by those soldiers of nature, though seldom one fourth of the number of the British. But the British officers had one advantage of them. This was the art of drawing up and reporting to their superiors plans of their battles, and exaggerated accounts of their great success, and the immense loss of the Indians, which were never thought of till long after the battle was over, and often while they were smarting under their severe defeat or surprise.

"When the Indians determine on war or hunting, they have stated preparatory, religious ceremonies, for purification, particularly by fasting, as the Israelites had.

"Father Charlevoix gives an account of this custom in his time. In case of an intention of going to war, he who is to command does not commence the raising of soldiers, till he has fasted several days, during which he is smeared with black—has no conversation with anyone—invokes by day and night, his *tutelar spirit*, and above all, is very careful to observe his dreams. The fast being over, he assembles his friends, and with a string of wampum in his hands, he speaks to them after this manner. 'Brethren! the Great Spirit authorizes my sentiments, and inspires me with what I ought to do. The blood of——is not wiped away—his body is not covered, and I will acquit myself of this duty towards him,' etc."

Mr. M'Kenzie in some measure confirms this account, though among different nations. "If the tribes feel themselves called upon to go to war the elders convene the people in order to obtain the general opinion. If it be for war, the chief publishes his intention to smoke in the sacred stem (a pipe) at a certain time. To this solemnity, meditation and fasting are required as preparatory ceremonials. When the people are thus assembled, and the meeting sanctified by the custom of smoking (this may be in imitation of the smoke of the incense offered on the altar of the Jews), the chief enlarges on the causes which have called them together, and the necessity of the measures proposed on the occasion. He then invites them who are willing to follow him, to smoke out of the sacred stem, which is considered as a token of enrollment." A sacred feast then takes place, and after much ceremony, usual on such occasions, "the chief, turning to the east, makes a speech to explain more fully the design of their meeting, then concludes with an acknowledgement for past mercies received, and a prayer for the continuance of them, from the master of life. He then sits down, and the whole company declare their approbation and thanks by uttering the word *Ho!*" (in a very hoarse, guttural sound, being the third syllable of the beloved name), "with an emphatic promulgation of the last letter. The chief then takes up the pipe, and holds it to the mouth of the officiating person" (like a priest of the Jews, with the incense), "who after smoking three whiffs, utters a short prayer, and then goes round with it from east to west, to every person present." The ceremony then being ended, "he returns the company thanks for their attendance, and wishes them, as well as the whole tribe, health and long life."

Do not these practices remind the reader of the many directions in the Jewish ritual, commanding the strict purification or sanctifying of individuals about to undertake great business or enter on important offices?

"The Indians, by oppression, diseases, wars, and ardent spirits, have greatly diminished in numbers, degenerated in their moral character, and lost their high standing as warriors, especially those contiguous to our settlements.

"The very ancient men who have witnessed the former glory and prosperity of their country, or who have heard from the mouths of their ancestors, and particularly from their beloved men (whose office it is to repeat their traditions and laws to the rising generations, with the heroic achievements of their forefathers), the former state of their country with the great prowess and success of their warriors of old times, they weep like infants when they speak of the fallen condition of their nations. They derive however some consolation from a prophecy of ancient origin and universal currency among them, that the men of America will, at some future period, regain their ancient ascendancy and expel the man of Europe from this western hemisphere. This flattering and consolatory persuasion has enabled the Seneca and Shawnee prophets to arrest, in some tribes, the use of intoxicating liquors, and has given birth, at different periods, to attempts for a general confederacy of the Indians of North America" (Clinton).

The compiler of *A Star in the West* was present at a dinner given by General Knox to a number of Indians, in the year 1789, at New York; they had come to the president on a mission from their nations.[7] The house was in Broadway. A little before dinner, two or three of the sachems, with their chief or principal man, went into the balcony at the front of the house, the drawing room being upstairs. From this they had a view of the city, the harbor, Long Island, etc. After remaining there a short time, they returned into the room, apparently dejected; but the chief more than the rest. General Knox took notice of it and said to him, "Brother! what has happened to you? You look sorry! Is there anything to distress you?" He answered: "I'll tell you, brother. I have been looking at your beautiful city—the great water—your fine country—and see how happy you all are. But then, I could not help thinking that this fine country and this great water was once ours. Our ancestors lived here—they enjoyed it as their own in peace—it was the gift of the Great Spirit to them and their children. At last the white people came here in a great canoe. They asked only to let them tie it to a tree, lest the waters should carry it away—we consented. They then said some of their people were sick, and they asked permission to land them and put them under the shade of the trees. The ice then came, and they could not go away. They then begged a piece of land to build wigwams for the winter—we granted it to them. They then asked for some corn to keep them from starving—we kindly furnished it to them, they promising to go away when the ice was gone. When this happened, we told them they must now go away with their big canoe; but they pointed to

7. The compiler of *A Star in the West* is, of course, Elias Boudinot.

their big guns round their wigwams, and said they would stay there, and we could not make them go away. Afterwards, more come. They brought spirituous and intoxicating liquors with them, of which the Indians became very fond. They persuaded us to sell them some land. Finally they drove us back, from time to time, into the wilderness, far from the water, and the fish, and the oysters—they have destroyed the game—our people have wasted away; and now we live miserable and wretched, while you are enjoying our fine and beautiful country. This makes me sorry, brother! And I cannot help it!"

From the great similarity of the manners and customs of the Indian natives and those recorded of the Jews, many learned men have come to the conclusion that the Indian tribes are none other than the descendants of the Ten Lost Tribes of Judah. If not, in what manner can we account for this similarity? Their religious emblems are nearly of the same import—their rites and ceremonies in many respects do not differ essentially—there is an evident approach in many instances between the two languages, and withal there is a *personal* resemblance. (There are but two mother tongues, it is said, among the northern Indians, including those tribes that inhabit the Mississippi, the Huron and Algonquian. There is not more difference between these than between the Norman and French.)[8]

The late Wm. Penn, who was acquainted with the natives before they became corrupted by the whites, was exceedingly struck with their appearance, and in one of his letters to a friend in England, he says, "I found them with like countenance with the Jewish race; and their children of so lively a resemblance to them, that a man would think himself in Duke's-place or Berry-street, in London, when he seeth them" (Penn's Works, 2d vol. 80p. year 1682). "They wore earrings and nose jewels; bracelets on their arms and legs; rings on their fingers, necklaces made of highly polished shells found in their rivers and on their coasts. Their females tied up their hair behind, worked bands round their heads, and ornamented them with shells and feathers, and are fond of strings of beads round several parts of their bodies. They use shells and turkey spurs round the tops of their moccasins, to tinkle like little bells, as they walk." Isaiah proves this to have been the custom of the Jewish women, or something much like it. "In that day, says the prophet, the Lord will take away the bravery of their tinkling ornaments about their feet, and their cauls, and their round tires like the moon. The chains and the bracelets and the mufflers. The bonnets and the ornaments of the legs, and the headbands, and the tablets, and the earrings; the rings and the nose jewels" (Isa. 3:18). They religiously observed certain feasts, and feasts very similar to those enjoined on the Hebrews, by Moses, as will hereinafter more

8. This paragraph does not seem to be from *A Star in the West*.

particularly be shown. In short, many, and indeed, it may be said, most of the learned men, who did pay any particular attention to these natives of the wilderness at their first coming among them, both English and Spaniards, were struck with their general likeness to the Jews. The Indians in New Jersey, about 1681, are described as persons straight in their limbs, beyond the usual proportion in most nations; very seldom crooked or deformed; their features regular; their countenances somewhat fierce, in common rather resembling a Jew than a Christian (Smith's History of New Jersey).

In general, the Indian languages are very "copious and expressive," considering the narrow sphere in which they move. In comparison with civilized nations, their ideas are few. In their language, we find neither cases nor declensions, a few or no prepositions. This has been remarked more particularly, as there is no language known in Europe, except the Hebrew, without prepositions. The public speeches of the Indians are short but bold, nervous, and abounding with metaphor. For instance, the speech made by Logan, a famous Indian chief, about the year 1775, was never exceeded by Demosthenes or Cicero. In revenge for a murder committed by some un- known Indians, a party of our people fired on a canoe loaded with women and children, and one man, all of whom happened to belong to the family of *Logan,* who had been long the staunch friend of the Americans, and then at perfect peace with them. A war immediately ensued, and after much blood- shed on both sides, the Indians were beat and sued for peace. A treaty was held, but Logan disdainfully refused to be reckoned among the suppliants; but to prevent any disadvantage from his absence, to his nation, he sent the following talk, to be delivered to Lord Dunmore at the treaty: "I appeal to any white man to say, if he ever entered Logan's cabin hungry, and he gave him no meat—if ever he came cold and naked, and Logan clothed him not. During the course of the last long and bloody war, Logan remained idle in his cabin, an advocate for peace. Such was his love for the white men, that my countrymen pointed as they passed and said, *Logan is the friend of white men.* I had thought to have lived with you, but for the injuries of one man. Colonel———the last spring, in cold blood, and unprovoked, murdered all the relations of Logan, not sparing even my women and children. There runs not a drop of his blood in the veins of any living creature. This calls on me for revenge. I have sought it. I have killed many. I have fully glutted my ven- geance. For my country, I rejoice at the beams of peace. But do not harbor a thought that mine is the joy of fear. Logan never felt fear. He will not turn on his heel to save his life. Who is there to mourn for Logan? No, not one."

"Great allowance must be made for translations into another language, especially by illiterate and ignorant interpreters. This destroys the force as well as beauty of the original.

"A writer (Adair) who has had the best opportunities to know the true idiom of their language, by a residence among them for forty years, has taken great pains to show the similarity of the Hebrew with the Indian languages, both in their roots and general construction; and insists that many of the Indian words, to this day, are purely Hebrew, notwithstanding their exposure to the loss of it to such a degree as to make the preservation of it so far, little less than miraculous."

Mr. Boudinot in his able work states, "as a matter of curiosity, that the Mohawks, in confederacy with the Five Nations, as subsisting at the first arrival of the Europeans in America, were considered as the lawgivers, or the interpreters of duty to the other tribes. Nay, this was so great, that all paid obedience to their advice. They considered themselves as supreme, or first among the rest. Mr. Colden says, that he had been told by old men in New England, that when their Indians were at war, formerly with the Mohawks, as soon as one appeared, their Indians raised a cry from hill to hill, a Mohawk! a Mohawk! upon which all fled like sheep before a wolf, without attempting to make the least resistance. And that all the nations around them have, for many years, entirely submitted to their advice, and pay them a yearly tribute of wampum. The tributary nations dare not make war or peace, without the consent of the Mohawks. Mr. Colden has given a speech of the Mohawks, in answer to one from the Governor of Virginia, complaining of the confederate nations, which shows the Mohawks' superiority over them, and the mode in which they corrected their misdoings. Now it seems very remarkable that the Hebrew word Mhhokek, spelled so much like the Indian word, means a lawgiver (or leges interpres) or a superior.

"Blind chance could not have directed so great a number of remote and warring savage nations to fix on, and unite in so nice a religious standard of speech, and even grammatical construction of language, where there was no knowledge of letters or syntax. For instance, A, oo, EA, is a strong religious Indian emblem, signifying, I *climb, ascend* or *remove* to another place of residence. It points to A-no-wah, the first person singular, and O E A, or Yah, He, Wah, and implies putting themselves under the divine patronage. The beginning of that most sacred symbol is, by studious skill and thorough knowledge of the power of letters, placed twice, to prevent them from being applied to the sacred name, for vain purposes, or created things.

"Though they lost the true meaning of their religious emblems, except what a very few of the more intelligent traders revive in their retentive memories of the old inquisitive magi, or beloved man; yet tradition directs them to apply them properly. They use many plain religious emblems of the divine name, as Y, O, he wah—Yah and Ale, and these are the roots of the prodigious number of words, through their various dialects. It is worthy of remembrance, that two Indians, who belong to far distant nations, without the knowledge of each other's language, except from the general idiom, will intelligibly converse together, and contract engagements without any interpreter, in such a surprising manner, as is scarcely credible. In like manner we read of Abraham, Isaac, and Jacob, travelling from country to country, from Chaldea into Palestine, when inhabited by various differing nations—thence into Egypt and back again, making engagements, and treating with citizens wherever they went. But we never read of any difficulty of being understood, or their using an interpreter.

"The Indians generally express themselves with great vehemence and short pauses, in their set public speeches. Their periods are well turned, and very sonorous and harmonious. Their words are specially chosen, and well disposed, with great care and knowledge of their subject and language, to show the being, power, and agency of the Great Spirit in all that concerns them.

"To speak in general terms, their language in their roots, idiom, and particular construction, appears to have the whole genus of the Hebrew, and what is very remarkable, and well worthy of serious observation, has most of the peculiarities of that language, especially those in which it differs from most other languages; and 'often both in letters and signification, synonymous with the Hebrew language.' They call the lightning and thunder, Eloha, and its rumbling noise Rowah, which may not improperly be deduced from the Hebrew word *Ruach,* a name of the third person in the holy Trinity, originally signifying 'the air in motion or a rushing wind' (Faber).

"The Indian compounded words are generally pretty long, but those that are radical or simple, are mostly short; very few, if any of them, exceed three or four syllables. And as their dialects are guttural, every word contains some consonants, and these are the essential characteristics of language. Where they deviate from this rule, it is by religious emblems, which obviously proceeds from the great regard they pay to the names of the Deity, especially to the great four lettered divine, essential name, by using the letters it contains, and the vowels it was originally pronounced with, to convey a virtuous idea; or by doubling or transposing them, to signify the contrary. In this, all the Indian nations agree. And as this general custom must proceed from one primary cause, it seems to assure us, that the people was not in a savage state when they first separated, and varied their dialects with so much religious care and exact art."

Mr. Boudinot, speaking of the Indian traditions as received by their nations, says, not having the assistance afforded by the means of writing and reading, they are obliged to have recourse to tradition, as du Pratz, 2nd vol., 169, has justly observed, "to preserve the remembrance of remarkable transactions or historical facts; and this tradition cannot be preserved, but by frequent repetitions; consequently many of their young men are often employed in hearkening to the old beloved men, narrating the history of their ancestors, which is thus transmitted from generation to generation.

"In order to preserve them pure and incorrupt, they are careful not to deliver them indifferently to all their young people, but only to those young men of whom they have the best opinion. They hold it as a certain fact, as delivered down from their ancestors, that their forefathers, in very remote ages, came from a far distant country, by the way of the west, where all the people were of one color, and that in process of time they moved eastward to their present settlements."

This tradition is corroborated by a current report among them, related by the old Chickasaw Indians to our traders, that now about 100 years ago, there came from Mexico, some of the old Chickasaw nation, or as the Spaniards call them, Chichemicas, in quest of their brethren, as far north as the Aquahpah nation, above one hundred and thirty miles above the Natchez, on the southeast side of the Mississippi River; but through French policy, they were either killed or sent back, so as to prevent their opening a brotherly intercourse with them, as they had proposed. It is also said that the Nauatalcas believe that they dwelt in another region before they settled in Mexico, that their forefathers wandered eighty years in search of it, through a strict obedience to the commands of the great spirit, who ordered them to go in quest of new lands, that had such particular marks as were made known to them; and they punctually obeyed the divine mandate, and by that means found out and settled that fertile country of Mexico.

Our southern Indians have also a tradition among them which they firmly believe, that of old time, their ancestors lived beyond a great river. That nine parts of their nation, out of ten, passed over the river, but the remainder refused and stayed behind. That they had a king when they lived far to the west, who left two sons. That one of them, with a number of his people, traveled a great way for many years, till they came to Delaware River, and settled there. That some years ago, the king of the country from which they had emigrated sent a party in search of them. This was at the time the French were in possession of the country on the River Allegheny. That after seeking six years, they found an Indian who led them to the Delaware towns, where they stayed one year. That the French sent a white man with them on their return, to bring back an account of their country, but they have never been heard of since.

It is said among their principal, or beloved, men that they have it handed down from their ancestors, that the book which the white people have was once theirs. That while they had it they prospered exceedingly; but that the pale people bought it of them, and learnt many things from it; while the Indians lost their credit, offended the Great Spirit, and suffered exceedingly from the neighboring nations. That the Great Spirit took pity on them and directed them to this country. That on their way they came to a great river, which they could not pass, when God dried up the waters and they passed over dry-shod. They also say that their forefathers were possessed of an extraordinary divine spirit, by which they foretold future events and controlled the common course of nature, and this they transmitted to their offspring, on condition of their obeying the sacred laws. That they did by these means bring down showers of plenty on the beloved people. But that this power, for a long time past, had entirely ceased.

The reverend gentlemen mentioned before, who had taken so much pains in the year 1764 or 5 to travel far westward, to find Indians who had never seen a white man, informed the writer of these memoirs that, far to the northwest of the Ohio, he attended a party of Indians to a treaty, with Indians from the west of the Mississippi. Here he found the people he was in search of—he conversed with their beloved man who had never seen a white man before, by the assistance of three grades of interpreters. The Indian informed him "that one of their ancient traditions was, that a great while ago, they had a common father, who lived toward the rising of the sun, and governed the whole world. That all the white people's heads were under his feet. That he had twelve sons, by whom he administered his government. That his authority was derived from the Great Spirit, by virtue of some special gift from him. That the twelve sons behaved very bad and tyrannized over the people, abusing their power to a great degree, so as to offend the Great Spirit exceedingly. That he being thus angry with them, suffered the white people to introduce spirituous liquors among them, made them drunk, stole the special gift of the Great Spirit from them, and by this means usurped the power over them, and ever since the Indians' heads were under the white people's feet. But that they also had a tradition, that the time would come, when the Indians would regain the gift of the Great Spirit from the white people, and with it their ancient power, when the white people's heads would be again under the Indians' feet."

Mr. M'Kenzie in his *History of the Fur Trade,* and his journey through North America, by the lakes, to the South Sea, in the year——, says "that the Indians informed him, that they had a tradition among them, that they originally came from another country, inhabited by wicked people, and had traversed a great lake, which was narrow, shallow and full of islands, where they had suffered great hardships and much misery, it being always winter, with ice and deep snows—at a place they called the Coppermine River, where they made the first land, the ground was covered with copper, over which a body of earth had since been collected to the depth of a man's height. They believe also that in ancient times their ancestors had lived till their feet were worn out with walking, and their throats with eating. They described a deluge, when the waters spread over the whole earth, except the highest mountain, on the top of which they were preserved. They also believe in a future judgment" (M'Kenzie's history, page 113).

The Indians to the eastward say that, previous to the white people coming into the country, their ancestors were in the habit of using circumcision, but latterly, not being able to assign any reason for so strange a practice, their young people insisted on its being abolished.

M'Kenzie says the same of the Indians he saw on his route, even at this day (*History*, page 34). Speaking of the nations of the Slave and Dogrib Indians, very far to the northwest, he says, "whether circumcision be practiced among them, I cannot pretend to say, but the appearance of it was general among those I saw."

The Dogrib Indians live about two or three hundred miles from the straits of Kamchatka. Dr. Beatty says, in his journal of a visit he paid to the Indians on the Ohio, about fifty years ago, that an old Christian Indian informed him that an old uncle of his, who died about the year 1728, related to him several customs and traditions of former times; and among others, that circumcision was practiced among the Indians long ago, but their young men, making a mock of it, brought it into disrepute, and so it came to be disused (*Journal*, page 89). The same Indian said that one tradition they had was that once the waters had overflowed all the land and drowned all the people then living, except a few, who made a great canoe and were saved in it (page 90). And that a long time ago, the people went to build a high place. That while they were building of it, they lost their language and could not understand one another, that while one, perhaps, called for a stick, another brought him a stone, etc. etc., and from that time the Indians began to speak different languages.

Father Charlevoix, the French historian, informs us that the Hurons and Iroquois, in that early day, had a tradition among them that the first woman came from heaven, and had twins, and that the elder killed the younger.

In an account published in the year 1644, by a Dutch minister of the Gospel, in New York, giving an account of the Mohawks, he says, "An old woman came to my house and told the family that her forefathers had told her that the Great Spirit once went out walking with his brother, and that a dispute arose between them, and the Great Spirit killed his brother." This is plainly a confusion of the story of Cain and Abel. It is most likely from the ignorance of the minister in the idiom of the Indian language, misconstruing

Cain being represented a great man for the Great Spirit. Many mistakes of this kind are frequently made.

Mr. Adair, who has written the history of the Indians, and who deserves great credit for his industry, and improving the very great and uncommon opportunities he enjoyed, tells us, that the southern Indians have a tradition, that when they left their own native land, they brought with them a sanctified rod, by order of an oracle, which they fixed every night in the ground; and were to remove from place to place on this continent, toward the rising sun, till it budded in one night's time. That they obeyed the sacred oracle, and the miracle at last took place, after they arrived on this side of the Mississippi, on the present land they possess. This was the sole cause of their settling there— of fighting so firmly for their reputed holy land and holy things—that they may be buried with their beloved forefathers.

This seems to be taken from Aaron's rod.

Colonel James Smith, in his *Journal of Events,* that happened while he was prisoner with the Caughnawaga Indians, from 1755 to 1759, says, "They have a tradition that in the beginning of this continent, the angels or heavenly inhabitants, as they call them, frequently visited the people, and talked with their forefathers, and gave directions how to pray, and how to appease the great being, when he was offended. They told them they were to offer sacrifice, burn tobacco, buffalo and deer's bones, etc. etc." (page 79).

The Ottawas say "that there are two great beings that rule and govern the universe, who are at war with each other; the one they call Maneto, and the other Matchemaneto. They say that Maneto is all kindness and love, and the other is an evil spirit that delights in doing mischief. Some say that they are equal in power; others say that Maneto is the first great cause, and therefore must be all powerful and supreme, and ought to be adored and worshipped: whereas Matchemaneto ought to be rejected and despised." "Some of the Wyandots and Caughnawagas profess to be Roman Catholics; but even these retain many of the notions of their ancestors. Those who reject the Roman Catholic religion, hold that there is one great first cause, whom they call Owaheeyo, that rules and governs the universe, and takes care of all his creatures rational and irrational, and gives them their food in due season, and hears the prayers of all those who call upon him; therefore it is but just and reasonable to pray and offer sacrifice to this great being, and to do those things that are pleasing in his sight. But they widely differ in what is pleasing or displeasing to this great being. Some hold that following nature or their own propensities is the way to happiness. Others reject this opinion al-together, and say, that following their own propensities in this manner is neither the means of happiness, nor the way to please the deity. My friend

Tecaughretanego, said, our happiness depends on our using our reason, in order to suppress these evil dispositions; but when our propensities neither lead us to injure ourselves nor others, we may with safety indulge them, or even pursue them as the means of happiness" (page 86).

Can any man, says Mr. Boudinot, read this short account of Indian traditions, drawn from tribes of various nations, from the west to the east, and from the south to the north, wholly separated from each other, written by different authors of the best characters, both for knowledge and integrity, possessing the best means of information, at various and distant times, without any possible communication with each other, and in one instance from ocular and sensible demonstration; written on the spot in several instances, with the relaters before them—and yet suppose that all this is either the effect of chance, accident, or design, from a love of the marvelous or a premeditated intention of deceiving, and thereby ruining their own well-established reputations?

Charlevoix was a clergyman of character, who was with the Indians some years and traveled from Canada to the Mississippi in that early day.

Adair lived forty years entirely domesticated with the southern Indians and was a man of learning and great observation. Just before the revolutionary war he brought his manuscript to Elizabethtown, in New Jersey, to William Livingston, Esq. (a neighbor of the writer) to have it examined and corrected, which was prevented by the troubles of a political nature, just breaking out. The Reverend Mr. Brainerd was a man of remarkable piety and a missionary with the Crosweek Indians to his death. Dr. Edwards was eminent for his piety and learning and was intimately acquainted with the Indians from his youth. Dr. Beatty was a clergyman of note and established character. Bartram was a man well known to the writer, and traveled the country of the southern Indians as a botanist, and was a man of considerable discernment, and had great means and knowledge; and M'Kenzie, in the employment of the northwest company, an old trader, and the first adventurous explorer of the country, from the Lake of the Woods to the southern ocean.

It is now asked, continues Mr. Boudinot, can anyone carefully and with deep reflection consider and compare these traditions with the history of the ten tribes of Israel, and the late discoveries of the Russians, Capt. Cook and others, in and about the peninsula of Kamchatka and the northeast coast of Asia and the opposite shores of America, of which little was before known by any civilized nation, without at least drawing strong, presumptive inferences, in favor of these wandering nations being descended from some oriental nation of the old world, and most probably, all things considered, being the lost tribes of Israel.

Let us look into the late discoveries, and compare them with the Indian traditions.

Kamchatka is a large peninsula, on the northeastern part of Asia. It is a mountainous country, lying between fifty-one and sixty-two degrees of north latitude, and of course a very cold and frozen climate. No grain can be raised there, though some vegetables are. Skins and furs are their chief exports. The natives are wild as the country itself and live on fish and sea animals with their reindeer. The islands in this sea, which separate it from the northwest coast of America, are so numerous that the existence of an almost continued chain of them between the two continents is now rendered extremely probable. The principal of them are the Kuril Islands, those called Bering and Copper Islands, the Aleutian Islands, and Fox Islands. Copper Island, which lies in fifty-four degrees north, and in full sight of Bering's Island, has its name from the great quantities of copper with which the northeast coast of it abounds (Mr. Grieve's history). It is washed up by the sea, and covers the shores in such abundance that many ships might be loaded with it very easily. These islands are subject to continual earthquakes and abound in sulphur. Alaska is one of the most eastwardly islands and probably is not far from the American coast. The snow lies on these islands till March, and the sea is filled with ice in winter. There is little or no wood growing in any part of the country, and the inhabitants live in holes dug in the earth. Their greatest delicacies are wild lily and other roots and berries, with fish and other sea animals. The distance between the most northeastwardly part of Asia and the northwest coast of America is determined by the famous navigator Capt. Cook not to exceed thirty-nine miles. These straits are often filled with ice, even in summer, and frozen in winter, and by that means might become a safe passage for the most numerous host to pass over in safety, though these continents had never been once joined, or at a much less distance than at present. The sea from the south of Bering Straits to the islands, between the two continents, is very shallow. From the frequent volcanoes that are continually happening, it is probable, not only that there has been a separation of the continent at Bering Straits, but that the whole space from the island to that small opening was once filled up with land; but that it had by the force and fury of the waters, perhaps actuated by fire, been totally sunk and destroyed, and the islands left in its room. Neither is it improbable that the first passage of the sea was much smaller than at present and that it is widening yearly, and perhaps many small islands that existed at the first separation of the continents have sunk or otherwise have been destroyed. These changes are manifest in almost every country.

Monsieur Le Page du Pratz, in the 2nd vol. of his *History of Louisiana,* page 120, informs us that, being exceedingly desirous to be informed of the origin of the Indian natives, made every inquiry in his power, especially of the nation of the Natchez, one of the most intelligent among them. All he could learn from them was that they came from between the north and the sun setting—being no way satisfied with this, he sought for one who bore the character of one of their wisest men. He was happy enough to discover one named Moneachtape, among the Yazoos, a nation about forty leagues from the Natchez. This man was remarkable for his solid understanding and elevation of sentiment, and his name was given to him by his nation as expressive of the man—meaning *"killer of pain and fatigue."* His eager desire was to see the country from whence his forefathers came—he obtained directions and set off. He went up the Missouri, where he stayed a long time, to learn the different languages of the nations he was to pass through. After long traveling he came to the nation of the Otters, and by them was directed on his way, till he reached the southern ocean. After being some time with the nations on the shores of the great sea, he proposed to proceed on his journey and joined himself to some people who inhabited more westwardly on the coast. They traveled a great way between the north and the sun setting, when they arrived at the village of his fellow travelers, where he found the days long and the nights short. He was here advised to give over all thoughts of continuing his journey. They told him "that the land extended still a long way in the direction aforesaid, after which it ran directly west, and at length was cut by the great water from north to south. One of them added, that when he was young he knew a very old man, who had seen that distant land before it was eaten away by the great water; and when the great water was low, many rocks still appeared in those parts." Moneachtape took their advice, returning home after an absence of five years.

This account given to du Pratz, in the year 1720, confirms the idea of the narrow passage at Kamchatka and the probability that the continents once joined.

It is remarkable that the people, especially the Kamchatkians, in their marches, never go but in Indian file, following one another in the same track. Some of the nations in this quarter prick their flesh with small punctures with a needle in various shapes, then rub into them charcoal, blue liquid, or some other color, so as to make the marks become indelible, after the manner of the more eastern nations.

Bishop Lowth, in his notes on the 16th verse of the 49th chapter of Isaiah, says, "This is certainly an allusion to some practice common among the Jews at that time, of making marks on their hands and arms by punctures on the skin, with some sort of sign or representation of the city or temple, to show their affection and zeal for it. They had a method of making such punctures indelible by fire or staining—and this art is practiced by traveling Jews all over the world at this day"—vide also his note on chap. 45, 5th verse.

Thus it is with our northern Indians; they always go in Indian file, and mark their flesh just as above represented.

The writer of this has seen an aged Christian Indian sachem, of good character, who sat for his portrait. On stripping his neck to the lower part of his breast, it appeared that the whole was marked with a deep bluish color in various figures, very discernible. On being asked the reason of it, he answered, with a heavy sigh, that it was one of the follies of his youth, when he was a great warrior, before his conversion to Christianity; and now, says he, I must bear it, as a punishment for my folly, and carry the marks of it to my grave.

The people of Siberia made canoes of birch bark, distended over ribs of wood, nicely sewed together. The writer has seen this exactly imitated by the Indians on the River St. Lawrence, and it is universally the case on the lakes. Col. John Smith says, "At length we all embarked in a large birch bark canoe. This vessel was about four feet wide and three feet deep and about thirty-five feet long; and though it could carry a heavy burden, it was so artfully constructed, that four men could carry it several miles, from one landing place to another; or from the waters of the lakes to the waters of the Ohio. At night they carry it on the land, and invert it, or turn it bottom up, and convert it into a dwelling house."

It also appears from the history of Kamchatka, written by James Grieve, that, in the late discoveries, the islands which extend from the south point of Kamchatka amount to thirty-one or thirty-two. That on these islands are high mountains, and many of them smoking volcanoes. That the passages between them, except in one or two instances, were but one or two days' row, at the time of the author's writing that history. They are liable to terrible inundations and earthquakes.

The following is collected from Mr. Steller's journal, as recorded in the above history: "The mainland of America lies parallel with the coast of Kamchatka, insomuch that it may reasonably be concluded that these lands once joined, especially at the Techukotskoi Noss, or Cape." He offers reasons to prove it: 1st. The appearance of both coasts, which appear to be torn asunder. 2nd. Many capes project into the sea from thirty to sixty versts. 3d. Many islands are in the sea which divides Kamchatka from America. 4th. The situation of the islands and the breadth of that sea. The sea is full of islands, which extend from the northwest point of America to the channel of Anianova. One follows another, as the Keruloski islands do at Japan. The American coast at sixty degrees of north latitude is covered with wood; but at Kamchatka, which is only fifty-one degrees, there is none for near fifty versts from the sea, and at sixty-two, not one tree is to be found. It is known also that the fish enter the rivers on the American coast earlier than they do in the rivers of Kamchatka. There are also raspberries, of a large size and fine taste, besides honeysuckles, cranberries, and blackberries in great plenty. In the sea there are seals, sea beavers, whales, and dogfish. In the country and in the rivers on the American coast, red and black foxes, swans, ducks, quails, plover, and ten kinds of birds not known in Europe. These particulars may help to answer the question, whence was America peopled; for though we should grant that the two continents never were joined, yet they lie so near to each other that the possibility of the inhabitants of Asia going over to America, especially considering the number of the islands, and the coldness of the climate, cannot be denied. From Bering's Island, on its high mountains, you can see mountains covered with snow, that appear to be capes, of the mainland of America. From all which it appears clearly, here was a probable means of a people passing from Asia to America, either on the mainland before a separation, or from island to island; or on the ice after a separation, by which the continent of America might have been peopled by the tribes of Israel wandering northeast and directed by the unseen hand of Providence, and thus they entered into a country wherein mankind never before dwelt.

It is not presumed that the ten tribes of Israel alone did this. Many of the inhabitants might have gone with them from Tartary or Scythia; and particularly the old inhabitants of Damascus, who were carried away in the first place by Tilgath-pilneser, before his conquest of the Israelites, and were their neighbors, and perhaps as much dissatisfied with their place of banishment, though for different reasons, as the Israelites, as well as from Kamchatka, on their way where they were stopped some time, as the Egyptians did with the Israelites of old. And indeed it is not improbable, as has before been hinted, that some few of other nations, who traded on the seas, might, in so long a course of time, have been driven by stress of weather and reached the Atlantic shores at different places; but the great body of people settling in North and South America must have originated from the same source.

Hence it would not be surprising to find among their descendants a mixture of the Asiatic languages, manners, customs, and peculiarities. Nay, it would appear rather extraordinary and unaccountable if this was not so. And if we should find this to be the case, it would greatly corroborate the fact of their having passed into America from the northeast point of Asia, according to the Indian tradition. We, at the present day, can hardly conceive of the facility with which these wandering northern nations removed from one part of the country to the other. The Tartars at this time, who possess that northern country, live in tents or covered carts and wander from place to place in search of pasture, etc.

The general character, manners, habits, and customs of the Indians have been very generally misrepresented. It is quite certain that, at the time of the discovery of this continent by Columbus, it was peopled by some thousands of tribes, scattered from the coast opposite Kamchatka to Hudson's Bay. Their exact number has never been ascertained, and at this time it is impossible— generation after generation and tribe after tribe have gone down to the grave, and of some great and powerful nations, there is not a solitary survivor left. It seems as if the destroying angel had passed over the country, and that the numerous and happy natives had looked on him and died. Mr. Boudinot mentions one hundred and ninety different nations, each having a *king* and *sachem.*

"Du Pratz, in his *History of Louisiana* (vol. 108–123), gives an account of the single nation of the Padoucas, lying west by northwest of the Missouri, in 1724, which may give a faint idea of the numbers originally inhabiting this vast continent. He says, 'the nations of the Padoucas is very numerous, extends almost two hundred leagues, and they have villages quite close to the Spaniards of New Mexico.' 'They are not to be considered as a wandering nation, though employed in hunting, summer and winter—page 121. Seeing they have large villages, consisting of a great number of cabins, which contain very numerous families. These are permanent abodes; from which one hundred hunters set out at a time with their horses, their bows, and a good stock of arrows.' 'The village where we were, consisting of one hundred and forty huts, containing about eight hundred warriors, fifteen hundred women, and at least two thousand children, some Padoucas having four wives.'—page 124. 'The natives of North-America derive their origin from the same country, since at bottom they all have the same manners and usages, as also the same manner of speaking and thinking.'

"Mr. Jefferson, late President of the United States, in his *Notes on Virginia,* has also given much useful information to the world on several important subjects relating to America, and among others, as to the numbers of the Indians in that then dominion. Speaking of the Indian confederacy of the warriors, or rather nations, in that state and its neighborhood, called 'the Powhatan confederacy,' says, it contained in point of territory, as he supposes, of their patrimonial country 'about three hundred miles in length, and one hundred in breadth. That there was about one inhabitant for every square mile, and the proportion of warriors to the whole number of inhabitants, was as three to ten, making the number of souls about thirty thousand.'

"Some writers state the number of their warriors at the first coming of Europeans to Virginia to be fifteen thousand, and their population fifty thousand. La Houtan says that each village contained about fourteen thousand souls, that is, fifteen hundred that bore arms, two thousand superannuated men, four thousand women, two thousand maids, and four thousand five hundred children. From all which, it is but a moderate estimate to suppose that there were six hundred thousand fighting men, or warriors, on this continent at its first discovery.

"In 1677, Col. Coursey, an agent for Virginia, had a conference with the Five Nations at Albany. The number of warriors was estimated at that time in those nations at the following rate. Mohawks three hundred, Oneidas two hundred, Onondagas three hundred and fifty, Cayugas three hundred, Senecas one thousand—total two thousand one hundred and fifty, which makes the population about seven thousand two hundred. Vide Chalmer's *Political Annals,* 606.

"Smith, in his *History of New York,* says that in 1756, the number of fighting men were about twelve hundred.

"Douglas, in his *History of Massachusetts,* says that they were about fifteen hundred in 1760.

"In 1764, Col. Boquet states the whole number of the inhabitants (he must mean fighting men) at fifteen hundred and fifty.

"Captain Hutchins, in 1768, states them at two thousand one hundred and twenty, and Dodge, an Indian trader, in 1779, at sixteen hundred, in the third year of the American revolutionary war. Many reasons may be assigned for the above differences—some may have stayed at home for the defense of their towns—some might be absent treating on disputes with their neighbors, or sickness, etc. etc.

"During the above war, 1776–7, the British had in their service, according to the returns of their agent—Mohawks three hundred, Oneidas one hundred and fifty, Tuscaroras two hundred, Onondagas three hundred, Cayugas two hundred and thirty, Senecas four hundred—In the whole fifteen hundred and eighty. The Americans had about two hundred and twenty, making up eighteen hundred warriors, equal to about six thousand souls.

"In 1783, Mr. Kirkland, missionary to the Oneidas, estimated the number of the Seneca warriors at six hundred, and the total number of the Six Nations, at more than four thousand.

"1790, he made the whole number of Indian inhabitants then remaining, including, in addition, those who reside on Grand River in Canada, and the Stockbridge and Brothertown Indians, to be six thousand three hundred and thirty.

In 1794, the Six Nations numbered seven thousand one hundred and forty-eight souls."

But what are these to the Southern Indians, and especially those of Mexico and Peru? I will give one example. Mons. Le Page du Pratz, in his *History of Louisiana,* written about the year 1730, assures us "that the nation of the Natchez, from whom the town of that name on the Mississippi is called, were the most powerful nation in North America—2nd vol. 146. They extended from the River Manchas or Iberville, which is about fifty leagues from the sea, to the River Wabash, which is about four hundred and sixty leagues from the sea, and that they had five hundred sachems in the nation." He further says "that the Chatkas or Flat-heads, near the River Pacha Ogulas, had twenty-five thousand warriors, but in which number, he supposes many were reckoned who had but a slight title to that name"—page 140.

A distinguishing trait in the character of the aborigines is that of unbounded hospitality. Mr. Bartram, who knew the Seminole Indians well, as he traveled among them considerably, says that they possess a vast territory, all East Florida, and the greatest part of West Florida, which being naturally cut and divided into thousands of islets, knolls, and eminences, by the innumerable rivers, lakes, swamps, savannas, and ponds, form so many secure retreats and temporary dwelling places that effectually guard them from any sudden invasion or attacks from their enemies. (The title of the Indians to this and almost any other portion of our southern country is *extinguished*!) And being such a swampy, hummocky country, furnishes such a plenty and variety of supplies for the nourishment of every sort of animal that I can venture to assert that no part of the globe so abounds with wild game or creatures fit for the food of man. Thus they enjoy a superabundance of the necessities and conveniences of life with the security of person and property, the two great concerns of mankind. They seem to be free from want or desires. No cruel enemy to dread; nothing to give them disquietude but the gradual encroachments of the white people. Thus contented and undisturbed, they appear as blithe and free as the birds of the air, and like them as volatile and active, tuneful and vociferous. The visage, action, and deportment of a Seminole, being the most striking picture of happiness in this life—joy, contentment, love, and friendship without guile or affectation—seem inherent in them, or predominate in their vital principle, for it leaves them but with the last breath of life.

To exemplify their kindness to strangers, he says "that having lost his way in traveling through their towns, he at a stand how to proceed, when he observed an Indian man at the door of his habitation, beckoning to him, to come to him." Bartram accordingly rode up to him. He cheerfully welcomed him to his house, took care of his horse, and with the most graceful air of respect led him into an airy, cool apartment, where being seated on cabins, his women brought in a refreshing repast, with a pleasant cool liquor to drink—then pipes and tobacco. After an hour's conversation, and Mr. Bartram informing him of his business, and where he was bound, but having lost his way, he did not know how to go on. The Indian cheerfully replied, that he was pleased that Mr. B. was come in their country, where he should meet with friendship and protection; and that he would himself lead him into the right path. He turned out to be the prince or chief of Whatoga. How long would an Indian have rode through our country, before he would have received such kindness from a common farmer, much less a chief magistrate of a country? Mr. Bartram adds to the testimony of Father Charlevoix, in favor of their good characters among themselves. He says they are just, honest, liberal, and hospitable to strangers; considerate, loving, and affectionate to their wives and relations; fond of their children; frugal and persevering, charitable and forbearing. He was weeks and months among them in their towns, and never observed the least sign of contention or wrangling; never saw an instance of an Indian beating his wife or even reproving her in anger.

Col. John Smith says, "When we had plenty of green corn and roasting ears, the hunters became lazy, and spent their time in singing and dancing. They appeared to be fulfilling the scriptures, beyond many of those who profess to believe them, in that of taking no thought for tomorrow, but in living in love, peace, and friendship, without disputes." In this last respect they are an example to those who profess Christianity—page 29.

"As the Israelites were divided into tribes, and had a chief over them, and always marched under ensigns of some animal peculiar to each tribe, so the Indian nations are universally divided into tribes, under a sachem or king, chosen by the people from the wisest and bravest among them. He has neither influence nor distinction, but from his wisdom and prudence. He is assisted by a council of *old, wise,* and *benevolent men,* as they call their priests and counsellors. Nothing is determined (of a public nature) but in this council, where everyone has an equal voice. The chief or sachem sits in the middle, and the council on each hand, forming a semi-circle, as the high priest of the Jews did in the Sanhedrim of that nation."

Mr. Penn, when he first arrived in Pennsylvania, in the year 1683, and made a treaty with them, makes the following observations in a letter he then wrote to his friends in England. "Every king has his council, and that consists of all the old and wise men of his nation, which perhaps are two hundred people. Nothing of moment is undertaken, be it war, peace, selling of land, or traffic, without advising with them. 'Tis admirable to consider how powerful the chiefs are, and yet how they move by the breath of the people. I have had occasion to be in council with them upon treaties for land, and to adjust the terms of trade. Their order is thus, the king sits in the middle of an half moon, and hath his council, the old and wise on each hand. Behind them, at a little distance sits the young fry, in the same figure. Having consulted and resolved their business, the king ordered one of them to speak to me. He came to me, and in the name of his king, saluted me. Then took me by the hand, and told me that he was ordered by his king to speak to me; and that now it was not he, but the king that spoke, because what he should say was the king's mind. During the time this person was speaking, not a man of them was observed to whisper or smile. The old were grave—the young reverent in their deportment. They spoke little, but fervently and with eloquence. He will deserve the name of *wise,* who out-wits them in any treaty about a thing they understand. At every sentence they shout, and say amen, in their way."

Mr. Smith, in his *History of New Jersey,* confirms this general statement. "They are grave even to sadness, upon any common, and more so upon serious occasions—observant of those in company, and respectful to the aged—of a temper cool and deliberate—never in haste to speak, but wait, for a certainty, that the person who spake before them, had finished all he had to say. They seemed to hold European vivacity in contempt, because they found such as came among them, apt to interrupt each other, and frequently speak altogether. Their behavior in public councils was strictly decent and instructive. Everyone, in his turn, according to rank of years or wisdom or services to his country. Not a word, whisper, or murmur, was heard while anyone spoke: no interruption to commend or condemn: the younger sort were totally silent. Those denominated kings, were sachems distinguished by their wisdom and good conduct. The respect paid them was voluntary, and not exacted or looked for, nor the omission regarded. The sachems directed in their councils, and had the chief disposition of their lands"—pages 141, 144.

Every nation of Indians have certain customs, which they observe in their public transactions with other nations, and in their private affairs among themselves, which is scandalous for anyone among them not to observe. And these always draw after them either public or private resentment, whenever they are broken. Although these customs may, in their detail, differ in one nation when compared to another, yet it is easy to discern that they have all had one origin. This is also apparent from every nation understanding them. Mr. Colden says, "Their great men, both sachems and captains, are generally poorer than the common people; for they affect to give away, and distribute all the presents or plunder they get in their treaties or in war, so as to leave nothing to themselves." There is not a man in the ministry of the Five Nations (of whom Mr. Colden was writing) who has gained his office otherwise than by merit. There is not the least salary, or any sort of profit annexed to any office, to tempt the covetous or the sordid; but on the contrary, every unworthy action is unavoidably attended with the forfeiture of their commission; for their authority is only the esteem of the people, and ceases the moment that esteem is lost. An old Mohawk sachem, in a poor blanket and a dirty shirt, may be seen issuing his orders, with as arbitrary an authority as a Roman dictator.

"As every nation, as before observed, has its peculiar standard or symbol, as an eagle, a bear, a wolf, or an otter, so has each tribe the like badge, from which it is denominated. When they encamp, on a march, they always cut the representation of their ensign or symbol, on the trees, by which it may be known who have been there. The sachem of each tribe is a necessary party in all conveyances and treaties, to which he affixes the mark of his tribe, as a corporation does that of the public seal.

"If you go from nation to nation, you will not find one who does not lineally distinguish himself by his respective family. As the family or tribe of the eagle, panther (which is their lion), tiger, buffalo (their ox or bull), and also the bear, deer, raccoon, etc. etc. So among the Jews, was the lion of the tribe of Judah—Dan was known by a serpent—Issachar by an ass, and Benjamin by a wolf. But the Indians, as the Jews, pay no religious respect for any of these animals, or for any other whatever.

"They reckon time after the manner of the Hebrews. They divide the year into spring, summer, autumn, or the falling of the leaf, and winter. Korah is their word for winter with the Cherokee Indians, as it is with the Hebrews. They number the years by any of these four periods, for they have no name for the year. And they subdivide these, and count the year by lunar months, or moons, like the Israelites, who also counted by moons. They call the sun and moon by the same word, with the addition of day and night, as the day sun, or moon—the night sun, or moon. They count the day by three sensible differences of the sun like the Hebrews—as the sun coming out— mid-day, and the sun is dead, or sunset. Midnight is half way between the sun going in and coming out of the water—also by mid-night and cock-crowing. They begin their ecclesiastical year at the first appearance of the first new moon of the vernal equinox, according to the ecclesiastical year of Moses. They pay great regard to the first appearance of every new moon. They name the various seasons of the year from the planting and ripening of fruits. The green eared moon is the most beloved or sacred, when the first fruits become sanctified, by being annually offered up; and from this period they count their beloved or holy things."

The greatest act of hostility toward a nation is to profane the graves of their dead. If one of their nation dies at a distance, they secure the body from birds and wild beasts; and when they "imagine the flesh is consumed, and the bones dried, they return to the place, bring them home, and inter them in a very solemn manner." The Hebrews, in like manner, carefully buried their dead but on any accident, they gathered their bones, and laid them in the tombs of their forefathers. Thus Jacob "charged his sons, and said unto them, I am to be gathered unto my people, bury me with my fathers, in the cave that is in the field of Ephron the Hittite." This was in Canaan. "There they buried Abraham and Sarah his wife; there they buried Isaac and Rebecca his wife;

and there I buried Leah." "And Joseph took an oath of the children of Israel, saying, God will surely visit you, and ye shall carry my bones from hence." "And Moses took the bones of Joseph with him" (Gen. 49:29, 31; 50:25; Exod. 13:19). "And the bones of Joseph, which the children of Israel brought up out of Egypt, buried they in Shechem," as above mentioned (Josh. 24:32). The Jews buried near their cities, and sometimes opposite to their houses, implying a silent lesson of friendship, and a caution to live well. They buried families together, but strangers apart by themselves.

When an old Indian finds that it is probable that he must die, he sends for his friends, and with them collects his children and family around him; and then, with the greatest composure, he addresses them in the most affectionate manner, giving them his last council and advising them to such conduct as he thinks for their best interests. So did the patriarchs of old, and the Indians seem to follow their steps, and with as much coolness as Jacob did to his children, when he was about to die.[9]

A very worthy clergyman, with whom the writer was well acquainted, and who had long preached to the Indians, informed him that many years ago, having preached in the morning to a considerable number of them, in the recess between the morning and afternoon services, news was suddenly brought, that the son of an Indian woman, one of the congregation then present, had fallen into a mill dam and was drowned. Immediately the disconsolate mother retired to some distance in deep distress and sat down on the ground. Her female friends soon followed her and placed themselves in like manner around her, in a circle at a small distance. They continued a considerable time in profound and melancholy silence, except now and then uttering a deep groan. All at once the mother, putting her hand on her mouth, fell with her face flat on the ground, her hand continuing on her mouth. This was followed, in like manner, by all the rest, when all cried out with the most melancholy and dismal yellings and groanings. Thus they continued, with their hands on their mouths, and their mouths in the dust a considerable time. The men also retired to a distance from them and went through the same ceremony, making the most dismal groanings and yellings.

Need any reader be reminded of the Jewish customs on occasions of deep humiliation, as in Job 21 and 5—"Mark me and be astonished, and lay your hand on your mouth." 29 and 9—"The princes refrained talking, and laid their hands on their mouths." 49 and 4—"Behold! I am vile, what shall I answer thee? I will lay my hand on my mouth." Micah 7 and 16—"The nations shall see and be confounded; they shall lay their hands on their

---

9. This, and the previous paragraph, appear to be Apess's interpolations. The following paragraph resumes the extracts from Boudinot.

mouth." Lament. 3 and 7—"He putteth his mouth in the dust, if so be, there may be hope." Prov. 30 and 32—"If thou hast thought evil, lay thine hand upon thine mouth."

The Choctaw Indians hire mourners to magnify the merit and loss of the dead, and if their tears do not flow, their shrill voices will be heard to cry, which answers the solemn chorus much better. However, some of them have the art of shedding tears abundantly. (Jer. 9:17, 19)—"Thus saith the Lord of Hosts, consider ye, and call for the mourning women, that they may come, and send for cunning women, that they may come for a voice of wailing is heard, etc."[10]

In Dobson's *Encyclopedia,* vol. 1, page 557, will be found some striking testimony in favor of the strict and rigid morality of the Indians. To that account I refer the reader, who will find an interesting sketch, entitled to credibility, of the advice given by a father (an Indian) to an only son. As far back as tradition reaches, it appears to have been the practice among the Indians to instruct their young men and women in their system of morality. For this purpose, teachers were appointed to instruct them in it. Many of them, however, after becoming acquainted with the manners and customs of the whites, doubted its efficacy, and acted accordingly. The late venerated Boudinot, in one of his last literary productions, relates the following circumstances.

"A minister preaching to a congregation of Christian Indians, west of Delaware, observed a stranger Indian, listening with great attention. After the service, the minister inquired who he was. It appeared, on inquiry, that he lived three hundred miles to the westward—that he had just arrived and gave this account of himself. "That his elder brother living in his house, had been many days and nights in great perplexity, wishing to learn to know the Great Spirit, till at length he resolved to retire into the woods, supposing that he should succeed better in a state of separation from all mankind. Having spent many weeks alone in great affliction, he thought he saw a man of majestic appearance, who informed him that there were Indians living to the southeast, who were acquainted with the Great Spirit and the way to everlasting life; adding that he should go home and tell his people, what he had seen and heard. For this reason, as soon as he had heard his brother speak, he determined to travel in search of the people he had described, till he found them; and since he had heard what had been said that day, the words had been welcome to his heart."

A missionary made a journey to the Shawnee country, the most savage of the Indian nations. He stopped at the first village he came to and lodged with

---

10. The Appendix in the 1829 edition of *A Son of the Forest* ended here. The material added to the Appendix in the 1831 edition from here to the end is also from Boudinot.

one of the chief men. He informed the chief of his business, and opened some truths of the Gospel to him by means of an interpreter who accompanied him. The chief paid great attention, and after some time told him that he was convinced that the missionary's doctrines were true, pointing out the right road. That the *Shawnee* had been long striving to find the way of life; but that he must own, with regret, that all their labor and researches had been in vain. That they, therefore, had lost all courage, not knowing what they should do further, to obtain happiness. The chief accompanied the missionary to the next village and persuaded him to lodge with a heathen teacher.

The missionary then preached to him, and told him that he had brought him the words of eternal life. This the Indian said was what they wanted, and they would hear him with pleasure. After some days, the heathen teacher said, I have not been able to sleep all night, for I am continually meditating upon your words, and will now open to you my whole heart. I believe what you say is the truth. A year ago I became convinced that we are altogether sinful creatures, and that none of our good works can save us; but I did not know what to do to get relief. I have therefore always comforted my people, that somebody would come and show us the true way to happiness, for we are not in the right way. And even but the day before you came, I desired my people to have a little patience, and that some teacher would certainly come. Now you are come, and I verily believe that the Great Spirit has sent you to make known his word to us.

Monsieur De Lapoterie, a French author, speaking of the Cherokees and other southern Indians, gives this account of them: "These Indians look upon the end of life, to be living happily; and for this purpose their whole customs are calculated to prevent avarice, which they think embitters life."

Nothing is more severe reflection among them than to say, *that a man loves his own.* To prevent the use and propagation of such a vice, upon the death of an Indian, they burn all that belongs to the deceased, that there may be no temptation for the parent to hoard up a superfluity of arms or domestic conveniences for his children. They cultivate no more land than is necessary for their plentiful subsistence and hospitality to strangers. At the feast of expiation, they also burn all the fruits of the earth and grain left of the past year's crops.

Mr. Brainerd informs us that, about one hundred and thirty miles from our settlements, he met an Indian, who was said to be a devout and zealous reformer. He was dressed in a hideous and terrific manner. He had a house consecrated to religious purposes. Mr. Brainerd discoursed with him about Christianity, and some of the discourse he seemed to like, but some of it he wholly rejected. He said that God had taught him his religion and that he would never turn from it, but wanted to find some who would heartily join him in it, for the Indians had grown very degenerate and corrupt. He said he had thoughts of leaving all his friends and traveling abroad in order to find some who would join with him, for he believed that the Great Spirit had good people somewhere, who felt as he did. He said that he had not always felt as he then did but had formerly been like the rest of the Indians, until about four or five years before that time. Then he said, that his heart was very much distressed, so that he could not live among the Indians, but got away into the woods and lived for some months. At length he said the Great Spirit had comforted his heart and showed him what he should do; and since that time he had known the Great Spirit and tried to serve him, and loved all men, be they who they may, so as he never did before. He treated Mr. Brainerd with uncommon courtesy and seemed to be hearty in it.

The other Indians said that he had opposed their drinking strong liquor with all his power; and if at any time he could not dissuade them from it, he would leave them and go crying into the woods. It was manifest that he had a set of religious notions of his own, that he had looked into for himself, and had not taken for granted upon bare tradition; and he relished or disrelished whatever was spoken of a religious nature, according as it agreed or disagreed with his standard. He would sometimes say, now *that* I like, so the Great Spirit has taught me, etc. Some of his sentiments seemed very just; yet he utterly denied the existence of an evil spirit and declared there was no such a being known among the Indians of old times, whose religion he supposed he was attempting to revive. He also said that departed souls went southward, and that the difference between the good and bad was that the former were admitted into a beautiful town with spiritual walls, or walls agreeably to the nature of souls. The latter would forever hover round those walls, and in vain attempt to get in. He seemed to be sincere, honest, and conscientious in his own way, and according to his own religious notions, which was more than could be said of most other pagans Mr. Brainerd had seen. He was considered and derided by the other Indians as a precise zealot, who made an unnecessary noise about religious matters, but in Mr Brainerd's opinion, there was something in his temper and disposition that looked more like true religion than anything he had observed among other heathen Indians.

Indian Hymn

Many shall come from the East and the West, and sit down with Abraham, Isaac, and Jacob, in the kingdom of God, when the children of the kingdom shall be thrust out.

> In da darke wood, no Indian nigh,
> Den me look heb'n, and send up cry
> Upon me knee so low—

Dat God on high—in shiny place,
See me in night wid teary face,
   Da priest did tell me so.

God send his angel, take me care,
He come himself and hear me pray'r,
   If inside heart do pray;
He see me now, he now me hear,
He say, poor Indian neber fear,
   Me wid you night and day.

Den me lub God wid inside heart,
He figh fo me, he take me part,
   He safe me life afore:
God lub poo Indian in da wood,
So me lub God, and dat be good,
   Me praise him two time more.[11]

The End

11. This strange, patronizing dialect poem has a slight but interesting subsequent history. It is reprinted in the *Red Man* (June 1889):1, the publication of the Carlisle Indian School. The newspaper was one of the leading propaganda organs in the movement to Americanize the Indians. The newspaper attributes it to Apess, though in fact it is from Boudinot. It would be intriguing to know where he found it, but the most mysterious question is why Apess would have chosen to reproduce it.

PART 2

*The Increase
of the Kingdom
of Christ:
A Sermon
and The Indians:
The Ten Lost
Tribes*

Nothing is known about where or when *The Increase of the Kingdom of Christ* was first delivered by Apess or what occasioned his decision to publish one of his sermons. *The Indians: The Ten Lost Tribes,* although clearly a companion piece for the concerns and ideas in the sermon, is a distinct essay. The sermon is Apess's most orthodox Christian expression. Although Native Americans provide a motif in the text, they are subordinated throughout to Apess's celebration of the coming triumph of evangelical Christianity. His conviction of the imminence of Christ's coming partakes fully of the millenarian optimism among contemporary Protestant revivalists. ✓ His catalog of all the instruments of God's good works repeats a commonplace of evangelical preaching in this period.

The rhetoric of the sermon is arguably regressive. By making the Indians objects and signs of the conversion of the world, his evangelical discourse controls and subjugates "the Indian." The theme of John the Baptist, a man of the wilderness, as the forerunner of one yet greater than himself and who will disappear when his superior appears, cannot but evoke the idea of Indians as precursors of a superior civilization which is to come after and to supplant them. Yet, it is important to note, Apess remains steadfastly committed to an egalitarian Christianity. Heaven is characterized as a place of utter equality, the mark of its most extreme difference from earthly kingdoms.

The writing seems to me exceptionally polished and rhetorically skillful. A good example is: "All that is good is in heaven. All that is glorious is there. All that is permanent is there. No change comes there—no sickness— no death—no grief—no wasting remorse—no bitter memory—no secret sting—no disturbing jealousy—no envy of the soul, pining away because another is great or beloved." In these words might also be heard echoes of his own history and of the longings which in some part moved him toward Christianity.

Increase
of the
Kingdom
of Christ

▲

He must increase (John 3:30)

This remarkable prediction was uttered by John the Baptist, who has been appropriately called the forerunner of Christ. It is the more remarkable because, contrary to the usual feelings of poor humanity, made up of flesh and blood, the same sentence which foretold the increase of the Savior also foretold that John, the mighty prophet of the wilderness, whose habitation was not with the beings of his race, should decrease[1]—should wane away before a greater than himself. It is an evidence of truth and disinterestedness when a prophet testifies against himself, and foretells his own failing influence and the rise of another; selfishness would take a different course and point to its own glory and aggrandizement. But we have the testimony of Jesus Christ himself, that John was the greatest of prophets; none born of woman ever surpassed him in stern dignity and grandeur of character. Like one apart from man, he came from the desert, girded with camel's hair, and preached repentance in a voice of thunder that shook Judea and filled Jordan with thousands, who came to signify how their sins should be washed away in the running stream. There was power in his words. There was that in them which could not pass away. Their meaning was not only that the single being of whom he spoke should increase but that his cause, his kingdom, his empire on earth, beginning in Christ, should swell and spread through all lands and extend its absorbing and powerful influences until time should be no more. John, in the greatness of his character, surrenders himself to decay and gives up his dispensation to decrease—but, with the strong and pervading visions of prophecy, he gives to his Savior and his God that increase which we, after a lapse of more than eighteen hundred years, see in the full and successful tide of glorious fulfillment.

1. "He must increase, but I *must* decrease" is the whole verse.

It is a blessed thing to stand on some of the great landmarks of time and be able to look back on a long line of prophecy fulfilled; and thus to have an unwavering confidence in what God has promised for future times. Ancient saints were happy to take on trust and realize by faith those things which have now become matters of history and present themselves before us to comfort and inspire us with new confidence in all our Heavenly Father has promised to his church.

In considering the grand subject of the increase of Christ, which we take to mean the kingdom of Christ on earth and in heaven, we are led to inquire, first, *What is the kingdom of Christ? And in what manner are we to expect its increase?*

1st. The kingdom of Christ is righteousness. The kingdoms of this world, with but few exceptions, are confederacies of wrong; the powerful trespass on the weak; the rich live in luxury and rioting, while the poor are enslaved and doomed to much servile drudgery, without any hope of bettering their condition. But, in the kingdom of Christ, the noble of the earth are on an equality with the poor and humble; no distinctions of birth, except that of being born again, are known. Every subject of Christ's kingdom strives to purify himself from all evil. He becomes righteous in his dealings toward his fellow man; and, in accordance with the spirit of the kingdom to which he belongs, he can enslave no man—he can oppress no man—he can only do to others as he would have others do to him.

In the kingdom of Christ every vicious principle and impure motive of the heart is sought out and corrected; the axe is laid at the root of the tree of human corruption, and the tall branches of pride and avarice, and lust and cruelty, wither, and in their place spring up the trees of Paradise, loaded with the fruits of the Spirit. The wicked man becomes holy; the drunkard becomes temperate; the robber restores that which he has taken. Large communities, long disturbed by quarrels and wars, strangely forget to fight and live in gentleness and peace. The profane man becomes one of whom it may be said—"Behold, he prayeth." Entire nations of idolatrous savages suddenly learn another worship and bow themselves in praise and adoration before the Great Spirit, for the first time revealed to them in the fullness of his glory through a suffering and risen Savior. The white man, who has most cruelly oppressed his red brother, under the influence of that Gospel which he has long professed to believe, and just now begins to feel, pours out unavailing tears over the wasted generations of the mighty forest hunters and, now they are almost all dead and buried, begins to pity and lament them. The soldier, red with the blood of a hundred battles, begins to pause over the motives which induce nations to draw the sword against each other and inquires within himself if it would not be nobler to forgive than to kill.

2nd. We are to expect the increase of the kingdom of Christ generally by the progressive spread of all those things which we have described as constituting that kingdom. But, in addition, there are many particular modes of increase, which we intend to notice as constituting a full ground of faith, hope, and assurance in this matter. Were we to expect the increase of the kingdom of Christ only through the progressive spread of good principles, communicated from man to man in the manner that philosophical or political principles are, we might well despair of the ultimate triumph of Christianity. But we have the most sure word of prophecy to rely upon, as in our text, which foretells the spread of the kingdom of grace, and in thousands of passages far more explicit. And we have not only the full and wide prospect of the promises of Jehovah, but, as we briefly remarked before, we have the long history of God's faithfulness, as well as a countless multitude of instances in which the saving power of his grace has been made known in the conversion of large masses of human beings from the error and darkness of sin. Through the glass of church history, we may look and see religion at its lowest ebb, when Jesus came a heavenly pilgrim into our wicked world. We see him select twelve, not from the noble and mighty on earth but from the walks of obscurity; we see him giving a commission to these twelve fishermen of Galilee to overthrow kingdoms, subvert the hoary institutions of idolatry, change the moral aspect of mighty and renowned countries, and lift up the standard of immortality where all had been rebellion and darkness before; we see the stupendous work to which these apparently powerless men were appointed, all accomplished before they died. The last one had not gone to his glorious rest before polished Greece and the tremendous power of the Roman Empire had bowed before them; the cross was raised above the golden eagles of the eternal city; Idumea, Spain, Gaul, and the distant isle of Britain had received apostolic visits, accompanied by the rushing wings of the Holy Ghost, sent down from heaven; the oracles of Delphos, the responses of the Sibyls, the orgies and human sacrifices of the Druids were all overthrown and silenced.

We have in church history the record of this grand transaction before us, to show us what can be done by what has been done. Although, at that era, the set time to favor Zion had not arrived, yet such was the glorious effects of the wide-spreading religion of Christ that the world were without excuse for not holding fast the treasure which worlds were too poor to purchase. This great treasure was rejected or prostituted to worldly purposes, and in a few centuries the world sunk into the dreamless slumber of the Dark Ages.

Secondly, the particular times when the kingdom of Christ has increased, or when it is destined to increase, have been in part noted. We have alluded to the remarkable increase in the early age of Christianity. There was another great increase at the period which has been called the Reformation, when a host of daring spirits came out from the bosom of the Papal Church and gave it its death wound. They fought nobly for Christ, and many thousands sealed their devotion to the cause of truth by pouring out their blood on the scaffold and at the stake. The slumber of the Scottish church was at a more recent period awakened by the lion voice of John Knox. Afterward, the English church, and indeed the whole world, slumbering together, heard the mighty call of the Spirit of God through the instrumentality of Wesley, and Whitefield, and Edwards, and the numerous worthies of the last generation. But it has been reserved for the present generation to witness more systematic efforts to promote the cause of Christ than ever before have been put in operation. To the usual means of grace have been added many societies and institutions for the promotion of godliness. Thousands of messengers run to and fro throughout the earth; the stores of information are increased, and the knowledge of the Lord, like a refluent wave, begins to roll over all lands. Bibles and tracts, and Bethel flags, and heralds of salvation to far distant lands multiply around us, and we see swift messengers go down to the ships and speed over the wide seas, that Christ may get to himself his great honor. The last thirty years have witnessed wonderful things for God. The stone which has begun to roll cannot stop; its onward course must be swifter as it bounds over the landmarks of coming time, into the gulf of eternity. The feeble hand of man, although by divine grace it can do much in promotion of Christ's kingdom, can do nothing against it. He must increase. And we have the satisfaction of a full belief that what our eyes see is but the beginning of those better days which shall fill the church with rejoicing and praise. Glory to God in the highest! The earth shall be full of his praise. The stone cut out of the mountain without hands shall fill the whole earth, crumbling haughty thrones to dust and rolling in thunder over unrepenting and hardened rebels.

Thirdly, we proceed to offer the reasons why the kingdom of Christ must increase.

1st. Because it is the purpose of God. Announced by prophecy, confirmed by promise upon promise, it is a most certain fact that Jesus shall reign over a world that has long rejected and despised him; because God, the Almighty Father, hath purposed from the beginning to reward him for his voluntary humiliation by crowning him Lord of all. Some eminent men have delighted to consider the kingdom of Christ over the hearts of men as resulting from, and made certain by, a compact made between him and his Father, and our Father—and there are scriptural reasons for this view of the subject; a compact in which the sovereignty over the redeemed millions of mankind was covenanted to the Eternal Son, in consequence of his great agency in the work of salvation. Heaven will be too narrow a space to sing the praises of redeeming love, and even an unending eternity not long enough to celebrate the dying love of the second person in the Godhead.

2nd. Because of God's love to his Son Jesus Christ. The bright and stern justice of the Father cannot look with approbation on sin; consequently, the salvation of any part of mankind, were there no daysman between a broken law and its angry voice calling for retribution and the lost sinner, would be rendered an impossibility. But God the Father loves his Son. He hath made him the firstborn of the Church on high—the first fruits of a triumphant resurrection from the dead—he is the chiefest among ten thousand, and one altogether lovely. Although on us, poor rebels at best, the high and perfect sovereign of the heavens cannot look with complacency, yet on Jesus our advocate he can look with the love which language is not mighty enough to utter or describe and say to him, "I will give thee the heathen for thine inheritance, and the uttermost parts of the earth for a possession."

Thus we see that not only the faithfulness of the Almighty mind stands pledged for the increase of the kingdom of righteousness but the love of God the Father to the Son secures the spread of religion over the whole earth. God loves his only begotten Son, and through him all that bear his image and are the true sheep of his fold. Christ and his Father are one in love. Whom Christ loveth, therefore, the Father loves; and those redeemed and sanctified souls who love the glorious being who surrendered into the arms of death all that was mortal about him for their salvation will also love God the Father. Thus, not only is the future increase of Christ's kingdom made sure by the strong passion of immortal love, but heaven also is a place of love between all that enter into its glorious circuit.

3rd. Another reason of the sure increase of the kingdom of Christ is found in the prevalence of wickedness and irreligion in some parts of the earth. As sure as sin now abounds, so sure shall grace much more abound. In this way we turn the arms of the enemy against himself. Satan may foolishly expect the victory, because he has now many provinces of the earth and many children in his own moral likeness scattered everywhere; but this renders the sudden and widespread success of Christ the more certain and inevitable. All that has gone before in the history of godliness among men shall be eclipsed and almost forgotten in the rich glories of a coming day, when the last entrenchment of the devil on earth shall be stormed by the soldiers of the cross, led on by the captain of their salvation.

4th. Another reason why Christ's kingdom must increase is that it is for the glory of God. The strong arm of Almighty power will gloriously defeat the enemy of man on his own ground, and will abase him, and chain him in the sight of his deluded followers, and cast him with his angels and all impenitent sinners into the bottomless pit. For a thousand years the hated form of the old dragon, the deceiver, shall not be seen on earth. Before all eyes in heaven, as well as all below the skies, the glory of God shall be vindicated by the overthrow, the writhings, the chains, and the torments of the old serpent, who has long deceived the nations.

5th. Another reason why we may expect an enlargement of the kingdom of Christ beyond any former parallel is that the ancient people of God, long despised as outcasts and wanderers among the nations, have not yet been gathered into the fullness of the Gentiles. They were cast out of their inheritance by reason of their stubborn and haughty spirit of unbelief; and their casting out was, as it were, life to the Gentile world—yet it is foretold in the sure word of prophecy that their return to the Gospel, which they have rejected for more than eighteen centuries, will be as life from the dead to all the living world. As this chosen people fell from their lofty eminence of religious knowledge, the clouds broke away over the heathen world, and the sun of righteousness shone through the ancient gloom of idolatry and superstition; but when they shall rise again in the grandeur of holy affections, having repented of their great sins, and looked on him whom they pierced and mourn, then shall unspeakable glory from heaven baptize all nations. The followers of the false prophet Mohammed, when they shall see the obstinate nation of Jews turning to God and gathering themselves from their long dispersions, shall abjure their Alcoran and take up the holy oracles as their guide and the Holy Jesus as their true prophet, who alone hath the words of eternal life. The great stumbling block before the chariot of Christianity shall then be removed. The ancient chosen people shall then be no more a scorn and a hissing among men. They have all along been precious in the sight of God, and whatever nation has favored them under the hard bondage which their sins cause them to suffer has apparently been blessed of heaven, while those who have added bitterness and cruelty to their burdens have drunk deeply of the cup of divine vengeance. Woe, woe to the nations who tread on the discarded jewels of Israel. Although in ruins, grandeur makes its high abode with the house of Judah and the house of Israel. The shield of the great Jehovah, veiled from human eyes by a thick cloud of judgment, still blazes like an orb of fire for their defense. Earth and hell are not able to accomplish their extermination, or to amalgamate these dispersed people with strange nations.

If, as many eminent men with apparently high presumption, if not unquestionable evidence, believe, the Indians of the American continent are a part of the long lost ten tribes of Israel, have not the great American nation reason to fear the swift judgments of heaven on them for nameless cruelties, extortions, and exterminations inflicted upon the poor natives of the forest?

We fear the account of national sin, which lies at the doors of the American people, will be a terrible one to balance in the chancery of heaven. America has utterly failed to amalgamate the red man of the woods into the artificial, cultivated ranks of social life. Has not one reason been that it was not the purpose of God that it should be done—for lo, the blood of Israel flowed in the veins of these unshackled, freeborn men?

Oh, when shall the sweet voice of mercy reach all my kindred according to the flesh! When shall the desert break out into songs of praise, loud and high, like the lion cry of Judah's warriors in their day of triumph! When shall the proud, strong, and fleet warriors of the western wilds, the remnants of powerful tribes, come up to the help of the Lord against the man of sin, as strong and as bold for Christ as they are in council, and in deeds of arms! Let us pray for Zion—and let us remember her scattered and peeled people in their sorrowful season of desertion. The lamp of Israel shall burn again, and the star of Judah shall rise again, never to go down, for it will shine over Bethlehem. We here among our scattered and benighted brethren according to the flesh find a reason for the greater increase of the kingdom of Christ, which takes hold of our heart and causes our bowels to yearn in sympathizing sorrow.

Fourthly, we are led to a consideration of some of the events of Providence, leading to, or introductory to, a more glorious increase of the kingdom of Christ.

1st. There will be—yea, there now is—a time of great sorrow and commotion upon the earth. Before Christ will take to himself the entire rule on earth, everything proud and haughty must be abased and brought low. The Savior will not permit of man-worship in his earthly kingdom. He must reign and be worshiped undivided and supreme. The haughty kings of the earth, the proud nobles, the oppressive and unjust governments, must all be dashed to pieces, or brought into a lamblike submission to Christ.

2nd. In effecting this great change among men there will, no doubt, be persecution toward Christianity. As soon as worldly men really perceive for what cause every throne on earth is shaking and distressed with terrifying fears, their anger will burn against Christians. As long as they suppose that all these changes are made by and for the benefit of the cause of liberty or the spirit of reform, they may not persecute Christians; but when the stubborn facts shall convince them that these revolutions, changes, and the shaking of the nations tend to one great end—the advancement of the kingdom of Christ on earth—it will be a wonder if great rage and persecution be not excited. The hope of the church under God is that religion will have attained such strength and prevalence before that discovery, it will not be in the power of wicked men to show their rage with such bloody malice as they would have done had the staff of power remained in their hands. To God alone let his saints look in the day of trouble. One sweet look of Almighty love upon the earth can control the maddening rage of man and fill all creation with the smiles of heavenly benevolence.

In conclusion of this subject we remark (1st.) that it will be in vain for sinners to oppose the increase of Christ's kingdom. There was a strange meaning in those words of the Baptist—*He must increase*. Earth and hell—the congregated hosts of bad men and devils—cannot blot out those words of prophetic import or prevent their fulfillment. The greater the number or the array against truth, the greater will be the overthrow of the enemy and the triumph of Christ—for he shall put all things under his feet. The war-horse and his rider, the spear and the chariot, the cannon and the battle-axe, all are useless against the unseen, spiritual hosts of the Lord. His kingdom grows in the heart; it cometh not by observation, neither can matter obstruct its course; the work of the Lord can increase even under the flames of persecution until the very persecutors in their turn are willing to become martyrs for that Gospel they have opposed. The Gospel takes hold of the heart of man, even while his hands hold the instruments of torture, and in a moment the lion becomes a lamb—the enemy becomes a friend—the opposer becomes an advocate and a martyr.

2nd. It is the duty of Christians more and more to pray, *thy kingdom come;* for every great spiritual good, God will be inquired of by the house of Israel. No great blessing and extension can come to the cause of godliness before much earnest prayer has been made by those whose duty it is to be co-workers together with God in the salvation of a ruined world. Unless Christians pray with earnest agony of desire for the increase of Christ's kingdom, they will feel no gladness when the event has come in its full glory. Praise only can spring from a deep and living interest in the cause. The hymns and anthems of loud joy will only be in the mouths of those who have prayed for the blessed event, with sincerity and perseverance.

3rd. It is the duty of Christians not only to pray but to labor to promote the increase of Christ's kingdom on earth. There is great need of labor as well as encouragement for it. The extraordinary exertions of Christians during the last thirty years have been like a powerful lever, exerting a mighty strength in overthrowing the old foundations of error and sin. Every blow has been effectual: Not one has returned void. And eternity alone shall show how much human instrumentality has had to do with the present encouraging state of things. It is a noble enterprise to conquer the world for Christ. Alexander and Napoleon could not have cherished bolder designs than the soldiers of the cross now have. Their columns are formed; their armor of battle is girded on, and high over their heads float the banners of Jehovah, the

Lord of Hosts. In letters of flame on the banners of the host is inscribed salvation. The trumpet of the Gospel sounds longer and louder. Young men, filled with higher ardor than their fathers were, rise up by thousands and enroll themselves in the army of immortality. The tribes of the wilderness are in motion. They begin to hear their Savior's voice, sweetly sounding like the voice of the turtledove among the waving trees of the forest. Arise, ye nations in your strength, and glorify your Redeemer with a voice that all creation may hear—with a song of praise that shall sound like the roar of many waters.

There are views of great moral sublimity connected with the subject of the increase of the kingdom of Christ. The heart of man is not large enough to conceive of them in all their glorious extent, nor is the intellect of man strong enough to contemplate them in their unveiled majesty.

The increase of the kingdom of Christ has always been of a twofold character. Christ is the foundation stone of his kingdom in two worlds. When the first redeemed sinner was brought into heaven, Christ's peculiar kingdom, which is the kingdom of redemption, commenced there. One by one, the saints before the flood were gathered into it, and Enoch came into it without the smell of the grave upon him. Thousands after thousands have gone to heaven, and every hour there are more following them, until now there are more there than there are on earth. Christ's kingdom above is greater than his kingdom below. When a good man dies and goes away to be here no more, he does not go into a land of strangers; all who have lived, felt like him, and died like him are in the upper world ready to welcome him to the Christian's only true home. All who have any true worth of character are there. There is Moses, the man of God—not in vexation of spirit and mourning because of rebellious countrymen but in glory and strength, more than when he stood on the banks of the Red Sea, parting its water like a wall of crystal on either hand. There are the long line of prophets and the millions who were gathered in under the old dispensation, and there is John the Baptist, the herald of the New Testament, which was to be sealed in holier blood than that of earth. There are the apostles of Christ and the precious early Christians who were hunted in mountains and dens and caves of the earth for their bold testimony for the truth. There are the reformers of a dark age, and the bright lights of the last generation, and the first fruits that have fallen from the shaken fig tree of the present day. All that is good is in heaven. All that is glorious is there. All that is permanent is there. No change comes there—no sickness—no death—no grief—no wasting remorse—no bitter memory—no secret sting—no disturbing jealousy—no envy of the soul, pining away because another is great or beloved. Happiness, like a broad, smiling sky, overspreads and surrounds all the inhabitants of the upper clime. No trumpet of war breaks in upon the groves of eternal rest. No scorching wind from the sandy desert withers the immortal flowers of Paradise. No enemy lurks in the shelter of the balmy trees to murder the chosen of God in secret places. No broken vows and broken hearts are there. No tombstones there to tell the sad tale of mortality and tears. No fields of war are there scathed with the breath of the red artillery, making desolation more desolate. No arrow shot from the Indian's strong bow flies whizzing and hot for blood through the tranquil air of the upper Eden.

If any ask why we linger on such contemplations as these, we answer that the upper world is the very heart of Christ's kingdom—the sum total of all its increase. It is the end of the Christian's journey. All the increase of Christ's kingdom on earth goes to swell the population of heaven. It was what our text meant when it declared that *He must increase*—that earth should be overspread with the knowledge of the Savior, and heaven filled to overflowing with the yellow harvest of souls ripened for glory. The connection between the kingdom of Christ above and the kingdom of salvation below is of a most intimate kind. The minds that belong to the one belong also to the other. The prayer of the one turns into the praise of the other. The cross of the one is the crown of the other; and victory over the flesh, the world, and the devil is inscribed on all the banners of heaven.

The consideration of Christ's upper kingdom is a theme so delightful that we pause longer on it than we should. After tarrying near the regions of bliss, it seems hard to descend and breathe the air of earth again. But from the sublime heights of our contemplations we will descend to where darkness still mingles with the light and nature struggles with grace. We come imploring sinners, with many tears, to look well to their state before the day of mercy shall have passed away. All who do not belong to the kingdom of Christ must, of necessity, belong to the kingdom of the adversary; for there is no middle kingdom. A high wall and a wide gulf separate the two states in the eternal world. Sinners, the day may come when you shall gaze from an unapproachable distance upon scenes of joy and glory and have for yourselves not a drop of water to cool your parched tongues. It is possible, and even very probable, that you may belong to the wrong kingdom. You may be far on the left hand, while some you have despised, and are now despising, may be on the right hand, the heirs of eternal blessedness, filling heaven with melodious music and songs of triumph. It is a bitter thing to trifle away one's own soul and one's own hopes of salvation. It is a fearful thing for a poor feeble worm to oppose single-handed strength against the rolling wheels of a mighty kingdom. The worm must be crushed, for the wheels of eternal empire cannot turn from their course to save the obstinate sinner's head. The steady and overwhelming increase of the kingdom of Christ sounds the knell of death to the incorrigible sinner's hope of impunity. The two ways which pass through the vale of time lead to places far removed from each other—lead to a kingdom of darkness and a kingdom of light and happiness. Let poor sinners beware lest they reach that point from whence there is no more redemption. Let them remember the solemn words—the redemption of the soul is precious, and it ceaseth forever. Let them remember that time hath a fleeting wing and flies terribly swift away to the judgment. Let them call after him with an exceeding loud and mournful cry, and he will not stay for them, nor regard their importunity. Now is the moment for instant reconciliation. A moment's delay is dangerous, for there is an hour in which a man may hate God and holiness, and the next hour he may love God and holiness, or be in eternity an heir of eternal woe. Strike hands, O sinner, with thine adversary, while thou art in the way with him, and be reconciled, lest harm come unto thee, and a great ransom be not able to deliver thee.

We turn from the heartrending prospects of the unholy, who will not be warned and persuaded to turn to Christ, to the sacramental host who have great conquests and triumphs through grace before them. While sinners mourn, saints may rejoice. The windows of heaven are opening in blessings above the heads of devoted Christians. While the wages of unrighteousness are hard, the recompense of those who serve God with all their might is exceedingly great. Great and rich crowns are hung up in heaven for them, and thrones are spread nearby the throne of the Ancient of Days and nearby the throne of the Lamb who died to redeem them from death. It is great gain to belong to Christ. In his blessed service a few days of labor and suffering are rewarded with a crown and a part in a glorious kingdom that hath no end.

Come, then, child of the promises, and share in the battle as thou wouldst share in the victory which is even now achieving over the man of sin. There is a great light of glory descending upon the American church. Revivals follow revivals, and the deep brown wilderness is vocal with the shouting and songs of the delivered tribes, long slaves to error but now emancipated and brought out of the wilderness of sin into the Canaan of Gospel liberty. Would not your hearts, my beloved friends, rejoice to hear the anthems of praise bursting from the hearts of twelve hundred church members in the woods of Canada? Yes, you would thank your heavenly father day and night could you see the same red men who painted themselves fearfully in the late war, sharpened their hatchets, made their knives keen for the scalp, and sought the blood of your soldiers, your women, and your children, now praying for you and blessing your good missionaries, who have followed them into the shadow of the wilderness and besought them to turn to the precious Savior and become heirs of the kingdom of grace. This is but a part of the good and great work, which is indeed so great and vast that the mind is not able to comprehend it all at once. We must look at detached parts and then add up the whole—and then not a thousandth part of the mercy of the Savior to poor, wretched, self-ruined man can be conceived by the human comprehension or told by the human tongue. Let expressive silence muse his praise.

Divine influence hath come down upon the nations, sternly rebuking their sins, and melting them down to tender and generous affections. Bless God for all his goodness, for it shall increase more and more on the earth—

> Till like a sea of glory,
> It spreads from pole to pole.

Amen.

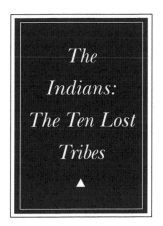

The
Indians:
The Ten Lost
Tribes

▲

In my travels from place to place, I have frequently met with persons who have impiously called in question the being, majesty, power, and justice of the God of the universe. That men have but *finite* conceptions of the *infinite* glory with which the great first cause is surrounded is too well established to admit a single doubt—as reason and good sense, the world over, teach us that we cannot fathom a measureless depth with a measured line.

Some have ever arraigned the *justice* of God. I have been asked, time and again, whether I did not sincerely believe that God had more respect to the white man than to the untutored son of the forest. I answer, and always answer such, in the language of Scripture. "No: God is no respecter of persons." I might meet a question of this kind by proposing another, viz., Is not the white man as sinful by nature as the red man? Uneducated, and unrenewed by divine grace, is he not a heathen, is he not an enemy to God and righteousness, prone to the commission of every crime, however flagrant in its nature and its tendencies? Does not the white man, however gifted, and eloquent, and learned, and popular, grow up and sicken and die?

With thinking men, those whose sentiments are worthy of regard, there is but one opinion, and that is that the soul of the Indian is immortal. And, indeed, the conviction rests with great force on the minds of many intelligent men, men of profound reasoning and deep and studious research, that the Indian tribes, now melting away like dewdrops in the morning's sun, are no less than the remnant of that people, the records of whose history has been blotted out from among the nations of the earth—whose history, if history they have, is a series of cruelties and persecutions without a parallel. That nation, peculiarly and emphatically blessed of God—his own highly favored and chosen people, preserved by the wondrous interposition of divine power, brought up out of Egypt and their cruel bondage by miraculous means, inducted into the promised land flowing with milk and honey, but strong in the purposes of rebellion—their murmurs rose to heaven, calling loudly for vengeance. And when the Savior of sinners made his humble appearance on the earth, to redeem its inhabitants from the thralldom of sin and death and restore them to the favor of heaven, they received him not; they disdained him, simply because he did not come in princely splendor, swaying the conqueror's scepter of blood and carnage, and dominion over the nations. They cried out, "He is not the Christ, crucify him, crucify him," and nailed the Lord of the universe to the cross. They, like Pharaoh, hardened their hearts. Suddenly, the storm of divine wrath overtook them—their city, over which he who suffered on the cross had shed the tears of sorrow, was razed to the ground, and the once warlike and powerful nation of Jews melted away before the overwhelming and countless legions of foes that rose up to chastise and crush them.

That the Indians are indeed no other than the descendants of the ten lost tribes, the subscriber has no doubt. He is one of the few remaining descendants of a once powerful tribe of Indians, and he looks forward with a degree of confidence to the day as being not far distant when ample justice shall be done the red man by his white brother—when he shall be allowed that station in the scale of being and intelligence which unerring wisdom designed him to occupy.

It is a matter of deep and lasting regret that the character of the Indians, who occupied this widespread and goodly heritage, when men of pale faces came over the pierceless solitudes of the mighty ocean, with their large canoes, and were received with all the kindly feelings of native innocence—I say that it is deeply to be regretted that their character should be so grossly misrepresented and misunderstood. They have been accused of cruelty and perfidy of the basest nature—of crimes and vices of the most degrading cast. Again and again are the people of this happy land referred back to the period of its early settlement, and their attention directed to the smoking ruins of villages and the cries of suffering and distress. Scenes like these, I grant, are sufficient to harrow up the mind; but in contemplating the sufferings of their early brethren, the whites seem almost to forget the corroding sorrows of the poor Indians—the wrongs and calamities which were heaped upon them. Follow them into the deep recesses of their wilderness solitudes, hear their long and loud complaints, when driven by the pale faces whom they had kindly received, and cheerfully, in the fullness of their friendship, sustained through days and months of sorrow, and want, and affliction, from their happy homes, the resting place of their fathers. Can you wonder, friends, that they should have resisted, manfully, against the encroachment of their white neighbors?

But I think that history declares that, when this continent was first discovered, that its inhabitants were a harmless, inoffensive, obliging people. ✓ They were alike free from the blandishments and vices of civilized life. They received the strangers from the "world beyond the waters" with every token of esteem; high-minded, noble, generous, and confident to a fault, they placed implicit confidence in the professions of their visitors; they saw not the aim and design of the white man, and the chains of a cruel bondage were firmly entwined around them before the illusion was dispelled; and when their eyes were opened, they beheld naught as the portion of their cup but servitude and sorrow. Hundreds of thousands perished before the face of the white man. Suffice it to say, what is already known, that the white man came upon our shores—he grew taller and taller until his shadow was cast over all the land—in its shade the mighty tribes of olden time wilted away. A few, the remnant of multitudes long since gathered to their fathers, are all that remain; and they are on their march to eternity.

Wm. Apess

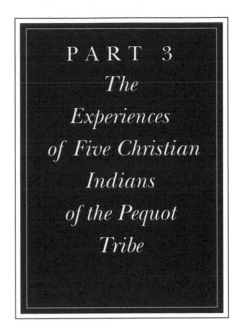

PART 3

The
Experiences
of Five Christian
Indians
of the Pequot
Tribe

The Experiences of Five Christian Indians of the Pequot Tribe (1833) may be, in its first edition, the most artfully constructed of Apess's books. The narration of his own life, which opens the book, articulates an almost unqualified condemnation of white people for what they have done to the natives of the continent. In form an account of his conversion, it is in effect an exploration of the barriers to achieving an affirmative identity as a Native American in the eastern United States in the first third of the nineteenth century.

The five conversion accounts which make up the main body of the book can be read as a variation on this theme, though in each of them the discovery that Christianity can be a faith open to all people is formative. With the important exception of Aunt Sally George, all of these people were effectively orphans and either raised in the households of whites or economically bound to them by other means. But for Aunt Sally, all of them can achieve a Christian faith only by overcoming not only the indifference of most whites to the state of Indian souls but also the unapologetic racism practiced by white professors of Christianity. How could an Indian espouse a faith which itself was used to justify his or her oppression? Hannah Caleb strikes this note, which recurs throughout the book: "the poor Indians, the poor Indians, the people to whom I was wedded by the common ties of nature, were set at naught by those professors of grace, merely because we were Indians." The power of Christian faith, then, is shown to be manifested not in whites but in each of these converts, who are, with it, able to overcome the enmity they feel toward white people and love them despite the absence of any reciprocation.

The life of Aunt Sally George is situated so as to heighten the impact of the critique of whites and of their limited grasp of the religion by which they mean to justify their claims to superiority over Native Americans. Her saintliness impresses itself in no small measure through Apess's reiteration that she was regarded as holy by all who encountered her, white people and Indians. She becomes almost luminous in the text in her power to overcome what the reader has come to understand as the nearly insuperable blindness and hypocrisy of white Christians. Though her account lacks the overt critique of the others, it, too, indicates the personal devastation of being a member of a despised and subordinated group. The conversion crisis in Aunt Sally George's life involves her decision to take her own life when she was a young woman and her being lifted by her prayers to Christ. She does not explain what moved her despair, but at this point in the book a reader needs no elaboration.

The placement of the final conversion account, Anne Wampy's, suggests the subtlety of Apess's grasp of Euro-Americans' images of Indians. Anne Wampy is a drunk, a basket maker, old and poverty-stricken, without children, as clearly at the end of the line as one might get. Only the intensity of her hatred of white people might modulate these enclosing stereotypes. Her conversion near the end of her life becomes, however, not a rejection of Indian ways but an overcoming of the oppression of white people, which she has internalized.

"Conversion," which for most white readers would conventionally have read as a synonym for assimilation, becomes the medium, instead, for an affirmation of Indian pride and autonomy. And whites, not Indians, become those in need of conversion. By expropriating the very language of white justification and turning it back upon them, Apess also engages in a linguistic conversion. His deliberate reversals of the vocabulary of subordination become explicit in the concluding essay, "An Indian's Looking-Glass for the White Man." Christ as a Jew is recalled as a man of color and whites as the most degraded people in his day. Those in need of conversion become the white "civilizers"; the true Christians, by both heritage and practice, become Native Americans: "If you can find a spirit like Jesus Christ and his Apostles prevailing now in any of the white congregations, I should like to know it."

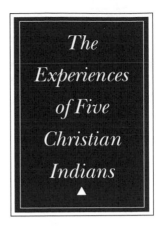

The Experiences of Five Christian Indians

▲

The Experience of the Missionary

It is not my intention to descend to particulars in this pamphlet, any farther than to notice the origin of my life for the purpose of giving the youth a transient view between their condition and mine; or those poor children of the forest, who have had taken from them their once delightful plains and homes of their peaceful habitations; their fathers and mothers torn from their dwellings, and they left to mourn, and drop a tear, and die, over the ruins of their ancient sires. Perhaps you may ask, Why is this? I answer, because of deception and power, assisted with the fiery waters of the earth—rum. Such, my young friends, was the case of this poor self-taught Indian youth, whose experiences you are about to read.

My parentage, according to the custom of the country, was none of the least—being the descendant of a chief, or the head officer of the nation. But this availed nothing with me; the land of my fathers was gone; and their characters were not known as human beings but as beasts of prey. We were represented as having no souls to save, or to lose, but as partridges upon the mountains. All these degrading titles were heaped upon us. Thus, you see, we had to bear all this tide of degradation, while prejudice stung every white man, from the oldest to the youngest, to the very center of the heart.

It was thought no crime for old and young to hiss at the poor Indians, the noblest work of God, who had met with great misfortunes, and lost everything they had, by those very persons who despised them; yea, look which way they would, they could see no friends, nor even hear a pleasant sound from the lips of the white. Yea, there was but little help for them.

When you read this, ask yourselves if ever you had such trials. If not, begin now to prize your privileges and show pity to those whose fates are wretched and cruel. I shall now enter more fully upon my experience in childhood. It will be well to speak to the point; I shall make but few remarks here, as I intend publishing, should the Lord spare my life, a book of 300 pages, 18 mo. in size; and there the reader will find particulars respecting my life.[1]

My parents were of the same disposition of the Indians, that is, to wander to and fro. And, although my father was partly white, yet he had so much of the native blood that he fashioned after them in traveling from river to river, and from mountain to mountain, and plain to plain, on their journey.

I was born at Colrain, Massachusetts, A.D. 1798, on the 30th day of January.[2] We lived here but a few months and then removed to Colchester, Connecticut, within about twelve miles of our native tribe; and there, to my sad misfortune, my father and mother parted, I being at this time but a babe, being not more than three years old, and I saw my mother's face no more for twenty years. I was then placed with my grandparents on my mother's side, who, my readers, were not the best people in the world: for they would at times drink New England rum, and then I was neglected. How awful it is to have parents who will drink spirituous liquors or alcohol and, by that, to neglect their dear little children and leave them to suffer. You will see how much I had to suffer on the account of rum.

During my stay with the old folks our fare was hard, there being five children of us, and our fare was about equal as to earthly comforts. Sometimes we had something to eat, and at other times nothing. Many are the times in which we have gone to bed supperless, to rest our little weary limbs, stretched upon a bundle of straw, and how thankful we were for this comfort; and in the morning we were thankful to get a cold potato for our breakfasts. We thought it good fare. There was a white man who lived about a mile off, and he would, at times, bring us some frozen milk, which for a time supplied the calls of nature. We suffered thus from the cold; the calls of nature, as with almost nakedness; and calumny heaped upon us by the whites to an intense degree.

Little children, how thankful you ought to be that you are not in the same condition that we were, that you have not a nation to hiss at you, merely because your skins are white. I am sure that I rejoice for you, that it is not the case. But to proceed: At a certain time, when my grandmother had been out among the whites, with her baskets and brooms, and had fomented herself with the fiery waters of the earth, so that she had lost her reason and judgment and, in this fit of intoxication, raged most bitterly and in the meantime fell to beating me most cruelly; calling for whips, at the same time, of unnatural size, to beat me with; and asking me, at the same time, question after

1. This seems unambiguously a reference to *A Son of the Forest,* not to an entirely new and second autobiography, and thus suggests that some, if not most, of "The Experience of the Missionary" was drafted before the writing of *A Son of the Forest* in 1828/29.
2. January 31 is the date he gives in *A Son of the Forest.*

question, if I hated her. And I would say yes at every question; and the reason why was because I knew no other form of words. Thus I was beaten, until my poor little body was mangled and my little arm broken into three pieces, and in this horrible situation left for a while. And had it not been for an uncle of mine, who lived in the other part of the old hut, I think that she would have finished my days; but through the goodness of God, I was snatched from an untimely grave.

The white man will say, "What cruel creatures, to use children so!" If I could see that this blame was attached to the poor degraded Indians, I should not have one word to say. But when not a whit of it belongs to them, I have the more to say. My sufferings certainly were through the white man's measure; √ for they most certainly brought spirituous liquors first among my people. For surely no such sufferings were heard of, or known among our people, until the burning curse and demon of despair came among us: Surely it came through the hands of the whites. Surely the red man had never sought to destroy one another as this bane of hell would! And we little babes of the forest had to suffer much on its account. Oh white man! How can you account to God for this? Are you not afraid that the children of the forest will rise up in judgment and condemn you?

Little children, if you have parents that drink the fiery waters, do all you can, both by your tears and prayers and friendly admonitions, to persuade them to stop; for it will most certainly ruin them, if they persist in it. But to proceed: I did not long continue in this situation but was relieved from it by my uncle making his complaint to the selectmen of the town, who took up my case and placed me for a while among some of the white neighbors, until I was healed of my wounds, although it was a year before I was able to help myself much without aid. Being now about five or six years old, it was agreed upon that I should live with this white family until I had arrived at the age of twenty-one. They, being Baptist people and having no children of their own, became more fond of me than is usual for people to be of adopted children and treated me with the utmost kindness, and particularly Mrs. Furman, who was very kind and generous. And as they had agreed to send me to school, accordingly, when I had arrived at the age of six years, they sent me to school. And this they continued to do for six successive winters, which was about all the education that I received. The amount of benefit which I have received from this, none can tell. To God be all the praise.

Things began now to wear a different aspect; and my little heart began again to be expanded, and I began to be inquisitive about many things. At times, the children of God would assemble around me, to worship the Great Spirit, something new to me. Of course I listened with great attention. Their songs were sweet, and as the oil of joy no doubt was in their hearts to indite their petitions, to nerve their admonitions, to send home the word to the hearts of those who heard it, doubtless made it the more interesting. And so it caught my youthful heart, being a constant hearer of these things. And my mind became more knitted together with them. And I would question Mrs. Furman respecting these things. She would give me a great many good, wholesome admonitions and tell me the young must die as well the old, and often point me to the graveyard and cite me to small graves and warn me to prepare to die. It would leave a powerful effect upon my mind, which was not easily effaced. I recollect the first time I visited a chapel for the worship of God. It being a new place, and looking to me somewhat fine to the eye, I took great liberties, was something like a country clown passing through populous villages and cities, staring all the while upon those fine piles of buildings which he saw, or like a rabble of boys and girls going to church to hear the Indian preach: something so indeed, and so much so that I lost my balance of behavior. And when I returned I received a short address, accompanied with a handsome present, that I have not yet forgotten; it weighed well with me, so that forever afterward I was enabled to keep my balance well. It would be well for heads of families to supply their children with such presents, when needed; it would save the country from much disgrace. But to proceed: When I was about eight years old, the preaching of the Gospel powerfully affected my mind, although I was ignorant of the plan of salvation through Jesus Christ; but I had no doubt but the word was spoken with divine authority, which not only drew tears of contrition from *me* but from many others. But being small, and of little note in the world, no one supposed that I wanted religion.

In those days, the aged thought the youth were not subjects of grace; such is the fact, although it may be surprising to many; so there was none to comfort the little Indian boy. How different now! Lord, help the youth who are exalted to heaven in point of privileges so to prize them, that they might not be thrust down to hell.

I would remark here that many rise up against this doctrine; but why not rise up against, or in opposition to, the state's prison and house of correction and even the gallows itself? These are places to punish the people for their crimes. Some say their crimes are punished here; indeed, this is a new doctrine. Whoever saw a crime in the state's prison, locked up to hard labor; or whoever saw a crime hung up by the neck? How absurd, then, to delineate such doctrine. Crime is crime and stands for what is, let scoffers say what they will; may grace be imparted to enlighten our eyes. But to return: For the profiting of the youth, I would speak a little further of the exercises of my mind. Although they could not believe that I wanted religion, yet the Spirit of the Lord followed me daily; and my mind was so overwhelmed that I could hardly contain myself to rest without giving vent to my feelings. But little did the people with whom I lived think that I was serious about a future state; and although I could weep to be at church, yet they would deny me at times, saying I only wanted to look at the boys and play with them. Those sudden rebuffs would dampen my serious thoughts, and I would turn away to wicked paths of vice and unite with wicked boys and break the Sabbath, by wandering to and fro about the swamps, hedges, ponds, and brooks, sporting with whatever came in our way. But when I came home at night and retired to rest, the darkness itself was a terror to me, as I would picture to my imagination that the fiends of night stood around me, ready to devour me. Then I would cry to the Lord to have mercy upon my poor soul and promise him, if he would spare me, I would do better. But, when the darkness was past, I, like Pharaoh, forgot my promise: Thus I was led on by wicked youths until I was almost ruined, until I was persuaded to leave my home and wander to and fro to seek my bread. This displeased Mr. Furman; he, supposing I had become discontented, had sought me out another place, without my consent, which displeased me and made me more discontented than ever, I being at this time about ten years of age, entirely unfit to choose for myself. But so it was; I was alone in the world, fatherless, motherless, and helpless, as it were, and none to speak for the poor little Indian boy. Had my skin been white, with the same abilities and the same parentage, there could not have been found a place good enough for me. But such is the case with depraved nature, that their judgment for fancy only sets upon the eye, skin, nose, lips, cheeks, chin, or teeth and, sometimes, the forehead and hair; without any further examination, the mind is made up and the price set. This is something like buying chaff for wheat, or twigs of wood for solid substance.

But to proceed with our story: The place that he had procured for me was with a people professing religion that belonged to the Presbyterian church, and withal very strict. They also thought much of themselves, he being formerly a judge, likewise a member of Congress, in the House of Representatives, and had sufficient to supply all the common calls of life, for all his household.[3] I went to try my new home; and while there on trial, they used me pretty fairly, made me a few presents suited to please children, etc. They had now secured my favor, as they thought; the agreement was now made that I should have clothing and schooling, so as to read and write, and plenty of work. Now this man is what is generally called an enlightened Christian.

But let us look at his proceedings and see if he was actuated by the spirit of Christ or the custom of the day: Hear, and then decide. And there was work

---

3. Judge Hillhouse in fact sat in the Continental Congress, never the House of Representatives.

enough. This part of the bargain was completely fulfilled on his part, and that was all. As to my fare, it was none of the best, though middling: It was not so bad as I have seen—I mean my table fare and lodging—but when we came to the clothing part, it was mean enough, I can assure you. I was not fit to be seen anywhere among decent folks, and of course there was no meeting for me to attend, although I had a desire. But this good man did not care much about the Indian boy. He wished to hear me read: I could make out to spell a few words, and the judge said, "You are a good reader." I hope he was a better judge at law. Now, some may think me hard, but truth will stand.

Now, the judge had family prayers and was exact in having all his family to hear him pray; so he would always have a repetition of words, and I soon could pray as well as he; and of course I did not care for his prayers any longer. I would remark, however, that a colored woman, who had lived with the judge for many years, told me that he once prayed, though previous to it there was one of the most powerful thunderstorms that ever was known in these parts; and after he had made that prayer he forgot to pray again.[4] I expect there are many such in the world. But to proceed: The poor little Indian boy, when the Sabbath came, had nowhere to go to worship God, and so, like all other little boys who are left alone in the world, would stroll about the lots and meditate upon past times and listen to the little songsters of the forest, which would chaunt the praise of God for me, while there was none to take me by the hand and lead me to the holy place or to the fountain of blessedness. Now, if my face had been white, it would have been a town talk. But as it was an Indian face, no matter whether it was dirty or poor or whether I had clothing or not. But the judge has gone to the great Judge above, who will do right. I would not live with him, and he sold me, as a farmer would sell his sheep for the slaughter, without any of my knowledge whatever, to Mr. Williams, of New London; and through hypocrisy alone they carried me along to my place of destination. I had now arrived at the age of about eleven years and a half, and now I found that I had a new home; and in fact, I was not so much displeased with it as some might suppose, for now I found myself in a comfortable situation—enough to eat and drink, and things comfortable to wear—whereas before I was quite destitute of many things. This improvement somewhat settled my mind, and I became more contented. But soon I found that all his household wished me to become their servant, from the cook to the clerk. This I did not stomach well; it was too much for one to bear, to call every man "master." I thought it beneath my dignity; of course, there

4. The contrast Apess is drawing is between rote and spontaneous prayers. For an evangelical, the only genuine prayer comes from the heart, not from memorization. The jab at the judge is sharp, for only once has he been known to utter a "real" prayer and that because he was so frightened by a thunderstorm as to give it out involuntarily.

was war in the wigwam—who should be master. But Mr. Williams settled with us all, and with me in particular, as he said he meant to make me a good boy, but at the same time told me that I must obey the heads of his family, and all this was perfectly right; and some good, I think, was accomplished. However, I never cried out like the poor African, "Massa, Massa—Mister, Mister," but called them by their regular names.

Things now went on smoothly for some time. The general and his family generally attended the Congregational church or society on the Sabbath, to hear the word of God dispensed; though neither he nor his family were religious, yet they used to be often there; and their example was good so far as it went; and so I had an opportunity to attend with them. My mind was much occupied about those who preach the Gospel, there being a difference between those who preach and those who read.[5] I could discover this; the preaching that I formerly attended was with divine power, which made the language of the speaker eloquent and sublime, and withal called the attention of those who heard it to seek the salvation of their souls; while that of the latter, being a selection of fine sentences, and read off in an elegant style, which only seemed to please the ear and lull the people to sleep. How much better, then, to study and trust in God than to study and trust to head and pen; for a curse is pronounced upon all such: "Cursed is he that putteth his trust in an arm of flesh." And what is the difference whether a preacher puts it in his own arm or the arm of his neighbor? Now, I have not said this because I am biased by any sectarian principle whatever; I should condemn it in one sect as much as in another. But what said our Lord? He said to his servants, "Go and preach the Gospel to every creature." Why did he not say, "Go, read my Gospel to every creature?" Therefore, no man who reads his sermon can be justified in so doing; for Jesus has said, "Now are ye my disciples, if ye do whatsoever I have commanded you." And if they who are the servants of God go astray, and do wrong continually, and place things where they ought not to be, no wonder the churches are all the time in commotion. But to proceed:

After I had attended the meeting a while, I had a desire to attend Methodist meeting, in the same neighborhood. This was altogether new to me; but it was interesting to attend them, and so much so that I desired to be a constant attendant of them. By these meetings I was led to look more into the plan of salvation, that it was free for all: "Whosoever would, let him come and take of the waters of life freely."

It was now that the Lord began to revive his work. The powers of darkness began to gather round, that the light of the Gospel might be shut out. Beelzebub was busy, both day and night, to prevent good. He employed

---

5. That is, between those who preach without a written text and those who read their sermons.

all that would work for him, from the pharisee to the educated scholar in the desk, even down to the peasant and drunkard that reeled around in gutters and mud puddles in the street. It was now that these people had to suffer much; they were openly called the scum and filth of the earth, deceivers, and, in a word, all the calumny that could be heaped upon them, by those who ought to have known better. It was said that it was a disgrace for any character of respectability to attend these meetings. But I can say this much about it; I believe it arose from sectarian bigots. Not that I could suppose that they (the Methodists) were free from it, but have as much as their neighbors; and it is the case with all sects, that they are more or less bigoted. And if they are, they need not join with the devil's crew, to do all the hurt they can to one another. This, to me, does not look much like religion.

But the work of God rolled on, like an overwhelming flood. Persecution seemed to cement the hearts of the brethren and sisters together, and their songs were sweet. Their prayers and exhortations were like arrows sticking in the heart of their King's enemy, while the preachers poured the thunders of the law upon them, as if God himself had spoken to them, as he did to the children of Israel from Mount Sinai, that they should fear and tremble at his word.

My heart now became much troubled, and I felt determined to seek the salvation of my soul, for their sayings did not affect me much (although they did not want me to attend their meetings), though I had neither respectability nor character to lose but was like the partridge upon the mountain, a mark for them all to shoot at, and hiss at, and quack at—which often put me in mind of the geese and crows.[6]

But, notwithstanding, this sectarian nonsense raged most bitterly, and I do suppose that they who could help it would not be willing for their dogs to go there to meeting, for fear of bringing disgrace upon themselves. I would to God that people were more consistent than what they are. Say, would you like to lose everything that was near and dear to you, merely because your skin is white? I had to do it, merely because I had a red one. Judge ye, if this is right; and if not, stop where you are, and cease to do evil and learn to do well. But again, as I had no character to lose, I became a constant attendant on these meetings, and although a sinner before God, yet I had no disposition to make sport of the people of God or his word. Why I mention this is because so many go on purpose to sport with one another and make derision of the people of God, and those, too, who call themselves gentlemen and ladies. Such, how-

---

6. The pronouns can confuse here. "Their sayings" are those of the "respectable," like the Williamses who scorned the Methodists as vulgar and disreputable, while "their meetings" are those of the Methodists who welcomed the boy.

ever, disgrace themselves and are, in the judgment of good men, and their Maker, below the beasts of the field. Shame! shame! shame! to be so indecent, who boast of so much correctness and purity! But, notwithstanding the people would be so bad, yet the "Lord had respect unto his people, and his ears were open to the cries of his servants, and his ears were open to their supplication"; and in answer to prayer, he was pleased to revive his work; the Holy Ghost moved upon the face of the congregation; and his children were built up, and gathered strength at every meeting, and were built up in the most holy faith of the Gospel, and soon the power of the Holy Ghost fell powerfully among the people, so that the cries of the wounded were distinctly heard at every part of the house. The great Physician of souls was present, to heal all that would come to him and seek his favor. Thus the work of God went on most powerfully, so much so that Satan and his army retreated, at times, before it; and then would gather around it like a thick cloud of darkness, and mimic the catamount, or owls of the forest, or the young lion, which had lost its mother, and roaring to be answered. But the Lord assisted his servants to overcome them, through the word of his testimony.

It was now that conviction settled upon my mind, more and more; and I was more serious than usual. But being young, only about fourteen years of age, was somewhat flighty; though when I considered how great a sinner I was before God, and how often I had grieved the good Spirit of the Lord, my distress for mercy was very great.

At one of these meetings I was induced to laugh, not because I wanted to but to hide my distress from those around me. Being among the young people, I did not wish for them to know it; but such was my seriousness that it could not be hid, and I became affected, even unto tears, until they coursed down my cheeks like rain. And when the bold persecutors saw it, they inquired if I was one of the Lamb's people.

Brother Hill was at this time preaching from these words: "Behold the Lamb of God, who taketh away the sins of the world." He spoke feelingly of his (Christ's) sufferings on the cross; of his precious blood, that flowed like a purifying river from his side; of his sustaining the accumulated weight of the sins of the whole world; and dying to satisfy the demands of justice, which could only be appeased by an infinite atonement. I felt convinced that Christ had died for all mankind; that age, sect, color, country, or situation made no difference. I felt assured that I was included in the plan of redemption, with all my brethren. No one can conceive with what joy I hailed this new doctrine, as it was called. It removed all my excuses, and I freely believed that all I had to do was to look in faith upon the Lamb of God, who made himself a free-will offering for unregenerated and wicked souls, upon the cross. My spirits were depressed; my crimes were arrayed before me; and no tongue can tell the anguish of soul I felt. After meeting, I returned home with a heavy heart, determined to seek the salvation of my soul.

This night I slept but little; at times I would be melted down into tenderness and tears; and then again, my heart would seem as hard as adamant. I was awfully tempted; the evil one would try to persuade me that I was not in the pale of mercy. I fancied that evil spirits stood around my bed; my condition was deplorable, and awful; and I longed for day to break, as much as the tempest-tossed mariner, who expected every moment to be washed from the wreck he fondly clings to; so it was with me, upon the wreck of the world, buffeted by Satan, assailed by the world; sometimes in despair; then believing against hope; my heart, at times, seemed almost broke, while the tears of contrition coursed down my cheeks like rain.

But sin was the cause of all this, and no wonder; I groaned and wept; I had often sinned, and my accumulated transgressions had piled themselves as a rocky mountain upon my heart; and how could I endure it? The weight thereof seemed to crush me down; in the night seasons, I had fearful visions, and would often start from my sleep and gaze around the room, as I was ever in dread of seeing the evil one ready to carry me off. I continued in this frame of mind for more than seven weeks. My distress, finally, became so acute that the family took notice of it; some of them persecuted me because I was serious and fond of attending meetings. Now persecution raged on every hand, within and without; and I had none to take me by the hand and say, "Go with us and we will do you good." But in the midst of difficulties, so great to one only little more than fourteen years of age, I ceased not to pray for the salvation of my soul: Very often my exercises were so great that sleep departed from me. I was fearful that I should wake up in hell. And one night I was in bed mourning, like the dove for her absent mate, I fell into a doze. I thought I saw the world on fire; it resembled a large bed of coals, red, and glowing with heat; I shall never forget the impression it made upon my mind. No tongue can tell or possibly describe the agony of my soul; for now I was greatly in fear of dropping into hell, that awful place, where the smoke of their torments ascendeth up forever and ever. I cried earnestly for mercy; then I was carried to another place where perfect happiness seemed to pervade every part, and the inhabitants thereof. Oh, how I longed to be among them and partake of their happiness. I sighed to be freed from pain and misery; I knew that nothing but the attenuated thread of life kept me from sinking into the awful lake which I beheld. I cannot think it is in the power of human language to describe the feelings that rushed upon my mind at that moment, or thrilled through my veins; everything seemed to bear the signet of reality. When I awoke, I was glad to find it was a vision and not a reality. I went on from day to day, with my head bowed down, seeking the Savior of sinners, but without success. The heavens appeared to be brass; my prayers wanted the wings of faith to waft them to the skies. The disease of my heart increased; the heavenly Physician had not stretched forth his hand and poured upon my soul the panacea of the Gospel; the scales had not fallen from my eyes; and no ray of celestial light had dispelled the darkness that had gathered around my soul; the cheering sound of sincere friendship fell not upon my ear. It seemed as if I was friendless, unpitied, and unknown; and at times I wished to become a dweller in the wilderness. Who can wonder, then, that I was almost in despair, surrounded by difficulties and apparent dangers? But I was resolved to seek the salvation of my soul with all my heart; to trust entirely to the Lord and, if I failed, to perish pleading for mercy at the foot of the throne. I now hung all my hopes upon the Redeemer, and clung with indescribable tenacity to the cross, on which he purchased salvation for my soul, "the vilest of the vile." The result was such as is always to be expected, when a lost and ruined sinner throws himself entirely on the Lord—*perfect freedom.* On the 15th day of *March,* in the year of our Lord, 1813, I heard a voice saying unto me, in soft and soothing accents, "*Arise, thy sins that are many are all forgiven thee; go in peace and sin no more.*" There was nothing very singular, save that the Lord stooped to lift me up, in my conversion.

I had been sent into the garden to work, and while there, I lifted up my heart to God, when, all at once, my burden and fears left me; my soul was filled with love; love to God, and love to all mankind. Oh, how my poor heart swelled with joy! And I would cry, "Glory to God in the highest." There was not only a change in my heart but everything around me. The scene was entirely changed; the works of God praised him, and I saw in everything that he had made his glory shine. My love now embraced the whole human family; the children of God, I loved most dearly. Oh, how I longed to be with them; and when any of them passed me, I would gaze at them until they were lost in the distance. I could have pressed them to my bosom, as they were more precious to me than gold, and I was always loath to part with them whenever we met together. The change, too, was visible in my very countenance. I enjoyed great peace of mind, and that peace was like a river, full, deep, and wide, and flowing continually. My mind was employed in contemplating the works of God and in praising his holy name. I dwelt so particularly upon his mercy and goodness that I could praise him aloud, even in my sleep, and when I awoke, it was glory to God and the Lamb, and my heart burnt continually with the love of God. Well might the poet say,

O for such love, let rocks and hills
    Their lasting silence break;
And all harmonious human tongues
    The Savior's praises speak.

I continued in this happy frame of mind for some time; it was very pleasant to live in the enjoyment of pure and undefiled religion, and naught could I see but seas of rest and waves of glory before me. I wanted only the wings of angels to waft me to Paradise, that I might dwell around the throne of God forever. But alas! I dwelt in a tent below, that held me fast and would not let me go, and here to resist the fiend, the Christian's foe—to war, and tug, and toil at the oar of prayer, till time with me no more should be; and then, if faithful to my Lord, with all the faithful saints should be.

But here I can say, I had none to make me the object of their care, to encourage me to press forward in the ways of well doing. But, on the other hand, persecution raged most bitterly, and soon I was deprived of that privilege that was near and dear to me: such as the privilege of class meetings, and other means of grace, that are usually among the Methodists; and being young, I was again led astray. How hard it is to be robbed of all our earthly rights and deprived of the means of grace, merely because the skin is of a different color; such had been the case with me.[7] I would ask the white man if he thinks that he can be justified in making just such a being as I am, or any other person in the world, unhappy; and although the white man finds so much fault because God has made us thus, yet if I have any vanity about it, I choose to remain as I am, and praise my Maker while I live that an Indian he has made.

But again: The burden that was heaped upon me, at this time, was more than I could bear, being only about fifteen years old, and I now began to relapse back again into my former state. I now became acquainted with wicked and silly youths, and one of them whose name was *Miner* and myself agreed to try some other parts of the world. Children as we were, we made the best arrangements for our journey that we could; and so off we started and steered our course for New York. With difficulties and fears, we arrived there. Many of the people thought that we were sailor boys, as we informed them that we had been privateering and had been taken and set on a shore near New London and were going home to New York, to our parents; and it being wartime, we informed the people all we knew about it. When we had arrived at New York City, and almost alone in the world, and but little economy to take care of ourselves, we thought best to engage in the war.[8] So I became a musician in the army, while my comrade went on board of a privateer.

We now parted, and I went with the soldiers to Canada, where I experi-

---

7. In the 1837 edition this is revised to "with us poor colored people." At the end of this paragraph a similar revision implicates his experience with that of all people of color: "that Indians he has made."

8. The War of 1812. Apess enlisted in April 1813 when he was fifteen.

enced all the horrors of war; fought in the great Battle of Lake Champlain, with General McComb, with Hampton and Wilkinson, at the Mills. After the war was over, I went to Montreal and from thence to upper Canada, Fort Niagara; from thence to Kingston, and through the wilderness, and saw many of my brethren, who ornamented the wood with their camps and chanted the wild beasts of prey with their songs.[9] Being now satisfied with these regions and their curiosities, I now began to think of home and those kindred friends who had long before buried me beneath the sods of the forest, to behold my face no more forever here, being gone so long, nearly five years.

This journey was not instructing to the paths of virtue but of vice— though I did not forget the past, and often recollected those happy moments, and sighed on account of my condition, but had no heart to pray, no pious parents to instruct me, no minister of God's holy word to notice me and pour into my ear the blessed truths of God, but a poor, destitute, helpless child of the forest, all alone in the world, as it were. I now made the best of my way home to my kindred in the flesh, and when I arrived there, I found them surprised and rejoiced to see me on this side of the grave. After a while I became more steady and began once more to attend the worship of God, and had a desire to return for my backsliding state to the worship of God, that I might enjoy his smiles again. For it was now that I had become wretched and miserable through the deceitfulness of sin, and bad examples of the white soldiers, and nothing but thick darkness gathered around me; and, apparently, my situation was worse than before. It was now harder to seek the Lord than it was when I was young, for now my sins were redoubled; and it appeared indeed that there was no mercy for me. And when I went to pray and call upon God for mercy, I was met by the enemy of souls, who very readily thrusted a dart at me filled with a message of despair, that there was nothing but eternal death for me; that I had committed the unpardonable sin, by having sinned against the Holy Ghost, and it was all in vain for me to try again for help in God; that he was sure that I should make up his host in hell.[10]

My distress became more acute than ever; but I attended the meetings where God's children meet and at last I made known my distress to them; and they, the dear children of God, comforted me, by saying that Christ would have mercy upon the worst of sinners, and encouraged me to pray; and then prayed with and for me.

---

9. Apess was around the Bay of Quinte in Ontario, with either a community of Mohawks on the northeast shore or a community of Mississaugas on the southwest shore.

10. The unpardonable sin was despair, that is, to believe that one's own sin and sinfulness were greater than God's love and power.

I sought the Lord for weeks and months, and at last I began to see that I had received some of his divine approbation: To say that I immediately had as clear an evidence as I had before, I cannot. But when I acknowledged myself a sinner before the people and confessed what a sinner I had been, then the light of God's countenance broke into my soul, and I felt as if I were on the wings of angels and ready to leave this world. I united with the Methodists, and was baptized by immersion, and strove to walk with them in the way to heaven, and can say that I spent many happy hours with them in the worship of God; and to this day, I most heartily rejoice that I was brought again from the dead to praise God. After a while, I began to exercise my gift in the way of prayer and exhortation and was blest in so doing. I began to be exercised more abundantly about the salvation of precious souls and began to have a desire to call sinners to repentance in a public way; and it appeared I could not rest in any other way. But I knew that I was weak and ignorant as to the letter; and not only so, I was already a hissing-stock and a byword in the world, merely because I was a child of the forest; and to add any more occasion to the weak and scornful family of the whites was more than I wished to do; but there was no peace for me, either by day or night. Go I must, and expose my ignorance to the world, and strive to preach, or exhort sinners to repentance. I soon found men like adders, with poison under their tongues, hissing around me; and to this day, I find now and then one hissing at me. My trials again were many, and apparently more than I could bear; but I entreated of God to show me my duty and prayed to him for a token of his grace, when I went to call sinners to repentance. The Lord heard my prayer, and sent down his awakening power, and convinced sinners of the error of their ways; but I was too unbelieving, believing that I was not the character that God should take to thresh the mountains of sin. The angel of the Lord appeared to me in the visions of the night and read some extracts of John's Gospel. It appeared that before me there was a plain, and upon that the sun shone delightfully; but it was a difficult place for me to reach, being a dark and winding way, through mire, but I reached it; here I was encouraged by the angel to persevere. It was now, when I awoke, that I was troubled still the more; and night and day it was preach, preach, though many thought it would be a miracle for such an ignorant creature as I to preach the Gospel. But it is a fact that I had a difficult road to travel before I really got to preaching; but I can say that I have seen the salvation of the Lord in so doing, and God has made me, the unworthiest of all his servants, the humble, happy instrument in bringing many to bow at his scepter. To him be all the glory forever.

I would now say that I have been a regular member in the Methodist Episcopal and Protestant Methodist church for about nine years; in the Methodist Episcopal church I was an exhorter for eighteen months. I left them in good standing, and with good credentials on April 11, 1829, and united with the Protestant Methodists, not because I had anything very special against the former, any further than their government was not republican.[11] Their religion is as good as it ever was. I have been in the Protestant church something like four years, as a preacher of the Gospel; and in that time have received holy orders as an authorized minister of Christ, to attend to the duties of a pastor; and I am no sectarian whatever, but boldly declare that I have preached for all that would open their doors; and all sects have bid me welcome; and this is as it should be. May God pour his Spirit upon them all, and all the world. Amen.

William Apess

THE EXPERIENCE OF THE MISSIONARY'S CONSORT
(Written By Herself)

I was born in Lyme, Conn., A.D. 1788 on the third day of January. My father was a descendant of one of the Spanish islands, or a native of Spain. My mother was an English woman, a descendant of the Woods family of Lyme. My father died when I was small, and like all other fatherless children, I had to be placed out among strangers. My mother, having but little property and not being able to sustain me, being a poor child, this was done before I had arrived at my sixth year, and among people, too, who neither feared God nor regarded man but blasphemed their blessed Maker, and that too with the greatest impunity. The woman was a proud and haughty person and often raged most bitterly at me, and that too for the most trivial things. I had no pious parents or guardians to teach me the paths of virtue; I never recollect any serious impression made on my mind while I lived with these people, by their admonitions. One day it was suddenly suggested to my mind that God saw me, and I was afraid to die. I was guilty before him, and I wished to find some place to hide from his presence; but, since I have found Jesus precious to my soul, I have regretted that I sought him not when I was young; but I had none to lead me to the blessed fountain of holiness, where my sins might be washed away; there was none that cared for my precious soul.

I was now residing at Mr. D. Gillet's, in Lyme, being now about twelve years of age, and about this time a circumstance happened that it was thought best that I should go home. I went home and there stayed about two months, as senseless to the reality of a future state as the beasts of the field. And then I was again bound out to Mr. Aniel Ely, in Lyme, where I continued until I was

11. In 1837, "as I then understood it" is added, further softening any hint of his estrangement from the Methodist Episcopal church.

eighteen years of age. Mr. Ely was a member of the Presbyterian church. He used to say his prayers every Saturday night and Sunday morning; after a few times in attendance, I could say his prayer as well as he. I used to be at church on the Sabbath, but Mr. Ely never told me I had a soul to save or to lose. I could not tell what I went to meeting for, unless it was to see and be seen, and learn fashions; what the minister said, I understood not, nor did it affect my mind. Thus, I went on, careless and prayerless, for about two years. When I had advanced to fourteen years of age, there arrived in our neighborhood a missionary, by the name of Bushnell. Before I heard him preach, he paid us a visit, and hearing much about him, I was anxious to see him but did not wish for him to see me. I was afraid of ministers and professors of religion; I thought them a better people than others; but after tea, the missionary made his appearance to us in the room where the children were, and there he very affectionately exhorted us all. This was the first time that I had ever been warned to seek the salvation of my soul. His words sank deep on my mind; I began to weep as soon as he had left me; I went out, and for the first time I ever felt the need of praying or of a Savior; I knelt and poured out my soul to God, that he would have mercy upon me; although I had never seen anybody kneel, yet it was impressed on my mind that I must, and from that time I cried to God earnestly every day, during some months.

The missionary preached that Sabbath, and I attended all his meetings; the word was with power to my heart; I think he was the first man of God I ever heard preach. During his stay, he visited at our house several times and would always admonish me: I was pleased to hear him but dare not make known the exercises of my mind to him. Mr. Bushnell expressed himself in such a way that it had a powerful effect and made a lasting impression on my mind; that was, when he saw me employed about my daily work here, he hoped that he should meet me in heaven. I felt myself such a vile wretch, I could not see why he should speak so to me, a poor sinner. But I was ignorant of the power of divine grace, that could fit me for that place. While Mr. B. stayed, my impressions were deeper and deeper, and I was daily resolved to seek the Lord and leave the vanities of the world behind me. But he soon left the place, and when he was gone, there was not one in the place that ever afterward presented the subject to me, only in the way of derision; even the children would laugh at me and say that Mr. B converted me. I had plenty of such aid from old and young.

Mr. Ely, although a member of the church, never mentioned the subject of religion to me while I lived with him. I pray God to have mercy upon all such church members. But through all the opposition and persecution I had, I strove to seek the salvation of my soul and cry to God to help me; this I did for about six months, but I was tormented without and within. Mrs. Ely was a stepmother in the house and very wicked, and withal a very great tyrant: Sometimes she would get angry at the other children and beat me, and for the most trifling thing. She would say to me at times, when I was meditating upon death and judgment, that my head was full of the evil one, and so much so that I could not attend to what she wanted me to. But this only grieved me, and I would sorrow and weep in secret places. Here I would remark how much little children have to undergo, who are fatherless and motherless in the world, and what was I but a child? How much I wanted a tender, and affectionate, and pious mother to take me by the hand and instruct me, or some pious friend. How much good it would have done to me; but I had none but a wicked and an unholy tyrant to discourage me. But I leave her, as she has long since gone to a just God who will do right. Poor woman, she died as she lived, a poor and impenitent sinner. About this time the Methodists came into the neighborhood and held meetings about a mile off: There was everything said about them but good. It was said that they had the devil among them, and I believed it and would as soon go to the house of ill fame as I would to their meetings. This prejudice only came, however, by the hearing of the ear, which made me as foolish as thousands of others have been on the same account.

However, I continued to pray, but I was alone and I had no one to communicate my feelings to but the Lord, and he, at times, gave me sweet peace of mind; but I did not know that it was religion. I had no pious father or godly pastor to look after me; nor mother in Israel to take me by the hand and drop an encouraging word of sympathy over me; nor friends—none of these blessings was I favored with, and I am sure that I did not want the world any more then than now. But having no pious instructor or Christian examples before me, the enemy of my soul became too powerful for me. I had a proud heart, a tempting devil, an alluring world to flatter and decoy me away, and to its force I yielded—cast off fear and restrained prayer. Oh, how horrible was my situation now, and I again slid into rude company, gave way to the pride of my heart, and my most besetting sins were music and dancing. And how thankful I am that I was never led away, as many poor females are, to disgrace themselves forever, and sometimes to swift destruction and to a miserable hell. I went on now in the way of folly, but not without conscience giving me a check at times, till I was 23 years of age. I would read my Bible; at times, I would be displeased with it, and the grand enemy of my soul would tempt me not to believe it, that it was a libel upon the world, and for a while I tried to believe it. But there was a passage that so forcibly struck my heart that I could not doubt its correctness; that is, "Except ye be converted and become as a little child, ye can in no wise enter the kingdom of heaven." The reason why I felt so indifferent, I suppose it originated from my being at Hartford, Conn., where I learned more evil than good; for I used to attend all the parties of recreation that came in my way; and in reading those sacred pages, they condemned my former proceedings, and my heart was not willing to submit to them. But I would remark further; while I lived in Hartford, although I used to frequent the ball chamber, yet when I returned home and meditated on death, judgment, and eternity, it would blast all my imaginary happiness, and my heart would sink in sorrow down, because I was such a sinner. And while here in the city of Hartford, I heard of the Methodists, but it was only in the way of derision. I heard of their camp meetings, that they had the most awful works that ever was known, or heard of; and I believed it—and took no pains to inform myself but lived on the credit of hearsay.

But although I was such a wicked sinner, I could not bear the thought of going to hell. Yet I went on in rebellion against God and did not seek for instruction; if I had, I do not doubt that I should have found it. Yet I felt sensible that without religion I must go to hell. But when I arrived to the age of twenty-one, I thought I would abandon all hopes of heaven, and if I went to hell, I should not go alone—that I should have plenty of company; so I though I would rest easy where I was; and if I should live to old age, then I would seek the Lord and get ready to die. But how little did I think of the uncertainty of life. But being now at my mother's home, and having been informed that the Methodist meetings were about two miles off, and was strongly invited by one of my neighbors to go to meeting with her. So, notwithstanding I had united to make derision of them with the rest of the wicked, yet for the first time I thought that I would go, though all the neighbors around, with the exception of a few, told the same sad tale. Yet, thought I, it is no harm for me to go and hear for myself—so I went. I think I never shall forget the preacher's text; it was in Acts 24:25, "And as he reasoned of righteousness, temperance," etc. And as the words fell from the preacher's lips, so it seemed to sink with weight into my heart—and its powerful effect was very great. I was convinced that I was a sinner and must be lost without a Savior. I saw that I was to blame for the sins I committed, and no one else. I began to tremble like a Felix. I saw it would not do to put off repentance until old age, for I saw that time was short, and eternity near, and life uncertain, and death certain.

I ever afterward attended the poor, despised Methodist meetings; and while sitting under the preaching of the Gospel, I felt myself such a lost sinner that at times I could not but just refrain from crying aloud for mercy. But I grieved the Holy Spirit again and again. I was afraid of persecution—not being willing to give up my good name and become a follower of the meek and humble Jesus. Though conviction for sin did so powerfully sit upon me at times, I knew not what to do; yet, when my young mates came where I was, or

I with them, I would join with them in their folly. Oh, how hard it was to give them up, and the vanities of this life, for an interest in Christ Jesus. It is a wonder of mercy that he did not give me up to hardness of heart and to a reprobate mind.

I wanted religion in my own way, and had a wish to have it and keep it to myself. I kept along in this way about a year. I recollect at a thanksgiving, while at home, my mother wished me to attend with her on an evening visit to a neighbor's house; but I felt very indifferent about going; but to please her I gave my consent. But before we got to the house, I heard music and dancing: I wished to return and go no farther, for I knew that I had promised the Lord that I would not dance any more. I told my mother I did not wish to join them—but she insisted on my going, saying that "I was not obliged to dance"; so I yielded and went along; and when we arrived there, I was very soon asked to dance, but I refused, with a determination not to. But my mother said that, if she was as young as Mary, she would. Hearing her say so, I thought, if she would if she was able, surely it would be no hurt for me—so I went onto the floor, but not willingly; and when I began to dance, it seemed as if the floor would sink. I felt awfully—a condemned sinner before God. However, I stayed and spent the evening with them. I mention this to show how much parents may do in keeping their children from the kingdom of God: But my mother was irreligious, and I regret to this day that I had no pious parents or teachers to instruct me. But, after all, it is a wonder that God did not take me out of the world and send me to hell.

After I had arrived at my twenty-fourth year, the Lord seemed to blast all my earthly joys and schemes by sickness and disappointments, but I could see the hand of God in this; but what could it be for I was not aware—but thought God was angry with me, and I did not know what he was going to do with me. Surely he led me in a way I knew not.

At that time I was away from home, nursing a sick woman. One night after I had retired, I was reading a hymn—"Come humble sinners, in whose breast"—and when I had come to this verse:

> I'll go to Jesus, though my sins
> Hath like a mountain rose;
> I know his courts, I'll enter in,
> Whatever may oppose.

I here viewed Jesus in the flesh, while upon earth, going about doing good, and his followers with him—and sinners falling at his feet, crying for mercy—and Jesus saying, "Son, daughter, go in peace and sin no more; for thy sins, which are many, are all forgiven thee." There was such a deep sense of my transgressions before me, that I had committed against a holy God, that

I could hardly contain myself. I thought, if he had been here, how gladly would I have fallen at his feet and implored forgiveness at his hand. I can truly say that I felt the need of mercy but did not know how to obtain it: There was no one near me that prayed, and what to do I did not know. A thousand thoughts rushed through me as in a moment of time, but I tried to raise my heart to God, which seemed to quiet me a little. I was afraid to go to sleep, but sometime in the night I fell into a doze, and when I awoke it was impressed powerfully on my mind that I must break off my sins and go in secret and pray—but how to I knew not, I had been such a sinner before God; but I tried to lift my heart to God and continued to do so a number of times during the day. I broke off from my outward sins and strove to do better, but did not reveal my mind to any. I went home, burdened with sin and guilt. I found no peace. There was a gloom spread over creation, and death seemed to be written on all, I said, and I wanted nothing but a preparation for it—for I had no desire for the things of this world—and sometimes I thought I took comfort in trying to pray and singing one of Dr. Watts's psalms—to hope, to love, to pray, is all that I require. The enemy of my soul told me that I was good enough, that I could pray and praise, and that was all God required of me.

I now went about to establish my own righteousness; I was a godly, formal saint; a pharisee within. I fear thousands build upon the same sandy foundation that I was then building upon. I praise God while I am writing, that he was jealous of his own glory and soon divested me of my rags of self-righteousness and opened my eyes and showed me whereabouts I was—that I was a guilty, wretched, helpless sinner before him, and he only kept me from sinking down to the abyss of woe. I now read my Bible; but it condemned me. I became angry at it, and with God, and wished to cast it from me, and I thought it hard for me to submit to his will or go to hell. I envied all the dumb beasts of the field, because they were innocent and had no souls. The very pains of hell got hold of me; and I thought, if hell were as bad as my conscience, it might well be called hell.

However, I went to meeting, and said nothing to anyone, nor they to me. It happened that I was at a house where one of the class was employed, a very pious man. I made known my mind to him, and he encouraged me to be faithful. I informed him that I wanted to attend class; he informed his leader, and I had an invitation to attend and was thankful for the privilege; and when they asked me the state of my mind, I told them the exercises and desires that I had; and they exhorted me to be faithful, to seek the Savior of sinners. But I was so hard and stubborn that I despaired of mercy at his hand. My mind was now led back to my former days, when the Spirit of the Lord strove with me— I saw I might have had religion then, but now there was no mercy for me—for I had sinned away my day of grace. The enemy said that God was unjust and would not forgive my sins, because I had sinned so long, and I must go to hell and had better put an end to my existence and know the worst of my case. Although I saw the justice of God in condemning me, yet I was not willing to be miserable forever. I felt dejected, and cast down, and forsaken, and I wept before the Lord. I was burdened, on account of my sins; and when I walked out it seemed as if the earth would sink under me, and I should go down to darkness and sorrow to receive the punishment due that my crimes had merited—the worst person then living was better than I was. I went mourning from day to day without any light of the Son to cheer the dungeon of my soul; pride, unbelief, self-will, all combined to keep me from the Savior of sinners. I doubted his power to save me, such a vile sinner as I was. I attended the meetings, and class, and from that dear people I was encouraged to press forward and obtain my object, the salvation of my soul. But when I was alone, my mind was filled with temptations and doubts and fears. I felt like a sinner justly condemned before God; I thought that if I should feel this distress for years, and then if God should pardon me, it would be an act of great mercy. I read my Bible and prayed, but my distress increased daily; my appetite forsook me: I wished for no kind of food whatever. And at night I was sleepless, and I had striven to make myself better by the works of the law—but that increased my pain the more.

The verse of a hymn came to me—"I can but perish if I go; I am resolved to try—for if I stay away, I know I shall forever die." I resolved to seek Jesus while I lived and, if I perished, to perish at his feet. My distress rolled on; I could not work. I could find no religion in reading or praying. I took my Bible one afternoon, not knowing where I was going; and it was rainy, so I thought I would stay until I found mercy, if mercy could be found. The Lord led me, for I never had been there before—for it was a complete shelter from the rain that was then falling. It was among the rocks; I spent the afternoon in reading, meditation, and prayer—hoping, believing, and doubting. I stayed there until it began to grow dark. Before I left the place I found some relief. I had some faith that Jesus had died to redeem my soul and had risen again for my justification.

When I got home it was so dark that I could not see to read. So I took my Bible and a lamp, and the first chapter that I opened to was John 19:30: "When Jesus therefore had received the vinegar, he said, It is finished; and he bowed his head and gave up the ghost." These words were applied to my heart—it seemed as if Jesus spoke to me himself and said, "All this I suffered for you, that you might live with me in heaven." The plan of salvation was now opened to my view. The Son of God was revealed to me by faith, in all his offices, as prophet, priest, and king. With pleasing grief and mournful joy, my spirit now was filled; that I had such a life destroyed, yet live by him I killed. I wept and grieved because Jesus had died to reveal so vile a wretch as I. My load of sin and fear of hell were gone; and then I was forcibly struck with these lines of the poet:

> Come mourning souls, dry up your tears,
> And banish all your guilty fears.

My burden of sin now left me; my tears were dried up. I felt a sweet peace in my soul but did not think this a change of heart.

I retired to rest, and there was a great calm. I awoke in the morning, and my soul was drawn out after God; and when I arose and looked around me upon the works of creation, everything wore a different aspect; everything I saw praised God; and I felt as if I had long been shut up in prison—my bonds were loosed, my chains were fallen off, and I was set at liberty. I wanted to proclaim to the whole world what God had done for my soul, and to my brethren and to my young mates, how happy I was and what a dear Savior I had found. I thought that I would go publish it without delay; but I was ignorant of the devices of Satan. He very readily informed me that if I did nobody would believe me. I listened to him and went not. I have been sorry ever since, that I was not obedient to the heavenly vision; I thought that, if a soul had been once cleansed from sin, that doubts and fears and darkness would never return to trouble that soul anymore—but in this I was mistaken, for they soon returned. On Sabbath morning, May 1813, I went to meeting as usual, but my mind was filled with darkness and unbelief. After preaching, we had a class for the dear children of God to relate the exercises of their minds; and while they were relating theirs, I felt encouraged to press forward, for some of them spoke the feelings of my heart. But I did not tell them the exercises of mine; and when they asked me, I told them I did not feel such a burden, and felt determined to persevere.

They gave me their pious admonitions, and I praised God for such a privilege to meet with his dear children. At the close of the meeting the preacher prayed earnestly for me. The Lord heard and answered the prayer, to the joy of my soul—for I felt peace with God through our Lord Jesus Christ and wanted to praise him aloud; but again I grieved the Holy Spirit of God and hid my talent in the earth, but they rejoiced and I kept silent—well might it be said that the fear of man bringeth a snare. I felt a love for the dear people of God and could join with them in worship but did not believe that God had converted me into his grace. I returned home praising God but was afraid that someone would hear me. I sung a verse of a hymn called the Good Shepherd:

> Come, good Lord, with courage arm us;
> Persecution rages here—

Nothing, Lord, we know can harm us,
While our Shepherd is so near.
Glory, glory be to Jesus,
At his name our hearts doth leap;
He both comforts us and frees us,
The good Shepherd feeds his sheep.

The last part of the verses spoke the sentiments of my heart. When I got home, I had a cross to take up, to confess to my mother. And the Lord gave me strength to do my duty; and after I had prayed with them, there was great peace that overspread my soul. I lived fearing and doubting until the next Thursday. And then I visited my brethren, where we had a prayer meeting— and then I strove to tell them what the Lord had done for my soul. So I lived along from one worship to another, and the old saints were instruments in the hands of God, in keeping me from falling a prey to the enemy of my soul and the alluring charms of this vain world.

The hearing of the old pilgrims' songs, and their sweet admonitions, attended to buoy me up and keep me from stumbling into the ditch of despair; for it stimulated me to move forward. And had it not been for them, I think I should have relapsed back again and sunk down into the cradle of carnal security—for it was a common saying, that after a soul was once converted, there was no more danger, although the word of God taught me different as well as his Spirit. But weak and feeble minds like mine are apt to be led astray. But I praise God for pious instructors, that pointed out the way and bade me persevere. Had they taught me different, no doubt I should have been like Mother Eve, who was so much deceived by the subtle foe—as you know that after God had told her not to eat the fruit of the garden which grew upon a certain tree, because it would be death. But Satan told her it would not be—but otherwise. And so he tells thousands; and it is to be feared that too many give way to his flattering charms and ruin their own souls.

But, friends, let them say what they will about the Methodists; I bless God that I ever knew them—for they taught me to believe in a present and full salvation, in order to obtain a crown of everlasting life. In June 1813, I joined the society,[12] and by this people, and the doctrines that they preached, I found it to be the power of God unto salvation to my poor soul. When I joined the Methodists, the preacher told me I must count the cost, that I must expect a great many falsehoods to be told about me. I found it even so. The wicked

12. This date appears as 1823 in the 1837 edition. I think the 1813 date is the probable one because Mary Woods seems to have fully converted by the time she and William Apess met—at a Methodist meeting.

soon began to accuse me of things that I had done which I never even had thought of. I tried by the aid of Heaven to keep a conscience void of offense before God and man; for I knew that I had peace with him. It is said that "He who will live godly in Christ Jesus shall suffer persecution." If they call the Master of the house Beelzebub, how much more will they of his household! So I resolved by the grace of God to persevere and give up all and take up the cross and follow Christ through evil report as well as good—for they that followed Jesus should not walk in darkness but have the light of life.

In July, myself and three other candidates were baptized by immersion by Elder Joel Winch, Salem, Conn. Truly the ordinance was blessed to me; it was a heaven below; a paradise, indeed, to my soul. I had such love, joy, and peace that I thought I never should doubt again—but in this I was mistaken; for it was not long before I doubted.

About August I went to camp meeting, hoping and praying that God would meet me there. I enjoyed myself well at the first of the meeting, but God had greater joy laid up for me. I tried in my weak way to exhort sinners and to be faithful to seek the salvation of their souls.

One day upon the campground, there was light from heaven shone into my soul, above the brightness of the sun. I lost sight of all earthly things— heaven was opened to my view, and the glory of the upper world beamed upon my soul. My body of clay was all that hindered my flying up to meet Jesus in the air. How long I remained in this happy frame of mind I do not know. But when I came to my recollection, my Christian friends were around me singing the sweet songs of heaven; and I thought I was in the suburbs of glory. And when I saw them, they looked like angels, for they were praising God. I felt the love of God like a river flowing into my soul. From that time until the close of the meeting, I was happy. I now returned home rejoicing in God my Savior. I thought that I never should be troubled with doubts and fears—but I was mistaken as before. The enemy of my soul tempted me, and I again gave way, and like Samson I lost all my strength, and I doubted of God's power to save me.

There was much said about sanctification, among our Methodist breth-ren—they said it was possible for God to cleanse us from all sin and urged the members of our church to seek it and not rest short of it—while others opposed it and said it was impossible to live without sin in this life and to be cleansed from all unrighteousness, boldly denying the power and efficacy of his blood. I was weak and unbelieving and finally doubted it myself, although I read it was the will of God, even our sanctification—and if we confess our sins, he is faithful and just to forgive us our sins, and the blood of Jesus cleanses us from all unrighteousness. I asked the Lord, in humble prayer, if this was attainable, and to show me what I am by nature, and what I ought to be by grace—for I was sure that I wanted as much grace as anybody in the world, to get through it.

I prayed daily for the Lord to enlighten me and teach me the way; for I wished to lay a sure foundation for the time to come. I continued my petition about one month; the Lord heard and answered my prayer and opened my eyes, and I saw if I was not fully saved from sin, and made holy, I could never enter into the kingdom of God, for God was holy, and heaven was a holy place, and without holiness no man should see the Lord.

I from that time read my Bible more diligently, and sought the Lord, by fasting and prayer, with a full determination not to stop, short of full redemption in the blood of Christ. I went to a quarterly meeting in Groton, Conn.; and there God manifested himself to me in such a powerful manner at that time that I fell prostrate upon the floor, insensible to all below; the last time I fell, I felt the blood of Jesus go through every avenue of the soul and body, cleansing me from the filthiness of the flesh and spirit. The Spirit bade me arise and tell what God had done for my soul; but I was again disobedient. After that, I was almost in despair, through unbelief. I struggled in darkness for some time; at last a divine ray of light broke into my soul. I then promised the Lord, if he would give me the evidence of full redemption in my heart, that I would proclaim it to all the world, come what would.

I attended a camp meeting, at Wilbraham, Mass. The power of the Lord was manifested in a wonderful manner, and there was a general cry among believers, for full redemption in the blood of Jesus; and I felt the cry in my own heart. I prayed, and cried, and struggled, and almost despaired of obtaining my object. But before the meeting closed, God in Christ showed himself mighty to save and strong to deliver. I felt the mighty power of God again, like electric fire, go through every part of me, cleansing me throughout soul, flesh, and spirit. I felt now that I was purified, sanctified, and justified. I had no fears. I could now shout victory through the blood of the Lamb. The words of the poet would best express my feelings:

> That sacred awe—that durst not move,
> All the silent heaven of love.

From that time until now, I have never doubted the power of God, to save all who by faith would come unto him; that is about seventeen years ago; and I find him still the same unchangeable, blessed Savior, his mercy always full and boundless as the ocean. I find it as good to my soul now as it was then; yea, I can say that it grows brighter and brighter, and do expect it will, even to the perfect day, if I am faithful. Then, through the merits of Jesus, I expect to hear the welcome sound, "Come, ye blessed of my Father, inherit the kingdom prepared for you from the foundation of the world," where all tears shall be wiped away from our eyes, and there with the happy throng shout and sing our sufferings over, around the throne of God. Then I should behold that great and innumerable company "that came out of great tribulation, and washed their robes, and made them clean and white in the blood of the Lamb," and have overcome, through the word of his testimony. There we shall be at rest, and the wicked shall cease from troubling us. Glory fills my soul while I meditate upon the moment when, through grace, I shall unite with them there.

I have now given you a sketch of the dealings of God with one of his most unworthy creatures. I am a spared monument of his mercy; and through his rich grace I hope to stand fast until he takes me from time to enter into his heavenly kingdom. May this be the happy lot of us all, is the prayer of your unworthy writer.

Mary Apess

THE EXPERIENCE OF HANNAH CALEB
(by the Missionary)

I was born in Groton, Conn. My mother died when I was about six years old. Her dying request was that I might be placed among educated people, who would teach me to read God's holy word. I accordingly was placed in a white family to be brought up. The gentleman's name, with whom I was placed, was Mr. James Avery, where I continued twelve years. They were a pious people, and by them I was instructed in the paths of virtue. But how much I have to regret that I did not take heed to my ways and, in the days of my youth, seek the salvation of my soul—then I should have been prepared to meet those troubles and trials which are incident to human life. But oh! how dark and dreary is the world without the sun! So is the way of sinners without the Sun of righteousness, to cheer and light up their dark and gloomy paths, through this wilderness world. But let us return: At the age of nineteen years I was married and had ultimately five children. My husband was a soldier in the French army and died in Canada, and with this trial I met with many more— the loss of all my dear children. And when the bosom friend, the darling of all my earthly career, was gone, with whom I should no more associate in time, it was almost too much for me to bear. But oh! when I turned to look for my children, at the seats and the table that they once surrounded, and at their pillows, which I had watched over with the affection of a fond mother, and had often pressed them to my breast, while tears fell like rain from their sparkling eyes upon my bosom, and had strove to hush them! But behold, they were no more, but all of them locked up in the cold caverns of the earth, and I their faces no more to behold in time—they were fled to the world of spirits, to him who had created them.

Thus my husband was gone—the darling of my heart—with my babes, the sweet objects of my care: Thus, being stripped of my earthly glory, I was left naked and wounded. I now became alarmed about my future welfare—for the Lord was at this time pleased to discover to me the lost condition of my poor soul. My conviction of sin was severe, but notwithstanding this, I was indifferent—not knowing how to help myself; but the anguish of my soul which I felt, no tongue can tell—for it was keen and pungent; and withal I felt a great enmity to the Christian religion, often wishing, in the depravity of my heart, I had been left like the rest of my kindred, ignorant and unknown. This may be surprising to some, but I can assure you there was a cause for this. I saw such a great inconsistency in their precepts and examples that I could not believe them. They openly professed to love one another, as Christians, and every people of all nations whom God hath made—and yet they would backbite each other, and quarrel with one another, and would not so much as eat and drink together, nor worship God together. And not only so, the poor Indians, the poor Indians, the people to whom I was wedded by the common ties of nature, were set at naught by those noble professors of grace, merely because we were Indians—and I had to bear a part with them, being of the same coin, when in fact, with the same abilities, with a white skin, I should have been looked upon with honor and respect.

But it is a fact that whites, with the same principle, would turn against their own kin, if the providence of God should have happened to change the shades of their complexion, although the same flesh and feelings. How must I feel, possessing the same powers of mind, with the same flesh and blood, and all we differed was merely in looks? Or how would you feel? Judge ye, though you never have been thrust out of society, and set at naught, and placed beyond the notice of all and hissed at as we have been—and I pray God you never may be. These pictures of distress and shame were enough to make me cry out, Oh horrid inconsistency—who would be a Christian? But I remark here that I did not understand frail nature as I ought, to judge rightly. And I would remark here that these feelings were more peculiar 70 years ago than now—what their feelings would be now, if the Indians owned as much land as they did then, I cannot say. I leave the man of avarice to judge.

But we observe further: The Lord was pleased in great mercy to continue the work of grace upon my heart, so I made bold to inquire by going from one Christian friend to another, asking questions about the way and what I must do to be saved. They said that I must pray, and look to the Lord as my Savior and friend. They told me that Jesus Christ died for sinners, even such as I, who was the chief of sinners. This encouraged me to pray, but I could find no comfort in so doing. I continued almost a year between hope and despair, wretched and miserable, without God and without hope in the world. The grand enemy of all good strove to decoy my mind away from my desired object and had well-nigh effected his scheme, for he suggested to me that there was no mercy for such sinners as I was. I used to roam whole days in my native forest, weeping and wailing on account of my sins, seeking the Savior of sinners—friendless, as I thought, unpitied and unknown. As I was walking by the side of a large pond, the enemy whispered to me to throw myself in and there end my days of sorrow and affliction. I was quick to obey. I got upon a log for that purpose; but a voice seemed to say to me, "Hannah, my mercy is as free for thee as this water, and boundless as the ocean." The tempter fled; my mind was calm, and I returned home, thinking that my distress would return no more; but in this I was disappointed. Soon all my doubts returned, and I could say with Job, "Thou hast shaken me to pieces; all my bones are out of joint." I was very weak, eating but just enough to keep soul and body united, often sleeping on the cold ground, and frequently not closing my eyes for nights together. However, I sometimes took great comfort in visiting the dear children of God, some of whom I went many miles to see, and hear them converse and pray for me. They pitied me and strove to comfort me, but all in vain.

I went out one evening, thinking that I should not return anymore, to behold my kindred in the flesh, or see the morning dawn; and there I prostrated myself before God and lifted up my hands to heaven, and, in the language of parting friends, I bade farewell to the moon, to the stars, and all creation, this earthly vision no more to behold in time. But withal I prayed that if it was God's will I might live a while longer—for I was not ready to die—and see those praying people, and hear one more prayer for my perishing soul, that I might be saved from hell and everlasting destruction, from the presence of God, and the glory of his power forever: For surely I thought it would be the place of my abode forever. But the Lord heard my prayer and spared me; and when the morning beamed forth, and my eyes caught her rising, I exclaimed, "Oh, that I might hear one more prayer for my poor soul." But it was suggested to me that Christians could not help me. I then turned from the world and the prayers of the saints and went into the wilderness and sat myself down, and I had an impression that I must sing. I thought, how could I sing of redeeming grace and dying love? Oh, the answer was, "Sing, for his mercy endureth forever." I must praise God for that; but where to begin I knew not, but thought I would try. So I began this way: "Glory to God the Father, glory to God the Son, glory to God the Holy Ghost, glory to God alone." After I had done singing, I had a desire to pray, but I thought, what shall I say? "Oh, I am a poor sinner. Lord have mercy upon me, a poor sinner." As I said so, glory seemed to break in upon my soul, and I was dissolved into the love of God, apparently, soul, body, and spirit. The heavens seemed to descend, and with them an innumerable company of angels, and the spirits of the just made perfect. They seemed to throng me; I was overcome with the vision. My whole soul was lost in wonder, love, and praise to God. I was enabled to join the heavenly company, and sing the wonders of redeeming grace and dying love.

My sins were all gone; I felt no longer their burden; I was transported, as it were, to the third heaven. This was about nine o'clock in the morning. Thus you see, my friends, that I was all night in prayer to God; and as I observed, the Lord pitied me and washed away all my sins. I then returned to my Christian friends with the lightness of an angel, with my heart tuned to sing the praise of God and the Lamb, with them, who had struggled so hard at the throne of grace for me. And I began to publish to them what the Lord had done for my soul, and warning sinners wherever I went to flee from the wrath to come.

Surely, I could say, "Old things are passed away, and behold, all things are become new." I could say there was no more enmity in my heart, that I loved white people as well as my own. I wonder if all white Christians love poor Indians. If they did, they would never hurt them anymore. And certainly, if they felt as I did, they would not. For I could say, as John said, "He that is born of God, has the witness in himself."

Thus I went on from day to day, in the service of my God, praising him all the while, and no cloud to darken my day. Oh, how happy, happy, was my soul, continually full of glory, glory.

Here the publisher would take the liberty of making a few remarks. Not being personally acquainted with Sister Caleb, I am not able to give her age and date of her conversion, precisely. But, being furnished by a young lady of respectability and piety with a copy, I have, therefore, no doubt of its authenticity. But nearly all my relations and a part of my family were acquainted with her personally. And here I would say a few things which you may place confidence in, respecting her. This dear child of the forest was translated into the kingdom of God, as near as we can learn, at the age of forty years; and as far as we can learn, she lived faithful through life. Sister Caleb was remarkable for her liberality, so that she not only had the precept but the example. She knew no sect but that of the Nazarenes; for she would go into all houses of worship and exhort sinners, and eat and drink at the Lord's table wherever it was spread, to show forth his death till he come; though she herself united to the Free-Will Baptists, to be under their watchful care.

Sister Caleb was also noted by all sects to be an example of piety; to all the world she was useful in temporal matters, such as teaching the young children of her tribe to read, while at other times she would instruct them and others, by precept and example, in the way to heaven and happiness. I can tell you, friends, that she lived in the faith of the Gospel; and thus lived and died our good sister, in the Lord, after nearly half a century from her conversion. She fell asleep in the arms of Jesus and went down to the grave with a joyful hope, big with immortality, of a glorious resurrection in Christ at the last trump, while her soul was wafted upon the wings of angels to the spirit land, to dwell around the throne of God forever and ever. There her trials are at an end; there she dwells in seas of rest, while before her, waves of glory roll, and shouts of glory echo from the throne.

W.A.

THE EXPERIENCE OF SALLY GEORGE
(by the Missionary)

I was born in Groton, Conn., 1779, and was brought up without any education, as to understanding the letter in any way whatever. And although there were many around us who were very zealous that we should have instruction, and be brought up well, yet but little was done toward it, I being left in general to wander to and fro, up and down the forest with my native kin. But surely I have many things to praise God for. Although I had not those inestimable privileges that some had and do have, yet I can say that I had some that many do not have, in time; there are many of my brethren who do not that are in the wide and western world. For they do not enjoy any instruction whatever. While poor me, although ignorant and unknown, yet I had some precious privileges: such as hearing God's holy word, and having good advice from those who were mothers in Israel. And, taught by the Spirit, they would beseech of me to be reconciled to God, and they were those of my own kin; and often they would do it with streaming eyes and melted hearts. Sometimes I would take a degree of interest in it, and at other times I would be quite indifferent about it; and at other times my young mates would lead me astray with their rudeness, being only about twelve or thirteen years old.

I continued in this way for some time, between hope and despair; but they continued to call after me, and the Holy Spirit seconded their efforts constantly, and often it was so powerful that my little heart would melt down into tenderness, and what to do with myself I knew not. I felt at times melancholy and dejected; but, notwithstanding this, I was encouraged by many to seek the salvation of my soul. But it was hard to leave my young mates; yet without religion I knew that I must be miserable and wretched forever. But what to do I did not know, and how to pray I knew not. I wandered up and down in the forest, weeping and mourning on the account of my sins, not knowing that I ever should enjoy happiness either in time or eternity. The enemy now would take the advantage of my youthful mind and suggest to me that there was no happiness for me, I must spend all the rest of my days in sorrow. The enemy of my soul followed hard after me and withal tempted me to destroy myself.

I had become now a wanderer alone, as it were, in my native woods; and one day as I was passing by a large, deep brook, the enemy of my soul tempted me to destroy myself in that place, by casting myself in. But I strove to raise my little heart to God, that he would have mercy upon my soul and save me. While thus exercised in prayer to God, for his kind protection, I fell to the earth as one dead, under the power of God. And while in this situation, I saw the pit of destruction opened for poor sinners; it was no imagination either, it was a solemn reality, it was plain before me. My soul was in sore distress, and I expected nothing but hell for my portion forever. I lay in this situation for some time as helpless as an infant, begging for the mercy of God, promising to him that I would be faithful to serve him all the days of my life. The Lord heard my prayer and sent down his melting grace into my soul; and before I arose from the ground I was translated into the kingdom of God's dear Son; for when I came to myself, I was praising God; there was a change in everything around me, the glory of the Lord shone around, all creation praised God, my burden and my fears were gone, the tempter had fled, and I was clothed, and in my right mind, sitting at the feet of Jesus.

I now returned home to my friends, and began to exhort my young mates to repentance, and to tell all that came in my way what the Lord had done for my soul. I then went to the church and told it there, and the dear children of God received me. I then with a servant of God went down to the banks of the river and was buried with Christ by immersion beneath the great water; and when I came up out of the water the glory of God descended and lighted upon my soul; and so I could rejoice continually, and say the one half was never told me about this Jesus whom many deride. *"Behold ye despisers, wonder and perish; I work a work in your day ye shall in no wise believe, though a man declare it unto you."* And although I could not read, the Spirit of the Lord was with me to instruct me in the way of holiness, and upon my heart was printed the image of my Savior, by the washing of regeneration and renewing of the Holy Ghost. My soul was bathed in the love of God, it was glory, and I was lost in wonder, love, and praise. I forgot all things here below and rode in the chariot of his love daily. Bless the Lord, O my soul, and all my powers, soul and body, praise him, for glory is his due forever and ever. Amen—so let it be.

* * *

I would remark here that this female was an aunt on my father's side, and we had a personal acquaintance with each other. She belonged to the same church that Sister Caleb did, and they were well acquainted with each other. She was a member of the church about thirty years, and for the most of the time, as far as I can learn, she lived in the life and power of religion. I have attended a great many meetings with Sister George, and I do not recollect that she ever had a barren season to her soul. She often meted out to my soul the sincere milk of the word, which gave me strength in the Lord to persevere. The Lord, of a truth, was with her. She was always diligent to seek Jesus in the way. The fences, the groves, the forest—all will witness to the fact.

Her organic power of communication, when tuned with heavenly zeal and burnt with heavenly love, was delightful, charming, and eloquent. I never knew her to speak unless the congregation was watered by an overwhelming flood of tears. She feared not to warn sinners to repentance while she lived. She was no sectarian; she would go among all orders of Christians and worship God with them, and was entirely free so to do. And I believe that she felt as much for her white neighbors as for her own kindred in the flesh.

She was counted almost a preacher; her language was free, lively, and animating. She was also very industrious and active; her limbs would play as lively over the ground as a deer. I have set out to walk with her twenty miles to a meeting, several times in my life, and generally, I had to keep upon the slow pace to keep up with her. In three hours and a half from the time we started, we were there. She was also skilled in doctoring the sick, and was useful wherever she went; and in this way procured for herself a very great share of Christian and friendly patronage among all who knew her. And while visiting the sick she would often pour into their ear the balm of consolation and refer them to the blessed Jesus, who could heal both soul and body. Where she met with the sin-sick soul, she would pour into their ears the oil of joy and point them to Jesus, who taketh away the sin of the world, the only sovereign remedy for sin-sick sinners. Our sister was noted generally by all for her piety through life.

At the close of her life, there was a remarkable circumstance which took place, that is, respecting a visit which she desired to make to a neighboring village about eight miles off. But I would remark that previous to this she was much debilitated in body, which was caused by a lingering disease, supposed to be somewhat dropsical and consumptive, and did not at times keep about but was confined to her bed. She lived a widow, and withal very comfortable, and used to entertain all her brethren that came to her. There were some of her brethren whom she desired to see, and said the Lord would give her strength to perform the journey; and so she arose, as it were, from a sickbed, and through the strength of the Lord she was enabled to go; and while there, she enjoyed some Christian conversation, had a few good meetings, and bade her brethren farewell, to meet no more in time; and returned home to die. She was now composed, and ready to die—and in two weeks afterward, she fell asleep in the arms of Jesus, without a struggle or a groan, May 6, 1824, aged forty-five years.

At the last, the fear of death was taken away, and her dying bed was glorious and interesting. Her friends were many, both natives and whites. The whites paid to her remains the last tribute of respect, which is due to Christians, and united in shedding the tears of sympathy and depositing her remains in the dark and lonesome caverns of the earth, there to remain, locked up in the cold and icy arms of death—till the blast of the Archangel shall blow out the sun and pour the stars upon the earth like rain; then shall her ransomed dust revive, and in the Savior's image rise. But while she sleeps in dust below, she bathes her weary soul in seas of heavenly rest, and not a wave of trouble rolls across her peaceful breast—Oh reader, strive to meet her there.

W.A.

The Experience of Anne Wampy
(by the Missionary)

In the year 1831, I was sent by the New York annual conference of the Protestant Methodists to visit this tribe and preach to them. Being my native tribe, I took pleasure in so doing; and when I arrived to the place of my destination, I found them a poor, miserable company. But I intend to speak further in another place and shall proceed with her experience.[13]

I commenced exhorting them to flee the wrath to come—there was an old veteran of the woods, who despised all that was said to her upon the subject of salvation and would use very bad language in her way, being not able to speak plain English. However, the Lord reached her heart, and many others, and there was a work of God among us. Sister Anne was brought to bow and humble herself at the feet of Jesus, after she had experienced the holy religion of Jesus. She then was free to tell the exercises of her mind, and not till then. We will give it to you in her own language; it is broken, but you can understand it. She began thus:

13. In the 1837 edition Apess revises this to begin: "In the year 1831, I visited the Pequot Indians, a small remnant left from the massacre of the whites, who are now lingering in a miserable condition upon the banks of the River Thames, apparently unpitied and unknown. But being an Indian, and somewhat connected with the tribe, I took pleasure in offering to them the word of life, and to warn them to flee from the wrath to come. It cannot be wondered at, that it excited attention among old and young."

When Christian come to talk with me, me no like 'em; me no want to see 'em; me love nobody; I want no religion. But Sister Amy no let me alone; she talk a great deal to me about Jesus. Sister Apess, too, come talk pray for me. I be afraid I should see 'em, and me no want to hear 'em; by me, by me come trouble very much, me very much troubled. Me no like Christians, me hate 'em, hate everybody. By me, by me very much troubled; me get sick, me afraid I die; me go pray, go off all alone in the woods; me afraid I go to hell, me pray. By me, by Jesus, come take me by the hand, lead me a great way off, show me one place look like hell; me come close to it so me feel it, me afraid I fall in, me cry to Jesus to have mercy on poor me. He take me by the hand again and lead me back, show me one great mountain all full of crevices; he say I must make that all smooth before I come again. I say hard work; I afraid I go to hell at last. I pray I look to Jesus. By me, by me give up; then me feel light, like one feather; me want to die, me want to fly—me want to go home; me love everybody, me want to drink no more *rum*. I want this good religion all the time.

She now began to exhort sinners. "I wish I could talk like white folks, me would tell everybody how I love Jesus." Then she said to the young people, "Don't do like I done, me old sinner, great many years me sin, do wickedly. Come, love Jesus; I want everybody to come love Jesus. Oh, how I love Jesus; me want everybody to pray for me, so I get to heaven where Jesus is." She looked upon me, just as I was about to leave her, and with streaming eyes said, "Pray for me that I go to heaven." And while I was thus beholding her face, and viewing the tears streaming down her furrowed cheeks, it did me good, for I beheld glory beaming in her countenance, which bespoke the expression of the inward man.

Our sister was born in Groton, Conn., A.D. 1760; lived in sin rising 70 years, brought up in ignorance and prodigality till old age, and then snatched as a brand from the burning, and translated into the glorious light of the Gospel, and made an heir of all things. How good and kind is God to all men; notwithstanding they live long in sin, and rebel against him, yet he is willing to have mercy upon all that will come unto him, let them be ever so great and unprofitable sinners.

Should this happen to fall into the hands of any old transgressor, that has not become wise above what is written, I hope they will remember that they will want Master Jesus as well as Sister Anne Wampy.[14] Lord help, Amen.[15]

William Apess

14. Apess added the following here in the 1837 edition: "Though many, no doubt, will even ridicule the idea of doing as this poor pagan, but in order for any sinner, rich or poor, to enter the

kingdom of heaven, they must be first purified in order to enter into so pure a place as heaven; and this is reasonable doctrine. Depend upon it, sinners, it was the intent of Christ's sufferings; and the end of his sufferings can be answered in no other way than upon the conditions of your repentance, and a reform of your wicked ways."

15. Anne Wampy was memorable to more than one person. The Reverend John Avery recalled her years later in his fine local history, *History of the Town of Ledyard, 1650–1900* (Norwich, CT: Noyes and Davis, 1901), 259–60: "I remember, when I was quite a small boy, one Ann[e] Wampy used to make an annual trip in the early spring past my home up through Preston City, Griswold and Jewett City, selling the baskets she had made the previous winter. When she started from her home she carried upon her shoulders a bundle of baskets so large as almost to hide her from view. In the bundle would be baskets varying in size from a half-pint up to five or six quarts, some made of very fine splints, some of coarse, and many skillfully ornamented in various colors. Her baskets were so good that she would find customers at almost every house. And after traveling a dozen or twenty miles and spending two or three days in doing it her load would be all gone. Then she would start on her homeward journey, and, sad to relate, before she had reached her home a large part of what she had received for her baskets would have been expended on strong drink."

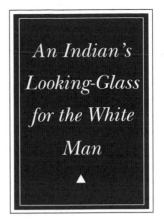

An Indian's
Looking-Glass
for the White
Man

▲

Having a desire to place a few things before my
fellow creatures who are traveling with me to the
grave, and to that God who is the maker and preserver both of the white man
and the Indian, whose abilities are the same and who are to be judged by one
God, who will show no favor to outward appearances but will judge righteousness. Now I ask if degradation has not been heaped long enough upon the
Indians? And if so, can there not be a compromise? Is it right to hold and
promote prejudices? If not, why not put them all away? I mean here, among
those who are civilized. It may be that many are ignorant of the situation of
many of my brethren within the limits of New England. Let me for a few
moments turn your attention to the reservations in the different states of New
England, and, with but few exceptions, we shall find them as follows: the most
mean, abject, miserable race of beings in the world—a complete place of
prodigality and prostitution.

Let a gentleman and lady of integrity and respectability visit these places,
and they would be surprised; as they wandered from one hut to the other they
would view, with the females who are left alone, children half-starved and
some almost as naked as they came into the world. And it is a fact that I have
seen them as much so—while the females are left without protection, and are
seduced by white men, and are finally left to be common prostitutes for them
and to be destroyed by that burning, fiery curse, that has swept millions, both
of red and white men, into the grave with sorrow and disgrace—rum. One
reason why they are left so is because their most sensible and active men are
absent at sea. Another reason is because they are made to believe they are
minors and have not the abilities given them from God to take care of
themselves, without it is to see to a few little articles, such as baskets and
brooms. Their land is in common stock, and they have nothing to make them
enterprising.

Another reason is because those men who are Agents, many of them are unfaithful and care not whether the Indians live or die; they are much imposed upon by their neighbors, who have no principle. They would think it no crime to go upon Indian lands and cut and carry off their most valuable timber, or anything else they chose; and I doubt not but they think it clear gain. Another reason is because they have no education to take care of themselves; if they had, I would risk them to take care of their own property.

Now I will ask if the Indians are not called the most ingenious people among us. And are they not said to be men of talents? And I would ask: Could there be a more efficient way to distress and murder them by inches than the way they have taken? And there is no people in the world but who may be destroyed in the same way. Now, if these people are what they are held up in our view to be, I would take the liberty to ask why they are not brought forward and pains taken to educate them, to give them all a common education, and those of the brightest and first-rate talents put forward and held up to office. Perhaps some unholy, unprincipled men would cry out, "The skin was not good enough"; but stop, friends—I am not talking about the skin but about principles. I would ask if there cannot be as good feelings and principles under a red skin as there can be under a white. And let me ask: Is it not on the account of a bad principle that we who are red children have had to suffer so much as we have? And let me ask: Did not this bad principle proceed from the whites or their forefathers? And I would ask: Is it worthwhile to nourish it any longer? If not, then let us have a change, although some men no doubt will spout their corrupt principles against it, that are in the halls of legislation and elsewhere. But I presume this kind of talk will seem surprising and horrible. I do not see why it should so long as they (the whites) say that they think as much of us as they do of themselves.

This I have heard repeatedly, from the most respectable gentlemen and ladies—and having heard so much precept, I should now wish to see the example. And I would ask who has a better right to look for these things than the naturalist himself—the candid man would say none.

I know that many say that they are willing, perhaps the majority of the people, that we should enjoy our rights and privileges as they do. If so, I would ask, Why are not we protected in our persons and property throughout the Union? Is it not because there reigns in the breast of many who are leaders a most unrighteous, unbecoming, and impure black principle, and as corrupt and unholy as it can be—while these very same unfeeling, self-esteemed characters pretend to take the skin as a pretext to keep us from our unalienable and lawful rights? I would ask you if you would like to be disfranchised from all your rights, merely because your skin is white, and for no other crime. I'll venture to say, these very characters who hold the skin to be such a barrier in the way would be the first to cry out, "Injustice! awful injustice!"

But, reader, I acknowledge that this is a confused world, and I am not seeking for office, but merely placing before you the black inconsistency that you place before me—which is ten times blacker than any skin that you will find in the universe. And now let me exhort you to do away that principle, as it appears ten times worse in the sight of God and candid men than skins of color—more disgraceful than all the skins that Jehovah ever made. If black or red skins or any other skin of color is disgraceful to God, it appears that he has disgraced himself a great deal—for he has made fifteen colored people to one white and placed them here upon this earth.

Now let me ask you, white man, if it is a disgrace for to eat, drink, and sleep with the image of God, or sit, or walk and talk with them. Or have you the folly to think that the white man, being one in fifteen or sixteen, are the only beloved images of God? Assemble all nations together in your imagination, and then let the whites be seated among them, and then let us look for the whites, and I doubt not it would be hard finding them; for to the rest of the nations, they are still but a handful. Now suppose these skins were put together, and each skin had its national crimes written upon it—which skin do you think would have the greatest? I will ask one question more. Can you charge the Indians with robbing a nation almost of their whole continent, and murdering their women and children, and then depriving the remainder of their lawful rights, that nature and God require them to have? And to cap the climax, rob another nation to till their grounds and welter out their days under the lash with hunger and fatigue under the scorching rays of a burning sun? I should look at all the skins, and I know that when I cast my eye upon that white skin, and if I saw those crimes written upon it, I should enter my protest against it immediately and cleave to that which is more honorable. And I can tell you that I am satisfied with the manner of my creation, fully— whether others are or not.

But we will strive to penetrate more fully into the conduct of those who profess to have pure principles and who tell us to follow Jesus Christ and imitate him and have his Spirit. Let us see if they come anywhere near him and his ancient disciples. The first thing we are to look at are his precepts, of which we will mention a few. "Thou shalt love the Lord thy God with all thy heart, with all thy soul, with all thy mind, and with all thy strength. The second is like unto it. Thou shalt love thy neighbor as thyself. On these two precepts hang all the law and the prophets" (Matt. 22:37, 38, 39, 40). "By this shall all men know that they are my disciples, if ye have love one to another" (John 13:35). Our Lord left this special command with his followers, that they should love one another.

Again, John in his Epistles says, "He who loveth God loveth his brother also" (1 John 4:21). "Let us not love in word but in deed" (1 John 3:18). "Let your love be without dissimulation. See that ye love one another with a pure heart fervently" (1 Peter 1:22). "If any man say, I love God, and hateth his brother, he is a liar" (1 John 4:20). "Whosoever hateth his brother is a murderer, and no murderer hath eternal life abiding in him" [1 John 3:15]. The first thing that takes our attention is the saying of Jesus, "Thou shalt love," etc. The first question I would ask my brethren in the ministry, as well as that of the membership: What is love, or its effects? Now, if they who teach are not essentially affected with pure love, the love of God, how can they teach as they ought? Again, the holy teachers of old said, "Now if any man have not the spirit of Christ, he is none of his" (Rom. 8:9). Now, my brethren in the ministry, let me ask you a few sincere questions. Did you ever hear or read of Christ teaching his disciples that they ought to despise one because his skin was different from theirs? Jesus Christ being a Jew, and those of his Apostles certainly were not whites—and did not he who completed the plan of salvation complete it for the whites as well as for the Jews, and others? And were not the whites the most degraded people on the earth at that time? And none were more so, for they sacrificed their children to dumb idols! And did not St. Paul labor more abundantly for building up a Christian nation among you than any of the Apostles? And you know as well as I that you are not indebted to a principle beneath a white skin for your religious services but to a colored one.

What then is the matter now? Is not religion the same now under a colored skin as it ever was? If so, I would ask, why is not a man of color respected? You may say, as many say, we have white men enough. But was this the spirit of Christ and his Apostles? If it had been, there would not have been one white preacher in the world—for Jesus Christ never would have imparted his grace or word to them, for he could forever have withheld it from them. But we find that Jesus Christ and his Apostles never looked at the outward appearances. Jesus in particular looked at the hearts, and his Apostles through him, being discerners of the spirit, looked at their fruit without any regard to the skin, color, or nation; as St. Paul himself speaks, "Where there is neither Greek nor Jew, circumcision nor uncircumcision, Barbarian nor Scythian, bond nor free—but Christ is all, and in all" [Col. 3:11]. If you can find a spirit like Jesus Christ and his Apostles prevailing now in any of the white congregations, I should like to know it. I ask: Is it not the case that everybody that is not white is treated with contempt and counted as barbarians? And I ask if the word of God justifies the white man in so doing. When the prophets prophesied, of whom did they speak? When they spoke of heathens, was it not the whites and others who were counted Gentiles? And I ask if all nations with the exception of the Jews were not counted heathens.

And according to the writings of some, it could not mean the Indians, for they are counted Jews. And now I would ask: Why is all this distinction made among these Christian societies? I would ask: What is all this ado about missionary societies, if it be not to Christianize those who are not Christians? And what is it for? To degrade them worse, to bring them into society where they must welter out their days in disgrace merely because their skin is of a different complexion. What folly it is to try to make the state of human society worse than it is. How astonished some may be at this—but let me ask: Is it not so? Let me refer you to the churches only. And, my brethren, is there any agreement? Do brethren and sisters love one another? Do they not rather hate one another? Outward forms and ceremonies, the lusts of the flesh, the lusts of the eye, and pride of life is of more value to many professors than the love of God shed abroad in their hearts, or an attachment to his altar, to his ordinances, or to his children. But you may ask: Who are the children of God? Perhaps you may say, none but white. If so, the word of the Lord is not true.

I will refer you to St. Peter's precepts (Acts 10): "God is no respecter of persons," etc. Now if this is the case, my white brother, what better are you than God? And if no better, why do you, who profess his Gospel and to have his spirit, act so contrary to it? Let me ask why the men of a different skin are so despised. Why are not they educated and placed in your pulpits? I ask if his services well performed are not as good as if a white man performed them. I ask if a marriage or a funeral ceremony or the ordinance of the Lord's house would not be as acceptable in the sight of God as though he was white. And if so, why is it not to you? I ask again: Why is it not as acceptable to have men to exercise their office in one place as well as in another? Perhaps you will say that if we admit you to all of these privileges you will want more. I expect that I can guess what that is—Why, say you, there would be intermarriages. How that would be I am not able to say—and if it should be, it would be nothing strange or new to me; for I can assure you that I know a great many that have intermarried, both of the whites and the Indians—and many are their sons and daughters and people, too, of the first respectability. And I could point to some in the famous city of Boston and elsewhere. You may look now at the disgraceful act in the statute law passed by the legislature of Massachusetts, and behold the fifty-pound fine levied upon any clergyman or justice of the peace that dare to encourage the laws of God and nature by a legitimate union in holy wedlock between the Indians and whites. I would ask how this looks to your lawmakers. I would ask if this corresponds with your sayings—that you think as much of the Indians as you do of the whites. I do not wonder that you blush, many of you, while you read; for many have broken the ill-fated laws made by man to hedge up the laws of God and nature. I would ask if they who have made the law have not broken it—but there is no other state in New England that has this law but Massachusetts; and I think, as many of you do not, that you have done yourselves no credit.

But as I am not looking for a wife, having one of the finest cast, as you no doubt would understand while you read her experience and travail of soul in the way to heaven, you will see that it is not my object. And if I had none, I should not want anyone to take my right from me and choose a wife for me; for I think that I or any of my brethren have a right to choose a wife for themselves as well as the whites—and as the whites have taken the liberty to choose my brethren, the Indians, hundreds and thousands of them, as partners in life, I believe the Indians have as much right to choose their partners among the whites if they wish. I would ask you if you can see anything inconsistent in your conduct and talk about the Indians. And if you do, I hope you will try to become more consistent. Now, if the Lord Jesus Christ, who is counted by all to be a Jew—and it is well known that the Jews are a colored people, especially those living in the East, where Christ was born—and if he should appear among us, would he not be shut out of doors by many, very quickly? And by those too who profess religion?

By what you read, you may learn how deep your principles are. I should say they were skin-deep. I should not wonder if some of the most selfish and ignorant would spout a charge of their principles now and then at me. But I would ask: How are you to love your neighbors as yourself? Is it to cheat them? Is it to wrong them in anything? Now, to cheat them out of any of their rights is robbery. And I ask: Can you deny that you are not robbing the Indians daily, and many others? But at last you may think I am what is called a hard and uncharitable man. But not so. I believe there are many who would not hesitate to advocate our cause; and those too who are men of fame and respectability—as well as ladies of honor and virtue. There is a Webster, an Everett, and a Wirt, and many others who are distinguished characters—besides a host of my fellow citizens, who advocate our cause daily. And how I congratulate such noble spirits—how they are to be prized and valued; for they are well calculated to promote the happiness of mankind. They well know that man was made for society, and not for hissing-stocks and outcasts. And when such a principle as this lies within the hearts of men, how much it is like its God—and how it honors its Maker—and how it imitates the feelings of the Good Samaritan, that had his wounds bound up, who had been among thieves and robbers.

Do not get tired, ye noble-hearted—only think how many poor Indians want their wounds done up daily; the Lord will reward you, and pray you stop not till this tree of distinction shall be leveled to the earth, and the mantle of prejudice torn from every American heart—then shall peace pervade the Union.

William Apess[16]

16. In the 1837 edition, *Experience of Five Christian Indians,* Apess removed this entire essay and substituted the following (entitled "An Indian's Thought") in its place and thus ended the book: "He would ask the white Christian thus: How can you let your light shine among Indians unless you do it by example? Proof of the Savior's light. Not by precept only, that he loved the world, but by example. Such as doing all manner of cures, by working miracles, to the astonishment of all the world; and to test his love for them, he laid down his life for them, even while they were enemies. Now, if we have his spirit, as we profess to have, we shall most certainly want the indigent of all classes made comfortable. And who that understands the history of the world, does not know that ignorance is the cause of the major part of the vices that exist in the world. Now, does not the white man know that it is his duty to educate the Indians, to help them build houses of worship, and such like, in order to raise them up and make them comfortable as yourselves? And do you not know it was the intent of Christ's dying to make you and them equal with himself in holiness and peace? Now, this is just the way you ought to feel toward all the race of mankind. And you can never make ignorant people know that you love them, unless you do something for them. And be it known to all men, that your light can never shine unless you do it by works of righteousness. Judge ye, what that is.—William Apess"

PART 4

*Indian
Nullification of the
Unconstitutional
Laws of Massachusetts
Relative to the
Marshpee Tribe; or,
The Pretended Riot
Explained*

The Mashpee Revolt of 1833–34 remains unknown to all but a few specialists in New England and Native American history. It involved a very small population of people, no one died or was injured, and it achieved a peaceful resolution, which was, on the whole, satisfactory to the Mashpee Indians and acceptable to the established powers in the Commonwealth of Massachusetts. It lacked, this is to suggest, the grand scale which seems, at least in the culture of the United States, prerequisite to historical memory. The apparently modest place the event holds in American history cannot be simply separated from the identity of its protagonists. Not only were they "Indians," but they were Indians who had welcomed black people and others of a similar "low order" into their community. And they were New England Indians at a time when the common presumption among white Americans was that they were no more. Those who survived were expected to welcome whatever kindnesses were doled out and otherwise to await quietly their ultimate extinction. William Apess, along with his compatriots among the Mashpees, intended to reverse these patterns of forgetfulness and neglect.

Apess's choice of a name for the protest reveals his sense of its potential significance and his ambition for it. The Nullification Crisis of 1832 had pitted a sovereign state of the Union against the federal government, provoking a major constitutional crisis which, in time, required a civil war to settle. Apess ✓ meant, and here he may be clearly distinguished from his brothers and sisters among the Mashpees, to have the revolt raise equally consequential questions, but about the political rights and status of America's first people. It is not ✓ fanciful to see him as one of the earliest indigenous leaders of an Indian rights movement. The near disappearance in historical consciousness of this important moment should be a reminder of how continuously Euro-Americans have marginalized Native Americans and deflected the troubling facts of an equally persistent exploitation.

White New Englanders' nearly hysterical reaction to the revolt, so fully documented in *Indian Nullification,* and especially to Apess, indicates how unusual, and how threatening, were the claims he advanced in the name of the Mashpees. The pressing of the Mashpees' grievances, however, might have been tolerated, barely, had Apess not had the genius and the presumption to expropriate the language of American democracy in the name of Native Americans. This assumption of equality shocked his auditors almost as much as his unhesitating reminders of their hypocritical observance of their proclaimed ideals. It was not a society, or a culture, accustomed to hearing African Americans, Native Americans, women, or the poor speak in their own voices in terms of their own choosing. More than a century would pass before even some of what Apess called for, in the name of all of his people, could be achieved.

The Mashpee Revolt was not, however, Apess's creation or simply a vehicle for his ideas. The Mashpees had struggled throughout the previous century to achieve a measure of autonomy in their civil and religious lives. The victory of the newly constituted United States in the American Revolution deprived them of a distant government, in England, more sympathetic to them than the Commonwealth of Massachusetts. The war weakened the community in other ways—chiefly and poignantly because so many of the men lost their lives fighting on the American side. When Gideon Hawley, the minister in Mashpee after the Revolution, succeeded in getting himself appointed guardian in 1789, he did so in the name of preventing further racial amalgamation among African Americans, Hessians, Mashpees, and others, thus "protecting" the Indians. The results of lost independence were evident in a decline not only in morale but also in population and in the economy. Steadily, but without success, two generations of the Mashpees had protested government by appointed overseers and religious worship administered by someone they neither chose nor wanted.

The documents in *Indian Nullification* make clear that the Mashpees already had leaders when Apess arrived. Blind Joe Amos, the Baptist preacher who ministered to most of the Mashpees, others in the Amos family, and the Coombs and Attaquin families, members of whom would figure in the leadership of the community for generations, did not suddenly blossom into prominence with the revolt. Apess unquestionably provided new energies and strategies, a catalyst for a renewal of persistent protest against white paternalism and exploitation, but his brilliant rhetorical and practical tactics could not have succeeded without a community that had a long tradition of opposition.

Indian Nullification, itself, is an odd book. Directly and indirectly, it is the work of many hands, more a documentary of the controversy than a singular account. Yet Apess's perspective and voice are unmistakable in it from the opening testimonials by the Mashpees' leaders and by Benjamin Franklin Hallett, the young reform newspaper editor, lawyer, and Democratic party activist whose advocacy of the Mashpees' cause was indispensable to its success. It seems probable that William G. Snelling functioned as the editor of the collection, assembling and ordering the documents and, I suspect, writing the awkwardly couched "Introduction," apparently by Apess although it is in the third person and unlike anything else, in style or tone, by him. It remains Apess's book, nonetheless, for it is unmistakably his first-person voice that comments throughout and shapes the entire document.[1]

1. Apess's notes to the text are included throughout within parentheses at the appropriate places. There is only one other change besides those detailed in the Textual Afterword that should be noted here. In the second and third paragraphs of page 183 and in the third paragraph of page 184, "Mr. Fiske" has been substituted for the "Mr. Fish" of the original. The context makes it virtually certain that J. J. Fiske, the counselor sent by the governor, is the person referred to, and not Reverend Phineas Fish, missionary to the Mashpees and their antagonist.

To the White People of Massachusetts.

The red children of the soil of America address themselves to the descendants of the pale men who came across the big waters to seek among them a refuge from tyranny and persecution.

We say to each and every one of you that the Great Spirit, who is the friend of the Indian as well as of the white man, has raised up among you a brother of our own and has sent him to us that he might show us all the secret contrivances of the pale faces to deceive and defraud us. For this, many of our white brethren hate him, and revile him, and say all manner of evil of him, falsely calling him an impostor. Know, all men, that our brother Apes is not such a man as they say. White men are the only persons who have imposed on us, and we say that we love our red brother, the Rev. William Apes, who preaches to us, and have all the confidence in him that we can put in any man, knowing him to be a devout Christian, of sound mind, of firm purpose, and worthy to be trusted by reason of his truth. We have never seen any reason to think otherwise.

We send this forth to the world in love and friendship with all men, and especially with our brother Apes, for whose benefit it is intended.

Signed by the three Selectmen of the Marshpee Tribe, at the Council House, in Marshpee.

Israel Amos
Isaac Coombs
Ezra Attaquin

March 19, 1835

Boston, October 2, 1834
To Whom It May Concern.

The undersigned was a native of the County of Barnstable, and was brought up near the Marshpee Indians. He always regarded them as a people grievously oppressed by the whites, and borne down by laws which made them poor and enriched other men upon their property. In fact the Marshpee Indians, to whom our laws have denied all rights of property, have a higher title to their lands than the whites have, for our forefathers claimed the soil of this State by the *consent of the Indians,* whose title they thus admitted was better than their own.

For a long time the Indians had been disaffected, but no one was energetic enough among them to combine them in taking measures for their rights. Every time they had petitioned the Legislature, the laws, by the management of the interested whites, had been made more severe against them. Daniel Amos, I believe, was the first one among them, who conceived the plan of freeing his tribe from slavery. William Apes, an Indian preacher, of the Pequot tribe, regularly ordained as a minister, came among these Indians to preach. They invited him to assist them in getting their liberty. He had the talent they most stood in need of. He accordingly went forward, and the Indians declared that no man should take their wood off their plantation. Apes and a number of other Indians quietly unloaded a load of wood, which a Mr. Sampson was carting off. For this, he and some others were indicted for a riot, upon grounds extremely doubtful in law, to say the least. Every person on the jury, who said he thought the Indians ought to have their liberty, was set aside. The three Indians were convicted, and Apes was imprisoned thirty days.

It was in this stage of the business, after the conviction, that I became the counsel of the Indians, and carried their claims to the Legislature, where they finally prevailed.

The persons concerned in the riot, as it was called, and imprisoned for it, I think were as justifiable in what they did, as our fathers were, who threw the tea overboard; and to the energetic movements of William Apes, Daniel Amos and others, it was owing that an impression was made on the Legislature, which induced them to do partial justice toward this long oppressed race. The imprisonment of those men, in such a cause, I consider an honor to them, and no disgrace; no more than the confinement of our fathers, in the Jersey prison-ship.

Benjamin F. Hallett,
Counsel for the Marshpee Indians

INTRODUCTION

The writer hopes that the public will give him credit for an intention to adhere rigidly to the truth in presenting his views of the late difficulties of the Marshpee tribe, as it is as much his wish as his intention to do justice to all his brethren, without distinction of color. Yet he is sensible that he cannot write truly on this subject without attracting the worst wishes of those who are enemies to liberty, or would reserve it exclusively to themselves. Could he speak without incurring such enmity, he would be most happy to do so; but he is fully aware that he cannot even touch this matter without exposing himself to certain calumny. This has been his portion whenever he has attempted to plead the cause of his ignorant and ever-oppressed red brethren. Nevertheless, he will endeavor to speak independently, as if all men were his friends and ready to greet him with thundering applause; and he would do so if their voices were to pronounce on him a sentence of everlasting disgrace. He writes not in the expectation of gathering wealth or augmenting the number of his friends. But he has not the least doubt that all men who have regard to truth and integrity will do justice to the uprightness of his intentions. (Heaven be praised! There are some such men in the world.) He is equally sure that the evidence contained in this little work will be satisfactory, as to all the points he wishes to establish, to all who are open to conviction.

It is true that the author of this book is a member of the Marshpee tribe, not by birth but by adoption. How he has become one of that unfortunate people, and why he concerns himself about their affairs, will now be explained to the satisfaction of the reader. He wishes to say, in the first place, that the causes of the prevalent prejudice against his race have been his study from his childhood upward. That their color should be a reason to treat one portion of the human race with insult and abuse has always seemed to him strange, believing that God has given to all men an equal right to possess and occupy the earth, and to enjoy the fruits thereof, without any such distinction. He has seen the beasts of the field drive each other out of their pastures, because they had the power to do so; and he knew that the white man had that power over the Indian which knowledge and superior strength give; but it has also occurred to him that Indians are men, not brutes, as the treatment they usually receive would lead us to think. Nevertheless, being bred to look upon Indians with dislike and detestation, it is not to be wondered that the whites regard them as on a footing with the brutes that perish. Doubtless there are many who think it granting us poor natives a great privilege to treat us with equal humanity. The author has often been told seriously, by sober persons, that his fellows were a link between the whites and the brute creation, an inferior race of men to whom the Almighty had less regard than to their neighbors and whom he had driven from their possessions to make room for a race more favored. Some have gone so far as to bid him remove and give place to that pure and excellent people who have ever despised his brethren and evil entreated them, both by precept and example.

Assumption of this kind never convinced William Apess of its own justice. He is still the same unbelieving Indian that he ever was. Nay, more, he is not satisfied that the learned and professedly religious men who have thus addressed him were more exclusively the favorites of his Creator than himself, though two of them at least have been hailed as among the first orators of the day, and spoke with an eloquence that might have moved stocks and stones. One of them dwells in New York and the other in Boston.[2] As it would avail him little to bespeak the favor of the world in behalf of their opinions by mentioning their names, he will proceed with the matter in hand, viz., the troubles of the Marshpee people, and his own trial.

Indian Nullification, etc.

It being my desire, as well as my duty as a preacher of the Gospel, to do as much good as in me lay to my red brethren, I occasionally paid them a visit, announcing and explaining to them the word of life, when opportunity offered. I knew that no people on earth were more neglected; yet, whenever I attempted to supply their spiritual wants, I was opposed and obstructed by the whites around them, as was the practice of those who dwelt about my native tribe (the Pequots) in Groton, Conn., of which more will be said in another place.

Being on a tour among my brethren in May 1833, I was often asked why I did not visit my brethren of Marshpee, of whom I had often heard. Some said that they were well provided and had a missionary, named Fish, who took care of their lands and protected them against the fraud of such of their neighbors as were devoid of principle. Others asserted that they were much abused. These things I heard in and about Scituate and Kingston, where I had preached. Some of those who spoke thus were connected with the missionary. The light thus obtained upon the subject being uncertain, I resolved to visit the people of Marshpee and judge for myself. Accordingly, I repaired to Plymouth, where I held forth on the civil and religious rights of the Indians, in Dr. Kendall's church, and was treated with Christian kindness by the worthy pastor and his people. Dr. Kendall gave me a letter of introduction to Mr. Fish, at Marshpee. Being unacquainted with the way, I strayed a little from it and found a number of good Congregationalists of the old school, who invited me to tarry and preach to them in the evening, which I did, to their acceptance; for they and their pastor desired me to remain and preach

2. I have been unable to identify either of the two men.

on the Sabbath, which, however, I could not consistently do. I proceeded thence to Sandwich, where I made my mission known to Mr. Cobb, the orthodox preacher, who appeared to be pleased.

Mr. Cobb said that he had agreed to exchange with Mr. Fish, on the Sabbath following, but as it was inconvenient for him to do so, he would give me a line to him. With this furtherance I set forward and arrived at Mr. Fish's house before sunset, informing those I met on the way that I intended to preach on the next day and desiring them to advise others accordingly. When I made my business known to Mr. Fish, he treated me with proper kindness and invited me to preach for him. When I awoke in the morning, I did not forget to return thanks to God for his fatherly protection during the night, and for preserving me in health and strength to go through the duties of the day. I expected to meet some hundreds of the tribe, and to hear from their lips the sweet song of salvation which should prepare their minds for the words of life, to be delivered by one of the humblest servants of God. I hoped that grace might be given to me to say something to my poor brethren that might be for their advantage in time and eternity, after which I thought I should see their faces no more. I looked to see them thronging around their missionary in crowds, and waited for this agreeable sight with great anxiety.

The time appointed for the service was half-past ten. When it arrived, we got into our carriages and proceeded to the meetinghouse, which was about two miles and a half distant. The sacred edifice stood in the midst of a noble forest and seemed to be about a hundred years old, circumstances which did not render its appearance less interesting. Hard by was an Indian burial ground, overgrown with pines, in which the graves were all ranged north and south. A delightful brook, fed by some of the sweetest springs in Massachusetts, murmured beside it. After pleasing my eyes with this charming landscape, I turned to meet my Indian brethren and give them the hand of friendship; but I was greatly disappointed in the appearance of those who advanced. All the Indians I had ever seen were of a reddish color, sometimes approaching a yellow, but now, look to what quarter I would, most of those who were coming were pale faces, and, in my disappointment, it seemed to me that the hue of death sat upon their countenances. It seemed very strange to me that my brethren should have changed their natural color and become in every respect like white men. Recovering a little from my astonishment, I entered the house with the missionary. It had the appearance of some ancient monument set upon a hilltop, for a landmark to generations yet unborn. Could Solomon's temple have been set beside it, I think no one would have drawn an architectural comparison. Beautiful as this place was, we had little time to admire it; something more solemn demanded our attention. We were to prepare ourselves for a temple more splendid than ever was built by hands.

When the congregation were seated, I arose and gave out the psalm. I now cast my eyes at the gallery, that I might see how the songsters who were tuning their harps appeared; but, with one exception, paleness was upon all their faces. I must do these *Indians* the justice to say that they performed their parts very well. Looking below, something new caught my attention. Upon two seats, reserved along the sides of the temple for some of the privileged, were seated a few of those to whom the words of the Savior, as well as his scourge of small cords, might be properly applied, "It is written that my house shall be called the house of prayer, but ye have made it a den of thieves"; for these pale men were certainly stealing from the Indians their portion in the Gospel, by leaving their own houses of worship and crowding them out of theirs. The law, perhaps, allowed them to do so. After singing and prayer, I preached one of my humble sermons, after which I attended a Sabbath school, in which a solitary red child might be seen here and there. By what I saw, I judged that the whites were much favored, while the little red children were virtually bidden to stand aside. I understood that the books that were sent to them had been given to the white scholars.

After a slight refreshment, the duty of worship was resumed; and I discovered that plain dealing was disagreeable to my white auditory. I inquired where *the Indians* were; to which Mr. Fish replied, that they were at a place called Marshpee, and that there was a person called *Blind Joe* who tried to preach to them, which was the cause of their absence. Though the said Joe was one of them, he had done them more harm than good. I asked why he did not imitate Blind Joe and get him to preach for him a part of the time. He answered that that could not be, that Joe was not qualified to preach and instruct. I replied that he could not, perhaps, be sure of that and that, if he had followed the course I had mentioned, it would at least have been the means of uniting the people, which would of itself have been great good. It was then concluded to have a meeting at Marshpee; and, in the afternoon of the next day, I paid the people of that place a visit in their meetinghouse. I addressed them upon temperance and education, subjects which I thought very needful to be discussed, and plainly told them what I had heard from their missionary, viz., that it was their general disposition to be idle, not to hoe the cornfields they had planted, to take no care of their hay after mowing it, and to lie drunken under their fences. I admonished them of the evil of these, their ways and advised them to consider any white man who sold them rum their enemy and to place no confidence in him. I told them that such a person deserved to have his own rum thrown into his face. I endeavored to show them how much more useful they might be to themselves and the world if they would but try to educate themselves, and of the respect they would gain by it. Then, addressing the throne of grace, I besought the Lord to have mercy on them and relieve them from the oppressions under which they labored. Here Mr. Fish cautioned me not to say anything about oppression, that being, he said, the very thing that made them discontented. They thought themselves oppressed, he observed, but such was not the case. They had already quite liberty enough. I suggested to him the propriety of granting them the privileges enjoyed by the whites about them; but he said that that would never do, as they would immediately part with all their lands. I told him that, if their improvement was his aim, he ought to go among them and inquire into their affairs, to which he replied that he did go at times but did not say much to them about their worldly concerns. He asked me if I thought it proper to preach about such things. I answered that I thought it proper to do good in any way, that a variety was not amiss, and that such a course would convince his flock that he had their welfare at heart.

I had now appointed to meet my brethren on Wednesday evening following, when I expected to bid them farewell forever; and in the meanwhile I had obtained a letter of introduction to Mr. Pratt, of Great Marshes. There I gave the audience a word in season, upon the subject of Indian degradation, which did not appear to please them much. I then visited Barnstable and, finding no resting place there for the sole of my foot, I journeyed as far as Hyannis, where I was entertained with hospitality and kindness. On the evening of the fourteenth day, I again preached on the soul-harrowing theme of Indian degradation; and my discourse was generally well received, though it gave much offense to some illiberal minds, as truth always will when it speaks in condemnation. I now turned my face toward Marshpee, to preach the word there.

I had made up my mind to depart early on the morrow, and therefore, that I might hear of their concerns and how they fared from their own mouths, I intended to commence my labors early in the day. I had not the least intention of staying with my brethren, because I saw that they had been taught to be sectarians rather than Christians, to love their own sect and to hate others, which was contrary to the convictions of my own experience as well as to the doctrine of Jesus Christ. What ensued led me to look farther into their case. The lecture I had delivered in the meetinghouse had wrought well, and a small pamphlet that contained a sketch of the history of the Indians of New England had had a good effect. As I was reading from it, an individual among the assembly took occasion to clap his hands and, with a loud shout, to cry, "Truth, truth!" This gave rise to a general conversation, and it was truly heartrending to me to hear what my kindred people had suffered at the hands of the whites.

Having partook of some refreshment, we again met to worship God in the schoolhouse; where I believe that the Spirit of the Lord was revealed to us.

Then, wishing to know more of their grievances, real or supposed, and upon their invitation, I appointed several meetings; for I was requested to hear their whole story and to help them. I therefore appointed the twenty-first of May, 1833, to attend a council to be called by my brethren. In the meanwhile I went to Falmouth, nine miles distant, where I held forth upon the civil and religious rights of the Indians. Some, who apparently thought that charity was due to themselves but not to the red men, did not relish the discourse; but such as knew that all men have rights and feelings, and wished those of others to be respected as well as their own, spoke favorably of it. Of this number was Mr. Woodbury, the minister, who thought it would do good. I then returned to Marshpee, to attend the council.

The meeting was held in the schoolroom. Business commenced at about nine in the morning and continued through the day. The first that arose to speak was an Indian, Ebenezer Attaquin by name. Tears flowed freely down his time-furrowed cheeks while he addressed us in a manner alike candid and affectionate. The house was well filled.

After listening patiently to the tale of their distresses, I counseled them to apply for redress to the governor and Council. They answered that they had done so, but *had never been able to obtain a hearing.* The white agents had always thrown every obstacle in their way. I then addressed them in a speech which they all listened to with profound attention.

I began by saying that, though I was a stranger among them, I did not doubt but that I might do them some good and be instrumental in procuring the discharge of the overseers and an alteration of the existing laws. As, however, I was not a son of their particular tribe, if they wished me to assist them, it would be necessary for them to give me a right to act in their behalf by adopting me, as then our rights and interests would become identical. They must be aware that all the evil reports calumny could invent would be put in circulation against me by the whites interested, and that no means to set them against me would be neglected. (Had the inspiration of Isaiah spoken these words, they could not have been more fully accomplished, as is known to the whites of Barnstable County, as well as the Indians.)

Mr. Ebenezer Attaquin, being one of the prayer leaders, replied first and said, "If we get this man to stand by us, we must stand by him, and if we forsake him after he undertakes for us, God will forsake us also."

Mr. Ezra Attaquin wished to know if I could not come and dwell with them, as so I could do them more good than if abiding at a distance. Mr. Ebenezer Attaquin said in reply that, if such a chance should be offered to a white man, he would be very glad to accept it.

I now inquired what provision could be made for me, if I should consent to their wishes. They answered that their means were small but that they would provide a house for me to live in and do what they could for my support. I said that, knowing their poverty, I did not expect much and gave them to understand that I could dig, and fish, and chop wood, and was willing to do what I could for myself. The subject of religious instruction was then discussed, and the inquiry was made, what should be done with their poor, blind brother (who was then absent among another sect). I answered that I was very willing to unite my labors with his, as there was plenty of work for both of us; and that, had I but half a loaf of bread, I would gladly divide it with him. It was then agreed that we should unite and journey together on the road toward heaven.

The case of Mr. Fish was next laid before the council, and complaints were made: that he had neglected his duty; that he did not appear to care for the welfare of the tribe, temporal or spiritual; that he had never visited some of the brethren at all, and others only once in five or seven years; that but eight or ten attended his preaching; that his congregation was composed of white people, to whom his visits were mostly confined; and that it seemed that all he appeared to care for was to get a living and make as much as he could out of the Indians, who could not see any reason to think him their friend. It was, therefore, agreed to discharge him, and three papers were drafted accordingly. One was a petition to the governor and Council, a second to the Corporation of Harvard College; the first complaining against the overseers and the laws relating to the tribe, and the second against the missionary set over them by Harvard College and the overseers. The third document was a statement of my adoption into the tribe and was signed by all present, and subsequently by others, who were not present but were equally desirous of securing their rights. It was as follows.

To all whom it may concern, from the beginning of the world
up to this time, and forever more.

Be it known, that we, the Marshpees, now assembled in the presence of God, do hereby agree to adopt the Rev. William Apes, of the Pequot tribe, as one of ours. He, and his wife, and his two children, and those of his descendants, forever, are to be considered as belonging to the Marshpee tribe of Indians. And we solemnly avow this, in the presence of God, and of one another, and do hereby attach our names to the same, that he may take his seat with us and aid us in our affairs. Done at the Council House in Marshpee, and by the authority of the same, May 21st, 1833.

Ebenezer Attaquin, *President*
Israel Amos, *Secretary*

To this instrument there are about a hundred signatures, which were affixed to the other papers above mentioned also. The resolutions which were sent to the two bodies were these:

Resolved, That we, as a tribe, will rule ourselves, and have the right to do so; for all men are born free and equal, says the Constitution of the country.

Resolved, That we will not permit any white man to come upon our plantation, to cut or carry off wood or hay, or any other article, without our permission, after the 1st of July next.

Resolved, That we will put said resolutions in force after that date (July next), with the penalty of binding and throwing them from the plantation, if they will not stay away without.

These resolutions were adopted by the tribe and put in force, as will be seen hereafter. It was hoped that, though the whites had done all they could to extinguish all sense of right among the Indians, they would now see that they had feelings as well as other men.

The petition to the Corporation of Harvard set forth the general dissatisfaction of the tribe with the missionary sent them by that honorable body, according to the intended application of the Williams Fund. The money was no more intended for Mr. Fish than for any other clergyman; neither had the Indians given him a call. They thought it right to let his employers know that he had not done his duty, because he not only received between five and six hundred dollars from the college but had possession of five or six hundred acres of the tribe's best woodland, without their consent or approbation, and converted them to his own exclusive use, pretending that his claim and right to the same was better than that of the owners themselves. Not liking this, the Indians solicited his discharge. The document runs thus:

To our white brethren at Harvard College and trustees of the Williams fund, that is under the care of that body, for the important use of converting the poor heathen in New England, and who, we understand, by means of that fund, have placed among us the Rev. Phineas Fish.

We thought it very likely that you would like to know if we, as a people, respected his person and labors, and whether the money was benefiting the Indians or not. We think it our duty to let you know all about it, and we do say, as the voice of one, with but few exceptions, that we as a tribe, for a long time, have had no desire to hear Mr. Fish preach (which is about ten years), and do say sincerely that we, as a body, wish to have him discharged, not because we have anything against his moral character, but we believe his labors would be more useful somewhere else, and for these reasons,

1st. We, as a people, have not been benefited by his preaching; for our moral character has not been built up, and there has been no improvement in our intellectual powers, and we know of no Indian that has been converted by his preaching.

2d. We seldom see him upon our plantation to visit us, as a people. His visits are as follows—To one house, one visit in one year—to another, two visits in five years—to another, one in seven—and to many, none at all. (We would here remark that Mr. Fish has not improved, but rather lost ground; for history informs us that such was the anxiety of the whites, that it was thought best to visit the Indians twice in one year, and preach to them, so as to save them.)

3d. We think that twenty years are long enough for one trial. Another reason is that you and the people think that we are benefited by that fund, or money paid to him for preaching to the Indians—and we are not. White people are his visitors and hearers. We would remark here that we have no objection to worship with our white neighbors, provided they come as they ought to come, and not as thieves and robbers, and we would ask all the world if the Marshpee Indians have not been robbed of their rights. We wonder how the good citizens of Boston, or any town would like to have the Indians send them a preacher and force him into the pulpit and then send other Indians to crowd the whites out of their own meeting house, and not pay one cent for it. Do you think the white men would like it? We trow, not; and we hope others will consider, while they read our distressing tale. It will be perceived that we have no objection if hundreds of other nations visit our meeting house. We only want fair play; for we have had foul play enough.

4th. We do not believe but that we have as good a right to the table of the Lord as others. We are kept back to the last, merely because our skins are not so white as the whites', and we know of no scriptures that justify him in so doing. (The writer would here observe, that he wonders any person guilty of a dark skin will submit to such unchristian usage, especially as the minister is as willing to shear his black sheep as his white ones. This being the case, ought he not to pay as much regard to them? Should he turn them loose to shift for themselves, at the risk of losing them?)

5th. We were never consulted as to his settlement over us, as a people. We never gave our vote or voice, as a tribe, and we fully believe that we are capable of choosing for ourselves, and have the right to do so, and we would now say to you, that we have made choice of the Rev. Wm. Apes, of the Pequot tribe, and have adopted him as one of ours, and shall hear him preach, in preference to the missionary, and we should like to have him aided, if you can do it. If not, we cannot help it—he is ours—he is ours.

Perhaps you have heard of the oppression of the Cherokees and lamented over them much, and thought the Georgians were hard and cruel creatures; but did you ever hear of the poor, oppressed and degraded Marshpee Indians in Massachusetts, and lament over them? If not, you hear now, and we have made choice of the Rev. Wm. Apes to relieve us, and we hope that you will assist him. And if the above complaints and reasons, and the following resolutions, will be satisfactory, we shall be glad, and rejoice that you comply with our request.

Resolved, That we will rule our own tribe and make choice of whom we please for our preacher.

Resolved, That we will have our own meeting house, and place in the pulpit whom we please to preach to us.

Resolved, That we will publish this to the world; if the above reasons and resolutions are not adhered to, and the Rev. Mr. Fish discharged.

The foregoing addresses and resolutions were adopted by a vote of the tribe, almost unanimous. Done at the Council House at Marshpee, May the 21st, 1833.

Ebenezer Attaquin, *President*
Israel Amos, *Secretary*

The Hon. Josiah Quincy, president of the college, promised to attend to this matter, said that he had long been satisfied that the money from the Williams Fund had not been applied to the object for which it was intended, and hinted at an intention to send no more to Mr. Fish till he should be better informed concerning the matter. (We understood that he actually did retain the money, though he never found leisure to make the inquiry alluded to.) He said that, had it been in the summer, he would have gone himself to the place. Summer has passed away, and we have seen no Mr. Quincy yet. We have heard that he was requested by several gentlemen to come and investigate our affairs, but we suppose he thinks that the poor Marshpees cannot have been wronged. However, as nothing has been done, we think it is time that the public should be made aware of our views and intentions.

Leaving Marshpee for New Bedford, I preached at several places on my way, and delivered lectures on Indian affairs. Many of the advocates of oppression became clamorous, on hearing the truth from a simple Indian's lips, and a strong excitement took place in that quarter.

Some feared that an insurrection might break out among the colored people, in which blood might be shed. Some called me an imposter, and others approved of my proceedings, especially the Quakers, whom I ever found benevolent and ready to help us. Their generous good will toward colored people of all races is well known. I feel bound to say, too, that there were others of the highest respectability in those parts who were anxious that their red brethren should obtain their rights and redress of their grievances.

When the time I had fixed for my return to my friends at Marshpee arrived, I turned thitherward and reached the place on the sixth of June. Here I met the blind preacher, whom I had never before seen. He bade me welcome and cordially agreed to join me in my labors, saying that God had listened to his prayers. He had for several years prayed for an assistant and now consented to labor in conjunction with me for the spiritual and temporal advantage of our brethren. We went through the plantation together. On the Sabbath there was a large meeting, and the assistance of God enabled me to preach to them, after which we set forth, as a delegation to the governor and Council in Boston. We stopped at several towns by the way, to discharge our duties as Christian ministers, and were kindly and hospitably received by the teachers.

When we arrived in Boston, we communicated our business to a certain doctor, who lived in Roxbury. He did not think so favorably of it as we had expected but, nevertheless, agreed to lay it before the board of trustees, which we presume he did, as he is a man of truth. We told him that we asked for justice, not money, and said that we wished the Marshpee Indians to avoid the meetinghouse, if it did not belong to them. With this we left him and have never heard from him from that day to this. He is gone where his deeds done in the flesh will receive their just reward, which I hope is a crown of blessedness and glory.

We did not find the governor in Boston, but were advised to wait on Mr. Armstrong, the lieut. governor. We showed him our petition and resolutions, which he said would avail us nothing, unless enforced. We answered that they would be enforced, at the appointed time. He then suggested that we might have been instigated to the measures in question by some of our enemies, probably meaning some of our unprincipled white neighbors. We replied that ill usage had been our only instigation and that no one had interfered in the matter. He advised us to deliver our petition to the Secretary of State, to be submitted to the Council at their next session, which we did.

This done, we called on one of the tribe who was engaged in the coasting business, and had done much to teach the Indians and to bring them to a right knowledge of their degraded condition. He said that he would willingly relinquish his business and join in the efforts of his brethren to shake off the yoke which galled them; and thereupon it was resolved to hold a convention on the twenty-fifth of June, for the purpose of organizing a new government. He desired to be there, and his name is Daniel Amos.

I now set out for Essex, where my family was living, accompanied by the blind preacher. I put my wife and little ones on board a small vessel, bound for Boston, while I and my blind brother returned thither by land. We all arrived safely and soon after embarked for Barnstable, where we arrived on the eighteenth of June and landed at a spot about twelve miles distant from the hospitable Indians. Here we found ourselves breathing a new atmosphere. The people were very little prepossessed in our favor, and we certainly owe them small thanks on the score of hospitality. We succeeded in obtaining the shelter of an old stable for two nights, by paying two dollars. We applied to one individual for accommodations during that time, for one of our party who was sick, but were refused. He said he had no room. If any white man should come to Marshpee and ask hospitality for a night or two, I do not believe that one of the whole tribe would turn him from his door, savages though they be. Does not he better deserve the name who took from us two dollars for sleeping in his stable? This usage made me think that in this part of New England prejudice was strong against the poor children of the woods, and that any aid we might receive must come from the more hospitable Indians, among whom we arrived on the twenty-first and rested till the twenty-fifth. We regarded ourselves, in some sort, as a tribe of Israelites suffering under the rod of despotic pharaohs; for thus far, our cries and remonstrances had been of no avail. We were compelled to make our bricks without straw.

We now, in our synagogue, for the first time, concerted the form of a government, suited to the spirit and capacity of freeborn sons of the forest, after the pattern set us by our white brethren. There was but one exception, viz., that *all* who dwelt in our precincts were to be held free and equal, *in truth*, as well as in letter. Several officers, twelve in all, were elected to give effect to this novelty of a government, the chief of whom were Daniel Amos, president, and Israel Amos, secretary. Having thus organized ourselves, we gave notice to the former board of overseers, and the public at large, of our intentions. This was the form of our proclamation.

Notice

Marshpee Plantation, June 25th, 1833

Having heretofore been distressed, and degraded, and robbed daily, we have taken measures to put a stop to these things.—And having made choice of our own town officers to act instead of the whites, and having acquainted the Governor of our affairs and resolutions, he has nothing against our putting them in force. (Here we were a little mistaken, not knowing in our ignorance that we were making the lieut. governor commander-in-chief and using his name to nullify the existing laws. Nevertheless, our mistake was not greater than many that have been made to pass current by the sophistry of the whites, and we acted in accordance with the spirit of the Constitution, unless that instrument be a device of utter deception.) And now we would say to our white friends, we are wanting nothing but our rights betwixt man and man. And now, rest assured that said resolutions will be enforced after the first day of July, 1833. Done at the National Assembly of the Marshpee Tribe, and by the authority of the same.

Daniel Amos, *President*
Israel Amos, *Secretary*

Hereupon the missionary and agents and all who put faith in them combined together to work our destruction, as is well known to all men.

We then proceeded to discharge all the officers appointed by the governor and Council, firmly believing that each and every one of the existing laws concerning the poor Israelites of Marshpee was founded on wrong and misconception. We also forwarded a letter and resolution to Gideon Hawley, to the effect that we were dissatisfied with his proceedings with regard to our affairs and with those of the other officers, that we desired their stay among us no longer, that we were seeking our rights and meant to have them, and we therefore demanded of them all a final settlement and warned them not to violate our regulations.

The resolution was as follows:

Resolved, That we will no longer accede to your terms after the first day of July next, 1833.

Done by the authority of the Marshpee Tribe.

Daniel Amos, *President*
Israel Amos, *Secretary*

We also proceeded to discharge the missionary, telling him that he and the white people had occupied our meetinghouse long enough and that we now wanted it for our own use. We likewise gave him notice that we had complained against him to the authorities at Harvard.

Those who had, as we think unlawfully, ruled us hitherto now awoke in astonishment and bestirred themselves in defense of their temporal interests. Mr. Hawley was dispatched to the governor at Worcester, to whom he represented the state of affairs in colors which we cannot acknowledge to have been faithful. He stated that the Indians were in open rebellion and that blood was likely to be shed. It was reported and believed among us that he said we had armed ourselves and were prepared to carry all before us with tomahawk and scalping knife; that death and destruction, and all the horrors of a savage war, were impending; that of the white inhabitants some were already dead and the rest dreadfully alarmed! An awful picture indeed.

However, several weeks previous to this the governor and Council had been apprised of what was going forward and had authorized one of the Council to visit the tribe, in order to hold counsel and, if possible, restore peace among them. But the first of July arrived before he came, and we did even as we had pledged ourselves to do, having in view no other end than the assertion and resumption of our rights. Two of the whites, indeed, proved themselves enemies to the Indians, by holding themselves in readiness to break up the new government and daring them to carry it into effect. They were brothers, and one of them has since gone to his reward. Their name was Sampson. They came, in defiance of our resolutions, to take away our wood in carts. As I was walking in the woods, I discovered them in the act of removing our property and called to him who was the owner of the teams to come near me. He complied and appeared much agitated as he approached. I mildly stated to him the views and intentions of the tribe, saying that it was not their design to wrong or harm any man in the least and that we wished them to desist till we should have had a settlement with the overseers, after which everything should be placed upon a proper footing. I begged them to desist, for the sake of peace; but it was to no purpose. They said that they knew what they were about and were resolved to load their teams. I answered that the men who owned the wood were resolved to carry their resolutions into force, and asked if they had not seen the notification we had posted up. One of them replied that he had seen but had not taken much notice of it. I again told them that the owners of the wood were at hand, and by the time one of the teams was laden, the Indians came up. I then asked William Sampson, who was a member of the missionary's church, if he would, even then, unload his team and wait till things were more quiet; to which he replied that he would not. I then, having previously cautioned the Indians to do no bodily injury to any man, unless in their own defense, but to stand for their rights and nothing else, desired them to unload the teams, which they did very promptly. One of the Sampsons, who was a justice of the peace, forbade them and threatened to prosecute them for thus protecting their own property, which had no other effect than to incite them to work more diligently. When they had done, I told the justice that he had, perhaps, better encourage others to carry away what did not belong to them and desired the teamsters to depart. They said they would, seeing that it was useless to attempt to load the carts. Throughout this transaction the Indians uttered neither a threat nor an unkind word, but the white men used very bitter language at being thus, for the first time, hindered from taking away what had always been as a lawful spoil to them hitherto.

The defeated Sampsons hurried off to get the aid of legal might to overcome right and were wise enough to trouble the Indians no further. The tribe were thus left in peaceable possession of all their property. Mr. Fish stated, in his report of the case, that we wanted possession of the mission house; but in this he was mistaken. No such thing was intended or even mentioned among us, though it is true that the meetinghouse and the two schoolhouses and all the land, excepting that on which Mr. Fish's house stood, were in our hands.

The Indians now made it part of their business to watch their property, being determined to disappoint the rapacity of the whites. They soon learned that the governor had sent an envoy to deal with them, and the news cheered their hearts not a little; for they earnestly wished for peace and quietness. A verbal message was brought, desiring us to meet him. We replied by asking why the agent did not come to us, if the governor had sent him for that purpose, instead of going to a tavern and calling on us to come to him there. I now suppose that this proceeding on his part was not so much his fault as that of one Ezra Crocker, who received twenty dollars *per annum* for entertaining the Indians in his house, and who not unfrequently thrust them out of doors. Nevertheless, we sent the agent an answer in writing, to the following effect.

To the Honorable Agent sent by the governor to
inquire into our affairs.

Dear Sir,

We are much gratified to see that the governor has noticed us so much as to inquire into our affairs. Your request could not be attended to yesterday; our people being very busy in the affairs of the day; but we will meet you with pleasure this morning at nine o'clock, at our meeting-house, there being no other place where we should like to see you for an interview.

Daniel Amos, *President*

July 4th, 1833

At the time appointed, we met the counselor, and he appeared to enjoy himself very well among us. When the meeting had been called to order, it was observed that the overseers were not present, and it was proposed to send for them, that they might have fair play and hear of what faults they were accused. They came, accompanied by the high sheriff of Barnstable County, the Hon. J. Reed of Yarmouth, and several other whites, who were invited to take seats among us. The excitement which pervaded Cape Cod had brought these people to our council, and they now heard such preaching in our meetinghouse as they had never heard there before—the bitter complainings of the Indians of the wrongs they had suffered. Every charge was separately investigated by our people, who gave the entire day to the work. The white persons present seemed very uneasy, often getting up, going out, and returning, as if apprehensive of some danger. The groundwork of their fears, if they had any, was this: Three of our people, who had been out in the morning hunting deer, had brought their guns into the meetinghouse, and this circumstance was thought, or pretended to be thought, by a few of our neighbors to portend violence and murder. Also, the counselor had brought a letter from the governor, indicating that he had been led, by wrong reports, to believe that something of the kind was likely to take place. ("In respect to the measures you may deem advisable, let them be confined in their adoption to an application of the *civil power*. If there is resistance, the Sheriff will, with your advice, call out the *posse comitatus,* and should there be reason to fear the inefficiency of this resort, I will be present personally, to direct any *military* requisitions," etc.)

This letter was read to the people, and was to them as a provocation and a stimulus. They thought it grievous that the governor should think they had put him in mind of his oath of office, to secure the Commonwealth from danger, and given him cause to call out perhaps fifty or sixty thousand militia; especially when the great strength and power of the Marshpee tribe was considered. To this supposed great demonstration of military power they might, possibly, have opposed a hundred fighting men and fifteen or twenty rusty guns. But it is written, "One shall chase a thousand, and two shall put ten thousand to flight"; so there might have been some reason for persons who believe the Bible to fear us. Who can say that little Marshpee might not have discomforted great Massachusetts? Nevertheless, the birthplace of American freedom was spared so great a disgrace; for the governor, very wisely, remained at home.

Toward the close of the day Mr. Fiske desired the Hon. Mr. Reed to explain to the Indians the laws, as they then stood, and the consequences of violating them. He told us that merely declaring a law to be oppressive could not abrogate it; and that it would become us, as good citizens whom the government was disposed to treat well, to wait for the session of the Legislature and then apply for relief. (Surely it was either insult or wrong to call the Marshpees citizens, for such they never were, from the Declaration of Independence up to the session of the Legislature in 1834.) "He went fully," says one reporter, whose name it may be well to omit, "into the situation of the tribe, in a very forcible and feeling manner, warning them against the rash measures they had already taken or adopted."

Mr. Fiske then pathetically stated his opinions concerning the awful consequences which would result from a violation of the laws, and spoke much at large of the parental feeling of government for the remnant of a once mighty and distinguished race. Wm. Apess replied that the laws ought to be altered without delay; that it was perfectly manifest that they were unconstitutional; and that, even if they were not so, there was nothing in them to authorize the white inhabitants to act as they had done. Being very anxious to learn what amount of good his brethren might expect, he spoke with an energy that alarmed some of the whites present considerably. The Hon. Mr. Reed questioned him as to his right to interfere. He replied that he had obtained it by the adoption of the tribe.

Mr. Reed, if I correctly understood him, answered that the Indians had no right to do such an act; no power to confer such a privilege. I replied that, if the plantation belonged to them, they undoubtedly had a right to give me leave to dwell upon it. Many other things he said, of which I could not see the reasonableness and propriety, and therefore we could not come to an agreement.

While these things were being done and said, as I have reason to believe, a warrant for my apprehension was put into the hands of the high sheriff, who, it appeared to me, was not very desirous to execute it. He approached me and, with some agitation, told me I must go with him to Cotuit; and added that if I did not accompany him peaceably he would have out the whole county of Barnstable. I was not conscious of giving any cause for this perturbation of mind, but I suppose others saw my conduct in a different light. It is admitted by all that nothing was done contrary to good order, though I admit that if I had refused to obey the warrant the sheriff would not have been able to enforce it. The fact is I was in no wise unwilling to go with him, or to have my conduct brought to the test of investigation, or to give all the satisfaction that might be required, had it appeared that I had done wrong. I was also very desirous to have the truth appear, viz., that it was not the intention or wish of the Marshpees to do violence or shed blood.

The sheriff told me that I should not suffer any injury or injustice and that I should have a hearing in the presence of my friend, Mr. Fiske. I went with him very quietly. The excitement ran very high, and almost all Cotuit was present at my examination. If wishes could have availed, I doubt not that I should have been ruined forever. I was arraigned on three charges: for riot, assault, and trespass; and pleaded Not Guilty.

The Messrs. Sampsons, four in number, were called, and testified as follows: That on the first day of July, between eight and nine A.M., they were carting wood from the Marshpee plantation; that they were hailed by Wm. Apess and forbidden by him to take any wood away until a settlement with the overseers should have been had; that the said Apess threatened them that he would call his men if they persisted, who would "*cut up a shine with them*" (the

Sampsons). (I do not recollect uttering this expression, and it is not one that I am in the habit of using. It surprised me much, too, that the Sampsons should all swear alike, when it was impossible that they could have heard alike. If I used the word "shine," it must have been in speaking to Mr. William Sampson, in a low tone, about fifty yards from the others.) They all agreed, however, that no unchristian temper was manifested and no indecorous language used. They admitted that they had no fear for their personal safety and that no harm was done to any of the persons concerned, save unloading their teams and ordering them to depart.

Now if I had taken any neighbor's wood without his leave, and he had thrown it out of my cart, and told me to go away, and had given me no farther molestation, I should think I had gotten off very easily. If a poor Indian wishes to get into a jail or penitentiary, that is just the course I would advise him to pursue. I leave it to the reader to say who were the persons aggrieved and injured, and that had the right to complain of trespass.

It was thought proper, by those who had the power so to do, to bind me over to appear and take my trial before the Court of Common Pleas, at the next session, in the sum of two hundred dollars, and sureties for the like amount were also required. Compliance was not difficult. I had only to send for Lemuel Ewer, Esq., of South Sandwich, who had, in former times, been the treasurer of the tribe, knew their wrongs, and was their friend. It was well for me that there was one man who knew on which side the right lay and had the courage to support it, for I verily believe that no other person would have dared to become my bondsman. I owe Mr. Ewer the justice further to say that he has done much to advance the interests of the Marshpee tribe, by giving information respecting them to the legislative body, for which we cannot easily show our gratitude.

The Cotuiters now waxed exceedingly wroth at what Mr. Ewer had done. Truth had been shot into their hearts, and if I should say that they bellowed like mad bulls and spouted like whales gored mortally by the harpoon, I do not think the figure of speech would be too strong. Mr. Crocker, the contractor or agent for our wood, felt himself especially aggrieved that I had gotten bail and was let loose upon the plantation, to hinder him in his business. His life, he thought, would be in danger. There was a great deal of loose talk and a pretty considerable uproar.

While I was waiting for Mr. Ewer to bail me, I had some conversation with the Hon. J. J. Fiske, who expressed himself concerned about the Indians and thought that something ought to be done. I said to him that my object was to get them righted, and allowed that I might possibly have gone too fast and far. In this I am now satisfied that I was mistaken. I believe that neither I nor any of my brethren went fast enough. I think there is no white man, Christian or infidel, who would have shown half so much forbearance as we did in the like circumstances. Mr. Fiske said he would do all he could for me, and I have no doubt that he did so. It was very proper in him to endeavor to quiet the whites. The Indians were already quiet and had no disposition to be otherwise.

Nevertheless, it seemed to be the common opinion that the imprisonment of Apess would frighten the rest of the tribe and cause them to forego their efforts to recover their rights. Had this been the case, they might have carted a few more good suppers and dinners out of our woods and have eaten them on their town meeting days, for two or three days together, twice in the year, and have thrown the bones and crusts to the poor, old, and ignorant among the natives, as they had done, year after year. The missionary, as usual, might have helped them to devour the spoil and have seen his flock degraded and abused before his eyes. Much was also said about the pains that had been taken to educate the Marshpees, and it was averred that, instead of going to the schools opened for them, they preferred going about the country picking berries and basket making. Mr. Crocker said he had been at great pains to induce the Indians to go to school. Let him who has been prejudiced against the Marshpees, by such argument, look at the legislative act of 1789, section 5, for the regulation of the plantation, prohibiting the instruction of the Marshpees in reading and writing, under pain of death. Who, then, dared to teach them?

Mr. Hawley, the former missionary, spent fifty or sixty years in Marshpee. He is mentioned in the history of Berkshire County, as a schoolmaster for the Mohawks, Oneidas, and Tuscaroras, in 1748, and nothing more is known of him, up to his arrival in Marshpee. Thither he came to teach, in A.D. 1757, and there he stayed till his death. What his care to educate the tribe was may be judged from the facts that he *did not teach one* Indian to read during his residence among them, as I am informed by those who knew him. He had probably imbibed the opinion that the natives were incapable of being taught and therefore spared himself trouble that he thought would be of no use. Nevertheless, he was willing to preach to them, and had a good portion of their land set off for his support. Truth obliges me to say that not one Indian was converted during the fifty years of his ministry. The neighboring whites were the sole recipients of the good resulting from his labors, if there was any. Speaking on this subject, the Reverend Cotton Mather Smith says that the arrangements for managing Indian schools were never thoroughly made, admirable as was the general plan and much as it promised. I think I may safely vouch for the truth and honesty of the reverend gentleman's admission.

Mr. Fish succeeded Mr. Hawley, in 1809, and was confirmed in his office by the authorities at Harvard and the white overseers at Marshpee. The arrangement was sanctioned by the General Court in 1811, contrary to law, as we think. Surely it takes two sides to make a bargain, and the consent of the Indians was never asked or obtained. Both of the divines mentioned above were willing to have the use of the property of the Marshpees, I fear, under a mere pretext of doing them good; and, therefore, that they and the overseers might have a support from the plantation, the owners were constantly proclaimed to be savages. I wonder what the whites would say, should the Indians take possession of any part of their property. Many and many a red man has been butchered for a less wrong than the Marshpees complain of.

Neither of the reverend gentlemen set up schools, and when the Marshpee children were put out to service, it was with the express understanding, as their parents all agree, that they should not be schooled. Many of those who held them in servitude used them more like dogs than human beings, feeding them scantily, lodging them hard, and clothing them with rags. Such, I believe, has always been the case about Indian reservations. I had a sister who was slavishly used and half starved; and I have not forgotten, nor can I ever forget, the abuse I received myself. To keep Indian children from hearing the Gospel preached in a land of Gospel privileges, in order that they might do work unbefitting the Sabbath at home, has been the practice, almost without an exception, wherever I have had opportunity to observe. I think that the Indians ought to keep the twenty-fifth of December (Christmas) and the fourth of July as days of fasting and lamentation, and dress themselves, and their houses, and their cattle in mourning weeds, and pray to heaven for deliverance from their oppressions; for surely there is no joy in those days for the man of color.

Let the reader judge, from what has been stated, what good the Marshpee Indians have derived from their two missionaries. I say boldly, none at all. On the contrary, they have been in the way of the good that would have been done by others. I say also that all the religious advantages the Indians have enjoyed have come from other ministers and members of other churches. I am equally sure that the money paid for our use, from the Williams Fund, has been a curse and not a blessing to us. Had some good Christian minister come to the tribe with half the sum, there is no doubt that God would have made him an instrument to raise up a respectable Christian society; whereas the fund has only served to build up the missionaries and the whites about the plantation. I am glad that it has done even this good, though it be to our enemies; for I am not of a spirit to envy the prosperity of others; I rejoice in it. But I sincerely think it is wrong in the whites to take the Gospel from the Indians, as they do in Marshpee, by occupying their meetinghouse and receiving the benefit of the missionary fund. I mean that the people about Cotuit and Marshpee go to our house and fill it, to our exclusion, without any charge; while the Indians are enforced by the laws which deprive them of the use of their own lands to pay a heavy tax, from which they derive no benefit. Is not depriving them of all means of mental culture the worst of all robberies? Can it be wondered that the Indians become more and more degraded? I presume all honest people will regret that such has been the case. It will be seen that both the missionaries and their white followers imbibed all the prejudices of the day and, by disseminating them, hindered others from doing us good. This is no excuse, however, for the government of this Commonwealth, whose duty it was to see that its red children were not abused in this way. We greatly fear that our white fathers did not much care about their colored children in Marshpee. At any rate, it may be some satisfaction to the philanthropists in the country to know how liberal they have been to their poor dependents.

To begin: The Indians owe nothing to the Commonwealth of Massachusetts, or to the inhabitants of New England generally, for religious instruction, excepting a single appropriation of four hundred dollars, made in 1816 or 1818, for repairing their meetinghouse. Four hundred dollars more were appropriated in 1831, for the purposes of erecting two schoolhouses; but not one cent for a teacher. (By an act of the Legislature in April last, 1835, *One Hundred Dollars* is hereafter to be appropriated annually, from the School Fund, for the public schools in Marshpee. For this liberal act the Marshpees are indebted to the representations made to the Committee on Education by their counsel, B. F. Hallett, Esq. This is an evidence of the paternal care of the Legislature, for which we can never be too grateful.)

The way the Marshpees have supported a school hitherto has been this. Some of them have lived abroad among the whites and have learned to read and write, with perhaps some small smattering of arithmetic. On returning to the tribe, they have taught others what they knew themselves, receiving pay from those who had the means and teaching the rest gratuitously. At the same time they have been compelled to support a preacher whom they did not wish to hear, and to pay, in one way or other, to the amount of four hundred dollars *per annum* to white officers, for doing them injury and not good. Thus then, in one hundred and forty years they have paid fifty-six thousand dollars to the whites, out of their own funds, in obedience to the laws of the Commonwealth. In return, the whites have given them one thousand in labor and money. Truly, the Commonwealth must make haste, or it will hardly be able to pay us the interest of our money. The principal we never expect to get.

Thus, though it is manifest that we have cost the government absolutely much less than nothing, we have been called state paupers, and as such treated. Those are strange paupers who maintain themselves, and pay large sums to others into the bargain. Heigh-ho! It is a fine thing to be an Indian. One might almost as well be a slave.

To return to the proceedings of the court at Cotuit: When suppertime was past, the Cotuiters were anxious to draw something out of me by questioning. They said they knew more about the matter than I did; that I had gotten myself into difficulty; and that Mr. Fish was a good man and had gained twenty members over to his church in twenty-five years. They might have added that these were infants, who became members merely by undergoing the rite of baptism. Perhaps they were very good members when they grew up—perhaps not.

Mr. Fish, alluding to the charge that but eight or ten of the Indians heard him preach, stated, in his memorial to the Legislature, that more than twice ten were upon his Sabbath school list. That might be true; but it was no answer to the charge. There may well have been on his list the names of so many persons, who attended neither his meeting nor his school. Nor had he denied the statements of the Indians in the least. I said to the gentlemen, who were rejoicing over my supposed downfall, that I was glad they had taken me into custody, as it would lead to an investigation of the whole ground in dispute. Mr. Ewer presently arrived; his bail was accepted, and I and my friends returned home.

On the seventh of July, I was again visited by the Hon. J. J. Fiske, who conversed freely with me on our religious affairs. He said it would be better for us to turn Congregationalists, as then we should probably be able to get assistance from the fund. I replied that I cared little by what name I was called, for I was no sectarian but could unite in the worship of God with all good Christians. It seemed to be the opinion of the Hon. J. J. Fiske that it was wrong for the Reverend Mr. Fish to receive the salary he did, without attending to the concerns of the Indians.

On the sixth, the head men of the tribe held a meeting and agreed to rescind the former meetings until the session of the Legislature, as the commissioner had fairly stated that whatever could be done for us would be done by that honorable body. We could do no less than accept a promise coming from so high an authority and await the leisure of our father, the Legislature, though he had neglected us and suffered us to be abused. Who could say but that he would uplift his voice and weep aloud, on hearing the story of our wrongs, as Joseph and his brethren did when they recognized each other? And indeed, though our tender parent proved a little hardhearted at first, by and by there was a little relenting toward his poor suffering babes of the woods, as will be seen in the proper place. The following notice was drawn up accordingly:

Whereas, certain resolutions have been made by us, the Marshpee Indians, in reference to our plantation, we do hereby solemnly declare, upon the security of the Governor's Counsel, (Meaning Envoy) that we shall be righted; and that there shall be a change of government, if necessary, and that the governor has pledged himself to do right, and that the property sold for money or otherwise disposed of, shall be refunded to us again, and that justice shall be done. Now, in consideration thereof, we do hereby guarantee to our white neighbors that they shall not be molested in their lawful concerns upon our plantation, provided that no white man meddles or interferes in any way whatever in our lawful affairs; and that you may understand that it is so, we say the resolutions are revoked, and we will wait with pleasure the sitting of the Legislature.

Done by the order of the Marshpee Tribe, July 6, 1833.

Daniel Amos, *President*

Israel Amos, *Secretary*

Soon after this, the commissioner departed, and I saw him no more till the sitting of the General Court. About this time our affairs got into the public prints, and it was reported through the whole land that there were hostile movements among the Indians at Cape Cod, or Buzzard's Bay. All the editors were very willing to speak on the favorite topic of Indian wrongs; but very few of them said anything about redress. On this head they were either silent or against us. Here and there was found one liberal and independent enough to speak in our behalf. Some of these articles shall be given, that it may be seen who were for or against our rights and privileges. It will be proper to state in the first place, however, that from July 4 to the sitting of the Court of Common Pleas, in September, there was little disturbance upon the plantation. We thought, from what we heard among the whites, that they were inclined to spare no pains to frighten us; but we listened patiently and remained quiet, according to our promise.

In August, we had a four-day meeting, which was the means of much good. Twelve Indians were redeemed from sin, and during the eighteen months that I have known them, the power of God has been manifested in the conversion of some thirty. God forbid that I should glorify myself; I only mention the circumstance to show that the Marshpees are not incapable of improvement, as their enemies would have the world suppose. But, under these circumstances, is it not natural for the Indians to think that their missionaries have cared less for saving their souls than for filling their own pockets, and that their thousands have been expended on them to very small purpose? I do think that the result of this meeting was in no wise pleasing to our white enemies.

At harvest time the reapers cut their grain and carried it to their granaries. But they were under the control of their taskmasters. A dispute arose. A woman whose husband was absent, doing business upon the great waters, claimed a portion of the grain, while the overseers maintained that it belonged to them. She applied for assistance to one of the true proprietors, who, in the presence of five or six men who were with the overseers' team, unloaded it and placed the grain where it ought to have been. I was present and happened to smile at this novel proceeding, which I suppose was the cause of a prosecution that presently took place for trespass. My horse had bitten off five or six rye heads in a rye field, for which enormity his owner was obliged to pay ten dollars, though the actual damage was not to the value of six cents. I will not retort the petty malice which prompted this mean act of revenge, by mentioning names. I now proceed to mark out the state of public feeling, by some extracts from the newspapers. The following is from the *New Bedford Press,* of June 1, 1833:

Marshpee Indians

The remnants of that race of men who once owned and inhabited the forests and prairies of the Old Colony that have now given place to large and populous villages and the busy hum of *civilized* man, are, it would seem, somewhat dissatisfied with the manner in which they are governed by the State authority. Communications illustrative of the condition of the *Marshpee Indians* in the County of Barnstable, have been forwarded to us by the agent of the tribe, by which it appears that they have been abused. Intelligence from other quarters comes fraught with bitter complaint, and there can be no manner of doubt that too ample room remains for the improvement of their condition. The communications at hand advise the Indians to stand out for their right to appoint their own overseers, and do all business now especially done by the State. That they ought to be allowed this privilege (if *privilege* it may be called), there is no question; but there is a question, whether this is the first important step to be taken. By a list of names which accompanies our advices, it appears that very few are able to write their own names, their mark being affixed instead; and in addition to this, we are informed that there are many who cannot even read. With this view of their condition the correct and efficient course to be pursued would seem to be that of sending *Education Missionaries* among them, that in contending for their rights, of which they say they are deprived, they may be enabled to act understandingly.

This may serve to show that the Marshpees had long been dissatisfied with their government and that very many complaints had been made, which will be illustrated by extracts from divers petitions, in another page. The next refers to the Marshpee trials and is signed in a manner signifying that the writer speaks advisedly, and from knowledge.

From the *Barnstable Journal* of July 18, 1833:

> Mr. Apes was arrested at the Marshpee Plantation on the 4th, by order of the Executive, and required to give bond for his good behavior.
>
> Mr. Apes now says, that this statement is not correct; that the Governor has ordered no such thing, and that he never was requested in all his life to give bond for his behavior.
>
> Much has been said in and out of the papers about the Indians in Marshpee. All that the Indians want in Marshpee is to enjoy their rights without molestation. They have hurt or harmed no one. They have only been searching out their rights, and in so doing, exposed and uncovered, have thrown aside the mantle of deception, that honest men might behold and see for themselves their wrongs. The Indians could spread columns before the world which would cause the hearts of good men to be sad, and recoil at the conduct of their white brothers. All that Mr. A. wishes is, that people would tell the truth.
>
> A Beholder

With regard to this article, I have to say that it speaks the truth. If an honest white man could look into our private affairs and know what wrongs we have suffered, it would change his complexion to a hue redder than the Indian's. But the crimes committed against our race cannot be enumerated here below. They will each and all, however, be judged at the bar of God, and it must be the comfort of the poor and oppressed, who cry for justice and find it not, that there is one who sees and knows and will do right. The next is from the *Boston Daily Advocate,* of July 12.

> Rev. Mr. Apes, who has been conspicuous in the Marshpee nullification, has, we learn, been taken and committed to jail in Barnstable county; upon what process, we are not informed, but we trust, for the honor of the State, that while our mouths are yet full of bitterness against Georgian violence, upon the Indians, we shall not imitate their example.

How true it is that men see the faults of others, rather than their own. If the good people of Massachusetts were as ready to do right as to have the Georgians do right, the Marshpee Indians might, perhaps, send a representative to the Legislature. I hope the remark will give no offense. The next is from the same print, of July 15, 1833.

> The Marshpee affairs, we are gratified to learn, are more quiet than they have been. The Indians took forcible possession of the Meeting-house the other day, and have retained it ever since, but no farther act has been committed on their part. They notified Mr. Fish that they had dismissed

him from their Parish, and also formally gave notice to the overseers that their offices were at an end. Hon. J. J. Fiske, of the Executive Council, has visited the Indians, by request of the Governor, and has, we learn, discharged the duty in a highly conciliatory and discreet manner. The Indians would not at first consent to see him, but being satisfied of the disposition of the Executive to listen to their grievances, they met Mr. Fiske alone in the Meeting-house, where, by their special request, the overseers also appeared. The Sheriff of the county, Hon. John Reed, and others, were also present. About one hundred of the Indians appeared, many of them armed with guns. They were perfectly under the command of Apes, but all of them conducted with propriety, and seemed peaceably disposed. Mr. Fiske heard their complaints for one day. Their demands were to have the overseers removed, and the books and funds, now in the hands of the Treasurer, transferred to them; and in fact to be left to the entire management of their affairs. It was explained to them that the Governor had no power to do this, if he were so disposed. That he could only change their overseers, and lay their complaints before the Legislature, who alone could alter the laws now governing the plantation. To this Apes would not agree, insisting that they should be relieved of the guardianship of the State, and that the Governor could do it at once.

He was questioned as to his own right to be on the plantation, to which he does not belong, and finding all argument useless with him, Apes was arrested in the assembly (where he was acting as moderator), upon a warrant for assault and trespass, in unloading the teams of Mr. Sampson. The Indians were perfectly quiet, and Apes having been bound over for his appearance to take his trial, in the sum of $200, he was immediately bailed by Mr. Ewer, a Justice of the Peace, and was not committed to jail, as has been represented. After his arrest, he expressed some contrition, and admitted he had gone too far. The ultimate understanding appears to be with the Indians, that they will offer no further resistance, but wait patiently for a redress of grievances, until the meeting of the Legislature, when they confidently expect to have their guardianship removed. As an evidence of their peaceable disposition, "President" Amos, at the request of Mr. Fiske, gave up the key of the Meeting-house, for Rev. Mr. Fish to occupy the pulpit, and asked as a favor, that the Indians might occupy it half the time. The result of the mission of Mr. Fiske, is therefore very favorable, and if a similar course is pursued hereafter, there will be no further difficulty with the tribe. They should be treated with all possible lenity and kindness, for the honor of the Commonwealth.

The Indians would not consent to see Mr. Fiske at first, because they did not like to meet their enemies off their own ground, and I presume they would not have consented to do so to this day. As to the counselor's meeting us alone, it was the special direction of the governor that he should hear the parties separately, because, supposing the government to be oppressive, it seemed to him that the Indians would be afraid to speak plainly in presence of their masters, or proffer their complaints. The Indians wished to do nothing in a corner, but rather to proceed with an open and manly spirit, that should show that they were unjustly accounted abject and willing slaves. As to my opinion of the powers of the governor, I have already admitted that I was in error; for I am not a man skilled in legal subtleties. My reason for pressing our claims so strongly was to make the way easy for my brethren, till something could be done for them. The Indians were requested to give up their own meetinghouse to a gentleman who did not come at their request, and to gather other people into it to suit his convenience. The Indians asked for their own house for only half the time, and even this was denied them. The law not bearing out their petition, they could only obtain it by force, and finding this to be the case, they forbore.

The question is: How can a man do good among a people who do not respect him or desire his presence, and who refuse to hear him preach? Yet Harvard College has forced such a one on the Marshpees against their will, right or wrong.

I heard a white lady observe that Mr. Fish was not a preacher for everyone, as though he was not fit to preach to any but us poor ignorant Indians. Nevertheless, if any people need a talented, enterprising preacher, we are the very ones. Some may suppose Mr. Fish to be a Unitarian. He was, when he was first settled at Marshpee; but his opinions underwent a change soon after, and he became what is commonly called an orthodox Congregationalist. In order to be a good one, he ought to make one more change—a change of inclination to force himself on poor Indians. One who has such an inclination cannot be a good member of any sect, or an honor to it. Such a person can be no ornament to any ecclesiastical body. I would not have it inferred from this that a breath of reproach is in my mind, or in those of my brethren, against any denomination of Christians. We love all who love the Lord Jesus in sincerity.

I expressed no contrition because I thought I had acted morally wrong, or had asked anything more than was right, but because I had mistaken the *law,* which in this case was a very different thing from justice.

The next article is from the *Barnstable Journal,* of July 25. It will serve to show that, though the matter had been perfectly explained to the inhabitants of Barnstable County, yet it contained some of our worst enemies as well as best friends. Our enemies were those in office, and those under their influence. The majority believed the Indians to be wronged and ought to have had redress; and these were unable to act in our behalf. Those who did act were either our enemies or persons who had no minds of their own and were led by them in all they did. Many of them did, nevertheless, sympathize with the Indians and pitied them when cast into prison, for all men can appreciate the blessing of liberty.

Marshpee Indians

Messrs. Editors,

We observed in one of your late papers, some editorial remarks which breathed a spirit of candor and good will towards us, and not of ridicule and sarcasm like that of your neighbor, the Patriot. Now Messrs. Editors, as our situation is but little understood, and the minds of the people much agitated, we feel a desire to lay before them some of the causes of the late excitement. We have long been under guardians, placed in authority over us, without our having any voice in the selection, and, as we believe, not constitutional. Will the good people of Massachusetts revert back to the days of their fathers, when they were under the galling yoke of the mother country? when they petitioned the government for a redress of grievances, but in vain? At length they were determined to try some other method; and when some English ships came to Boston, laden with tea, they mustered their forces, unloaded and threw it into the dock, and thereby laid the foundation of their future independence, although it was in a terrible war, that your fathers sealed with their blood a covenant made with liberty. And now we ask the good people of Massachusetts, the boasted cradle of independence, whom we have petitioned for a redress of wrongs, more grievous than what your fathers had to bear, and our petitioning was as fruitless as theirs, and there was no other alternative but like theirs, to take our stand, and as we have on our plantation but one harbor, and no English ships of tea, for a substitute, we unloaded two wagons loaded with our wood, without a wish to injure the owners of the wagons. And now, good people of Massachusetts, when your fathers dared to unfurl the banners of freedom amidst the hostile fleets and armies of Great Britain, it was then that Marshpee furnished them with some of her bravest men to fight your battles. Yes, by the side of your fathers they fought and bled, and now their blood cries to you from the ground to restore that liberty so unjustly taken from us by their sons.

Marshpee

The next article is from the *Boston Daily Advocate*. In the editorial remarks will be discerned the noble spirit of independence and love of right, which are prominent characteristics of Mr. Hallett's character and which induced him, throughout the controversy, to lend the aid of his columns to the poor and oppressed descendants of the people who welcomed his forefathers to their shores. He is not ungrateful for the kindness showed them in a time so remote. I think it my duty to say of him that he has been fruitful of good works in behalf of all the oppressed. We Indians have tried his integrity and have found it sound metal. He gave us the aid of his extensive learning and undeniable talent, and carried our cause before the Legislature with no other end in view than the good of the Commonwealth and of the Marshpee tribe, and a strong desire to wipe from the character of his native state the foul blot of our continued wrongs. He never asked where his pay was to come from, but exposed the iniquities which had been transacted in the affairs of the Marshpee people, without hesitation, fear, or favor, a course he has steadily pursued to this day. We acknowledge his doings as acts of pure benevolence toward us, and we say that the sons of the Pilgrim fathers may well be proud of such a brother. Had others been only a little like him we should have had no reason to complain; and we recommend him as an example to all who may hereafter have dealings with Indians. Let them do as he has done, and they will be honored as he is. To be sure, it is no great matter to be loved and honored by poor Indians; but the good will of even a dog is better than his ill will. The rich man fared sumptuously every day, while the poor one was lying at his gate, feeding on the crumbs that fell from his table, and the dogs only had compassion on him. They both died; and we read that God sent a convoy of angels to bring the poor man safe home. The rich man doubtless had a splendid funeral; but we do not hear that he had any favor from his Maker. Oh ye who despise Indians, merely because they are poor, ignorant, and copper-colored; do you not think that God will have respect unto them?

The Marshpee Indians

We have received a genuine communication from one of the Marshpee Indians, and as we verily believe that tribe is in many respects wronged by the whites, and neglected by their legal guardians, the Legislature, we are desirous of giving them a hearing, that justice may be done them, if it be a possible matter to get such a thing as justice and good faith from white men toward Indians. Undoubtedly some of their supposed grievances are imaginary and much exaggerated, but others are real, and tend greatly to depress them. We have had an overflow of sensibility in this quarter toward the Cherokees, and there is now an opportunity of showing to the world whether the people of Massachusetts can exercise more justice and less cupidity toward their own Indians than the Georgians have toward the Cherokees. We earnestly exhort the Marshpeeians to abstain from all acts of violence, and to rely with full confidence upon the next Legislature for redress. That body has heretofore treated their claims too lightly, but there is a growing disposition to hear and relieve their grievances. A memorial from the tribe, setting forth the wrongs of which they complain, would unquestionably receive prompt attention. The laws by which they are exposed to the cupidity of their white neighbors, are extremely defective, and require a thorough reform. Our correspondent, who we believe speaks the sentiments of the tribe, shall be heard for himself, and we hold our columns free to publish any facts, on either side of this question, which may be offered to the public.

"Marshpee, Aug. 5, 1833

"Mr. Hallett,

"*Dear Sir*—With regret I say that your white brethren still think it a privilege to impose upon us here. The men upon our plantation were gathering their hay harvest, and the poor women whose husbands were at sea, who had let out their land, confidently expected to have their share, but it was taken from them by unjust men, and not so much as a spear of it left to sustain them, or even the promise of help or aid in any way; it was not taken for debt and no one knows for what. The overseers have now become displeased, and choose at this time to use their great power. I hope we shall not have to call upon the State to protect us, but if we are imposed upon in this manner, we believe we shall. And while we are willing to be still and peaceable, we think that those of our white friends, with the light they possess, ought to show as much of the spirit of kindness as poor ignorant Indians. The Legislature has bound the poor Indians as they have. The Indians would propose one thing. We have some white men here who will smuggle rum, and sell it to the Indians, and as they have no license, they ought to be stopped. We are happy to say that many of our Indians are temperate, but we wish them all to be, and we want some way to have a stop put to these things, for these white men are ten times worse than any of the Indians. I might name a Fuller, a Chadwick, and a Richardson; we really wish that the honorable Legislature would place guardians over them, to keep them from wasting our property in this way. While I was absent, there was a man that sued me for trespass, and tried the case without my information. What kind of law is this? I had the liberty of baiting my horse in a field. A man had rye in a field he did not hire, but took it upon shares. My horse got in his rye, but six cents would pay all the damage. But the action is not damage, but trespass, and that done unknown to me.

"It is impossible to give you the details of wrongs imposed upon the

Indians. We are to be accused by our enemies, tried by them, and condemned by them. We can get redress nowhere, unless we trouble the government all the while, and that we are delicate to do.

"Now we believe that some of these things published abroad would do good, and we should have more peace.

"Yours, most obediently"

We have received another communication from Marshpee, upon the same subject:

"Having seen several articles in your paper, relating to the Marshpee tribe, we perceive that your paper is free, not muzzled. Marshpee Indians speak for themselves. It is not to be doubted but that the public would like to hear the Indians speak for themselves. It has been represented that the Indians were troublesome, and war-like movements were among us. If to make an inquiry into our rights by us, is war-like, so it is. Otherwise than this we know nothing about it, and we know of none that has a disposition to shed blood. It is true that the day the Hon. J. J. Fiske, of the Governor's Council, was present with us, in a council at the meeting-house, the Indians, three in number, were out in the morning, hunting deer, and when they came to the meeting-house, they had their business to attend to, and could not conveniently go four or five miles to put up their muskets, neither did we see the propriety of their so doing. We believe that a just man would not have trembled at an old rusty musket.

"We are hard to believe, that any people, served as we have been here, would more kindly submit to it, than we have. We think now we have submitted long enough, and we thought it no crime to look, or ask after our rights. But we found our white neighbors had thrown their chains of interest around our principal stock, so much so that we began to think they soon would drag both interest and principal all away. And no wonder they began to cry out, when they saw that the Indians were likely to unhook their chains, and break their hold. We believe white men had more war in their hearts than any of the Indians.

"We are willing to hint a few things. We thought white men would do well, that they were trusty. We doubt not but what they be among themselves; but we scarcely believe that they care much for the poor Indians, any further than what they can get out of them. It is true we have land in Marshpee. We can stay upon it; but we have had to pay one dollar per cord, to the overseers, for our own wood, and take it or carry it just where these men said. Our meadows were taken from us and rented out to white people, our pastures also. About twelve hundred cords of our wood has been cut the last year, and we judge the minister has cut one hundred and fifty cords for his share. And in a word, they did as they pleased. The poor could get a pound of meat, or a half peck of corn, and one quart of molasses for two weeks. Much might be said, but we forbear. It is true that we have had a preacher, but we do not believe that he cares anything about us. Neither had we any hand in his settlement over us. To be sure, he likes to stay with us, but we think it is because he gets so much good pay. But five or six adult persons attend his preaching, there being *not one Indian male* belonging to his church. This gentleman has cut much wood, to the dissatisfaction of the Indians; and it is true they have passed resolutions that they will not hear him preach. Yet he wants to stay with us.

"Interest[ed] men tremble and threaten, but we fear not, and sincerely hope they will soon tremble before God, and prepare to meet their Judge, who will do right, and who will have no regard for skins or color.
                                                                "Think of the Indians"

We turn from this judicious and liberal article to one that is less favorable. It is from the *Barnstable Journal*, of August 22, 1833.

The Indians

We learn from South Sandwich that the Indians, constituting the Marshpee tribe, intend to petition at the sitting of the next Legislature, for a redress of grievances, and a revision of the code of laws by which they are governed. The recent revolt among them, and the measures adopted to make known their situation and treatment, by themselves, and by those who have avowed their friendship toward them (its validity time will determine), gave rise to considerable excitement. An inquiry into the state of affairs was instituted, which terminated, as far as we have been able to learn, to the satisfaction of those employed in the investigation, that some of the evils under which they are labouring are real, and rendered so by the laws of the Commonwealth, but many imaginary. We do not doubt that the state of society among them is low and degraded, comparatively speaking, but what contributes to keep them in this situation we are unable to say, unless it be, that the plantation has been a resort of the vagrant, the indolent, and those whom refined society would not allow among them. If this is the case, and we believe it has been, something should be done, either among the Indians, or by the Legislature, to remedy the evil. We have understood also, that certain individuals, located contiguous to the plantation, retail ardent spirits to them in quantities as large as they are able to pay for. If this be the fact, such men should be ferreted out, and in justice to the Indians, to the community about them, and to the laws of the land, they should be made to suffer, by being exhibited to public derision, and by the penalty of the act prohibiting the retail of spirits. If they have not the power, and no one feels willing to go forward in shutting up these poisonous springs, give them the power, and if they do not exercise it, let them suffer.

Mr. Apes is among them, and attended the "Four Days Meeting," held during the present of month, which we are told was managed with good order and regularity.

The writer here says that the Indians are vile and degraded, and admits that they can be improved. He gives no explanation of the causes of their degradation. If the reader will take the trouble to examine the laws regarding the Marshpees, he will see those causes of the inevitable and melancholy effect and, I am sure, will come to the conclusion that any people living under them must necessarily be degraded. The *Journal*, however, does us the small justice to admit that we are not so degraded but that we can hold a meeting of four days' duration with propriety and moderation. What, then, might we not do, were proper pains taken to educate us?

The next two extracts are from the *Boston Advocate* of September 10 and 11, 1833.

The Marshpee Indians

We are mortified for the honor of the State, to learn from Barnstable County, that the Court of Common Pleas and Sessions there (Judge Cummins) have tried and convicted William Apes and six Indians of the Marshpee tribe, upon charges connected with the efforts of the Indians to obtain justice from their white masters. Apes is very popular with the Indians, and this persecution of him, which at least was unnecessary, will inflame them the more.

The papers say the conviction was for *riot*. This cannot be, for there was no riot, and no riot act read. Apes and his associates prevented a man from carrying wood off the plantation. They were, perhaps, wrong in doing so, but the law which takes this wood from the Indian proprietors, is as unjust and unconstitutional as the Georgia laws, that take the gold mines from the Cherokees. Could the question of property have been tried, the act of stopping their own wood, by the Indians, could not have been made even trespass, much less riot. It is said that Apes and the rest were indicted under some obsolete law, making it a misdemeanor to conspire against the laws. We have looked for such an act, but cannot find it in the Statute Book.

At any rate, law or no law, the Indians were indicted and convicted. They were tried by their opponents, and it would be impossible to get justice done them in Barnstable County. An impartial jury could not be found there. It is the interest of too many to keep the Indians degraded. We think the conviction of these Indians is an act of cruelty and oppression, disgraceful to the Commonwealth. The Marshpee Indians are wronged and oppressed by our laws, nearly as much as ever the Cherokees were by the Georgians. But it is useless to call for the exercise of philanthropy at *home*. It is all expended *abroad*.

An attempt was made to indict some of the white harpies, who are selling rum to the Indians, without license. Those men got clear, and are still suffered to prey on the poor Indians; but to stop a load of wood, which in reality belonged to the Indians themselves, was an outrage which the Court were ready enough to punish! Is it creditable to let the *white* spiders break through the laws, while we catch and crush the poor Indian flies?

The Indians

William Apes and the Marshpee Indians, who were tried before the Court of Common Pleas in Barnstable County, were ably defended by Mr. Sumner, of this city. Apes was sentenced by Judge Cummings, to thirty days imprisonment in the common jail. One other was sentenced to ten days imprisonment, and the rest were not tried. When the sentence was pronounced, several Indians who were present, gave indications of strong excitement at what they conceive to be a tyrannical persecution. It is much to be feared, that this unnecessary and apparently vindictive course, pursued by the overseers and their friends, after the Indians had become quiet, and resolved to wait patiently for redress from the Legislature, will inflame them to acts of violence, and give the whites who wish to oppress them, further advantages over them.

We have visited the greater part of the tribe recently, in their own dwellings, and we know how strongly and unanimously they feel upon the subject of what they really believe to be, their slavery to the overseers. If, therefore, the course we have pursued, and mean to pursue, in laying their claims to justice before the public, entitles us to be listened to as a friend, we beg them to abstain from all acts which violate even the unjust and hard laws by which they are now held in bondage. Resistance will furnish their enemies with the strongest weapons against them, and discourage their friends. Let them endure patiently, till the next Legislature meets, and if there is any virtue or honesty in our public men, the rights of the Marshpee Indians will be secured.

In our last article we said that it was impossible for the Indians to have an impartial jury in Barnstable. We did not mean that this arose from all the whites being opposed to the Indians. They have many friends in Barnstable County, who think them deeply injured, and who have no interest in keeping them degraded, in order to enjoy the privileges which too many whites now have, at the expense of the tribe. We alluded to the influences that would be used upon the jury, as in the case of Apes, where we learn, that three individuals, favorable to the Indians, but having formed no opinion in that case, were excluded from the regular jury. One of them was set aside, for saying he thought the Indians ought to be free. We are still at a loss to know under what law these Indians were found guilty of riot, in preventing their own wood from being carried off their own land. Where are all our Cherokee philanthropists, at this time?

The injustice of the proceedings of the Barnstable Court of Common Pleas and Sessions is here fitly exposed. In empaneling the jury, it is certain that no name of one favorably inclined toward the Indians was selected, and there are many who do not scruple to say that it was the determination of the court to condemn them, right or wrong. Nevertheless, it appeared, from the evidence brought, that no fear or alarm whatever had been occasioned to the complainants, and that all they had to complain of was having been hindered from taking away the Marshpees' wood.

It may not be amiss to say here that, when the honorable judge said he thought it would be well to postpone the case till the next session, the district attorney, Mr. Warren, replied that he did not think it would be proper, because such a course would involve the Commonwealth in extra expense. I should like to ask what thanks are due to the learned gentleman from the Commonwealth, for subjecting it to continued reproach and disgrace for the sake of a few dollars. Or, can it be that there is no disgrace in persisting in wrong toward Indians? Let those who think so, think so still; but there are many who think otherwise, and there is one above who knows that they think rightly.

When the witnesses and the pleadings had been heard, the jury retired, for the sake of decency, and presently returned with a verdict of *guilty*. I thought that His Honor appeared to be pleased with it. The judgment was suspended about two hours, when the court again sat, and the matter was called up. There was not a little said concerning the case. Messrs. Reed, Sumner, Holmes, and Nye, of Yarmouth, Boston, Rochester, and Sandwich, all professional men, were opposed to the course pursued by the court and thought that an exposition of the law to us and reprimand would be productive of a better effect than imprisonment, or other severe punishment, which they justly believed would do no good whatever. Their judgment has since been confirmed by public opinion, and by the acts of the Legislature.

Since this affair took place, I have been kindly informed by a gentleman of Barnstable that my punishment was not half severe enough. I replied that, in my mind, it was no punishment at all; and I am yet to learn what punishment can dismay a man conscious of his own innocence. Lightning, tempest, and battle, wreck, pain, buffeting, and torture have small terror to a pure conscience. The body they may afflict, but the mind is beyond their power.

The gentleman above mentioned and one other have frequently said to the Marshpees, "If you will only get rid of Apess, and drive him off the plantation, we will be your friends." This has been their continued cry since I began to use my poor endeavors to get the Indians righted; and if it is not now universally believed that it is impossible to benefit and befriend the Indians while I am among them, it is not because they have spared any pains to propagate the doctrine. One would think, to hear these gentlemen talk, that they have a strong desire to benefit the Marshpees; and the question naturally arises, what steps they would take to this end, if they had the power. If we are to judge of the future by experience of the past, we may reasonably suppose that they would profit the tribe by getting possession of their property and making their own advantage of it.

The *Taunton Gazette* found fault with the government of the Commonwealth, for having placed the Marshpees under its laws contrary to their wish and consent, and denies its right so to do. This may be considered as in some degree indicative of the feeling of the good people of Taunton; and there are many other towns in Massachusetts where a kindly feeling is entertained for our persecuted race. We believe the wish to relieve us from bondage is general throughout the state, and we earnestly hope that a few designing men will not be able to accomplish their selfish ends, contrary to the will of a majority of the people.

The next article is from the *Boston Advocate*, of December 4, 1833.

Temperance among the Indians at Marshpee

The Indians met upon the 11th of October to take into consideration the cause of temperance, and to investigate the evils that King Alcohol has practised upon us, by infusing into our heads fancied riches, fame, honor, and grandeur, making us the sovereigns of the whole earth. But having been so often deceived, beat, abused and tyrannized over, and withal cheated, and robbed, and defrauded by this tyrant, and to cap the climax, almost deprived of our senses, burnt and nearly frozen to death, and all our expectations cut off as to the comforts of life, it was agreed upon (after an appropriate address from the Rev. William Apes, setting forth the evils of intemperance and its awful effects in wasting away our

race, like the early dew, before the morning sun) by our most influential
people to attack this mighty champion, and if possible, overcome him,
and shut him up in prison, and set a seal upon him, that he shall deceive
our nation no more. Accordingly a Temperance Society was formed, and
the following officers were elected: Rev. William Apes, President; Rev.
Joseph Amos, Vice President; Dea. I. Coombs, and Thomas Hush, Re-
cording Secretaries; Dea. C. Hinson, Corresponding Secretary; Executive Committee, Oakes Coombs, Joseph Tobey, Frank Hicks. Forty-two of
the tribe united in the pledge of Temperance.

Nov. 14. We met again, and the President again addressed the meeting,
much to the satisfaction of the people. After which many others gave
spirited addresses, setting forth the evils of intemperance, in a most
pathetic manner. It has caused a wonderful effect, and our brethren are
enlisting to take hold and shut up our great enemy in prison, and choke
him to death by total abstinence. Friends of Temperance help.

The Society passed the following resolutions:

Resolved, That we will not countenance the use of ardent spirits among
us, in any way whatever; and that we will do all in our power to suppress
it. That we will not buy it ourselves, nor suffer it to be in our houses,
unless ordered by a physician.

Resolved, That this Society shall meet monthly, to regulate itself, and if
anyone is found to break their pledge, the same shall be excluded,
without speedy repentance.

Voted, That the above be printed. Sixty-one is found upon our list.

Christopher Hinson, *Cor. Sec'y*

Marshpee, Nov. 15

It appears from this that Indians can be temperate, and have a disposition and desire to benefit themselves. It shows, too, that they are capable of
organizing societies, and taking care of their own concerns, as well, to say the
least, as any equal number of persons in the Commonwealth; for they certainly feel more strongly interested for themselves than others can be for
them.

It will be seen that little was done concerning our tribe, from the session
of the court at Barnstable up to the meeting of the Legislature, though the
opposition to us had wealth, talent, and power in its ranks. Clergymen,
lawyers, physicians, counselors, governor, senators, and representatives were
arrayed against us; and we Marshpees account all who opposed our freedom,
as Tories, hostile to the Constitution and the liberties of the country. This is
our sincere opinion of them, and it is to us a thing inexplicable that His
Excellency, the then governor, should have seen fit to place himself at their

head. (His Excellency Levi Lincoln, who proposed to raise a regiment to exterminate our tribe, if we did not submit to the overseers.) We desire to thank our Maker that they found themselves in the minority of the people and fell in the esteem of Christian and benevolent persons who heard of their conduct. We thank the majority of the controllers of public affairs, that they had more sense than to think of holding the rightful lords of the soil in bondage any longer, for the gratification of selfish and unjust men. Honorable is it to Massachusetts that there are enough good and upright men in authority to counteract the measures of those of a different character and remedy the evils they may occasion.

I shall now proceed to present to my brethren an Indian's appeal to them, and the laws framed by the Legislature for the oppression and moral and political destruction of the Marshpees and in bygone days. My comments thereupon will be omitted, because, should I say all the subject suggests, it would swell my book to a bulk that would be wearisome to the reader.

An Indian's Appeal to the White Men of Massachusetts

As our brethren, the white men of Massachusetts, have recently manifested much sympathy for the red men of the Cherokee nation, who have suffered much from their white brethren; as it is contended in this State, that our red brethren, the Cherokees, should be an independent people, having the privileges of the white men; we, the red men of the Marshpee tribe, consider it a favorable time to speak. We are not free. We wish to be so, as much as the red men of Georgia. How will the white man of Massachusetts ask favor for the red men of the South, while the poor Marshpee red men, his near neighbors, sigh in bondage? Will not your white brothers of Georgia tell you to look at home, and clear your own borders of oppression, before you trouble them? Will you think of this? What would be benevolence in Georgia, the red man thinks would be so in Massachusetts. You plead for the Cherokees, will you not raise your voice for the red man of Marshpee? Our overseers are not kind; they speak, you hear them. When we speak for ourselves, our voice is so feeble it is not heard.

You think the men you give us do us good, and that all is right. Brothers, you are deceived; they do us no good. We do them good. They like the place where you have put them. Brothers, our fathers of this State meet soon to make laws; will you help us to enable them to hear the voice of the red man?

Marshpee, Dec. 19, 1833

This appeal was published in several of the public prints, in order to make our dissatisfaction manifest.

The next extract is from the *Boston Advocate* and shows what opposition was made to the reading of our petition in the House of Representatives. The article says all that can be said for itself. (The counsel for the Indians, B. F. Hallett, Esq., could not find a member of the House from Barnstable County who would present the petition. The Indians will not forget that they owed this act of justice to Mr. Cushing of Dorchester.)

Petition of the Marshpee Tribe of Indians

Yesterday morning, in the House, Mr. Cushing of Dorchester, presented the petition of the Proprietors and inhabitants of the Marshpee Plantation, signed by 79 males and 92 females on the plantation, and in behalf of 79 males and 37 females, who are absent from the plantation, and say they will not return to live under the present laws, in all 287: praying for the privilege to manage their own property; for the abolition of the overseership, that they may be incorporated as the town of Marshpee, with the right to make municipal regulations; that one or more Magis-. trates may be appointed among them; and for a repeal of the existing laws relating to their tribe, with the exception of the law preventing their selling their lands, which they pray may be retained; and for a redress of grievances.

[The Memorial sets forth in detail, the complaints of the tribe, and was drawn up among themselves, without assistance. It is represented here by Deacon Coombs, Daniel Amos, and William Apes, all of them well informed Indians, who are deputed by the tribe, and were present in the House yesterday.]

Mr. Cushing moved that the petition be read and referred to a special Committee, to be joined by the Senate.

Mr. Swift of Nantucket, said there was a statement to be made from the Governor and Council, on the subject of the difficulties with the Indians, and he hoped the petition would be laid on the table without being read.

Mr. Allen of Pembroke, hoped the motion to read the petition would not prevail. We should have in a few days a statement from the Governor and Council, and he hoped nothing would be done until that was received, to prejudice the House.

Mr. Cushing of Dorchester, was not aware that any objections could be made to the reading of the petition, which he considered as a matter of course; nor could he see how a knowledge of the matter could prejudice the House. He presumed the House would not take upon itself to refuse to hear the petition of the humblest individual, and he did not fear that they could not control their minds so far as to be ready to give a fair hearing to the other side. The intimation that some document was to come from another source, did not go at all to show that the petition ought not to be read. Whether the statement which gentlemen said was to be made, was in aid or explanation of the petition did not appear, but the subject was before the House, and ought to receive the attention due to it.

Mr. Lucas of Plymouth, said (as far as we could hear him) that the difficulty in the Marshpee tribe had been caused by an itinerant preacher, who went there and urged them to declare their independence. They proceeded to extremities, and the Governor and Council sent a commissioner to examine the affair, and he made a report to the Council, and until that was heard, he hoped nothing would be heard from the Indians. It ought first to come before the House. The petition originated no doubt, from the itinerant preacher, who had been pouring into their ears discontent until they had a riot, and the rioters were prosecuted with the preacher among them, and he was convicted and imprisoned. Whether any of the petitioners were among those rioters or not, he did not know.

Mr. Allen of Pembroke, said he had not heard the gentleman from Plymouth. It was not his wish to prevent the petitioners being heard at a proper time, but he thought the House ought to hear the other side, before any course was taken.

Mr. Robinson of Marblehead, hoped that the attempt would not be persisted in, to withhold from these Indians the common indulgence of having their petition read.

Mr. Loring of Hingham, understood that this was the same petition which went before the Governor and Council [Mr. L. was misinformed; it is a different petition], and as it was very long, it would take up time unnecessarily to read it. He hoped it would be laid on the table.

Mr. Allen of Worcester, thought those who opposed the reading were in fact increasing the importance of the petition by that course. If the House should refuse to hear it read, a course he did not remember had ever been adopted toward any respectful petition, from any quarter, it would become a subject of much more speculation than if it took the ordinary course.

Mr. H. Lincoln of Boston, was surprised to hear an objection raised to the reading of this petition. It was due to the character of the House, and to our native brethren the petitioners, whose agents were here on the floor, that they should be heard, and heard patiently. He hoped that out of respect to ourselves, and from justice to the petitioners, their petition would find every favor, which in justice ought to be extended to it.

Mr. Swift of Nantucket, again urged that the petition ought not to be read, until the report from the Governor and Council was first heard.

Mr. Chapman.—"The petitioners have a constitutional right to be heard. I know not of what value that provision is which gives a right to petition, if the House can refuse to hear the petition. They do not ask for action, but to be heard. It can be read and laid on the table. So long as I hold a seat in this House, my hand shall be raised to give a hearing to the humblest individual who presents a petition for redress of grievances."

Mr. Loring of Hingham hoped the idea could not be entertained that they wished to throw this subject out of the House. He wanted the whole subject should be brought up, and not that this petition should go in first. It was not his wish to prevent the petitioners being heard.

The Speaker put the question, shall the petition be read? and it was carried in the affirmative, nearly every hand in the House being raised. In the negative we saw but five hands. The petition was then read by the Speaker.

Mr. Roberts of Salem moved that it be laid on the table and printed for the use of the House, as there must be a future action of the House upon it. The motion was carried without objection.

The attempt to prevent the petition of the Marshpee Indians from being read, was repelled in the House with an unanimity which shows the value the Representatives place upon the right of petitioning. The poor Indians are without advice or counsel to aid them, for they have no means to fee lawyers, but they will evidently find firm friends in the House ready to do them justice. This is no party question. It involves the honor of the State. Let all be done for them that can be wisely done in a spirit of paternal kindness. Let it not be shown that our sympathy for Indians extends only to those at the South, but has no feeling for our own.

From the same:

The Marshpee Indians

The laws which regulate this remnant of a once powerful tribe of Indians, are not familiar to many, and it is one great defect in the present system, that these laws are so difficult of access, and so complex that the Indians neither know nor comprehend them; and it cannot be expected that they should live contentedly under oppressive regulations which they do not understand. Should any new laws be passed, they ought to be as simple as possible, and be distributed for the use of the Indians.

By the Act of 1788, Ch. 38, Vol. 1 of Laws, page 342, new provisions were made, the previous act of 1788, Ch. 2, being found insufficient "to protect them and their property against the arts and designs of those who may be disposed to take advantage of their weakness." The wisdom of the whites, at that time, invented the following provisions for that purpose:

Section 1. A Board of five Overseers was established (afterwards reduced to three), two to be inhabitants of Barnstable County, and three from an adjoining County. (Now two are inhabitants of Barnstable and one of Plymouth County.) These Overseers were vested with full power to regulate the police of the plantation; to establish rules for managing the affairs, interests and concerns of the Indians and inhabitants. They may improve and lease the lands of the Indians, and their *tenements;* regulate their streams, ponds and fisheries; mete out lots for their particular improvement; control and regulate absolutely, their bargains, contracts, wages, and other dealings, take care of their poor, and bind out their children to suitable persons.

The Overseers are directed to hold stated meetings, elect a moderator, secretary and treasurer, and may appoint and remove guardians over any of the Indians, to act under the Overseers, and to carry their regulations into effect, the guardians to give bonds to the Overseers.

By section 2, the Overseers or the guardians they appoint have power to demand and receive all property or wages owing to said Proprietors or any of them, by any person, and may sue in their own names for its recovery, or for any trespass, fraud or injury done to their lands or them. They may settle all accounts and controversies between the Indians or any white person, for voyages or any services done by them, and may bind the children of poor proprietors by indenture, to suitable persons.

Sect. 3. No lease, covenant, bond or bargain, or contract in writing, is of any validity unless approved by the Overseer or guardian; and no Indian proprietor can be sued for any goods sold, services done, &c. or for money, unless the account is first approved by the Overseers.

[This, it is said, enables the Overseers to sanction the accounts of those who sell to the Indians upon the expectation of obtaining the favor of the Overseers, and opens a door for connivance.]

Sect. 4. The Overseers are to keep a fair account of all monies, wages, &c. they receive, and all proceeds of the plantation, and shall distribute to the proprietors their respective shares and dues, after deducting reasonable expense of conducting their business, *paying their just debts* (of which the Overseers are made the judges), and providing for the sick and indigent, from the common profits, and reserving such sums as can be spared conveniently, for the support of religious instruction, and schooling children. The accounts to be laid before the Governor annually. The Governor and Council appoint the Overseers and displace them at pleasure.

Sect. 5. The Indian Proprietors are prohibited giving any one liberty to cut wood, timber or hay, to milk pine trees, carry off any ore or grain, or to plant or improve any land or tenement, and no such liberty, unless approved by the Overseers, shall bar an action on the part of the Overseers to recover. The lands shall not be taken in execution for debt and an Indian committed for debt may take the poor debtor's oath, his being a *proprietor* to the contrary notwithstanding.

The last act relating to this tribe, was passed Feb. 18, 1819, Chap. 105, 2d vol. of Laws, page 487. It provides that no person thereafter shall be a proprietor of the Plantation, except a child or lineal descendant of some proprietor, and in no other way shall this *right,* as it is called, be acquired. Other inhabitants are called members of the tribe.

The Overseers are to keep a record of names, or census, of all who are proprietors, and all who are residents or members of the tribe, a return of which is to be made to the Governor the last of December.

The Overseers, in addition to all former power, are invested with all the powers and duties of guardians of the Indians, whenever such office of guardian shall be vacant. [A very blind provision, by the way, which it may be as difficult for white men as for Indians to understand.]

Any person selling ardent spirits to an Indian, without a permit in writing from the Overseer, from some agent of theirs or from a respectable physician, may be fined not more than fifty dollars, on conviction; and it shall be the duty of the Overseer to give information for prosecuting such offenders.

The Overseer may bind out to service, for three years at a time, any proprietor or member of the tribe, who in their judgment has become an habitual drunkard and idler, and they may apply his earnings to his own support, his family's, or the proprietors generally, as they think proper.

All real estate acquired or purchased by the industry of the proprietors and members (meaning of course without the limits of the plantation) shall be their sole property and estate, and may be held or conveyed by deed, will, or otherwise.

If any Indian or other person shall cut or take away any wood, timber, or other property, on any lands *belonging* to the proprietors or members which is not set off; or if any person not a proprietor or member, shall do the same on lands that have been set off, or commit any other trespass, they shall be fined not over $200, or imprisoned not over two years. The Indians are declared competent witnesses to prove the trespass. No Indian or other person is to cut wood without a permit in writing, signed by two Overseers, expressing the quantity to be cut, at what time and for what purpose; and the permit must be recorded in their proceedings before any wood or timber shall be cut.

[Of this provision, the Indians greatly complain, because it gives them no more privilege in cutting their own wood than a stranger has, and because under it, as they say, the Overseers oblige them to pay a dollar or more a cord for all the wood they are permitted to cut, which leaves them little or no profit, and compels the industrious to labor merely for the support of the idle, while the white men, who have their teams, vessels, &c. can buy their permits and cut down the wood of the plantation in great quantities, at much greater profit than the Indian can do, who has nothing but his axe, and must pay these white men a dollar or more for carting his wood, and a dollar or more to the Overseers, thus leaving him not enough to encourage industry.]

All accounts of the Overseers are to be annually examined by the Court of Common Pleas for Barnstable, and a copy sent by the Overseers to the Governor.

Any action commenced by the Overseers, does not abate by their death, but may be prosecuted by the survivors.

All fines, &c. under the act, are to be recovered before Courts in Barnstable County, one half to the informer, and the other to the State. These are all the provisions of the law of 1819, and these are the provisions under which the tribe is governed.

As I suppose my reader can understand these laws and is capable of judging of their propriety, I shall say but little on this subject. I will ask him how, if he values his own liberty, he would or could rest quiet under such laws. I ask the inhabitants of New England generally how their fathers bore laws, much less oppressive, when imposed upon them by a foreign government. It will be at once seen that the third section takes from us the rights and privileges of citizens *in toto,* and that we are not allowed to govern our own property, wives, and children. A board of overseers are placed over us to keep our accounts and give debt and credit, as may seem good unto them.

At one time, it was the practice of the overseers, when the Indians hired themselves to their neighbors, to receive their wages and dispose of them at their own discretion. Sometimes an Indian bound on a whaling voyage would earn four or five hundred dollars, and the shipmaster would account to the overseers for the whole sum. The Indian would get some small part of his due, in order to encourage him to go again and gain more for his white masters, to support themselves and educate their children with. And this is but a specimen of the systematic course taken to degrade the tribe from generation to generation. I could tell of one of our masters who has not only supported himself and family out of the proceeds of our lands and labors but has educated a son at Harvard, at our expense.

It is true that, if any Indian elected to leave the plantation, he might settle and accumulate property elsewhere and be free; but if he dared to return home with his property, it was taken out of his hands by the board of overseers, according to the unjust law. His property had no more protection from their rapacity than the rest of the plantation. In the name of heaven (with due reverence), I ask: What people could improve under laws which gave such temptation and facility to plunder? I think such experiments as our government have made ought to be seldom tried.

If the government of Massachusetts do not see fit to believe me, I would fain propose to them a test of the soundness of my reasoning. Let them put our white neighbors in Barnstable County under the guardianship of a board of overseers and give them no privileges other than have been allowed to the poor, despised Indians. Let them inflict upon the said whites a preacher whom they neither love nor respect and do not wish to hear. Let them, in short, be treated just as the Marshpee tribe have been; I think there will soon be a declension of morals and population. We shall see if they will be able to build up a town in such circumstances. Any enterprising men who may be among them will soon seek another home and society, which it is not in the power of the Indians to do, on account of their color. Could they have been received and treated by the world as other people are, there would not be so many living in Marshpee as there are by half.

The laws were calculated to drive the tribes from their possessions and annihilate them as a people; and I presume they would work the same effect upon any other people; for human nature is the same under skins of all colors. Degradation is degradation, all the world over.

If the white man desired the welfare of his red brethren, why did he not give them schools? Why has not the state done something to supply us with teachers and places of instruction? I trow, all the schooling the Marshpee people have ever had they have gotten themselves. There was not even a house on the plantation for the accommodation of a teacher till I arrived among them. We have now a house respectable enough for even a white teacher to lodge in comfortably, and we are in strong hopes that we shall one day soon be able to provide for our own wants, if the whites will only permit us to do so, as they never have done yet. If they can but be convinced that we are human beings, I trust they will be our hindrance no longer.

I beg the reader's patience and attention to a few general remarks. It is a sorrowful truth that, heretofore, all legislation regarding the affairs of Indians has had a direct tendency to degrade them, to drive them from their homes and the graves of their fathers, and to give their lands as a spoil to the

"Manner of Instructing the Indians" [frontispiece for *Indian Nullification*]. The caption for this engraving echoes the tone in much of *Indian Nullification* and *Eulogy on King Philip*, Apess's final works. In both pieces, Apess views most Euro-Americans as patently hypocritical in their actions and their rhetoric regarding Native Americans. He is especially damning of the pretensions of Christians and Christian missionaries. "Instructing" here, then, is but the most transparent veil for "destroying," an equivalence repeated in Apess's frequent play on "conversion," not in the sense of helping Native Americans toward the Christian faith but in the sense of stealing their lands, quite another kind of conversion. Courtesy, American Antiquarian Society.

general government, or to the several states. In New England, especially, it can be proved that Indian lands have been taken to support schools for the whites and the preaching of the Gospel to them. Had the property so taken been applied to the benefit of its true owners, they would not and could not have been so ignorant and degraded a race as they now are, only forty-four of whom, out of four or five hundred, can write their names. From what I have been able to learn from the public prints and other sources, the amount annually derived to the American people from Indian lands is not far from six millions, a tax of which they have almost the sole benefit. In the meanwhile, we daily see the Indian driven farther and farther by inhuman legislation and wars, and all to enrich a people who call themselves Christians and are governed by laws derived from the moral and pious Puritans. I say that, from the year of our Lord, 1656, to the present day, the conduct of the whites toward the Indians has been one continued system of robbery.

I suppose many of my readers have heard of the late robbery at Barnegat and are ready to say that the like has never been known in this country, and seldom in any other. Now, though two-thirds of the inhabitants, not excluding their magistrates, have been proved to be thieves, I ask, was their conduct worse or even so bad as that constantly practiced by the American people toward the Indians? I say no; and what makes the robbery of my wronged race more grievous is that it is sanctioned by legal enactments. Why is it more iniquitous to plunder a stranded ship than to rob, and perhaps murder, an Indian tribe? It is my private opinion that King Solomon was not far wrong when he said, "Bring up a child in the way he should go, and when he is old he will not depart from it." He might have said with equal propriety, "in the way he should *not* go." I am sorry that the Puritans knew no better than to bring up their children to hate and oppress Indians. I must own, however, that the children are growing something better than their fathers were, and I wish that the children of Barnegat had had better parents.

The next matter I shall offer is in two more articles from the *Boston Advocate*. The first is by the editor.

The Indians

The arms of the State of Massachusetts, which appear at the head of all official acts, and upon the seals of office, are an Indian with his bow and arrows. Over his head is an arm holding the sword of Justice. Is this sword designed to protect or oppress the Indians? The Legislature now have the opportunity to answer this question, and as they answer, will be the record in history. The principal community of Indians in this State, the Marshpee tribe, have presented their complaints before the Legislature. Though an unwise attempt was made by some few of the Representatives from the neighborhood of the Indians, to prevent the reading of their petition, it was received with marked kindness by the House, and ordered to be printed, a favor which the Indians did not think of asking.

There is evidently a disposition in the House to prove that our sympathies are not confined merely to the Georgia Indians, for political effect.

Mr. Hallett,

I perceive that your paper has spoken a good word now and then for the native Indians of Massachusetts. There is no class of human beings in this State, who have more need of a candid and humane advocate.

I do not know much about the remnants of a once noble and hospitable race, and yet I know enough to make me grieve for them, and ashamed of the State.

For about two hundred years, the laws have prohibited Indians from selling their lands to whites, within this Commonwealth. This restriction, designed originally to protect the natives against fraud, has, upon the whole, had an unfavorable effect upon their happiness. If they had been at liberty to dispose of their land and depart with the proceeds, or even without the proceeds, to seek some new location, they would in all probability have been happier. Nor have these prohibitory laws had even the poor effect to protect them from the rapacity of their white neighbors. These have contrived to clip the corners of those simple people, and to get hold of their pleasant and fertile valleys in a very surprising manner, considering the strictness of the law.

But the great ground of complaint is, that no native Indian, or descendant, is allowed by us *to be a man, or to make himself a man*, whatever may be his disposition and capacity. They are all kept in a state of vassalage, under officers, appointed sometimes by the Governor, and sometimes by the Legislature. The spot of his own ground, which he may cultivate, is annually rented out to the Indian by an overseer; and provisions are doled out to the tribe according to the discretion of *"Guardians," "Trustees,"* &c. Their accounts are presented to the Governor and Council, who allow, and the Treasurer of the Commonwealth pays them as a matter of course. I dare not say whether those accounts are in all cases correct, or not. If they are, we ought to be thankful to the honesty of the Trustees, &c. not to the wisdom of the Legislature in providing checks upon fraud.

But the effect upon the *Indians* is the great question. This is decidedly bad. They are treated more like dogs than men. A state of tutelage, extending from the cradle to the grave; a state of utter dependence, breaks down every manly attribute, and makes of human creatures, designed to walk erect, creeping things.

But there is another very great evil, if I am rightly informed, which calls loudly for the interposition of the Legislature. The Marshpee and other Indian communities in this State, are not included within the jurisdiction of any incorporated town. The consequence is, that they are without police, except what the Trustees and other officers appointed by them, exercise. These officers never live among them; and the consequence is, that the Indian grounds are so many *Alsatias*, where the vagrant, the dissipated, and the felonious do congregate. Nor is this the fault of the native. It is the fault of their State; which, while it has demolished Indian customs, has set up no regular administration of municipal laws in their stead. Thus I am informed, that at Gayhead, spirituous liquors are retailed without license, and that *it is considered* that there is no power which can reach the abuse. There are many industrious and worthy people among these natives who are anxious for improvement, and to promote the education and improvement of their people, but a degrading personal dependence on the one hand, and the absence of nearly all incentives and all power to do good on the other, keeps them down.

The *paupers* among these natives, who are at some seasons of the year a majority or nearly all of them, are supported by the State, and there must be a great opportunity and temptation to the agents of the government to wrong these poor people. The agents always have the ear of the government, or rather they *are* the government. The Indians have nobody to speak for them. They are kept too poor to pay counsel. I think it is not too much to say that almost any degree of injustice, short of murder, might be done them without any likelihood of their obtaining redress.

Why should not this odious, and brutifying system be put an end to? Why should not the remaining Indians in this Commonwealth be placed upon the same footing as to rights of property, as to civil privileges and duties, as other men? Why should they not *vote*, maintain schools (they have volunteered to do this in some instances), and use as they please that which is their own? If the contiguous towns object to having them added to their corporations, let them be incorporated by themselves; let them choose their officers, establish a police; maintain fences and take up stray cattle. I believe the Indians desire such a change. I believe they have gone as far as they are allowed to introduce it. But they are fettered and ground to the earth.

I am informed that many of the stoutest *whalers* are produced among our small Indian tribes. I am also informed, that they are defrauded by the whites of a great part of their wages, which would otherwise amount to large sums. If some respectable men could be trained up and fostered among these people, their intelligence and influence would be invaluable to educate, protect and guide their seafaring brethren. Under such auspices, they would, after the years of peril, return and settle down with snug independence, be a blessing to their brethren, and respectable in the sight of all. Now they are so knocked about, so cheated, preyed upon and brutalized, that they think of nothing, and *hope* nothing, but sensual gratifications; and in consequence, die prematurely, or live worse than to die.

The Christian philanthropists of Massachusetts little know the extent of evil, which there is in this respect. I entreat them, I entreat the constituted authorities, to look to it.

William Penn

I use these pieces chiefly because they partly correspond in truth and spirit with what I have already said. Let our friends but read the laws, and they will see what the sword of the Commonwealth is intended for. In the second article there is a grievous mistake. It says that the government has assisted us. The Marshpee Indians have always paid their full share of taxes, and very great ones they have been. They have defrayed the expense of two town meetings a year, and one of two of the white men whose presence was necessary lived twenty-five miles off. The meetings lasted three or four days at a time, during which these men lived upon the best, at our cost, and charged us three dollars a day and twenty-five cents a mile, traveling expenses, going and coming, into the bargain. This amounts to thirty-five dollars a trip; and as there were, as has already been said, two visitations a year, it appears that we have paid seventy dollars a year to bring one visitor, whose absence would have been much more agreeable to us than his presence. Extend this calculation to the number of seven persons, and the other expenses of our mis-government, and perhaps some other expenditures not mentioned, and see what a sum our tax will amount to.

The next article is from the *Boston Advocate* of December 27, 1833.

The Marshpee Indians

It was stated in the Barnstable Journal the other day, and has been copied into other papers, that the Marshpee Indians were generally satisfied with their situation, and desired no change, and that the excitement, produced principally by Mr. Apes, had subsided. We had no doubt this statement was incorrect, because we had personally visited most of the tribe, in their houses and wigwams, in August last, and found but one settled feeling of wrong and oppression pervading the whole; not a new impulse depending upon Mr. Apes or any other man, but the result of the unjust laws which have ruled them like a complete despotism.

The Overseers are not so much to blame as the laws. We doubt not they have acted honestly; but, in the spirit of the laws, they have almost unavoidably exercised a stern control over the property and persons of the tribe. In fact the laws, as they now stand, almost permit the Overseers, with impunity, to sell the Indians for slaves. They can bind them out as they please, do as they please with their contracts, expel them from the plantation almost at will, and in fact use them nearly as slaves. We do not think they have intentionally done wrong to the Indians, but the whole system of government is wrong; and hence the unalterable dislike the Indians have to their Overseers. No better men could be appointed, that we know of; but the best men must play the tyrant, if they execute the present laws, designed as they are to *oppress,* and not to protect the poor Indians.

We have known these Indians, from our youth up. They live near our native home. The first pleasure we ever derived from the exercise of benevolence, was in satisfying the calls of their women and children for bread, at our father's door, and we always found them kind hearted to those who were kind to them. We have often met with them to worship in their rural meeting-house, and have again and again explored with the angling rod, the romantic stream, abounding with the nimble trout, which courses through their plantation.

For these reasons, and these alone, we felt it our duty to give them an opportunity to be heard through the columns of our paper, while all others were closed to them, or cold to their complaints. If we can do them any good, we shall have a full reward in the act itself. We have it already in the simple tribute of gratitude, which they have unexpectedly bestowed upon our poor services.

They have sent us a communication, which is signed by the best men in the tribe. We know most of these names, and they belong to the most sensible and most industrious to be found on the plantation. Will other papers publish this simple appeal to the justice of the white men? It is useless to say after this, that the Indians of Marshpee are content with their condition. Something must be done for them.

Marshpee Indians

"Mr. Hallett,

"It has been stated in some of the papers that the Marshpee Indians are generally satisfied with their situation, and the conduct of the Overseers, and want no change. It is also said that the most industrious men on the plantation are opposed to petitioning the Legislature to give them the management of their own property; and they would all have been quiet, if it had not been for Mr. Apes.

"Now we know something of our own rights without being told by Mr. Apes, or anyone. We have confidence in Mr. Apes, and have seen no reason to doubt that he means well; but our dissatisfaction with the laws and the Overseers was the same as it is now, long before Mr. Apes came among us, and he will have our confidence no longer than while we are satisfied he does right. If he does wrong, we shall oppose him as soon as any man, but so long as he honestly aids us in seeking for our rights, we shall be in his favor. He is only one of us, and has no more authority over the tribe than any other member of it. He has been adopted into the tribe, according to the Indian custom; and as long as he deserves our confidence, we shall regard him as a friend.

"But it is unfair to attempt to prejudice the public against us, while we are petitioning for our rights. It is not true that the Indians are satisfied. The Legislature ought not to be deceived by such stories from interested men. There is a universal dissatisfaction with our condition, and unless something is done to relieve us, the whole tribe must suffer, and they will feel as if they must give up all hope of improving their condition. We wish you to publish this with our names, that the public may not be deceived.

"Daniel B. Amos, Oaks A. Coombs, James Hush, Ezra Attaquin,
Isaac Coombs, James Lowes, Christopher Hinson, George Cannada,
Aaron Keeter, Richard Simon, Joseph Pocknet,
Daniel X [his mark] Pocknet, Nicholas Pocknet, Peter X Squib,
David Wilbur, Joseph X Squib, William X Jones,
Jacob X Pocknet, Isaac X Simons, Israel Amos, David Mingo.

"N. B. There could be a host of names procured, but we think here are enough to satisfy the whole earth that we are *not* satisfied to remain in bondage.

"We also feel very grateful for the patriotic and benevolent course that the worthy editor, Mr. Hallett, has pursued, in laying our claims and oppression before the public, especially as he has done it without asking the least compensation. We rejoice to find such friends, for we believe them to be Christians, and impartial philanthropists.

"Gentlemen and ladies of other papers are not forgotten. The Indian's heart swells with gratitude to them for noticing us; and we wish that editors who are friends to our rights, would please notice the above.

"Done at a regular meeting at Marshpee, Dec. 23, 1833.

"Daniel B. Amos, *Sec'y*

Marshpee, Dec. 23, 1833"

I quote these articles only because they serve to show that there was a disposition prevalent among the editorial fraternity to prejudice the people at large against the rights and liberties of the Indians.

After our petition had been presented, our delegates obtained admission into the Hall of the Representatives, where they were privileged to tell their own story. Our enemies endeavored to hinder them even of this, though without success; and thankful are we that they did not succeed. It will be seen from the following that the delegation were not unmindful of their duty.

The address of the Marshpee Indians at Boylston Hall, last evening, was listened to with great attention, by a crowded house, and with approbation, too, if we may judge from the repeated marks of applause.

The address at the State House last Friday evening was also attended by an overflowing house. We were unable to get in, and cannot, therefore, say what effect was produced by it.

The next is from the *Liberator* of Jan. 25, 1834.

The Marshpee Indians

This is a small tribe, comprising four or five hundred persons, residing at the head of Cape Cod, in Barnstable County. They have long been under the guardianship of the State, treated as paupers, and subjected to the control of a Board of Overseers. A memorial from them was presented to the Legislature last week (written entirely by one of their number), in which they set forth the grievances which are imposed upon them, the injustice and impolicy of the laws affecting their tribe, the arbitrary and capricious conduct of the Overseers, and the manner in which they are defrauded of the fruits of their labor; and earnestly beseech the Legislature to grant them the same liberty of action as is enjoyed by their white brethren, that they may manage their own concerns, and be directly amenable to the laws of the State, and not to their present Overseers.

A delegation from this tribe is now in this city, consisting of Deacon Coombs, Daniel Amos, and William Apes. The use of the Hall of the House of Representatives having been granted to them, they made a public statement of their situation and wants to a crowded audience on Friday evening last, principally composed of members of the House; and were listened to most respectfully and attentively.

Deacon Coombs first addressed the assembly, in a brief but somewhat indefinite speech; the purport of which was, that, although by taking side with the Overseers, he might have advanced his own interests, he nevertheless chose to suffer with his people, and to plead in their behalf. Their condition was growing more and more intolerable; excessive exactions were imposed upon them; their industry was crippled by taxation; they wished to have the Overseers discharged.

Daniel Amos next addressed the meeting. He said he was aware of his ignorance; but although his words might be few, and his language broken, he as deeply sympathized with his suffering constituents, as any of his tribe. He gave a short sketch of his life, by which it appeared that he went at an early period on a whaling voyage, and received some bodily injury which incapacitated him from hard labor for a long time. He sought his native home, and soon experienced the severity of those laws, which, though enacted seemingly to protect the tribe, are retarding their improvement, and oppressing their spirits. The present difficulties were not of recent origin. He stated, with commendable pride, that he had never been struck for ill-behavior, nor imprisoned for crime or debt; nor was he ashamed to show his face again in any place he had visited; and he had been round a large portion of the globe. The memorial before the Legislature had been read to the tribe; some parts had been omitted at their request; and nothing had been sent but by their unanimous consent. After vindicating the character of Mr. Apes, and enumerating some of the complaints of the tribe,

He was followed by William Apes, who, in a fearless, comprehensive and eloquent speech, endeavored to prove that, under such laws and such Overseers, no people could rise from their degradation. He illustrated the manner in which extortions were made from the poor Indians, and plainly declared that they wanted their rights as men and as freemen. Although comparatively ignorant, yet they knew enough to manage their own concerns more equitably and economically than they were then managed; and notwithstanding the difficulties under which they labored, their moral condition was improving. There was not so much intemperance among them as formerly; many of the tribe were shrewd, intelligent and respectable men; and all that was necessary to raise up the entire mass from their low estate, was the removal of those fetters and restrictions which now bind them to the dust. Mr. Apes described the cause and the extent of the disturbance which took place last summer, and which resulted in his imprisonment. The head and front of their offending was in going into the woods, and unloading a cart, and causing it to be sent away empty. The reason for that procedure was, that they wished no more wood to be cut until an investigation of their rights had been made. They used no violence; uttered no oaths; made no threats; and took no weapons of defense. Everything was done quietly, but firmly. Mr. Apes wished to know from whence the right to tax them without their consent, and at pleasure, and subject them to the arbitrary control of a Board of Overseers, was derived? He knew not himself; but he feared it was from the color of their skin. He concluded by making a forcible appeal to the justice and humanity of the Legislature, and expressing his confidence that the prayer of the memorialists would not be made in vain.

In several instances, the speakers made some dextrous and pointed thrusts at the whites, for their treatment of the sons of the forest since the time of the pilgrims, which were received with applause by the audience. They were all careful in their references to the conduct of the Overseers; they wished to say as little about them as possible; but they wanted their removal forthwith.

This is the first time our attention has been seriously called to the situation of this tribe. It is a case not to be treated with contempt, or disposed of hastily. It involves the rights, the interests, and the happiness of a large number of that race which has been nearly exterminated by the neglect, the oppression, and the cruelty of a superior number of foreign invaders.

In the enslavement of two millions of American people in the Southern States, the tyranny of this nation assumes a gigantic form. The magnitude of the crime elevates the indignation of the soul. Such august villainy and stupendous iniquity soar above disgust, and mount up to astonishment. A conflagration like that of Moscow, is full of sublimity, though dreadful in its effects; but the burning of a solitary hut makes the incendiary despicable by the meanness of the act.

In the present case, this State is guilty of a series of petty impositions upon a feeble band, which excite not so much indignation as disgust. They may be, and doubtless are, the blunders of legislation; the philanthropy of proscriptive ignorance; the atoning injuries of prejudice, rather than deliberate oppression. No matter who are the Overseers (we know them not), nor how faithfully they have executed the laws. The complaint is principally against the State; incidentally against them. They may succeed, perhaps, in vindicating their own conduct; but the State is to be judged out of the Statute Book, by the laws now in force for the regulation of the tribe. Fearing, in the plenitude of its benevolence, that the Indians would never rise to be men, the Commonwealth has, in the perfection of its wisdom, given them over to absolute pauperism. Believing they were incapable of self-government as free citizens, it has placed them under a guardianship which is sure to keep them in the chains of a servile dependence. Deprecating partial and occasional injustice to them on the part of individuals, it has shrewdly deemed it lawful to plunder them by wholesale, continually. Lamenting that the current of vitality is not strong enough to give them muscular vigor and robust health, it has fastened upon them leeches to fatten on their blood. Assuming that they would be too indolent to labor if they had all the fruits of their industry, it has taken away all motives for superior exertions, by keeping back a portion of their wages. Dreading lest they should run too fast, and too far, in an unfettered state, it has loaded them with chains so effectually as to prevent their running at all. These are some of the excellencies of that paternal guardianship, under which they now groan, and from which they desire the Legislature to grant them deliverance.

We are proud to see this spontaneous, earnest, upward movement of our red brethren. It is not to be stigmatized as turbulent, but applauded as meritorious. It is sedition, it is true; but only the sedition of freedom against oppression; of justice against fraud; of humanity against cruelty. It is the intellect opposed to darkness; the soul opposed to degradation. It is an earnest of better things to come, provided the struggling spirit be set free. Let this tribe have at least a fair trial. While they remain as paupers, they will feel like paupers; be regarded like paupers; be degraded like paupers. We protest against this unnatural order of things; and now that the case has come under our cognizance, we shall not abandon it hastily.

We are aware that another, and probably an opposite view of this case is to be laid before the public, on the part of a commissioner delegated by the Governor and Council, to inquire into the difficulties which have arisen between the tribe and the Overseers. We shall wait to get a glimpse of it before we pass judgment upon it. Whatever may be alleged either against the Indians or against those who hold a supervision over them, or whatever may be said in favor of them both; we have felt authorized to make the foregoing remarks, upon an examination of the laws enacted for the government of these discordant parties. An augmentation, diminution, or change of the Board of Overseers, will not remedy the evil. It lies elsewhere; in the absolute prostration of the petitioners by a blind legislation. They are not, and do not aspire to be an independent government, but citizens of Massachusetts.

Fortunately, there is a soul for freedom in the present Legislature. A more independent House of Representatives has never been elected by the people. The cries of the Indians have reached their ears, and we trust affected their hearts. They will abolish a needless and unjust protectorate. The limb, which is now disjoined and bleeding, will be united to the body politic. What belongs to the red man shall hereafter in truth be his; and, thirsting for knowledge and aspiring to be free, every fetter shall be broken and his soul made glad.

About this time the opposition of our enemies increased to a flood. Yet we remained undismayed, for we knew that we had the right on our side. So we endured the shots of their sharpshooters against us patiently. The following, from the *Boston Courier* of January 28, 1834, will show to what I allude.

Late in the month of June last, an extraordinary proceeding was had by the Marshpee tribe of Indians, residing on their plantation in Barnstable County, under the protection and guardianship of this Commonwealth. Excited, as it has since appeared, by the turbulent spirit of a stranger and intruder, they assembled in what they termed a town meeting, and adopted resolutions declaring their independence of the government of Massachusetts, abjuring the authority of the laws, and proclaiming that after the first day of July then next, they should assume the management of their own affairs; and, *that "they would not permit any white man from that day, to come upon their Plantation to cut or carry off any wood, hay, or other article, without their permission, under the penalty of being bound and thrown from the Plantation."*

To allay the excitement which had been created among these misguided people, and to ascertain and remove, as far and as speedily as possible, any just cause of complaint, the most prompt measures were adopted by the Executive. A discreet and confidential agent was despatched to the plantation with instructions to make thorough examination into their grievances, real or supposed, and to become acquainted with their condition, and what their interest and comfort required. He was especially charged to represent to them the parental feelings and regard of the government of the Commonwealth towards them; to assure the head men, that, if the Overseers appointed by the State, had been unjust or unkind, they should forthwith be removed, and others appointed in their stead, and the wrongs sustained at their hand amply redressed, but that the guardianship, originally imposed for their security against the frauds and wicked devices of unprincipled white men, and continued under frequent assurances, *by the Indians themselves,* of its necessity, could not be suspended by the authority of the Governor and Council. That this rested with the Legislature, to which, after careful investigation of their complaints, a proper representation would be made by the Executive. He was also directed to caution them against heeding the counsels of those who would excite them to disquiet in their present situation, and to admonish them, that disorder and resistance to any rightful authority would meet with immediate and exemplary correction, through the civil tribunals.

On reaching the plantation, the agent found these deluded people in a state of open rebellion against the government of the State, having with force, seized upon the Meeting-house, rescued from the Overseers a portion of property in their possession, chosen officers of their own, and threatened violence to all who should attempt to interfere with them, in the measures of *self-government* which they had assumed. These threatenings and outrages had already created great alarm among the white inhabitants in the neighborhood, and induced to apprehensions of more serious consequences. Through the firmness and prudence of the agent, sustained by the advice and good offices of several intelligent citizens of the County, the leader in the sedition was arrested for a breach of the peace, and delivered over to the civil authority. An inquiry into the conduct of the Overseers subsequently conducted by the agent in the presence of the head men, and the conciliatory, and friendly explanations offered to the tribe, of their relations to the government of the State, resulted in inducing them to rescind their former violent resolves, and restored quiet to the plantation.

A minute and interesting report by the gentleman to whom this delicate service was assigned, embracing an historical account of the tribe, and describing their present condition, character and numbers, with the situation, value, and improvement of their property, and the manner in which the guardianship constituted by law has been exercised over them, accompanies this communication. The Indians have received an assurance, that the attention of the Legislature shall be invited to their complaints, and the report will not fail to assist in the deliberations to which the subject may give occasion.

Does it not appear from this, and from his message, that the ex-governor is a man of pure republican principles? He seems to consider the Marshpees as strangers and thinks they ought to be driven to the wilds of the Far West, in humble imitation of that wise, learned, and humane politician, Andrew Jackson, L.L.D.

I do consider that neither I nor any of my brethren enjoy any political rights; and I desire that I and they may be treated like men, and not like children. If any among us are capable of discharging the duties of office, I wish them to be made eligible, and I wish for the right of suffrage which other men exercise, though not for the purpose of pleasing any party by our votes. I never did so, and I never will. Oh, that all men of color thought and felt as I do on this subject.

I believe that Governor Lincoln had no regard whatever for our rights and liberties; but as he did not get his ends answered, I shall leave him to his conscience. The following from Mr. Hallett, of the *Advocate*, fully explains his message:

The Marshpee Indians

The current seems to be setting very strong against extending any relief to our red brethren. Governor Lincoln's ex-message has served to turn back all the kind feelings that were beginning to expand toward the Marshpee tribe, and force and intimidation are to be substituted for kindness and mercy.

We cannot but think that Massachusetts will be dishonored by pursuing the stern course recommended by Ex-Governor Lincoln, who seems, by one of his letters to Mr. Fiske, to have contemplated almost with pleasure, the prospect of superintending in person, military movements against a handful of Indians, who could not have mustered twenty muskets on the plantation.

We now see how unjust we have been to the Georgians in their treatment of the Cherokees, and if we persist in oppressing the Marshpee Indians, let us hasten to *unresolve* all the glowing resolves we made in favor of the Georgia Indians. If Governor Lincoln is right in his unkind denunciation of the poor Marshpee Indians, then was not Governor Troop of Georgia right, in his messages and measures against the Cherokees? If the Court at Barnstable was right in imprisoning the Indians for attempting to get their rights, as they understood them, and made their ignorance of the law no excuse, were not the Courts of Georgia justifiable in their condemnation of the Cherokees, for violations of laws enforced against the will of the helpless Indians?

Oh, it was glorious to be generous, and magnanimous, and philanthropic toward the Cherokees, and to weep over the barbarities of Georgia, because that could be turned to account against General Jackson; but when it comes home to our own bosoms, when a little handful of red men in our own State, come and ask us for permission to manage their own property, under reasonable restrictions, and presume to resolve that all men are free and equal, without regard to complexion; Governor Lincoln denounces it as *sedition,* the Legislature are exhorted to turn a deaf ear, and the Indians are left to their choice between submission to tyrannical laws, or having the militia called out to shoot them. How glorious this will read in history!

The next is from the *Barnstable Patriot,* of February 5, 1834, of a different character.

Marshpee Indians

Mr. Editor,

William Apes, Deacon Coombs, and Daniel Amos, are now in Boston, where they are much caressed, by the good citizens, and are styled the "*Marshpee Deputation;*" and we see in the Boston papers notices that the "Marshpee Deputation will be present at the Tremont Theatre, by invitation." (Mr. Apes did not attend.) That the Marshpee Deputation will address the public upon the subject of their grievances, in the "*Representative Hall,*" "in Boylston Hall," &c. And we learn at their "*talk,*" in the Representative Hall, they drew a large audience, and that audience was so indiscreet (not to say indecorous or riotous), as to cheer and applaud Apes in his ribaldry, misrepresentation and nonsense. Really, it looks to us, as if there was much misunderstanding upon the subject of the

Marshpee difficulties. If there is anything wrong we would have it put right; but how does the case appear. At the time of Apes' coming among them, they were quiet and peaceable, and their condition, mentally, morally, and pecuniarily improving. At this time, and when this is the condition and situation of the Indians, comes this intruder, this disturber, this riotous and mischief-making Indian, from the Pequot tribe, in Connecticut. He goes among the inhabitants of Marshpee, and by all the arts of a talented, educated, wily, unprincipled Indian, professing with all, to be an apostle of Christianity; he stirs them up to sedition, riot, *treason!* Instigates them to declare their independence of the laws of Massachusetts, and to *arm themselves* to defend it.

We need not follow, minutely, the transactions which rapidly succeeded this state of things. We will merely remark that, in that time of rebellion, prompt, efficient, but mild measures were taken by the Executive, to quell the disturbances, and restore good faith. An agent was sent by the Governor, to inquire into the cause, and if possible, to remove it. That agent found it to be his duty to arrest Apes (that *pious* interloper), as a riotous and seditious person, and bind him over for trial, at the Common Pleas Court. He was there tried; and, in our opinion, never was there a fairer trial. He was convicted; and, in our opinion, never was there a more just conviction, or a milder sentence. After the performance of his sentence, Apes is again at work stirring up new movements. And having strung together a list of *imaginary* grievances, and false allegations, and affixed a great number of names, without the knowledge or consent of many of the individuals, he goes to the Legislature, with two of his ignorant, deluded followers, pretending to be *"the Marshpee Deputation,"* and asks redress and relief.

We would be the last to object to their receiving redress and relief; and we doubt not they will obtain, at the hands of the Legislature, all they ought to have. But who is the *"Marshpee Deputation,"* that is showing off to such advantage in the city? It is William Apes, the convicted rioter, who was the whole cause of the disgraceful sedition at Marshpee the last summer; who is a hypocritical *missionary,* from a tribe in Connecticut; whose acquaintance with the Marshpeeans is of *less than a year's* standing. And he is endeavoring to enlist public sympathy in *his* favor, *in advance,* by lecturing in the Hall of Representatives, upon that pathetic and soul-stirring theme, Indian degradation and oppression; vilifying and abusing the irreproachable pastor of the plantation, Mr. Fish; stigmatizing and calumniating the Court and Jury who tried and convicted him, and flinging his sarcasms and sneers upon the Attorney and Jury who indicted him. And for *all this,* he is receiving the *applause* of an audience, who *must be* ignorant of *his* character; and blinded by the pretences of this impostor. And as far as that audience is composed of Legislators, their conduct, in permitting Apes to enlist their passions and feelings in his favor, pending a Legislative investigation of the subject, is reprehensible.

But, there is no fear that the matter will not be set right. That the investigation by the intelligent agent last summer, (Mr. Fiske,) and the investigation now going on by a committee of the Legislature, will show the true character of Apes, and point out the real wants and grievances of the Indians; and that the remedy will be applied, to the satisfaction of the Indians and the discomfiture of that renegade impostor and hypocritical interloper and disturber, Apes, there is little doubt; that *such* may be the result, is the sincere wish of

The True Friends of the Indians

The spirit in which this unrighteous piece is written speaks for itself and is its own antidote. However, it is just what we might expect from a liberal paper of the liberal town of Barnstable—so one gang of partisans call it. Deliver us from a "patriot," who would set his face against all good and destroy the people themselves. These writers, if there be more than one of them, seem to have some idea of piety and religion. I therefore advise them to pluck the motes out of their own eyes, that they may see clearly enough to make better marks with their pens. The editor and his correspondents (if he did not write the article himself) have rendered themselves liable to a suit for defamation; but I think it best to let them go. I will not touch pitch. The discomforted, hypocritical impostor, renegade, and interloper will forgive, and pray for them. He will not render evil for evil, though sorely provoked.

Nevertheless, I feel bound to say to these excellent friends of the Marshpees, who wished them to remain crushed under the burden of hard laws forever and ever, that they will go down to their graves in the disappointment, which, perhaps, will cause them to weep away their lives. I should be sorry to hear of that and exhort them to dry their tears, or suffer a poor Indian to wipe them away.

Notwithstanding all that was said and done by the opposition, the Marshpee deputation left the field of battle with a song of triumph and rejoicing in their mouths, as will presently be seen. I shall give a brief sketch of the proceedings of one of the most enlightened committees that ever was drafted from a legislative body. Everything was done to sour their minds against the Indians that could be done, but they were of the excellent of the earth, just and impartial.

The committee was composed of Messrs. Barton and Strong, of the Senate, and Messrs. Dwight of Stockbridge, Fuller of Springfield, and Lewis of Pepperell, of the House. Benjamin F. Hallett, Esq., appeared as counsel for the Indians.

Lemuel Ewer, Esq., of South Sandwich, was a witness, and the only white one who was in favor of the Indians. The Indian witnesses were Deacon Coombs, Daniel B. Amos, Ebenezer Attaquin, Joseph B. Amos, and William Apes.

On the other side appeared Kilburn Whitman, Esq., of Pembroke, as counsel for the overseers; Messrs. J. J. Fiske of Wrentham and Elijah Swift of Falmouth, both of the Governor's Council; the Reverend Phineas Fish, the Marshpee missionary, sent by Harvard College; Judge Marston, Nathaniel Hinckley, and Charles Marston, all of Barnstable; Gideon Hawley of South Sandwich, Judge Whitman of Boston, and two Indians, Nathan Pocknet and William Amos, by name. It was a notable piece of policy on the part of the overseers to make a few friends among the Indians, in order to use them for their own purposes. Thus do pigeon trappers use to set up a decoy. When the bird flutters, the flock settle round him, the net is sprung, and they are in fast hands. Judge Whitman, however, could not make his two decoy birds flutter to his satisfaction, and so he got no chance to spring his net. He had just told the Indians that they might as well think to move the Rock of Gibraltar from its base as to heave the heavy load of guardianship from their shoulders; and, when he first came before the committee, he said he did not care a snap of his finger about the matter, one way or the other. But he altered his mind before he got through the business and began to say that he should be ruined if the bill passed for the relief of the Indians and was, moreover, sure that Apes would reign, king of Marshpee. The old gentleman, indeed, made several perilous thrusts at me in his plea; but, when he came to cross-examination, he was so pleased with the correctness of my testimony that he had nothing more to say to me. I shall now leave him, to attend to his friend, Judge Marston.

This gentleman swore in court that he thought Indians an inferior race of men, and, of course, were incapable of managing their own affairs.

The testimony of the two decoy pigeons was that they had liberty enough, more than they knew what to do with. They showed plainly enough that they knew nothing of the law they lived under. The testimony of the Reverend Mr. Fish was more directly against us. Some may think I do wrong to mention this gentleman's name so often. But why, when a man comes forward on a public occasion, should his name be kept out of sight, though he be a clergyman? I should think he would like to make his flock respected and respectable in his speech, which he well knew they never could be under the then existing laws. Is it more than a fair inference that it was self-interest that made him do otherwise, that he might be able to continue in possession of his stronghold? If he had said to the Indians, like an honest man, "I know I have no right to what is yours, and will willingly relinquish what I hold of it," I do not doubt that the Indians would have given him a house and a life estate in a farm, and perhaps have conveyed it to him in fee simple, if he had behaved well. Such a course would have won him the love and esteem of the Indians, and his blind obstinacy was certainly the surest means he could have taken to gain their ill will. He may think slightly of their good opinion, and I think from his whole course of conduct that we are as dogs in his sight. I presume he could not die in peace if he thought he was to be buried beside our graves.

It is the general fault of those who go on missions that they cannot sacrifice the pride of their hearts in order to do good. It seems to have been usually the object to seat the Indians between two stools, in order that they might fall to the ground, by breaking up their government and forms of society, without giving them any others in their place. It does not appear to be the aim of the missionaries to improve the Indians by making citizens of them. Hence, in most cases, anarchy and confusion are the results. Nothing has more effectually contributed to the decay of several tribes than the course pursued by their missionaries. Let us look back to the first of them for proofs. From the days of Eliot to the year 1834, have they made one citizen? The latter date marks the first instance of such an experiment. Is it not strange that free men should thus have been held in bondage more than two hundred years, and that setting them at liberty at this late day should be called *an experiment* now?

I would not be understood to say, however, that the Reverend Mr. Fish's mission is any criterion to judge others by. No doubt, many of them have done much good; but I greatly doubt that any missionary has ever thought of making the Indian or African his equal. As soon as we begin to talk about equal rights, the cry of amalgamation is set up, as if men of color could not enjoy their natural rights without any necessity for intermarriage between the sons and daughters of the two races. Strange, strange indeed! Does it follow that the Indian or the African must go to the judge on his bench, or to the governor, senator, or indeed any other man, to ask for a helpmeet, because his name may be found on the voter's list, or in the jury boxes? I promise all concerned that we Marshpees have less inclination to seek their daughters than they have to seek ours. Should the worst come to the worst, does the proud white think that a dark skin is less honorable in the sight of God than his own beautiful hide? All are alike, the sheep of his pasture and the workmanship of his hands. To say they are not alike to him is an insult to his justice. Who shall dare to call that in question?

Were I permitted to express an opinion, it would be that it is more honorable in the two races to intermarry than to act as too many of them do. My advice to the white man is to let the colored race alone. It will considerably diminish the annual amount of sin committed. Or else let them even *marry* our daughters, and no more ado about amalgamation. We desire none of their connection in that way. All we ask of them is peace and our rights. We can find wives enough without asking any favors of them. We have some wildflowers among us as fair, as blooming, and quite as pure as any they can show. But enough has been said on this subject, which I should not have mentioned at all, but that it has been rung in my ears by almost every white lecturer I ever had the misfortune to meet.

I will now entreat the reader's attention to the very able plea of Mr. Hallett, upon our petition and remonstrances. The following are his remarks after the law which gave us our liberty was passed by his exertions in our cause:

I will now briefly consider the "documents, relating to the Marshpee Indians," which have been presented and printed, this session, by the two Houses.

The first is a Memorial, signed by seventy-nine males and ninety-two females, of the Plantation. Of the seventy-nine males, sixty-two are Proprietors, and forty-four write their own names. They are all united in wishing to have a change of the laws, and a removal of the Overseership, but desire that their land may not be sold without the mutual consent of the Indians and the General Court.

This memorial represents, 1. That no particular pains has been taken to instruct them. 2. That they are insignificant because they have had no opportunities. 3. That no enlightened or respectable Indian, wants Overseers. 4. That their rulers and the minister have been put over them, without their consent. 5. That the minister, (Mr. Fish,) has not a male member in his church of the Proprietors, and they believe twenty years would have been long enough for him to have secured their confidence. 6. That the laws which govern them and take away their property, are unconstitutional. 7. That the whites have had three times more benefit of the Meeting-house and the minister, than they have had. 8. That the business meetings for the tribe, have been held off the plantation, at an expense to them. 9. That their Fishery has been neglected and the whites derived the most benefit from it. [The Overseers admit that the Herring Fishery has not been regulated for fifty years, although in 1763, it appears it was deemed a highly important interest, and in 1818, the Commissioners reported that it ought to be regulated for the benefit of the Indians to the exclusion of the whites.] 10. That the laws discourage their people, who leave the plantation on that account. 11. That men out of the tribe are paid for doing what those in it are capable of doing for the plantation. 12. That the whites derive more benefit than themselves, from their hay, wood and timber. 13. That the influence of the whites has been against them, in their petitions for the past years. 14. That they believe they have been wronged out of their property. 15. That they want the Overseers discharged, that they may have a chance to take care of themselves. 16. That very many of their people are sober and industrious, and able and willing to do, if they had the privilege. All these statements will be found abundantly proved.

This memorial comes directly from the Indians. It was drawn up among them without the aid of a single white man. They applied to me to prepare it for them. They happened to select me, as their counsel, simply because I was born and brought up within a few miles from their plantation, and had known their people from my infancy. I told them to present their grievances in their own way, and they have done so. Not a line of the memorial was written for them.

On the other side, opposite to their memorial for self-government, is the remonstrance of *Nathan Pocknet* and forty-nine others, the same Nathan Pocknet, who in 1818 petitioned for the removal of the Overseership. This remonstrance was not prepared by the Indians. It came wholly from the Rev. Mr. Fish, and the Overseers. It speaks of the "unprecedented impudence" of the Indians, and mentions a *"Traverse Jury."* No one who signed it, had any voice in preparing it. It shows ignorance of the memorial of the tribe, by supposing they ask for liberty to sell their lands; and ignorance of the law, by saying that the Overseers have not power to remove nuisances from the plantation.

This remonstrance is signed by fifty persons, sixteen males and thirty-four females; seventeen can write. Of the signers, *ten* belong to Nathan Pocknet's family. Ten of the males are Proprietors, of whom two are minors, and one a person non compos. Of the non-proprietors, one is a convict, recently released from State prison, who has no right on the Plantation. Two of the Proprietors, who signed this remonstrance (John Speen and Isaac Wickham), have since certified that they understood it to be the petition for Mr. Fish, to retain his salary, but that they are entirely opposed to having Overseers and to the present laws.

Thus it is shown that out of the whole Plantation of 229 Proprietors, but *five* men could be induced, by all the influence of the Minister and the Overseer, to sign in favor of having the present laws continued, and but *eleven* men out of the whole population of 312. The signers to the memorial for a change of the laws are a majority of all the men, women and children belonging to the Plantation, at home and abroad.

Another document against the Indians who ask for their liberty, is the memorial of the Rev. Phineas Fish, the missionary. Of the unassuming piety, the excellent character, and the sound learning of that reverend gentleman, I cannot speak in too warm terms. I respect him as a man, and honor him as a devoted minister of the gospel. But he is not adapted to the cultivation of the field in which his labors have been cast. Until I read this memorial, I should not have believed that a severe expression could have escaped him. I regret the spirit of that memorial, and in its comparison with that of the Indians, I must say it loses in style, in dignity and in Christian temper.

In this memorial, Mr. Fish urges upon the Legislature the continuance of the laws of guardianship as they now are, and especially the continuance of the benefits he derives from the property of the plantation. What are the reasons he gives for this? Do they not look exclusively to his own benefit, without regard to the wishes of the Indians?

He states, as the result of his ministry, twenty members of the tribe added to his church in *twenty-two* years. This single fact proves that his ministry has failed of producing any effect at all proportioned to the cost it has been to the Indians. Not from want of zeal or ability, perhaps, but from want of adaptation. If not, why have other preachers been so much more successful than the missionary? There never has been a time that this church was not controlled by the whites. Mr. Fish now has but five colored members of his church, and sixteen whites. Of the five colored persons, but one is a male, and he has recently signed a paper saying he has been deceived by Mr. Fish's petition, which he signed, and that he does not now wish his stay any longer among them.

On the other hand, "blind Jo," as he is called, a native Indian, blind from his birth, now 28 years of age, has educated himself by his ear and his memory, has been regularly ordained as a Baptist minister, in full fellowship with that denomination, and has had a little church organized since 1830. The Baptist denomination has existed on the plantation, for forty years, but has received no encouragement. Blind Jo has never been taken by the hand by the missionary or the Overseers. The Indians were even refused the use of *their* Meeting-house, for the ordination of their blind minister, and he was ordained in a private dwelling. Though not possessing the eloquence of the blind preacher, so touchingly described in the glowing and chaste letters of Wirt's British Spy, yet there is much to admire in the simple piety and sound doctrines of "Blind Jo"; and he will find a way to the hearts of his hearers, which the learned divine cannot explore.

There is another denomination on the plantation, organized as "The Free and United Church," of which William Apes is the pastor. This denomination Mr. Fish charges with an attempt to *usurp* the parsonage, wood-land and the Meeting-house; he denounces, as a *"flagrant act,"* the attempt of the Indians to obtain the use of *their own Meeting-house,* and appeals to the sympathies of the whole civilized community to maintain *by law* the Congregational worship, which, he says, "is the most ancient form of religious worship there"! "Why should Congregational worship be excluded to make room for others?" asks the Rev. Mr. Fish. "Where will be the end of vicissitude on the adoption of such a principle, and how is it possible, amid the action of rival *factions,* for pure religion to be promoted?" [Pages 7, 8, 9, of Mr. Fish's memorial. Senate, No. 17.] Is this language for a Christian minister to address to the Legislature of Massachusetts? To petition for an established Church in Marshpee? Can he ever have read the third Article of the Bill of Rights, as amended?

What has been the result of these "rival factions," in Marshpee? Blind Jo and William Apes, have *forty-seven* Indian members of their churches (fourteen males), in good standing, collected together in three years. The missionary has baptized but twenty in twenty-two years. The Indian preachers have also established a total abstinence Temperance Society, without any aid from the missionary, and there are already sixty members of it, who, from all the evidence in the case, there is no reason to doubt, live up to their profession.

I do not say this to detract from the good the missionary has done; I doubt not he has done much good, and earnestly desired to do more; but when he denounces to the Legislature other religious denominations, as *usurpers* and *"rival factions,"* it is but reasonable that a comparison should be drawn between the fruit of his labors and that of those he so severely condemns.

I confess, I am struck with surprise, at the following remarks, in the memorial of the Rev. Mr. Fish. Speaking of the complaint of the Indians respecting their Meeting-house, that it is not fit for respectable people to meet in, being worn out; he says, "As it was built by a *white* Missionary Society, and repaired at the expense of the *white* Legislature of the State, perhaps the *whites* may think themselves entitled to some wear of it, and being no way fit for *respectable* people, the church and congregation hope they may the more readily be left unmolested in their accustomed use of it." [Page 4.] Again he says of the complaints of the Indians, that they were forbidden to have preaching in their School-houses. "The School-houses, built by the munificence of the State, began to be occupied for *Meeting-houses,* soon after their erection, and have been more or less occupied *in this fashion!* ever since; and your memorialist desires to affirm that *in this perversion* of your *liberal purpose,* he had no share whatever!!"

Is this possible? Can it be a *perversion* of buildings erected for the mental and moral improvement of the Indians, that religious meetings should be held there, by ministers whom the Indians prefer to the Missionary?

The inequality in the appropriations for religious instruction, is re-marked upon by the Commissioner, Hon. Mr. Fiske, who says in his report that if the present appropriations are to be restricted to a Con-gregationalist minister, some further provision, in accordance with re-ligious freedom, ought to be made for the Baptist part of the colored people. [Page 29. No. 14.]

I regret too, the unkind allusion in the Rev. Mr. Fish's memorial to Deacon Coombs, the oldest of the Marshpee delegation, formerly his deacon, and the last Proprietor to leave him. He says the deacon "once walked worthy of his holy calling." Does he mean to insinuate he does not walk worthily now? I wish you, gentlemen, to examine Deacon Coombs, who is present, to inquire into his manner of life, and see if you can find a Christian with a white skin, whose heart is purer, and whose walk is more upright, than this same Deacon Coombs. In point of character and intelligence, he would compare advantageously with a majority of the Selectmen in the Commonwealth.

With the religious concerns of Marshpee, I have no wish to interfere. I only seek to repel intimations that may operate against their prayer for the liberties secured by the Constitution. Neither do I stand here to defend Mr. Apes, who is charged with being the leader of the "sedition." I only ask you to look at the historical evidence of the existence of discon-tent with the laws, ever since 1693, and ask if Mr. Apes has been the author of this discontent. Let me remind you also, of the fable of the Huntsman and the Lion, when the former boasted of the superiority of man, and to prove it pointed to a statue of one of the old heroes, standing upon a prostrate lion. The reply of the noble beast was, "there are no *carvers* among the lions; if there were, for one man standing upon a lion, you would have twenty men torn to pieces by lions." Gentlemen, by depressing the Indians, our laws have taken care that they should have no *carvers*. The whites have done all the *carving* for them, and have always placed them *undermost*. Can we blame them, then, that when they found an educated Indian, with Indian sympathies and feelings, they employed him, to present their complaints, and to enable them to seek redress? Look at this circumstance, fairly, and I think you will find in it the origin of all the prejudice against William Apes, which may be traced to those of the whites who are opposed to any change in the present government of Marshpee. If aught can be shown against him, I hope it will be produced here in proof, that the Indians may not be deceived. If no other proof is produced, except his zeal in securing freedom for the Indians, are you not to conclude that it cannot be done? But his individual character has nothing to do with the merits of the question, though I here pronounce it unimpeached.

I will allude to but one other suggestion in the memorial of the Rev. Mr. Fish [page 10]. To show the necessity of continuing the present laws, he says, "already do we witness the force of example in the visible increase of crime. But a few weeks since, a peaceable family was fired in upon, during their midnight repose; while I have been writing, another has been committed to prison for a high misdemeanor."

Now what are the facts, upon which this grave allegation against the whole tribe is founded? True, a ball was fired into a house on the plantation, but without any possible connection with the assertion of their rights by the Indians, and to this day it is not known whether it was a white man or an Indian who did it. The "high misdemeanor," was a quarrel between Jerry Squib, an Indian, and John Jones, a white man. Squib accused Jones of cheating him in a bargain, when intoxicated, and beat him for it. The law took up the Indian for the assault, and let the white man go for the fraud.

Respecting then, as we all do, the personal character of the missionary, can you answer his prayer, to continue the present government, in order to protect him in the reception of his present income from the lands of the Indians? Are the interests of a whole people to be sacrificed to one man? What says the Bill of Rights? "Government is instituted for the common good, for the protection, safety, prosperity, and happiness of the *people,* and not for the *profit,* honor or *private interest* of any *one* man, family, or class of men."

I have now only to consider the report of the Commissioner, Mr. Fiske, who visited Marshpee in July last. The impartiality, candor and good sense of that report, are highly honorable to that gentleman. Deriving his first impressions from the Overseers and the whites, and instructed as he was with strong prepossessions against the Indians, as rebels to the State, the manner in which he discharged that duty, deserves a high encomium. He has my thanks for it, as a friend of the Indians. As far as the knowledge of the facts enabled the Commissioner to go, in the time allowed him, the conclusions of that report, substantiate all the positions taken in defense of the rights of the Indians. The Commissioner was instructed by the then Governor Lincoln, to inform the Indians that the government had no other object than their best good; "let them be convinced that their grievances will be inquired into, and a *generous* and *paternal* regard be had to their condition." They were so convinced, and they come here now, for a redemption of this pledge.

But his Excellency seems to have been strangely impressed with the idea of suppressing some rebellion, or another Shays' insurrection. Mr. Hawley, one of the Overseers, had visited the Governor, at Worcester, and because a few Indians had quietly unloaded a wood-cart, the calling out of the militia seems to have been seriously contemplated by the following order, issued to the Commissioner, by the Governor, dated July 5. "Should there be reason to fear the insufficiency of the *posse comitatus, I Will be present personally, to direct any military requisitions."*

Think of that, gentlemen of the Committee! Figure to yourselves his Excellency, at the head of the Boston and Worcester Brigades, ten thousand strong, marching to Marshpee, to suppress an insurrection, when scarce twenty old muskets could have been mustered on the whole plantation?

With the utmost respect for his Excellency, I could not refrain on reading this "order of the day," from exclaiming, as Lord Thurlow did, when a breathless messenger informed him that a rebellion had broken out in the Isle of Man, "Pshaw—a tempest in a tea pot."

Let us not, however, because the Indians are weak and inoffensive, be less regardful of their rights.

You will gather from the Report of Mr. Fiske, conclusive evidence of the long-continued and deep-rooted dissatisfaction of the Indians with the laws of guardianship, that they never abandoned the ground that all men were born free and equal, and they ought to have the right to rule and govern themselves; that by a proper exercise of self-government, and the management of their own pecuniary affairs, they had it in their power to elevate themselves much above their present state of degradation, and that by a presentation of new motives for moral and mental improvement, they might be enabled, in a little time, to assume a much higher rank on the scale of human existence. And that the Legislature would consider their case, was the humble and earnest request of the natives.

Is not the conclusion then, from all the facts in the case, that the system of laws persisted in since 1763, have failed as acts of paternal care? That the true policy now is to try acts of kindness and encouragement, and that the question of rightful control over the property or persons of the Indians beyond the general operation of the laws, being clearly against the whites; but one consideration remains on which the Legislature can hesitate: the danger, that they will squander their property. Of the improbability of such a result, Mr. Fiske informs you in his report [page 26].

He found nearly all the families comfortably and decently clad, nearly all occupying framed houses, and a few dwelling in huts or wigwams. More than thirty of them were in possession of a cow or swine, and many of them tilled a few acres of land around their dwellings. Several pairs of oxen, and some horses are owned on the plantation, and the Commons are covered with an excellent growth of wood, of ready access to market. Confine the cutting of this wood to the natives, as they desire, and they never can waste this valuable inheritance.

Mr. Fiske also says in his report [page 30], "that it is hardly possible to find a place more favorable for gaining a subsistence without labor, than Marshpee." The advantages of its location, the resources from the woods and streams, on one side, and the bays and the sea on the other, are accurately described, as being abundant, with the exception of the *lobsters*, which Mr. Fiske says are found there. The Commissioner is incorrect in that particular, unless he adopts the learned theory of Sir Joseph Banks, that *fleas* are a species of lobster!

Is there, then, any danger in giving the Indians an opportunity to try a liberal experiment for self-government? They ask you for a grant of the liberties of the constitution; to be incorporated and to have a government useful to them as a people.

They ask for the appointment of magistrates among them, and they ask too for an *Attorney* to advise with; but my advice to them is, to have as little as possible to do with Attornies. A revision of their laws affecting property by the Governor and Council, would be a much better security for them than an Attorney, and this they all agree to. Is there anything unreasonable in their requests? Can you censure other States for severity to the Indians within their limits, if you do not exercise an enlightened liberality toward the Indians of Massachusetts? Give them then substantially, the advantages which they ask in the basis of an act which I now submit to the Committee with their approval of its provisions. Can you, gentlemen, can the Legislature, resist the simple appeal of their memorial? "Give us a chance for our lives, in acting for ourselves. O! white man! white man! the blood of our fathers, spilt in the revolutionary war, cries from the ground of our native soil, to break the chains of oppression and let our children go free."

The correctness of Mr. Hallett's opinions are demonstrated in the following article.

Other editors speak ill enough of Gen. Jackson's treatment of the southern Indians. Why do they not also speak ill of all the head men and great chiefs who have evil entreated the people of Marshpee? I think Governor

Lincoln manifested as bitter and tyrannical a spirit as Old Hickory ever could, for the life of him. Often and often have our tribe been promised the liberty their fathers fought, and bled, and died for; and even now we have but a small share of it. It is some comfort, however, that the people of Massachusetts are becoming gradually more Christianized.

From the *Daily Advocate:*

The Marshpee Indians

The Daily Advertiser remarks that the Indian tribes have been sacrificed by the policy of Gen. Jackson. This is very true, and we join with the Advertiser in reprehending the course pursued by the President toward the Cherokees. If Georgia, under her *union* nullifier, Governor Lumpkin, is permitted to set the process of the Supreme Court at defiance, it will be a foul dishonor upon the country.

But while we condemn the conduct of General Jackson toward the Southern Indians, what shall we say of the treatment of our own poor defenseless Indians, the Marshpee tribe, in our own State? The Legislature of last year, with a becoming sense of justice, restored to the Marshpee Indians a *portion* of their rights, which had been wrested from them, most wrongfully, for a period of *seventy-four* years. The State of Massachusetts, in the exercise of a most unjust and arbitrary power, had, until that time, deprived the Indians of all civil rights, and placed their property at the mercy of designing men, who had used it for their own benefit, and despoiled the native owners of the soil to which they hold a better title than the whites hold to any land in the Commonwealth. These Indians fought and bled side by side, with our fathers, in the struggle for liberty; but the whites were no sooner free themselves, than they enslaved the poor Indians.

One single fact will show the devotion of the Marshpee Indians to the cause of liberty, in return for which they and their descendants were placed under a despotic guardianship, and their property wrested from them to enrich the whites. In the Secretary's Office, of this State, will be found a muster roll, containing a "Return of men enlisted in the first Regiment of Continental troops, in the County of Barnstable, for three years and during the war, in Col. Bradford's Regiment," commencing in 1777. Among these volunteers for that terrible service, are the following names of Marshpee Indians, proprietors of Marshpee, viz.

Francis Webquish, Samuel Moses, Demps Squibs, Mark Negro, Tom Caesar, Joseph Ashur, James Keeter, Joseph Keeter, Jacob Keeter, Daniel Pocknit, Job Rimmon, George Shawn, Castel Barnet, Joshua Pognit, James Rimmon, David Hatch, James Nocake, Abel Hoswitt, Elisha

Keeter, John Pearce, John Mapix, Amos Babcock, Hosea Pognit, Daniel Pocknit, Church Ashur, Gideon Tumpum.

In all twenty-six men. The whole regiment, drawn from the whole County of Barnstable, mustered but 149 men, nearly *one-fifth* of whom were volunteers from the little Indian Plantation of Marshpee, which then did not contain over one hundred male heads of families! No white town in the County furnished anything like this proportion of the 149 volunteers. The Indian soldiers fought through the war; and as far as we have been able to ascertain the fact, from documents or tradition, all but one, fell martyrs to liberty, in the struggle for Independence. There is but one Indian now living, who receives the reward of his services as a revolutionary soldier, old Isaac Wickham, and he was not in Bradford's regiment. Parson Holly, in a memorial to the Legislature in 1783, states that most of the women in Marshpee, had lost their husbands in the war. At that time there were *seventy* widows on the Plantation.

But from that day, until the year 1834, the Marshpee Indians were enslaved by the laws of Massachusetts, and deprived of every civil right which belongs to man. White Overseers had power to tear their children from them and bind them out where they pleased. They could also sell the services of any adult Indian on the Plantation they chose to call idle, for three years at a time, and send him where they pleased, renewing the lease every three years, and thus, make him a slave for life.

It was with the greatest effort this monstrous injustice was in some degree remedied last winter, by getting the facts before the Legislature, in spite of a most determined opposition from those who had fattened for years on the spoils of poor Marshpee. In all but one thing, a reasonable law was made for the Indians. That one thing was giving the Governor power to appoint a Commissioner over the Indians for three years. This was protested against by the friends of the Indians, but in vain; and they were assured that this appointment would be safe in the hands of the Governor. They hoped so, and assented; but no sooner was the law passed, than the enemies of the Indians induced the Governor to appoint as the Commissioner, the person whom of all others they least wished to have, a former Overseer, against whom there were strong prejudices. The Indians remonstrated, and besought, but in vain. The Commissioner was appointed, and to all appeals to make a different appointment, a deaf ear has been turned. It seems as if a deliberate design had been formed somewhere, to defeat all the Legislature has done for the benefit of this oppressed people.

The consequences have been precisely what the Indians and their friends feared. Party divisions have grown up among them, arising out of the want of confidence in their Commissioner. He is found always on the side of their greatest trouble; the minister who unjustly holds almost 500 acres of the best land in the plantation, wrongfully given to him by an unlawful and arbitrary act of the State, which, in violation of the Constitution, appropriates the property of the Indians to pay a man they dislike, for preaching a doctrine they will not listen to, to a *white* congregation, while the native preachers, whom the Indians prefer, are left without a cent, and deprived of the Meeting-house, built by English liberality for the use of the Indians. The dissatisfaction has gone on increasing. The accounts with the former Overseers remain unadjusted to the satisfaction of the Selectmen. The Indians have no adviser near them in whom they can confide; those who hold the power, appear regardless of their wishes or their welfare; no pains is taken by the authorities to punish the wretches who continue to sell rum to those who will buy it; and though the Indians are still struggling to advance in improvement, every obstacle is thrown in their way that men can devise, whose intent it is to get them back to a state of vassalage, that they may get hold of their property. All this, we are satisfied, from personal inspection, is owing to the injudicious appointment made by Gov. Davis, of a commissioner, and yet the Governor unfortunately seems indisposed to listen to any application for a remedy to the existing evils.

The presses around us, who are so eloquent in denouncing the President for his conduct towards the Southern Indians, say not a word in behalf of our own Indians, whose fathers poured out their blood for our Independence. Is this right, and ought the Indians to be sacrificed to the advantage a single man derives from holding an office of very trifling profit? Let us look at home, before we complain of the treatment of the Indians at the South.

The following extract refers to the act passed to incorporate the Marshpee District, after so much trouble and expense to the Indians. I should suppose the people of Massachusetts would have been glad to have done us this justice, without making so much difficulty, if they had been aware of the true state of facts.

The Marshpee Act

Restoring the rights of self-government, in part, to the Marshpee Indians, of which our legislation has deprived them for one hundred and forty years, passed the Senate of Massachusetts yesterday, to the honor of that body, without a single dissenting vote. Too much praise cannot be given to Mr. Senator Barton, for the persevering and high-minded manner in which he has prepared and sustained this act. With two or three exceptions, but which, perhaps, may not be indispensable to the success of the measure, it is all the Indians or their friends should desire, under existing circumstances. The clause reserving the right of repeal, is probably the most unfortunate provision in the act, as it may tend to disquiet the Indians, and to give the Commissioner a sort of threatening control, that will add too much to his power, and may endanger all the benefits of the seventh section. This provision was not introduced by the Committee, but was opposed by Messrs. Barton and Strong, as wholly unnecessary. [*Daily Advocate*]

Small Matter

In the resolve allowing fees to the Marshpee Indians, who have attended as witnesses this session, the high-minded Senator Hedge of Plymouth, succeeded in excluding the name of William Apes, as it passed the Senate; but the House, on motion of Col. Thayer, inserted the name of Mr. Apes, allowing him his fees, the same as the others. Mr. Hedge made a great effort to induce the Senate to non-concur, but even his lucid and *liberal* eloquence failed of its *noble* intent, and the Senate concurred by a vote of 13 to 6. Mr. Hedge must be sadly disappointed that he could not have saved the State twenty-three dollars, by his manly efforts to injure the character of a poor Indian. Mr. Hedge, we dare say, is a descendant from the pilgrims, whom the Indians protected at Plymouth Rock! He knows how to be *grateful!* [*Daily Advocate*]

It appears that I, William Apess, have been much persecuted and abused, merely for desiring the welfare of myself and brethren, and because I would not suffer myself to be trodden underfoot by people no better than myself, as I can see. In connection with this, I say I was never arraigned before any court, to the injury of my reputation, save once, at Marshpee, for a pretended riot. An attempt to blast a man merely for insisting on his rights, and no more, is a blot on the character of him who undertakes it and not upon the person attempted to be injured, let him be great or small in the world's eyes. I can safely say that no charge that has ever been brought against me, written or verbal, has ever been made good by evidence in any civil or ecclesiastical court. Many things have been said to my disparagement in the public prints. Much was said to the General Court, as that I was a gambler in lotteries and had begged money from the Indians to buy tickets with. This calumny took its rise from certain articles printed in the *Boston Gazette*, written, as I have good reason to believe, by one Reynolds, a proper authority. He has been an inmate of the state prison, in Windsor, Vermont, once for a term of two years, and again for fourteen, as in part appears by the following certificate of a responsible person.

Concord, N.H., June 27, 1832

To all whom it may concern.

This may certify, that *John Reynolds,* once an inmate of Vermont State Prison, and since a professed Episcopal Methodist, and also a licensed local preacher in Windsor, Conn. came to this place about June, 1830, recommended by Brother J. Robbins, as a man worthy of our patronage; and of course I employed him to supply for me in Ware and Hopkinton (both in N.H.), in which places he was for a short time, apparently useful. But the time shortly arrived when it appeared that he was pursuing a course that rendered him worthy of censure. I therefore commenced measures to put him down from preaching; but before I could get fully prepared for him, he was gone out of my reach. I would however observe, he wrote me a line from Portsmouth, enclosing his license, also stating his withdrawal from us; and thus evaded trial. We have, therefore, never considered him worthy of a place in any Christian church since he left Hopkinton, in May, 1831. And I feel authorized to state, that he does not deserve the confidence of any respectable body of people.

E. W. Stickney, Circuit Preacher,
In the Methodist Episcopal Church

His wrath was enkindled and waxed hot against me, because I thought him scarce honorable enough for a high priest and could not enter into fellowship with him. I opposed his ordination as an elder of our church, because I thought it dishonor to sit by his side; and he therefore tried to make me look as black as himself, by publishing things he was enabled to concoct by the aid of certain of my enemies in New York. They wrote one or two letters derogatory to my character, the substance of which Reynolds took the liberty to publish. For this I complained of him to the grand jury in Boston, and he was indicted. The following is the indictment:

The Jurors for the Commonwealth of Massachusetts, on their oath present, that John Reynolds of Boston, Clerk, being a person regardless of the morality, integrity, innocence and piety, which Ministers of the Gospel ought to possess and sustain, and maliciously devising and intending to traduce, vilify and bring into contempt and detestation one William Apes, who was on the day hereinafter mentioned, and still is a resident of Boston aforesaid, and duly elected and appointed a minister of the gospel and missionary, by a certain denomination of Christians denominated as belonging to the Methodist Protestant Church; and also unlawfully and maliciously intending to insinuate and cause it to be believed, that the said William Apes was a deceiver and impostor, and guilty of crimes and offences, and of buying lottery tickets, and misappropriating monies collected by him from religious persons for charitable purposes, and for building a Meeting-house among certain persons called Indians,

On the thirteenth day of August now last past, at Boston aforesaid, in the County of Suffolk aforesaid, unlawfully, maliciously, and deliberately did compose, print and publish, and did cause and procure to be composed, printed and published in a certain newspaper, called the "Daily Commercial Gazette," of and concerning him the said William Apes, and of and concerning his said profession and business, an unlawful and malicious libel, according to the purport and effect, and in substance as follows, that is to say, containing therein among other things, the false, malicious, defamatory and libellous words and matter following, of and concerning said William Apes, to wit: *convinced at an early period of my* (meaning his the said Reynolds) *acquaintance with William Apes* (meaning the aforesaid William Apes), *that he* (meaning said William), *was not what he* (meaning said William), *professed to be; but was deceiving and imposing upon the benevolent and Christian public* (meaning that said William Apes was a deceiver and impostor), *I* (meaning said Reynolds), *took all prudent means to have him* (meaning said William), *exposed, and stopped in his* (meaning said William), *race of guilt* (meaning that said William had been guilty of immorality, dishonesty, irreligion, offences and crimes); *these men* (meaning one Joseph Snelling and one Norris), *were earnestly importuned to investigate his* (meaning said William), *conduct, and enforce the discipline* (meaning the discipline of the church), *upon him* (meaning said William), *for crimes committed since his* (meaning said William's) *arrival in this city* (meaning said city of Boston, thereby meaning that said William Apes had been guilty of crimes in said Boston), *though well acquainted with facts, which are violently presumptive of his* (meaning said William's) *being a deceiver, his* (meaning said William's) *friends stand by him* (meaning said William's) *and will not give him* (meaning said William) *up, though black as hell* (meaning that said William was a deceiver, and of a wicked and black character). *When I am informed that he* (meaning said William) *is ordained* (meaning as a minister of the gospel), *that he* (meaning said William) *is by permission of the brethren travelling, and permitted to collect money to build the house aforesaid* (meaning the aforesaid Meeting-house), *for his* (meaning said William's) *Indian brethren to worship God in, I shudder not so much because he* (meaning said William) *is purchasing Lottery Tickets* (meaning that said

William was purchasing Lottery Tickets, and had spent some of the said money for that purpose), *but because I know of his* (meaning aforesaid William's) *pledge to the citizens of New York and elsewhere,* to the great injury, scandal, and disgrace of the said William Apes, and against the peace and dignity of the Commonwealth aforesaid.

Samuel D. Parker, Attorney of said Commonwealth, within the County of Suffolk

Parker H. Peirce, Foreman of the Grand Jury

A true Copy.—Attest, Thomas W. Phillips, Clerk of the Municipal Court of the City of Boston

Subsequently, I entered civil actions against two others, for the same offense, and had them held to bail in the sum of fifteen hundred dollars, with sureties. This soon made them feel very sore. They had put it in my power to punish them very severely for giving rein to their malignant passions, and they asked mercy. I granted it, in order to show them that I wanted nothing but right, and not revenge, and that they might know that an Indian's character was as dearly valued by him as theirs by them. Would they ever have thus yielded to an Indian, if they had not been compelled? I presume it will satisfy the world that there was no truth in their stories, to read their confessions, which are as follows:

Extract from a letter written by David Ayres,
to Elder T. F. Norris, dated New Orleans, April 12, 1833.

"I have arrived here this day, and expected to have found letters here from you, and some of my other brethren respecting Apes' suit. I never volunteered in this business, but was led into it by others, and it is truly a hard case that I must have all this trouble on their account."

Extract of a letter written by David Ayres
to William Apes, dated July 1, 1833.

"I am, and always have been your friend, and I never expected that any things I wrote about you, would find their way into the public papers. I am for peace, and surely I have had trouble enough. I never designed to injure you, and when all were your enemies, I was your warm friend."

Extract from a letter written by G. Thomas to
Rev. Thomas F. Norris, dated New York, July 12, 1833.

"William Apes might by some be said to be an excepted case; but when this is fairly explained and understood, this would not be the fact. My good friends of Boston, and my active little brother Ayres, are to blame for this, and not me. I had no malice against him, I never had done other than wish him well, and done what I hoped would turn out for the best; but knowing he was liable to error (as) others, and the case being placed in such colors to me, I awoke up; and being pressed to give what I did in detail as I thought, all for the good of the cause and suffering innocence; but I am sorry I ever was troubled at all on the subject; I thought that brother Reynolds was a fine catch; but time I acknowledge is a sure tell-tale. And by the by, they have caught me, and eventually, unless Apes will stop proceedings, I must bear all the burthen. Reynolds has got his neck out of the halter, and Ayres is away South, and may never return; and poor me must be at all the trouble and cost, if even the suit should go in my favor. Can I think that Apes will press it? No. I think he has not lost all human milk out of his breast, and will dismiss the suit; and, as to my share of the cost, if I was able, that should be no obstacle. If he will stop it all, if my friends do not settle it, I will agree to, as soon as I am able."

I hereby certify, that I have copied the foregoing passages from the letters purporting to be from David Ayres and G. Thomas, respectively, as above mentioned, and that said passages are correct extracts from said letters. I further certify, that, as the Attorney of said William Apes, I acted for him in the suits brought by him against said Thomas and Ayres for libel, that while said suits were pending, said Apes manifested a forgiving and forbearing disposition, and wished the suits not to be pressed any further than was necessary to show the falsehood of the statements of said Ayres and Thomas, and contradict them; and, that he expressed himself willing to settle with them upon their paying the cost, and acknowledging their error, in consequence of which, by direction from him, after he had perused said letters, I accordingly discharged both suits, the bail of said Thomas and Ayres paying the costs, which amounted to fifty dollars.

I further certify, that during my acquaintance with said Apes, which commenced as I think, in March last, I have seen nothing in his character or conduct, to justify the reports spread about him, by said Thomas and Ayres; but on the contrary, he has appeared to me to be an honest and well disposed man.

Henry Kinsman, No. 33, Court Street

Boston, November 30, 1833

I, the subscriber, fully concur in the above statement.

James D. Yates, Elder of the
Methodist Protestant Church

The original confession of Reynolds being lost, I trust that the following certificate will satisfy the reader that it has actually had existence.

To whom it may concern.

This is to certify that I have repeatedly seen, and in one instance, copied a paper of confession and *retraction* of Slanders, which the writer stated he had uttered, and published in papers of the day, against William Apes, the preacher to the Marshpee tribe of Indians, signed, John Reynolds, and countersigned as witness, by William Parker, Esq. The copy taken of the above mentioned confession by the subscriber, was sent to the Rev. T. R. Witsil, Albany, N.Y.

> Thomas F. Norris, President of the
> Protestant Methodist Conference, Mass.

Attest, James D. Yates
Boston, May 7, 1835

Nevertheless, lest this should not be sufficient, I am prepared to defend myself by written certificates of my character and standing among the whites and natives (the Pequot tribe), in Groton. They are as follows:

We the undersigned, native Indians of the Pequot tribe, having employed Rev. William Apes as our Agent, to assist us, and to collect subscriptions and monies towards erecting a house to worship in, do hereby certify, that we are satisfied with his agency; and that we anticipated that he would deduct therefrom, all necessary expenses, for himself and family, during the time he was employed in the agency, as we had no means of making him any other remuneration.

By permission, Frederick X Toby,
    Lucretia George,
By permission, Mary X George,
By permission, Lucy X Orchard,
    William Apes,
By permission, Margaret X George

I, Pardon P. Braton of Groton, in the County of New London, and State of Connecticut, of lawful age, do depose and say, that I was present when the above signers attached their names to the above certificate, by them subscribed, and am knowing to their having full knowledge of the facts therein contained; and further the deponent saith not.

Pardon P. Braton

Groton, Dec. 3, 1832

County of New London, ss.—Groton, Dec. 3, 1832.

Personally appeared, Pardon P. Braton, and made solemn oath to the truth of the above deposition, by him subscribed.

Before me,

William M. Williams, *Justice of the Peace*

Groton, Indian Town, Conn.

This may certify, that we, the subscribers, native Indians of the Pequot tribe, do affirm by our signatures to this instrument, that William Apes, Senior, went by our request as Delegate, in behalf of our tribe, to New York Annual Conference, of the Methodist Protestant Church, April 2, 1831.

The above done at a meeting of the Pequots, Oct. 6, 1830.

William Apes, Jr. Minister of the Gospel,
and Missionary to that tribe.

As witness our hands, in behalf of our brethren,

By permission, Mary X George,

By permission, Lucy X Orchard,

William Apes,

By permission, Margaret X George

I, Pardon P. Braton of Groton, New London County, State of Connecticut, do depose and say, that I am acquainted with the Pequot tribe of Indians empowering William Apes, Sen. as their Delegate to the New York Conference, as is above stated; and further the deponent saith not.

Pardon P. Braton

Groton, Dec. 3, 1832

New London County, ss.—Groton, Dec. 3, 1832.

Personally appeared, Pardon P. Braton, and made solemn oath to the truth of the above deposition, by him subscribed.

Before me,

William M. Williams,
Justice of the Peace

To all whom it may concern.

This may certify, that we, the undersigners, are acquainted with William Apes and his tribe, of Pequot, and that we live in the neighborhood with them, and know all their proceedings as to their public affairs, and that Mr. Apes, as far as we know, has acted honest and uprightly; and that he has done his duty to his Indian brethren, as far as he could consistently. And that he has duly made known his accounts, and appropriated the monies that was in contemplation for the Indian Meeting-house, for the Pequot tribe; and we also certify that said monies shall be duly appropriated.

Dated North Groton, Conn, Aug. 28, 1832.

Jonas Latham,
Asa A. Gore,
John Irish,
William M. Williams

An Inquiry into the Education and Religious Instruction of the Marshpee Indians

On the subject of the means taken to educate the Indians, I will say a few words in addition to what has already been said, because we wish to show that we can be grateful when we have favors bestowed on us. Up to 1835, the state had done nothing for education in Marshpee, except build us two school-houses in 1831.

Last winter the subject came up in the Legislature of distributing the School Fund of the state among the towns. A bill was reported to the House, in which Marshpee was made a school district and entitled to receive a dividend, according to its population by the United States census. Now, this was meant well, and we feel obliged to the committee who thought so much of us as this; but had the law passed in that shape, it would have done us no good, because we have no United States census. The people of Marshpee, nor the selectmen, knew nothing of this law to distribute the School Fund, and our pretended missionary, Mr. Fish, never interested himself in such matters; but our good friend Mr. Hallett, at Boston, thought of us and laid our claims before the committee, by two petitions which he got from the selectmen and from himself and the commissioner. We are told that the chairman of the School Committee, Hon. A. H. Everett, took much interest in getting a liberal allowance for education in Marshpee. He was once before a warm friend to the Cherokees, and his conduct now proved that he was sincere. He presented the petitions and proposed a law which would give us one hundred dollars a year forever, for public schools in Marshpee, which was the largest sum that had been asked for by our friend Mr. H. A number of gentlemen spoke in favor of this allowance, and all showed that a spirit of kindness, as well as justice toward the long-oppressed red men, begins to warm the hearts of those who make our laws, and rule over us. We trust we are thankful to God for so turning the hearts of men toward us.

The bill passed the House and also the Senate, without any objection, and it is now a law of the state of Massachusetts, that the Marshpee Indians shall have one hundred dollars every year, paid out of the School Fund, to help them educate their children. Our proportion as a district, according to what other towns receive, would have been but fifteen dollars. By the aid of our friends, and particularly of our counsel (Mr. H.), who first proposed it, we shall now receive one hundred dollars a year; and I trust the Indians will best show their gratitude by the pains they will take to send their children to good schools and by their raising as much more money as they can, to get good instructors, and give the rising generation all the advantages which the children of the whites enjoy in schooling. This will be one of the best means to raise them to an equality, and teach them to put away from their mouths forever the enemy which the white man, when he wanted to cheat and subdue our race, first got them to put therein, to steal away their brains, well knowing that their lands would follow.

The following are the petitions presented to the Legislature, which will give some light on the history of Marshpee.

To the Honorable General Court:

The undersigned are Selectmen and School Committee of the District of Marshpee. We understand your Honors are going to make a distribution of the School Fund. Now we pray leave to say that the State, as the guardians of the Marshpee Indians, took our property into their possession, so that we could not use a dollar of it, and so held it for sixty years. We could make no contract with a school-master, and during that time, till 1831, we had no school house in Marshpee, and scarcely any schools. We began to have schools about five years ago, but still want means to employ competent white teachers to instruct our children. Our fathers often petitioned the Legislature to give them schools, but none were given till 1831, when the State generously built us two school-houses.

We also beg leave to remind your Honors that our fathers shed their blood for liberty, and we their children have had but little benefit from it. When a continental regiment of four hundred men were raised in Barnstable county, in 1777, twenty-seven Marshpee Indians enlisted for the whole war. They fought through the war, and not one survives. After the war our fathers had sixty widows left on the Plantation, whose husbands had died or been slain. We have but one man living who draws a pension, and not a widow. We pray you, therefore, to allow to Marshpee, out of the School Fund, a larger amount in proportion than is allowed to other towns and districts who have had better means of education, and to allow us a certain sum per year—and as in duty bound, will ever pray.

Ezra Attaquin,

Isaac Coombs,
Israel Amos,
Selectmen and School Committee
of Marshpee District

To the Honorable, the Senate and House of Representatives
in General Court assembled:

The undersigned beg leave to represent in aid of the petition of the Selectmen and School Committee of the District of Marshpee, praying for a specific appropriation from the School Fund for the support of public schools in said district, that we are acquainted with the facts set forth in said petition, and believe that the cause of education could nowhere be more promoted in any District in the Commonwealth than by making a specific annual allowance to said Marshpee District. The Legislature have made a specific annual appropriation of fifty dollars to the Indians on Martha's Vineyard for public schools, and the undersigned are of opinion, that an annual appropriation of double that amount, would be no more than a fair relative proportion for the District of Marshpee. It is highly important that the District should be able to employ competent white teachers, until they can find a sufficient number of good teachers among themselves, which cannot be expected until they have enjoyed greater means of education than heretofore. The undersigned therefore pray that the petition of said Selectmen may be granted, by giving a specific annual allowance to said District.

Benj. F. Hallett, Counsel for the Marshpee Indians
Charles Marston, Commissioner of Marshpee

Here it will be seen that the missionary for the Indians on Martha's Vineyard did not go to sleep over his flock or run after others and neglect what ought to be his own fold, as did the missionary Mr. Fish, whom Harvard College sent to the Marshpees and pays for preaching to white men. Mr. Bayley, the white missionary on the Vineyard, as I understand, took pains to send a petition to Boston, and he got fifty dollars a year for our brethren there, of which we are glad. From all we can judge of Mr. Fish, we should have sooner expected that, instead of trying to help our schools, he would oppose our getting anything for schools, as he also opposed our getting our liberty. He has done nothing for us, about our schools, and even tried to set the Indians against their counsel, Mr. Hallett, by pretending he had lost his influence. When Mr. Fish does as much for our liberty, and for our schools, as Mr. Hallett has done, we will listen to his advice.

Mr. Bayley, the missionary on the Vineyard, we understand, has but two hundred dollars a year from Harvard College, while Mr. Fish, at Marshpee, has between four and five hundred and wrongly uses as his own about five hundred acres of the best land on the plantation belonging to the Indians. The Legislature, in 1809, took this land from the Indians, without any right to do so, as we think, and thus compel them, against the Constitution, to pay out of their property a minister they never will hear preach. Is this religious liberty for the Indians? Mr. Fish is now cutting perhaps 200 cords of wood, justly belonging to the Indians, when there is scarce five who will go and hear him preach in the meetinghouse erected by the British Society for propagating the Gospel among the Indians and given to the Indians, but in which Mr. Fish now preaches to the whites (having but one colored male member of his church; he is not an Indian, nor an original proprietor) and keeps the key of it, for fear that its lawful owners, the Indians, should go in it, without his leave. He will not let them have it for holding a camp meeting or for any religious purpose.

Last August we invited Mr. Hallett to come and address us on temperance and to explain to us the laws. We appointed to meet at the meetinghouse, as the most central place. Mr. Fish at first refused to let the Indians go into their own meetinghouse, and the people began to assemble under the trees, when it was proposed for the selectmen to go and ask for the key, that they might see if Mr. Fish would refuse it. At this moment, a white man who had been there some time, and had tried to pick a quarrel with Mr. Hallett and the Indians (this was Mr. Alvin Crocker, who had formerly enjoyed more benefits from the plantation than he does under the new law) said he was sent by Mr. Fish with the key and would let the people in, if they would promise to come out when *he* told them to. Mr. Hallett declined going in on such terms and proposed to hold the meeting under the trees. This shamed the messenger of Mr. Fish, and he opened the door, and the people went in, where Mr. Hallett addressed them. While the Indians were thus gratified in meeting their friends, and in hearing good advice from Mr. Hallett on temperance and their affairs, Mr. Fish's messenger interrupted the speaker, in a very abrupt and indecent manner, and tried to bring on a quarrel and break up the meeting. Captain George Lovell, always a friend to the Indians, tried to keep Mr. Crocker still, and Mr. Hallett declined having any controversy; yet the man persisted in his abuse until he broke up the meeting. Had it been thought best, this insulting ambassador would have been put out of the house as a common brawler and disturber; but Mr. Hallett forbore to have any controversy with him. He afterward met the Indians in their schoolhouses and delivered two addresses without interruption from the emissaries of Mr. Fish. This is a sample of the way the Indians have been treated about their own meetinghouse. In some of the old petitions, the Indians speak of this meetinghouse as *our* meetinghouse, and it was built for them without a dollar from the white men of this country, except when the Legislature, at the petition of the Indians, repaired it in 1816. And now, no Indian can go inside of it but by the permission of Mr. Fish, whom they will not hear preach.

It seems that the Indians are not to have the benefit of anything given to them. It must all go to the whites. The whites have our meetinghouse and make Marshpee pay about one-third the support of a minister they will not hear preach. The other two-thirds comes from a fund. In 1711, a pious man named Williams died in England, and in his will he said, "I give the remainder of my estate to be paid yearly to the College of Cambridge, in New England, or to such as are usually employed to manage the blessed work of *converting the poor Indians* there, to promote which, I design this part of my gift."

This was the trust of a dying man, given to Harvard College, that great and honorable literary institution. And how do they fulfill the solemn trust? They have been and still are paying about five hundred dollars a year to a missionary for preaching to the whites. This missionary, by his own statement [see Mr. Hallett's argument], shows he has added to his church *twenty* members from the tribe of over three hundred persons, in *twenty-two years*. Is not this more expensive, in proportion to the good done, than any heathen mission on record? Mr. Fish has now been preaching in Marshpee *twenty-four years*. In that time he has received from the Williams Fund, given solely to convert the poor Indians, about five hundred dollars a year, as nigh as can be ascertained, which is *twelve thousand dollars* for persuading twenty colored persons to join his church. This is six hundred dollars for every member added to his church, and if his other pay is added, it amounts to nine hundred dollars for each member.

Besides this, Mr. Fish has derived an income, we think, not much, if any, short of two hundred and fifty dollars a year, from the woodland, pasturage, marshes, meetinghouse, house lot, etc., which he has wrongfully held and used of the property of the Indians. Add this to his pay from Harvard College, and he has had *eighteen thousand dollars*, of money that belonged to the Indians and which, if it had been laid up for a fund, would have supplied missionaries for all the Indians in New England, according to the will of the pious Mr. Williams. We respect the president and trustees of Harvard College. They are honorable men and mean to do right, but I ask them to look at this statement, then to read the will of Mr. Williams, and laying their hands upon their heart, to ask in the presence of the God of the Indian as well as the white man whether they have done unto the Indians of New England and their children as they would that the Indians should do unto them and their children. We are told that we might bring a suit in equity, or in some way, to compel the trustees of the Williams Fund to distribute it as the pious donor meant, not for the conversion of the whites, even to the taking away from the

Indians of their meetinghouse and lands, but for "the blessed work of converting the poor Indians," as Mr. Williams says in his will.

But it is hard for Indians to contend in the courts of white men, against white men. We can have none of our people to decide such questions, and what could we do against all the power and influence of the Corporation of Harvard College? If the president and fellows of Harvard College prefer to deal unjustly by the poor Indians, and violate the trust of Mr. Williams, by giving the funds to the whites instead of the poor Indians, they must submit to the wrong, we suppose, for there are none strong enough to help them. They can take the money from the Indians but cannot compel them to hear a preacher they dislike.

Some people may say that William Apess wants to get what Mr. Fish has, but all he asks is that Harvard College and the state will not support an *established religion* in Marshpee but leave the Indians free to choose for themselves. Mr. Williams did not give his property to the Marshpee Indians more than to any others. It was designed for all the Indians in New England, and we cannot see what right Harvard College has to give it all for the whites near Marshpee and the Indians on Martha's Vineyard. If they are afraid that Blind Joseph or William Apess, the Indian preachers, should have any of this money if it is withdrawn from Mr. Fish, let them take it and send a missionary among the Marshpee Indians they like. Or let them employ a man, some Eliot, if they can find one, to visit all the Indians in New England, to find out their condition and spiritual wants and try to relieve them. This would be doing some good with money that is now only used to disturb the Indians, to take from them their meetinghouse, to create divisions among them, and turn what the pious Williams meant for a blessing into a curse to the Indians. What would the pious Williams say to Harvard College, could he visit Marshpee on a Sabbath? He might go to the meetinghouse built for the Indians by the society in England, of which I believe he was a principal member. He would find a white man in the pulpit, white singers leading the worship, and the body of the church occupied by seventy or a hundred white persons of the neighboring villages, scarcely one of whom lives on the plantation. Among these he would see four, five, six, or possibly ten persons with colored skins, not but one male among them belonging to the church. He would probably think he had made a mistake and that he was in a white town and not among the Indians. He might then go to the house of Blind Joseph (the colored Baptist preacher), or to the schoolhouse in Marshpee, and he would there find twenty, thirty, or forty Indians, all engaged in the solemn worship of God, united and happy, with a little church, growing in grace. He might then visit the other schoolhouse, at the neck, where he would find William Apess, an

Indian, preaching to fifty, sixty, or seventy, and sometimes a hundred Indians, all uniting in fervent devotion. After the sermon, he would hear a word of exhortation from several of the colored brethren and sisters, in their broken way, but which often touches the heart of the Indian, more than all the learning that Harvard College can bestow. He would hear the Indians singing praises to God and making melody in their hearts if not in their voices. What would he say then, when told that Harvard College had paid twelve thousand dollars of his funds for converting the poor Indians to the white minister, who had made twenty members in twenty-four years, while the two Indian preachers, with forty-seven members to their churches, added in three years, were like St. Paul, laboring with their own hands for a subsistence?

All the Indians ask of Harvard is, take away your pretended gift. Do not force upon us a minister we do not like and who creates divisions among us. Let us have our meetinghouse and our land, and we will be content to worship God without the help of the white man.

This meetinghouse might as well be in India as in Marshpee, for all the benefit the Indians have of it. It is kept locked all the time, with the key in Mr. Fish's possession. It is seen that he would not let the Baptist church of Indians have it to ordain their beloved pastor, Blind Joseph, in, and we see how it was granted to the Indians when they wanted it for Mr. Hallett to address them last summer. Not only were we forbidden the use of the meetinghouse, but even the land which the Legislature unconstitutionally, as we think, took from the Indians to give to Mr. Fish is considered by him too holy to be defiled by the Indians, who are its true owners.

Last summer, sometime in July, my church desired to have a camp meeting, of which we had had one before, attended, as we believe, with a great blessing. We selected a spot some distance from the meetinghouse, in a grove, beside the river; but though not in sight of the meetinghouse, it was on the ground which Mr. Fish thinks has been set apart for his sole use. After the notice was given of the camp meeting, I received from Mr. Fish the following note, which is here recorded as an evidence of the Christian spirit with which a church in Marshpee, consisting of thirty-five members, who were Indians, was treated and molested in their worship by the missionary Harvard College has paid so liberally to "convert the poor Indians," and who had but five Indians in his church, not one being a male member.

Marshpee, July 19, 1834

Mr. Wm. Apes,

Sir,—Perceiving by a notice in the "Barnstable Journal," of last week, that you have appointed a Camp-meeting, to commence on the 30th inst.

and to be holden on the Parsonage, and in the vicinity of the Meeting-house,

This is to forbid the proceeding altogether!

You have no pretence for such a measure; and if you persist in your purpose to hold such a Meeting, either near the *Meeting-house,* or on *any part of the Parsonage allotment,* you must consider yourself *responsible for the consequences.*

I am &c.

Phineas Fish

Rev. William Apes

Soon after this, the selectmen, one of whom was a member of my church, applied to Mr. Fish respecting holding the camp meeting on the parsonage. The place selected could not have disturbed Mr. Fish, any more than people passing in carriages in the main road. We had no meetinghouse, our school-houses would not hold the people, and we had no other means but to erect our tents and worship God in the open air. A pious family of whites from Nantucket came on the ground and began erecting their tent. Mr. Fish came there in person and ordered them off. The man told him that he had his family there and had no other shelter for the night but his tent, which he should not remove but would do so the next day, if he found that he was trespassing on any man's rights. But, he added, if Mr. Fish turned him off, he would publish his conduct to the world. Mr. Fish's interference to break up our religious meeting created much talk, and finally he wrote the following letter to the selectmen, after which we went on and had our meeting, in a quiet, orderly, and peaceful manner, and we believe it was a season of grace, in which the Lord blessed us.

To the Selectmen of Marshpee.

On mature thought, and in compliance with your particular request, I consent to your holding the Camp-meeting, which is this day commenced, on the spot near the river, where the first tent was erected. I consent (I say), on the following conditions, viz: That you undertake that no damage come upon the parsonage property, either wood land, or Meeting-house; that no attempt be made to occupy the Meeting-house; that there be no attempt on the Sabbath, or any other day, to interrupt the customary worship at the Meeting-house, and, *that peace, order, and quietude* be maintained during the time of the Camp-meeting. It is also distinctly understood, that this license is of *special favor,* and *not conceded as your right,* and no way to be taken as a ground for similar requests in future, or for encouraging any future acts of annoyance, vexation, or infringement of the quiet possession of the privileges, secured to me by the *Laws*. And that should any damage be done in any way as aforesaid, you will consider yourselves responsible to the proper authorities.

With my best wishes for your welfare, your friend,

Phineas Fish

Marshpee, July 30, 1834

The reader may now ask, how came Mr. Fish in possession of this property, which he claims to hold by the laws? I am at liberty to publish here the following views of the law and the facts in the case, drawn up by legal counsel whom the selectmen have consulted. And here I take my leave.

Opinion as to the Title Rev. Phineas Fish Has
to the Parsonage, So Called, in Marshpee

The first act of the General Court which interfered with the right of the Indians to sell their own lands, all of which they owned in common in Marshpee Plantation (including what is now called the parsonage), was in 1650, which provides that no person shall *buy* land of any Indian without license of the General Court. In 1665, this was extended to grants for term of years. In 1693, the Indians were put under guardianship.

In 1701, an Act was passed specially to protect the Indians in the enjoyment of their lands. [Col. Laws, page 150.] It also shows why the restriction in the sale of their lands was adopted.

"Whereas, the government of the late Colonies of the Massachusetts Bay and New Plymouth, to the intent the native Indians might not be injured or defeated of their just rights and possessions, or be imposed on and abused in selling and disposing of their lands, and thereby deprive themselves of such places as were suitable for their settlement", did inhibit the purchase of land without consent of the General Court, notwithstanding which, sundry persons have made purchases, &c.; therefore, all such purchases of lands were vacated, with the exception of towns, or persons who had obtained lands from the Indians, and also by virtue of a grant or title made or derived by or from the General Court. All leases of land from Indians for any term or terms of years to be void, unless license was obtained for such lease from the County Court of Sessions. *Provided,* nevertheless, that nothing in this act shall be held or deemed in any wise to hinder, defeat, or make void any bargain, sale, or lease of land made by an Indian to another Indian or Indians.

1718: This is the first act which took from the Indians their civil capacity to make contracts. It says, "Whereas, notwithstanding the care taken and provided (by the former act), a great wrong and injury happens to said Indians, natives of this country, by reason of their being drawn in by small gifts, or small debts, when they are in drink, and out of capacity to trade, to sign unreasonable bills or bonds for debts which are soon sued, and great charge brought upon them, when they have no way to pay the same, but by servitude"; therefore no contract whatever shall be recovered against any Indian native, unless entered into before two Justices of the Peace in the County, both to be present when the contract is executed by the Indian.

The act of 1725, recognizes the rights of Indians to employ persons to build houses on *their own lands*. Their own lands then were the commons, including the parsonage.

In 1763, Marshpee was incorporated as a District, including the land now called the parsonage. *"Be it enacted,* &c. that all the lands *belonging* to the Indians and mulattos in Mashpee be erected into a district, by the name of Mashpee." The Proprietors are empowered to meet *"in the public meeting house"* [the one now claimed by Mr. Fish] to elect a Moderator, five Overseers, two to be Englishmen, a town Clerk and Treasurer, being Englishmen, two Wardens, and one or more Constables. The majority of the Overseers had the sole power to regulate the fishery, to lease such lands and fisheries as are held in common, not exceeding for two years, and to allot to the Indians their upland and meadows. This act was to continue for three years and no longer. It does not appear ever to have been revived. The revolutionary war intervened, and there is no act after 1766, until the act of 1788, after the revolutionary war, which last act put the Indians and their lands under strict guardianship.

In this interval between 1766 and 1788, the only transaction on which Mr. Fish can found any claim to the parsonage took place. There was then either no law existing which could empower any person to sequester and set apart the lands of the Indians, or the law of 1693 (if that of 1763 had expired) was revived, by which the guardianship again attached to the Indians. The Indians, it is believed, continued to choose their own Overseers, under the charter of 1763, after it had expired, and without any authority to do so. It was the only government they had during the troubles of the revolution.

We now come to the first evidence of anything relating to the parsonage land being set apart from the common land. This was in 1783, and the following is the Deed from the Records of Barnstable County, and the only deed relating to this property.

Deed of Marshpee Parsonage

Know all Men by these Presents, That we, Lot Nye, Matthias Amos, Moses Pognet, Selectmen, and Israel Halfday, Joseph Amos and Eben Dives, of the district of Marshpee, *for the support of the Gospel in said Marshpee in all future generations, according to the discipline and worship of the Church in this place, which is Congregational,* do allot, lay out, and *sequester* forever, a certain tract of land, being four hundred acres more or less, lying within the Plantation of Marshpee, and *being Indian property,* which is to lay as a parsonage forever and to be *improved and used for the sole purpose aforesaid;* and the said tract or parcel of land for the said Parsonage, is situated on the East side of Marshpee river, and bounded as follows, viz: Beginning at a certain spring of fresh water which issues from the head of a small lagoon on the East side of Marshpee river aforesaid, and runs into said river a small distance below, and South of the spot where negro Scipio and his wife Jemimai had their house, which is now removed, and from thence running due East into the land until it comes to the great road which leads into Marshpee Neck, so called, and from thence North-wardly bearing Eastward as the said road runs until it comes to the great road, which is the common road from Barnstable to Falmouth, and then bounded by the last mentioned road Northwardly, and running West-wardly until it comes to Ashir's road, then crossing Falmouth road and running in Ashir's path till it comes to Marshpee river aforesaid, and then upon the said river Southwardly, and on the East side, until it comes to the first station, leaving Quokin, and Phillis his wife, quiet in their posses-sions which tract of land (except Mary Richards' fields and plantation), which is within the said boundaries and wood for Mary's own use, and fencing stuff for her fences as they now stand, with all the appurtinances and privileges thereunto belonging, shall be forever for the important purpose of propagating the Gospel in Marshpee, without any let, hin-drance or molestation. In confirmation whereof, we have hereunto set our hands and seals, this seventh day of January, one thousand and seven hundred and eighty-three. 1783.

> Lot Nye,
> Matthias X Amos, his mark,
> Moses X Pognet,   "

N.B. Before the insealing the premises, reserve was made by the signers of this instrument, for the heirs of Mary Richards, that they forever be allowed her in her life time, and Abraham Natumpum and his heirs, be allowed severally to enjoy and possess Scipio's cleared spot of land, and fencing stuff for the same.

> Israel X Halfday, his mark
> Joseph X Amos,   "
> Eben X Dives,   "

In possession of Gideon Hawley, Simon Fish.

Received November 10, 1800, and is recorded in the 25th Book of Records, for the County of Barnstable, folio 139, and compared.

Attest, Ebenezer Bacon, *Register*

Lot Nye was a white man, a great Indian speculator. The other five were Indians, two calling themselves Selectmen. Now what power had these men in 1783, to sequester four hundred acres of the common land of the Indians, for any purpose? If they were Selectmen, and had any power, that power was expressly limited by the act of 1763, to leasing lands for a term not exceeding two years. Here they undertook to make a perpetual grant, a sort of dedication of the property to a certain purpose. If they could dispose of one acre so, they might, with equal propriety, have disposed of the whole Plantation. The Indians were all tenants in common, and no dedication or transfer of the common land could be made, without a legal partition, or the consent of every individual tenant. If the pretended Selectmen acted for the Indians, they could only do so by power of attorney to act for all the tenants in common. There is no other possible legal way by which land, the fee of which is owned by tenants in common, can be transferred, either in fee or in occupancy out of their possession forever. But besides, no act of the Indians was then valid unless confirmed by the General Court. This deed, therefore, of 1783, was void at the time. It seems nothing was done with it, until 1800, *seventeen years* after, when it was recorded in the Barnstable County Registry of Deeds, at whose instigation does not appear. Now, in 1800, when this deed was recorded, the Indians were legally minors, and could do no act, and make no contract. All the power their Selectmen had, in 1783, was taken away. They were under five Overseers, who had power to improve and *lease* the lands of the Indians and their tenements, but no power to sell, sequester, or dedicate any part of them. The Overseers had no power to take a dollar from the Indians for religious worship. While this was the condition of the Indians under the law of 1789 (which continued in full force, with an additional act in 1819, till the new law of 1834), the deed was recorded in 1800, *seventeen years* after it was made by persons who had no power at all to make such a deed. The professed object was to set apart 400 acres, of the common land, lying in Marshpee, "*and being Indian property,*" for a parsonage, forever. The clear title then was in the Indians as tenants in common, for the deed so declares it, in 1783. The parsonage was their property then. How has it ever been conveyed out of their hands? The purpose for which this land was to be used, as sequestered by Lot Nye, etc. was for the sole purpose aforesaid, viz. "for the support of the Gospel in Marshpee in all future generations, according to the discipline and worship of the Church in this place, which is Congregational." And this property, says the deed, "shall be forever for the important purpose of propagating the Gospel in Marshpee, without any let, hindrance or molestation."

This, then, was the design of the original signers of this deed, who had no right to sign such a deed at all. Their object was to promote the Gospel in Marshpee, but how has it turned out? The property has been used for twenty-four years to pay a minister who preaches to the whites, and whom the Indians, with very few exceptions, will not hear. Is not this a gross perversion of the design of the donors, even if they had any power to have made this grant? No lawyer will pretend that the grant was not void, under this deed alone. There was no grantee, no legal consideration, and no power to convey. The deed remained on record until 1809, when the following act was passed by the Legislature, attempting to confirm a deed made 26 years before, by men who had no power to make such deed.

Commonwealth of Massachusetts,
House of Representatives, June 15, 1809.

On the representation of the Overseers of the Indian Plantation of Marshpee, in the County of Barnstable, stating in behalf of said Indians, that it would be conducive to their interests, that a certain grant and allotment of lands therein described, *formerly owned by said Indians,* for the support of the gospel ministry among them, should be confirmed and rendered valid.

Resolved, That a certain grant or allotment of land made by Lot Nye, Matthias Amos, Moses Pognet, Isaac Halfday, Joseph Amos, and Eben Dives, of the District of Marshpee, in the County of Barnstable, as appears by their deed by them, and by them signed, sealed and executed, on the seventh day of January, one thousand seven hundred and eighty-three, and recorded in the Registry of Deeds, in and for said County of Barnstable, in the fifty-fifth book thereof, and 139th folio of said book, said land being 400 acres more or less, according to said deed, be and the same hereby is confirmed and rendered valid to all intents and purposes by them in their said deed expressed, and the said tract of land shall be and remain forever as a parsonage, for the use and benefit of a Congregational gospel minister, as expressed and declared in their said deed. Sent up for concurrence.

Timothy Bigelow, *Speaker*
In Senate, June 19, 1809

Read and concurred.

H. G. Otis, *President*

June 19, 1809, Approved, C. Gore.
[True copy.]

Now, if the deed was not valid in 1783, without the concurrent action of the General Court, it could not be made valid by an act of the General Court 26 years afterward. Besides, the land had been in possession of the Indians, by virtue of their title, more than twenty years after the making of the pretended deed. The power of the grantors, if they ever had any power, had long expired, and Marshpee was governed by new laws. We might as well hold that an act passed by the House of Representatives in 1783 could be made valid by a concurrence of the Senate in 1809.

It is plain, therefore, that unless the General Court had power without the consent of the Indians to sequester this land in 1809, the setting of it apart from the common land is wholly void, and an act of mere arbitrary power. But the General Court never assumed the power to convey any land, for any purpose, belonging to the Indians without their consent. Where and how was their consent given to this act of 1809? They were minors in law, and could give no such consent. Their Overseers could give none for them, for their power only extended to allotting laws to the Indians, and *leasing* them. The pretense, therefore, that this was done at the request of the Overseers gives no strength to the act.

Let another fact be remarked. The original sequestration in 1783 was to promote the Gospel in Marshpee. The General Court profess to confirm and render valid the deed of Lot Nye and others, but they say that this four hundred acres "shall be and remain forever as a parsonage, for the use and benefit of a Congregational gospel minister, *as expressed . . . in their said deed.*"

Now, no such thing is expressed in their deed. There is not a word about a Congregational *minister;* only "for the support of the Gospel, . . . according to the discipline and worship of the Church in this place, which is Congregational."

The General Court, therefore, gave a construction to the deed which the deed never warranted. The whole proceeding must be illegal and void. The fee still remains in the Indians, and no power existed to take it from them without their whole consent as tenants in common, which they have never given, and could not give, because they were in law minors. Mr. Fish was sent to Marshpee as a minister, and ordained in 1811. The Indians, as a society, never invited him to come, or settled him. They never gave him possession of the land or Meeting[-]house. They were then minors in law, and could give no consent. The white Overseers and Harvard College were the only powers that undertook to give Mr. Fish possession of the property of the Indians. It is true, he has held it twenty years, but the statute of quiet possession does not run against minors. The Indians were declared minors, and could bring no action in court.

This is the true history of the parsonage and meetinghouse now wrongfully held by Mr. Fish. Have not the Indians a right to their own property? Has the Legislature and Harvard College a right to establish a religion by law in Marshpee, and take the property of the Indians to support a minister they will not hear? Where did the General Court get any power to give away the property of the Indians, any more than the lands of white men, held in common? They cannot take the property of the Indians to support a private individual. Was it then a public use? But the Constitution says "no part of the property of any individual, can with justice be taken from him, or applied to public uses, without his own consent, or that of the representative body of the people, and whenever the public exigencies require that the property of any individual should be appropriated to public uses, he shall receive a reasonable compensation therefor." Apply this to the act of the General Court, by which Mr. Fish holds four hundred acres of the common land of the Indians, against their consent, and for which they never received a dollar, and answer. Is not the Constitution violated, every day he is suffered to remain on the plantation, against their consent, subsisting on the property of the poor Indians, not to benefit them, but to preach to the whites?

Look at this subject also, in connection with religious freedom. The old article of the Constitution gave the Legislature power to *require* the towns to provide for public worship at their own expense, where they neglected to make such provisions themselves; but it also provided that the towns, etc. "shall at all times have the exclusive right of electing their public teachers, and of contracting with them for their support and maintenance."

This right the Indians have never had in regard to Mr. Fish, nor did they neglect to support worship, and if they did, the Legislature had no power to take their property and set it apart, but might impose a tax or a fine.

But what says the amended article on this subject of religious freedom? "The several religious societies of this Commonwealth (the Indian as well as the white man), whether corporate or unincorporate, shall ever have the right to elect their pastors or religious teachers, to contract with them for their support, to raise money for the erecting and repairing houses of public worship, for the maintenance of religious instruction, and all religious sects and denominations, demeaning themselves peaceably, and as good citizens, shall be equally under the protection of the law."

Are the Indians at Marshpee protected in the same manner the whites are, in their religious freedom? The Indians think not, and with good reason; and yet they cannot get redress. They have warned Mr. Fish to leave their property; they have dismissed him as their minister, if he ever were such, and have forbidden his using their Meeting[-]house, or carrying off their wood. But he persists in holding and using their property, as they say wrongfully, and even prohibits their having a religious meeting in the woods, without his consent. He is, it is stated, at this time employing men to cut and cart wood off the plantation, for his support, and it is supposed he will thus take of the property really belonging to the Indians, about two hundred cords of wood the present year.

Now if this land belongs in common to the Marshpee Indians, as they contend it does, Mr. Fish and the white men he employs (and it is understood he employs no others) violate the law of 1834, and are liable to indictment. That law says "that no person other than proprietors or inhabitants of said District, shall ever cut wood [upon the common lands], or transport the same therefrom. And every person offending against this provision, shall be liable to indictment therefor, and upon conviction, shall pay a fine of not less than fifty, nor more than one hundred dollars, to the use of said District." In this mode, by indicting the white men employed by Mr. Fish to cut and carry off wood, the question could be tried, which is simply whether the fee of the parsonage is in the Indians, or whether it is in Mr. Fish, who never had any deed of it in any way. The parsonage was common land in 1783. Has it been legally changed since in its title, is the question. But even in this matter, as we are informed, the courts of justice which are open to white men are closed to the poor Indians. At the last session of the court in Barnstable, the Selectmen of Marshpee complained against the white men employed by Mr. Fish, for cutting wood on their common lands. The District Attorney, on ascertaining that the wood was taken from the parsonage, so-called, undertook to decide the whole question, before it went to the court, as it is stated to us, and without any examination as to Mr. Fish's title, refused to act upon the complaint. Had the indictment been found, the question could have gone to the Supreme Court, and been there settled. The Indians now must either submit to be wronged until some prosecuting officer will hear their complaints, or they must apply for an injunction to stop Mr. Fish cutting any more of their wood. These are believed to be substantially the facts and the law, in this case. They are left with a candid public to consider, and to form their opinion on, if they cannot be shown to be unfounded.

It should be understood that the Committee who reported the act of 1834, giving the new law to the Indians, did not decide any question touching the parsonage. They treated all the plantation as lands owned in common. It has been said that the Chairman of the Committee, Mr. Barton, had given an opinion that Mr. Fish was entitled to hold the property. This is incorrect. To obviate such an impression, Mr. Hallett, the counsel for the Indians, wrote to Mr. Barton, and received the following reply, which will fully explain the position in which the question was left by the Legislature. In the views expressed by Mr. Barton, Mr. Hallett fully concurs. Too much praise cannot be given to Mr. Barton for the zeal, patience, and ability with which he discharged the duties of Chairman of the Committee.

Worcester, July 1, 1834

Dear Sir,

I last evening received your favor of the 28th ult. The Committee of the Legislature, who had in charge the Marshpee business, intentionally avoided expressing any opinion in regard to the tenure by which Mr. Fish held the parsonage. In our report we merely adverted to the facts, that in 1783, Lot Nye, and several Indians granted 400 acres of the common land, "to be forever for the important purpose of propagating the Gospel in Marshpee." There were no grantees named in the deed. In 1809, the General Court confirmed this grant of a parsonage, to be held forever for a Congregational Gospel Minister. We found Mr. Fish in possession of the parsonage, *as such a minister.* But whether by virtue of said grant, and his settlement at Marshpee he could hold the parsonage, *as a sole corporation,* we regarded it as a question of purely a judicial character, and one with which it was "not *expedient,*" and might we not have added *proper,* "for the Legislature to interfere." If Mr. Fish has rights under these grants, and by virtue of his settlement, I know you will agree with me, that the Legislature can do nothing to divest him of them. And if he had no such right, we were not disposed to create them. I am entirely satisfied with the course which the Committee took in relation to the parsonage; and the circumstance that questions are now agitated in relation to it, show that in one particular, at least, the Committee acted judiciously. We left the parsonage precisely as we found it; leaving to another branch of the government the appropriate responsibility of settling all questions growing out of the grant of 1783, the confirmation of 1809, and the settlement of Mr. Fish. Could we by legislation settle those questions, it might have been our duty to do so, for the sake of the harmony of the District. But it seems to me that any such attempt would have had a tendency to create new difficulties, rather than to diminish old ones.

A word in regard to my advice to Mr. Fish. I received a letter from Mr. Fish some time since, in which he expressed some apprehensions that an attempt would be made by the natives to take possession of the Meeting-house, parsonage, &c. His letter enclosed rather a singular communication, signed by the Selectmen of Marshpee. I did not keep a copy of my answer to Mr. Fish, but recollect distinctly the substance of it. I alluded to the authority of the Legislature in the premises as I have above. That they intended to leave the parsonage as they found it, without undertaking to limit or modify the effect of former acts. That the appropriate mode for the natives to ascertain their rights to, or to obtain possession of, the parsonage, &c. was by resorting to the courts. That any forcible attempt by single individuals to obtain possession of the Meeting-house, &c. would be a trespass; that if numbers combined for that purpose, it would constitute a riot. I take it I hazarded no professional reputation by giving these opinions. For you very well know, that they would be correct, Mr. Fish being in peaceable possession of the premises, whether he were so by seisin or disseisin, by right or by wrong. I hope, my dear sir, that our experiment in regard to the affairs of our Marshpee friends may yet succeed. If not, I think we may console ourselves as one of old did: that if Rome must fall, we are innocent.

I am, very respectfully yours,

J. Barton

The Legislature having thus left the question, to be decided by the Courts, if Mr. Fish insists on holding the parsonage, the inquiry must arise on legal principles: How was Mr. Fish settled in Marshpee, and by what right does he, as a sole corporation, or otherwise, hold the parsonage, as an allotment set apart forever for the support of a Congregational minister, in Marshpee? Harvard College, in which he was then, or had been, a tutor, sent him there as a missionary under the Williams Fund. The Legislature took no part whatever in the settlement. The Overseers permitted him to take possession of the meetinghouse and the parsonage land, so-called, and it is understood that they consented he should cut the annual growth of the wood off the parsonage. But even admitting that the Overseers could so dispose of the property of the Indians, for promoting a particular religious worship in Marshpee (which is explicitly denied), could they convey anything to Mr. Fish beyond the period of their own existence? By the law establishing the Overseers, they had no power beyond leasing land for two years. How then, could the Overseers grant for life to Mr. Fish the improvement of the parsonage and meetinghouse? They might have given it to him from year to year, while they were in office, but on the abolition of the Overseers, in 1834, and a restoration of civil rights to the owners of the fee of the parsonage, the Marshpee Proprietors, how could Mr. Fish continue to hold the parsonage against their will? Was it by virtue of his settlement, so that he now claims the land as a sole corporation? But a minister cannot be settled or constituted a sole corporation, without a parish to settle him. "A minister of a parish seized of lands in its *right* as parsonage lands, is *a sole corporation,* and on a vacancy, the parish is entitled to the profits"; 2d Dane's Abrg. 342, 7 Mass. Rep. 445. Mr. Fish is not seized of a parsonage in right of any parish or religious society, and therefore he cannot be a sole corporation. In point of fact, there was no legal parish in

Marshpee when Mr. Fish went there and took possession, under the Overseers, and not in right of the parish. A parish or precinct, as the law then was, must be a corporation entitled and required to support public worship, and having all the powers and privileges necessary for that purpose. (See 8th Mass. Rep. 91.) And where there has been no parish as such created in a town, the town itself will be considered a parish. (15 Mass. Rep. 296.) Marshpee was not a town. The Marshpee Indians were minors in law, and there was no legal parish to settle a minister, or to hold a parsonage, and no one to make contracts as such. Harvard College had no power to settle a minister in Marshpee, nor had the Overseers any such power. Their supervision was temporal and not ecclesiastical. Besides, the actual Congregational society which subsisted in Marshpee, when Mr. Fish was sent there, in 1811, was composed of a majority of *whites*. Mr. Fish himself testified before the Committee, that the church at Marshpee, in 1811, consisted of sixteen whites and but five colored persons. The church members were a majority of whites, so that even had the church voted to settle Mr. Fish, it would have been a vote of white men having no interest in the premises, and not of Indian Proprietors. Mr. Fish admits that the church passed no vote. It was asserted by one of the old Overseers, Mr. Hawley, that five Indians called on him, after Mr. Fish had preached there, and personally expressed a wish to have him stay with them, but there was no official act, and no vote of the church or society, and no assent of the Proprietors of Marshpee in any form.

Who were the Congregational church, and who the society in Marshpee, in 1811? A regularly gathered Congregational church is composed of several persons associated by covenant or agreement of church fellowship (9th Mass. 277), and a church cannot exist for any legal purposes, except as connected with a congregation or some regularly constituted religious society. (16 Mass. 488.) Where there are no special powers given to the church by the Legislature, the church cannot contract with or settle a minister, but that power resides wholly in the parish, of which the members of the church, who *are inhabitants,* are a part. (9 Mass. Reports, 277. Burr *vs.* First Parish in Sandwich.)

We have seen that there was no legal parish in Marshpee, in 1811, and therefore the Congregational church, if there were such then, had no power to settle Mr. Fish, even had they done so, which they did not. A parish may elect a public teacher, and contract to support him, without the consent of the church, if he be ordained by a council invited by the parish; but in Mr. Fish's case, he was ordained by the request and under the direction of the President and Corporation of Harvard College, the Trustees of the Williams Fund, with the assent of the Overseers. There is then no ground whatever for assuming that Mr. Fish ever was settled legally over a Congregational parish in Marshpee, so as to establish him a sole corporation, to hold the lands belonging to the Proprietors of Marshpee, under the dedication deed of 1783. If that deed, and the subsequent act of 1809, conveyed anything, the conveyance was for the use of the inhabitants as a parsonage, there being no parish in Marshpee, distinct from the Plantation. In such case, it would be held to be a grant to Marshpee (that is, the town), for the use of its ministers (14 Mass. 333). The grant, therefore, could it be regarded as such, was to the whole Proprietors of Marshpee, and they must first settle a minister before he could claim the use of the grant as a minister of the parish.

Neither has Mr. Fish, even if he had been legally settled, any just right, under the deed of 1783, to take the whole parsonage, because that deed states the principal object of the sequestration of the land to be, for the important purpose of promoting the Gospel in Marshpee, and merely referred to the only worship then known there, which was Congregational. When Mr. Fish went there in 1811, there was a Baptist church, and they objected to his taking possession of the parsonage.

There is a case in point in the 13th Mass. Rep. 190, which decides that, where the original Proprietors of a township appropriated a lot of land for a parsonage, and at the same time voted that they would endeavor that a Congregational minister should be settled in the township, such vote ought not to be construed to limit the benefit of the parsonage to a minister of the Congregational order, and that if the inhabitants of the parish should become Christians or any other Protestant sect, they would be entitled to the land, and that a Congregational society, incorporated as a full parish, would have no right to the parsonage. Neither can a parish convey a parsonage to a minister to be held by him in his personal right. By this decision, the Baptist or Methodist church in Marshpee have as good claim to the parsonage as Mr. Fish has.

The dedication, or whatever it may be called, of Marshpee parsonage was made by Lot Nye, etc. in 1783, and confirmed in 1809, by the General Court. Mr. Fish did not become a minister in Marshpee until 1811. Whoever settled him there, for the Indians did not, made no stipulation as to the income of the parsonage, which could bind the Plantation. The society only could make such stipulation, and they did not act in the premises. The Overseers could make no stipulation either to bind the parish or the proprietors, because their power only extended to giving a lease of land not exceeding two years. In the case of Thompson *vs.* the Catholic Congregational Society in Rehoboth (5th Pickering, 469), it was settled that where there was a ministerial fund in a parish, and the society settled a minister stipulating to pay him a salary, without taking any notice of the income of the fund, he must be considered as accepting the salary as a full compensation, and the society are entitled to the fund. Harvard College settled Mr. Fish in Marshpee, and agreed to pay him about five hundred dollars, or two-thirds the proceeds of the Williams Fund. The society to which Mr. Fish was sent to preach took no notice of the parsonage, nor did the Proprietors of Marshpee; hence Mr. Fish cannot hold the proceeds of the parsonage by right of succession, or by stipulation, either from the society or the Marshpee Proprietors, and therefore the Proprietors of Marshpee are entitled to the parsonage.

There is one other consideration that might legally deprive Mr. Fish of his rights in the parsonage, even if he acquired any by the transaction in 1811, which is denied. When he went to Marshpee, and first preached there, he was of the Unitarian faith, and so continued some time. Subsequently (and most undoubtedly from high conscientious motives), he became Orthodox in his creed, and has remained so ever since. [This fact has been named by the President of Harvard College, as one reason why the Williams Fund has continued to be diverted from its proper use; the delicacy Harvard College felt at dismissing Mr. Fish, lest it should be ascribed to persecution, for his change of sentiments from Unitarian to Orthodox.]

But if Mr. Fish claims to hold the parsonage by the *"laws,"* he must be governed by the decision of the Court in the celebrated case of Burr *vs.* the first parish in Sandwich. Mr. Burr was settled a Unitarian, and became Orthodox, and this the Supreme Court decided was just cause for the parish to dismiss him. Chief Justice Parsons said, in that case, that "according to the almost immemorial usage of Congregational churches, before the parish settle a minister, he preaches with them as a candidate for settlement, with the intent of declaring his religious faith, and if he is afterwards settled, it is understood that the greater part of the parish and church agree in his religious sentiments and opinions. If afterwards the minister adopts a new system of divinity, the parish retaining their former religious belief, so that the minister would not have been settled on his present system, in our opinion the parish have good cause to complain." On this ground the Court decided that Mr. Burr had forfeited his settlement.

The principle is the same applied to the relation Mr. Fish holds to the Marshpee Indians. He was placed over them by others, and the Indians are now compelled either to lose all the benefits of their own parsonage or to hear a man in whose doctrines they do not believe, and whom they cannot consent to take as their spiritual teacher.

Upon a full investigation into this branch of the inquiry, there seems to be no legal or equitable ground on which Mr. Fish can claim to hold the parsonage and Meeting[-]house against the Proprietors, and he must, therefore, be regarded as a trespasser, liable to be ejected, and the men he employs to cut and cart wood from the plantation are liable to indictment under the new law of 1834.

The invalidity of title is, however, a still stronger ground against Mr. Fish's right of adverse occupancy, which he now holds, and a case in principle precisely like this has been decided by the Supreme Court of Massachusetts. It occurred in 1798, before there was a reporter of the Supreme Court. Hon. John Davis, United States District Judge, was counsel for the Indians, and Samuel Dexter for the defendant. It was tried on a demurrer before the Supreme Court in Barnstable, upon an action of ejectment, Proprietors of Marshpee *vs.* Ebenezer Crocker. Judge Paine delivered the opinion of the Court in favor of the Indians. Judge Benjamin Whitman of Boston was also, we believe, concerned in the cause. The substance of the case, as stated by Judge Davis and Judge Whitman, was thus:

Ebenezer Crocker of Cotuit had furnished an Indian woman (known as the Indian Queen) with supplies for many years. She occupied, and claimed in severalty as her own, a valuable tract of about 200 acres of land on the Marshpee Plantation, called the neck, of which tract she gave a deed in fee, sometime before her death, to said Crocker, in consideration of the support he had given her. The consideration at that time was not very greatly disproportioned to the value of the land. After her death, she having left no heirs, the grantee, Mr. Crocker, who was an influential member of the General Court, petitioned that body and procured a full confirmation of the deed to him, in the same manner the General Court, in 1809, confirmed the parsonage deed of 1783, except that there was not so long a time intervening between Mr. Crocker's receiving the deed from the Indian Queen in her lifetime and its full confirmation by the General Court after her death.

This took place previous to the law of 1788, putting the Indians under guardianship, when either the law of 1693 or the charter of 1763 was in force. (In June 1763, the governor and Council appointed Thomas Smith, Isaac Hinckley, and Gideon Hawley, "pursuant to an act empowering them to appoint certain persons to have the inspection of the Plantation of Marshpee.") When the white Overseers came in, in 1798, they found Crocker in possession of this land, under the above title, and they employed Judge John Davis, as counsel, to vacate the deed and the act of the General Court. Judge Davis brought an action of ejectment against Crocker (not in the name of the Overseers), but in the name of the Proprietors of Marshpee, whose property, he claimed, was as tenants in common, on the ground that the old Queen, though she occupied it in severalty during her life, could not, as one tenant in common, convey the interest of her co-tenants in common. It was tried in the Supreme Court, and the deed was set aside, for insufficiency of title. This insufficiency of title vitiated the conveyance on the ground that the old Queen had no power to convey when she made the deed, and that the General Court had no power to make good, by a resolve, a title originally invalid.

Crocker also set up the claim of quiet possession, for thirty years, which it was supposed would secure the title; but the Court decided that this gave no title, and the land was restored to the Indians, and now forms a portion of their common land. Mr. Crocker of course, lost all he had furnished to the old Queen, and in this respect, his case was harder than it would be, were Mr. Fish dispossessed of the parsonage after enjoying it for twenty-four years, without any title thereto. It would be difficult for any lawyer to show why Crocker's deed, confirmed by the General Court, should have been set aside in 1798, and Lot Nye's deed, of the parsonage, be held valid in 1834.

On referring to my minutes of the trial of the petition of the Indians, for their liberty, in 1834, before a Committee of the Legislature, I find the following facts stated by Reverend Phineas Fish, who was a witness before that Committee. They will throw some light on the subject of inquiry.

Rev. Phineas Fish, sworn. Testifies that he was ordained at Marshpee in 1811. Was invited there by the Overseers of Marshpee. There were five persons of color belonging to the church, and sixteen whites. At the ordination, a white man rose up and protested against it. He said all were not satisfied. It was not a vote of the Indians by which he was settled, and no vote of the church was taken. Five Indians had expressed a wish that he would remain. He received two-thirds of the Williams Fund, from Harvard College. It had varied from 390 to 433 dollars. Received about 150 dollars per year from the woodland of the parsonage. Has built a dwelling house and made improvements on an acre and a half of land of the plantation, of which he holds a deed from the Overseers, confirmed by a resolve of the General Court.

Mr. Gideon Hawley testified that the Meeting-house was built by the funds of the English Society for propagating the Gospel, before 1757, when his father was sent as a missionary to the Indians, by the London Missionary Society. In 1817, five hundred dollars were granted on petition of the Indians, as a donation by the Legislature, to repair the church for the Marshpee Indians. After Mr. Fish had preached in Marshpee, 5 Indians came to Mr. Hawley and expressed a wish he would stay with them. There was no vote and no record. Before his father came to Marshpee, in 1757, Bryant, an Indian preacher, used to preach to the Indians, in the Meeting-house. The missionary (Mr. Hawley) received one hundred dollars annually, from Harvard College, of the Williams Fund. In 1778, the Indians gave the missionary, Mr. Hawley, two hundred acres of land, which witness inherits. [The validity of this title is not disputed.]

Hon. Charles Marston (one of the Overseers) testified that Mr. Fish had a

Sunday School, principally composed of white children. He did not recollect ever seeing more than eight colored children in it. There were more whites. The Overseers paid the schoolmistress seven and sixpence a week, and she board herself. To an Indian, who kept school in winter, were paid twelve and nineteen dollars a month. The whites who attend Mr. Fish's meeting never pay anything to him or the church. When the tax was required in parishes, many whites got rid of their tax by attending Mr. Fish's meeting. There was always twice as many whites as blacks in the society. Last summer (1833), he counted eighteen colored persons, and twice that number of whites. Mr. Dwight, one of the Committee, asked, if so many whites being there did not tend to discourage the Indians from being interested in the meeting. Mr. Marston thought it might.

Deacon Isaac Coombs, who had been twenty years a deacon in Mr. Fish's church, changed his sentiments, and was baptized by immersion. He testified before the Committee of the Legislature, that when he told Mr. Fish he had been baptized again, Mr. Fish said "that was rank poison, and that he should expect some dreadful judgment would befall me." Deacon Coombs, who is sixty years old, testified also, that the Meeting-house was built for the use of the Indians. No one could remember when it was built. There was but one colored male church member when Mr. Fish came to Marshpee, in 1811. He further stated to the Committee that his family got discouraged going to Mr. Fish's meeting, from the preference he gave to the whites. He did not come to see his family, and lost his influence by taking part with the guardians against the Indians. There was a difficulty in Mr. Fish's meeting about the singing. The colored people were put back, and the whites took the lead. Mr. Fish has 50 or 60 acres of pasture, East of the river, besides the parsonage.

I have thus given my views of the law and the facts touching the parsonage in Marshpee, in order that the Indians and their Selectmen, who have desired legal advice on the subject, may fully understand their rights. I am confident they will never attempt to obtain those rights except in a legal and peaceable way. The Courts at Barnstable, it is said, are closed to them, in the way pointed out by the law, the District Attorney refusing to prosecute the men who cut wood on the parsonage. I invite the attention of that acute and learned officer, Charles H. Warren, Esq., to the points made in this opinion, well assured that if it can be refuted by any professional gentleman, it can be done by him. If he cannot do so, I hope he will permit the title of the parsonage to be brought before the Court, under an indictment for cutting wood contrary to the act of 1834. I regret the necessity of presenting arguments to dispossess Mr. Fish of what he doubtless supposes he lawfully holds; but I am looking for the rights and the property of the Indians, and am not at liberty to consult personal feelings that would certainly induce me to favor the Rev. Mr. Fish, as soon as any man in his situation. I think it as important to him as to the Indians, that the title to the parsonage should be settled, for there will be feuds, and divisions, and strifes, as long as that property remains as it now is, wrongfully taken and withheld from the Indians, to support an "Established Church," in Marshpee. With this view I have proposed to Mr. Fish, in behalf of the Indians, to make up an amicable suit, before the Supreme Court, and obtain their opinion, and the parties be governed by it. The Indians are ready to submit it to such an arbitration. Mr. Fish declines. The only other remedy is an injunction in chancery to stop the cutting of wood. The Indians are not well able to bear the expense, at present, or this course would be taken to recover their property. Until some legal decision is had, Mr. Fish cannot but see, from an examination of the legal grounds set forth herein, that there are strong reasons for regarding him as holding in his possession that which rightfully belongs to another. The public will not be satisfied, until the rights of the Indians are fully secured. I have always been desirous that Mr. Fish should not be disturbed in his house lot, and for my own part, it would give me pleasure, should the Indians, immediately on getting legal possession of their own parsonage, unanimously invite him to settle over them. But so long as he withholds from them their property, it cannot be expected that they should receive him as their spiritual teacher. It is in direct violation of the Constitution and of religious freedom.

Benjamin F. Hallett,
Counsel for the Marshpee Indians

Boston, May 20, 1835.

The selectmen of Marshpee District, are at liberty to make such use of the foregoing as they think proper.

Concluding Observations

If, in the course of this little volume, I have been obliged to use language that seems harsh, I beg my readers to remember that it was in defense of the character of the people under my spiritual charge and of my own. The Marshpees have been reviled and misrepresented in the public prints as much more indolent, ignorant, and degraded than they really are, and it was necessary for their future welfare, as it depends in no small degree upon the good opinion of their white brethren, to state the real truth of the case, which could not be done in gentle terms. The causes which have retarded our improvement could not be explained without naming the individuals who have been the willing instruments to enforce them.

For troubling my readers with so much of my own affairs, I have this excuse. I have been assailed by the vilest calumnies, represented as an exciter of sedition, a hypocrite, and a gambler. These slanders, though disproved, still continue to circulate. Though an Indian, I am at least a man, with all the feelings proper to humanity, and my reputation is dear to me; and I conceive it to be my duty to the children I shall leave behind me, as well as to myself, not to leave them the inheritance of a blasted name. In so doing, I humbly presume to think, I have not exceeded the moderation proper for a Christian man to use.

William Apess

PART 5
Eulogy

on

King Philip,

as Pronounced

at the Odeon, in

Federal Street,

Boston

The *Eulogy on King Philip* was delivered twice, the first time on January 8 and the second on January 26, in a shortened version. The reasons for its being repeated can only be surmised from the text of the newspaper notices that announced it, promising "his full view of the mission cause, as there was some dissatisfaction at the previous one at the Odeon." It is clear that he was asked to repeat the address, though there is no indication of any sponsorship of the first address. We can guess that Apess meant, if no one else did, to observe the 160th anniversary of Philip's death and thus to honor him. It may have pleased him that he was still able to generate controversy, and especially around what had for almost ten years been the focus of his speaking and writing. Apess had long been unsparing about the falsity of "Christian" missionaries to the Indians who shamed and humiliated those to whom they had supposedly come in the name of Christ, a savior, as Apess liked to remind people, who was himself not white and whose salvation was for all, no matter their color, class, gender, or nationality. He condemned not only the most egregious behavior of those ministers who assisted or directly joined in land deals at the expense of Native Americans but also the mistaking of Christianity as an instrument of Euro-American notions of what constituted civilization.

The main body of the speech concentrates on a detailed account, with Philip at its center, of the early history of the encounters between New England Native Americans and the English. The attention to detail and the insistence on recalling this history can be seen in Apess's earlier writing, especially, of course, in his inclusion of the Appendix to *A Son of the Forest.* Unlike the Appendix, however, the *Eulogy* concerns itself only with New England history, although Apess is careful to insist that the treatment by whites of Indians there is symptomatic of the pattern everywhere in the United States. The best modern histories of the encounters between New England Native Americans and the Anglo-Americans confirm the interpretative stance Apess takes. Accurate though it is, Apess always deploys this history to move his larger indictment of white culture and his insistence that its destructiveness will eventually turn back on its progenitors.

In choosing Philip and early New England Anglo-Indian history as his emphasis, Apess had some precedent. Some Anglo-American writers had already provided portraits of these years that were sympathetic to the Indians, damned the Pilgrims and Puritans, and portrayed Philip as a noble and tragic hero. The difference has to do with Apess's insistence on giving this history a contemporary resonance, connecting the past treatment of Indians to present policy and calling for change. For him, history was to be not an excuse for nostalgia or vain regret but an accounting of what had been and what might yet be done differently.

These two occasions were his last in the public eye. And the *Eulogy* was his final publication of himself to a society that briefly noticed and then forgot him.

I do not arise to spread before you the fame of a noted warrior, whose natural abilities shone like those of the great and mighty Philip of Greece, or of Alexander the Great, or like those of Washington—whose virtues and patriotism are engraven on the hearts of my audience. Neither do I approve of war as being the best method of bowing to the haughty tyrant, Man, and civilizing the world. No, far from me be such a thought. But it is to bring before you beings made by the God of Nature, and in whose hearts and heads he has planted sympathies that shall live forever in the memory of the world, whose brilliant talents shone in the display of natural things, so that the most cultivated, whose powers shown with equal luster, were not able to prepare mantles to cover the burning elements of an uncivilized world. What, then? Shall we cease to mention the mighty of the earth, the noble work of God?

Yet those purer virtues remain untold. Those noble traits that marked the wild man's course lie buried in the shades of night; and who shall stand? I appeal to the lovers of liberty. But those few remaining descendants who now remain as the monument of the cruelty of those who came to improve our race and correct our errors—and as the immortal Washington lives endeared and engraven on the hearts of every white in America, never to be forgotten in time—even such is the immortal Philip honored, as held in memory by the degraded but yet grateful descendants who appreciate his character; so will every patriot, especially in this enlightened age, respect the rude yet all-accomplished son of the forest, that died a martyr to his cause, though unsuccessful, yet as glorious as the *American* Revolution. Where, then, shall we place the hero of the wilderness?

Justice and humanity for the remaining few prompt me to vindicate the character of him who yet lives in their hearts and, if possible, melt the prejudice that exists in the hearts of those who are in the possession of his soil, and only by the right of conquest—is the aim of him who proudly tells you, the blood of a denominated savage runs in his veins. It is, however, true that there are many who are said to be honorable warriors, who, in the wisdom of their civilized legislation, think it no crime to wreak their vengeance upon whole nations and communities, until the fields are covered with blood and the rivers turned into purple fountains, while groans, like distant thunder, are heard from the wounded and the tens of thousands of the dying, leaving helpless families depending on their cares and sympathies for life; while a loud response is heard floating through the air from the ten thousand Indian children and orphans, who are left to mourn the honorable acts of a few—civilized men.

Now, if we have common sense and ability to allow the difference between the civilized and the uncivilized, we cannot but see that one mode of warfare is as just as the other; for while one is sanctioned by authority of the enlightened and cultivated men, the other is an agreement according to the pure laws of nature, growing out of natural consequences; for nature always has her defense for every beast of the field; even the reptiles of the earth and the fishes of the sea have their weapons of war. But though frail man was made for a nobler purpose—to live, to love, and adore his God, and do good to his brother—for this reason, and this alone, the God of heaven prepared ways and means to blast anger, man's destroyer, and cause the Prince of Peace to rule, that man might swell those blessed notes. My image is of God; I am not a beast.

But as all men are governed by animal passions who are void of the true principles of God, whether cultivated or uncultivated, we shall now lay before you the true character of Philip, in relation to those hostilities between himself and the whites; and in so doing, permit me to be plain and candid.

The first inquiry is: Who is Philip? He was the descendant of one of the most celebrated chiefs in the known world, for peace and universal benevolence toward all men;[1] for injuries upon injuries, and the most daring robberies and barbarous deeds of death that were ever committed by the American Pilgrims, were with patience and resignation borne, in a manner that would do justice to any Christian nation or being in the world—especially when we realize that it was voluntary suffering on the part of the good old chief. His country extensive, his men numerous, so as the wilderness was enlivened by them, say, a thousand to one of the white men, and they also sick and feeble—where, then, shall we find one nation submitting so tamely to another, with such a host at their command? For injuries of much less magnitude have the people called Christians slain their brethren, till they could sing, like Samson: With a jawbone of an ass have we slain our thousands and laid them in

1. Philip's father was the Pokanoket sachem Massasoit who, as the rest of the *Eulogy* makes clear, became the Pilgrims' crucial ally.

heaps. It will be well for us to lay those deeds and depredations committed by whites upon Indians before the civilized world, and then they can judge for themselves.

It appears from history that, in 1614, "There came one Henry Harly unto me, bringing with him a native of the Island of Capawick [Chappaquiddick], a place at the south of Cape Cod, whose name was Epenuel. This man was taken upon the main by force, with some twenty-nine others," very probably good old Massasoit's men (see Harlow's Voyage, 1611),[2] "by a ship, and carried to London, and from thence to be sold for slaves among the Spaniards; but the Indians being too shrewd, or, as they say, unapt for their use, they refused to traffic in Indians' blood and bones." This inhuman act of the whites caused the Indians to be jealous forever afterward, which the white man acknowledges upon the first pages of the history of his country. (See Drake's *History of the Indians*, 7.)

How inhuman it was in those wretches, to come into a country where nature shone in beauty, spreading her wings over the vast continent, sheltering beneath her shades those natural sons of an Almighty Being, that shone in grandeur and luster like the stars of the first magnitude in the heavenly world; whose virtues far surpassed their more enlightened foes, notwithstanding their pretended zeal for religion and virtue. How they could go to work to enslave a free people and call it religion is beyond the power of my imagination and outstrips the revelation of God's word. O thou pretended hypocritical Christian, whoever thou art, to say it was the design of God that we should murder and slay one another because we have the power. Power was not given us to abuse each other, but a mere power delegated to us by the King of heaven, a weapon of defense against error and evil; and when abused, it will turn to our destruction. Mark, then, the history of nations throughout the world.

But notwithstanding the transgression of this power to destroy the Indians at their first discovery, yet it does appear that the Indians had a wish to

---

2. Apess's own notes will appear throughout this text within parentheses. He seems to have confused Thomas Hunt's 1614 capture of about twenty Indians for sale as slaves with the exploits of Edward Harlow. Whereas Hunt tried unsuccessfully to sell his captives in Spain, Harlow commanded an expedition in 1611 to kidnap Indians for the purpose of making them guides for the English. Among those Harlow captured was Epenow (Epenuel), a sachem from Martha's Vineyard. Epenow spent three years with Sir Ferdinando Gorges, the commander of the Plymouth fort in England who had an interest in colonizing New England. He told Gorges stories of fabulous gold mines. In 1614 Gorges sent an expedition back to find the mines, only to have Epenow leap overboard as the ship approached the island. Epenow's countrymen assisted him by showering the boat with a barrage of arrows, wounding the captain and a number of his crew. From Neal Salisbury, *Manitou and Providence: Indians, Europeans, and the Making of New England, 1500–1643* (New York: Oxford University Press, 1982), 95.

be friendly. When the Pilgrims came among them (Iyanough's men),[3] there appeared an old woman, breaking out in solemn lamentations, declaring one Captain Hunt had carried off three of her children, and they would never return here. The Pilgrims replied that they were bad and wicked men, but they were going to do better and would never injure them at all. And, to pay the poor mother, gave her a few brass trinkets, to atone for her three sons and appease her present feelings, a woman nearly one hundred years of age. O white woman! What would you think if some foreign nation, unknown to you, should come and carry away from you three lovely children, whom you had dandled on the knee, and at some future time you should behold them and break forth in sorrow, with your heart broken, and merely ask, "Sirs, where are my little ones?" and some one should reply: "It was passion, great passion." What would you think of them? Should you not think they were beings made more like rocks than men? Yet these same men came to these Indians for support and acknowledge themselves that no people could be used better than they were; that their treatment would do honor to any nation; that their provisions were in abundance; that they gave them venison and sold them many hogsheads of corn to fill their stores, besides beans. This was in the year 1622. Had it not been for this humane act of the Indians, every white man would have been swept from the New England colonies. In their sickness, too, the Indians were as tender to them as to their own children; and for all this, they were denounced as savages by those who had received all the acts of kindness they possibly could show them. After these social acts of the Indians toward those who were suffering, and those of their countrymen, who well knew the care their brethren had received by them—how were the Indians treated before that? Oh, hear! In the following manner, and their own words, we presume, they will not deny.

December (O.S.)[4] 1620, the Pilgrims landed at Plymouth, and without asking liberty from anyone they possessed themselves of a portion of the country, and built themselves houses, and then made a treaty, and commanded them to accede to it. This, if now done, it would be called an insult, and every white man would be called to go out and act the part of a patriot, to defend their country's rights; and if every intruder were butchered, it would be sung upon every hilltop in the Union that victory and patriotism was the order of the day. And yet the Indians (though many were dissatisfied), without the shedding of blood or imprisoning anyone, bore it. And yet for their

3. Iyanough of Cummaquid was one of the sachems who were counted as allies of the Plymouth colony until Miles Standish lashed out against a "conspiracy" of Massachusett leaders in 1623, killing seven. From Salisbury, *Manitou and Providence,* 130–34.
4. Old Style. Dates were ten days earlier than they would be currently.

kindness and resignation toward the whites, they were called savages and made by God on purpose for them to destroy. We might say, God understood his work better than this. But to proceed: It appears that a treaty was made by the Pilgrims and the Indians, which treaty was kept during forty years; the young chiefs during this time was showing the Pilgrims how to live in their country and find support for their wives and little ones; and for all this, they were receiving the applause of being savages. The two gentleman chiefs were Squanto and Samoset, that were so good to the Pilgrims.[5]

The next we present before you are things very appalling. We turn our attention to the dates 1623, January and March, when Mr. Weston's colony came very near starving to death; some of them were obliged to hire themselves to the Indians, to become their servants, in order that they might live.[6] Their principal work was to bring wood and water; but, not being contented with this, many of the whites sought to steal the Indians' corn; and because the Indians complained of it, and through their complaint, some one of their number being punished, as they say, to appease the savages. Now let us see who the greatest savages were; the person that stole the corn was a stout athletic man, and because of this they wished to spare him and take an old man who was lame and sickly and that used to get his living by weaving, and because they thought he would not be of so much use to them, he was, although innocent of any crime, hung in his stead. O savage, where art thou, to weep over the Christian's crimes? Another act of humanity for Christians, as they call themselves, that one Captain Standish, gathering some fruit and provisions, goes forward with a black and hypocritical heart and pretends to prepare a feast for the Indians; and when they sit down to eat, they seize the Indians' knives hanging about their necks, and stab them to the heart. The white people call this stabbing, feasting the savages. We suppose it might well mean themselves, their conduct being more like savages than Christians. They took one Wittumumet,[7] the chief's head, and put it upon a pole in their fort and, for aught we know, gave praise to their God for success in murdering

5. Samoset, an Abenaki whose people had experience trading with the English, and Squanto, a well-traveled captive who had been taken to England at one time, arranged for the March 1621 meeting between the Pokanoket and the English that resulted in a treaty. The treaty, in addition to symbolizing the mutual good will between the Pokanoket and the colonizers, freed Squanto to live with the English, whom he served as an interpreter, guide, and diplomat. From Salisbury, *Manitou and Providence*, 114–16.

6. Thomas Weston, a non-Separatist London merchant, formed a second colony in 1622 at Wessagusset, north of the Plymouth colony, consisting of sixty single men, most of whom had arrived earlier at Plymouth without adequate provisions. Ibid., 125.

7. Wituwament, a Massachuset sachem, was lured into an English home and killed with his own knife as part of Standish's preventive attacks to frustrate the Massachuset "conspiracy." Ibid., 130.

a poor Indian; for we know it was their usual course to give praise to God for this kind of victory, believing it was God's will and command for them to do so. We wonder if these same Christians do not think it the command of God that they should lie, steal, and get drunk, commit fornication and adultery. The one is as consistent as the other. What say you, judges, is it not so, and was it not according as they did? Indians think it is.

But we will proceed to show another inhuman act. The whites robbed the Indian graves, and their corn, about the year 1632, which caused Chicataubut to be displeased, who was chief, and also a son to the woman that was dead.[8] And according to the Indian custom, it was a righteous act to be avenged of the dead. Accordingly, he called all his men together and addressed them thus: "When last the glorious light of the sky was underneath this globe, and birds grew silent, I began to settle, as is my custom, to take repose. Before my eyes were fast closed, methought I saw a vision, at which my spirit was much troubled. A spirit cried aloud, 'Behold, my son, whom I have cherished, see the paps that gave thee suck, the hands that clasped thee warm, and fed thee oft. Can thou forget to take revenge of those wild people that have my monument defaced in a despiteful manner, disdaining our ancient antiquities and honorable customs? See, now, the sachem's grave lies, like unto the common people of ignoble race, defaced. Thy mother doth complain and implores thy aid against these thievish people, now come hither. If this be suffered, I shall not rest quiet within my everlasting habitation.'" War was the result. And where is there a people in the world that would see their friends robbed of their common property, their nearest and dearest friends; robbed, after their last respects to them? I appeal to you, who value your friends and affectionate mothers, if you would have robbed them of their fine marble, and your storehouses broken open, without calling those to account who did it. I trust not; and if another nation should come to these regions and begin to rob and plunder all that came in their way, would not the orators of the day be called to address the people and arouse them to war for such insults? And, for all this, would they not be called Christians and patriots? Yes, it would be rung from Georgia to Maine, from the ocean to the lakes, what fine men and Christians there were in the land. But when a few red children attempt to defend their rights, they are condemned as savages by those, if possible, who have indulged in wrongs more cruel than the Indians.

But there is still more. In 1619 a number of Indians went on board of a ship, by order of their chief, and the whites set upon them and murdered them without mercy; says Mr. Dermer, "without the Indians giving them the least provocation whatever."[9] Is this insult to be borne, and not a word to be

8. A Massachusett who led a band of fifty to sixty followers. Ibid., 184.
9. Captain Thomas Dermer led expeditions to New England on behalf of Ferdinando Gorges in

said? Truly, Christians would never bear it; why, then, think it strange that the denominated savages do not? O thou white Christian, look at acts that honored your countrymen, to the destruction of thousands, for much less insults than that. And who, my dear sirs, were wanting of the name of savages—whites, or Indians? Let justice answer.

But we have more to present; and that is the violation of a treaty that the Pilgrims proposed for the Indians to subscribe to, and they the first to break it. The Pilgrims promised to deliver up every transgressor of the Indian treaty to them, to be punished according to their laws, and the Indians were to do likewise. Now it appears that an Indian had committed treason by conspiring against the king's life, which is punishable with death; and Massasoit makes demand for the transgressor, and the Pilgrims refuse to give him up, although by their oath of alliance they had promised to do so.[10] Their reasons were, he was beneficial to them. This shows how grateful they were to their former safeguard and ancient protector. Now, who would have blamed this venerable old chief if he had declared war at once and swept the whole colonies away? It was certainly in his power to do it, if he pleased; but no, he forbore and forgave the whites. But where is there a people, called civilized, that would do it? We presume, none; and we doubt not but the Pilgrims would have exerted all their powers to be avenged and to appease their ungodly passions. But it will be seen that this good old chief exercised more Christian forbearance than any of the governors of that age or since. It might well be said he was a pattern for the Christians themselves; but by the Pilgrims he is denounced, as being a savage.

It does not appear that Massasoit or his sons were respected because they were human beings but because they feared him; and we are led to believe that, if it had been in the power of the Pilgrims, they would have butchered them out and out, notwithstanding all the piety they professed.

Only look for a few moments at the abuses the son of Massasoit received. Alexander being sent for with armed men, and while he and his men were breaking their fast in the morning, they were taken immediately away, by order of the governor, without the least provocation but merely through suspicion.[11] Alexander and his men saw them and might have prevented it but did not, saying the governor had no occasion to treat him in this manner;

1619 and 1620. The incident Dermer recounted occurred in the summer of 1620 when an English crew coasting along Massachusetts Bay invited some Pokanokets onto the ship and then murdered them.

10. This passage refers to Squanto, who plotted against Massasoit but was protected by the Pilgrims, who needed his aid.

11. Alexander was the eldest son of Massasoit and Philip's brother. Apess's account captures what seems actually to have occurred.

and the heartless wretch informed him that he would murder him upon the spot if he did not go with him, presenting a sword at his breast; and had it not been for one of his men he would have yielded himself up upon the spot. Alexander was a man of strong passion and of a firm mind; and this insulting treatment of him caused him to fall sick of a fever, so that he never recovered. Some of the Indians were suspicious that he was poisoned to death. He died in the year 1662. "After him," says that eminent divine, Dr. Mather,[12] "there rose up one Philip, of cursed memory." Perhaps if the Doctor was present, he would find that the memory of Philip was as far before his, in the view of sound, judicious men, as the sun is before the stars at noonday. But we might suppose that men like Dr. Mather, so well versed in Scripture, would have known his work better than to have spoken evil of anyone, or have cursed any of God's works. He ought to have known that God did not make his red children for him to curse; but if he wanted them cursed, he could have done it himself. But, on the contrary, his suffering Master commanded him to love his enemies and to pray for his persecutors, and to do unto others as he would that men should do unto him. Now, we wonder if the sons of the Pilgrims would like to have us, poor Indians, come out and curse the Doctor, and all their sons, as we have been by many of them. And suppose that, in some future day, our children should repay all these wrongs, would it not be doing as we, poor Indians, have been done to? But we sincerely hope there is more humanity in us than that.

In the history of Massasoit we find that his own head men were not satisfied with the Pilgrims, that they looked upon them to be intruders and had a wish to expel those intruders out of their coast; and no wonder that from the least reports the Pilgrims were ready to take it up. A false report was made respecting one Tisquantum, that he was murdered by an Indian, one of Coubantant's men.[13] Upon this news, one Standish, a vile and malicious fellow, took fourteen of his lewd Pilgrims with him, and at midnight, when a deathless silence reigned throughout the wilderness; not even a bird is heard to send forth her sweet songs to charm and comfort those children of the woods; but all had taken their rest, to commence anew on the rising of the glorious sun. But to their sad surprise there was no rest for them, but they were surrounded by ruffians and assassins; yes, assassins, what better name can be given them? At that late hour of the night, meeting a house in the wilderness, whose inmates were nothing but a few helpless females and children; soon a voice is heard—"Move not, upon the peril of your life." I

12. This is Increase Mather, Cotton Mather's father. Both wrote virulently against Indians, but it was Increase Mather who wrote most at length on King Philip's War.

13. Tisquantum was another name for Squanto. Coubantant was a sachem at Nemasket who had kidnapped Squanto and another of Plymouth's Indian advisers in August 1621.

appeal to this audience if there was any righteousness in their proceedings. Justice would say no. At the same time some of the females were so frightened that some of them undertook to make their escape, upon which they were fired upon. Now, it is doubtless the case that these females never saw a white man before, or ever heard a gun fired. It must have sounded to them like the rumbling of thunder, and terror must certainly have filled all their hearts. And can it be supposed that these innocent Indians could have looked upon them as good and trusty men? Do you look upon the midnight robber and assassin as being a Christian and trusty man? These Indians had not done one single wrong act to the whites but were as innocent of any crime as any beings in the world. And do you believe that Indians cannot feel and see, as well as white people? If you think so, you are mistaken. Their power of feeling and knowing is as quick as yours. Now this is to be borne, as the Pilgrims did as their Master told them to; but what color he was I leave it. But if the real sufferers say one word, they are denounced as being wild and savage beasts.

But let us look a little further. It appears that in 1630 a benevolent chief bid the Pilgrims welcome to his shores and, in June 28, 1630, ceded his land to them for the small sum of eighty dollars, now Ipswich, Rowley, and a part of Essex.[14] The following year, at the July term, 1631, these Pilgrims of the New World passed an act in court, that the friendly chief should not come into their houses short of paying fifty dollars or an equivalent, that is, ten beaver skins. Who could have supposed that the meek and lowly followers of virtue would have taken such methods to rob honest men of the woods? But, for this insult, the Pilgrims had well-nigh lost the lives and their all, had it not been prevented by Robbin, an Indian, who apprised them of their danger. And now let it be understood, notwithstanding all the bitter feelings the whites have generally shown toward Indians, yet they have been the only instrument in preserving their lives.

The history of New England writers say that our tribes were large and respectable. How, then, could it be otherwise, but their safety rested in the hands of friendly Indians? In 1647, the Pilgrims speak of large and respectable tribes. But let us trace them for a few moments. How have they been destroyed? Is it by fair means? No. How then? By hypocritical proceedings, by being duped and flattered; flattered by informing the Indians that their God was a going to speak to them, and then place them before the cannon's mouth in a line, and then putting the match to it and kill thousands of them. We might suppose that meek Christians had better gods and weapons than cannon; weapons that were not carnal, but mighty through God, to the

14. This is Mascononomo, and the "Pilgrims" he is welcoming were actually the Puritans of the Massachusetts Bay Colony, whose governor was John Winthrop.

pulling down of strongholds. These are the weapons that modern Christians profess to have; and if the Pilgrims did not have them, they ought not to be honored as such. But let us again review their weapons to civilize the nations of this soil. What were they? Rum and powder and ball, together with all the diseases, such as the smallpox and every other disease imaginable, and in this way sweep off thousands and tens of thousands. And then it has been said that these men who were free from these things, that they could not live among civilized people. We wonder how a virtuous people could live in a sink of diseases, a people who had never been used to them.

And who is to account for those destructions upon innocent families and helpless children? It was said by some of the New England writers that living babes were found at the breast of their dead mothers. What an awful sight! And to think, too, that these diseases were carried among them on purpose to destroy them. Let the children of the Pilgrims blush, while the son of the forest drops a tear and groans over the fate of his murdered and departed fathers. He would say to the sons of the Pilgrims (as Job said about his birthday), let the day be dark, the 22nd day of December 1622;[15] let it be forgotten in your celebration, in your speeches, and by the burying of the rock that your fathers first put their foot upon. For be it remembered, although the Gospel is said to be glad tidings to all people, yet we poor Indians never have found those who brought it as messengers of mercy, but contrawise. We say, therefore, let every man of color wrap himself in mourning, for the 22nd of December and the 4th of July are days of mourning and not of joy. (I would here say, there is an error in my book; it speaks of the 25th of December, but it should be the 22nd. See *Indian Nullification*.) Let them rather fast and pray to the great Spirit, the Indian's God, who deals out mercy to his red children, and not destruction.

O Christians, can you answer for those beings that have been destroyed by your hostilities, and beings too that lie endeared to God as yourselves, his Son being their Savior as well as yours, and alike to all men? And will you presume to say that you are executing the judgments of God by so doing, or as many really are approving the works of their fathers to be genuine, as it is

15. Apess, as he makes clear later in the speech, takes December 22 as the day the Pilgrims landed and stepped on Plymouth Rock. They in fact arrived in Massachusetts in December 1620. The landing at the rock is a piece of later mythology, which grew up alongside a celebration of the Founding Fathers. These twin icons in Euro-American culture each found an early and supreme articulator in Daniel Webster. Apess is, very consciously, I think, echoing and disputing Webster's reverential reading both of the "Fathers" and of the Pilgrims. The relevant speeches, among the best-known cultural expressions in Apess's day, are Webster's "First Settlement of New England" delivered at Plymouth on December 22, 1820, and his "Adams and Jefferson" delivered in Faneuil Hall, Boston, on August 2, 1826, the year the two men died on July 4—an irresistibly evocative coincidence.

certain that every time they celebrate the day of the Pilgrims they do? Although in words they deny it, yet in the works they approve of the iniquities of their fathers. And as the seed of iniquity and prejudice was sown in that day, so it still remains; and there is a deep-rooted popular opinion in the hearts of many that Indians were made, etc., on purpose for destruction, to be driven out by white Christians, and they to take their places; and that God had decreed it from all eternity. If such theologians would only study the works of nature more, they would understand the purposes of good better than they do: that the favor of the Almighty was good and holy, and all his nobler works were made to adorn his image, by being his grateful servants and admiring each other as angels, and not, as they say, to drive and devour each other. And that you may know the spirit of the Pilgrims yet remains, we will present before you the words of a humble divine of the Far West. He says, "The desert becomes an Eden." Rev. Nahum Gold, of Union Grove, Putnam, writes under the date June 12, 1835, says he, "Let any man look at this settlement, and reflect what it was three years ago, and his heart can but kindle up while he exclaims, 'what God has wrought!' the savage has left the ground for civilized man; the rich prairie, from bringing forth all its strengths to be burned, is now receiving numerous enclosures, and brings a harvest of corn and wheat to feed the church. Yes, sir, this is now God's vineyard; he has gathered the vine, the choice vine, and brought it from a far country, and has planted it on a goodly soil. He expects fruit now. He gathered out the stones thereof, and drove the red Canaanites from trampling it down, or in any way hindering its increase" (*New York Evangelist*, August 1).

But what next should we hear from this very pious man? Why, my brethren, the poor missionaries want money to go and convert the poor heathen, as if God could not convert them where they were but must first drive them out. If God wants the red men converted, we should think that he could do it as well in one place as in another. But must I say, and shall I say it, that missionaries have injured us more than they have done us good, by degrading us as a people, in breaking up our governments and leaving us without any suffrages whatever, or a legal right among men? Oh, what cursed doctrine is this! It most certainly is not fit to civilize men with, much more to save their souls; and we poor Indians want no such missionaries around us. But I would suggest one thing, and that is, let the ministers and people use the colored people they have already around them like human beings, before they go to convert any more; and let them show it in their churches; and let them proclaim it upon the housetops; and I would say to the benevolent, withhold your hard earnings from them, unless they do do it, until they can stop laying their own wickedness to God, which is blasphemy.

But if God was like his subjects, we should all have been swept off before now; for we find that, of late, Pilgrims' children have got to killing and mobbing each other, as they have got rid of most all the Indians.[16] This is worse than my countrymen ever did, for they never mobbed one another; and I was in hopes that the sons of the Pilgrims had improved a little. But the more honorable may thank their fathers for such a spirit in this age. And remember that their walls of prejudice was built with untempered mortar, contrary to God's command; and be assured, it will fall upon their children, though I sincerely hope they will not be seriously injured by it—although I myself now and then feel a little of its pressure, as though I should not be able to sustain the shock. But I trust the Great Spirit will stand by me, as also good and honorable men will, being as it were the last, still lingering upon the shores of time, standing as it were upon the graves of his much injured race, to plead their cause and speak for the rights of the remaining few. Although it is said by many that the Indians had no rights, neither do they regard their rights; nor can they look a white man in the face and ask him for them. If the white man did but know it, the Indians knows it would do no good to spend his breath for naught. But if we can trust to Roger Williams's word in regard to Indian rights: He says, no people were more so; that the cause of all their wars were about their hunting grounds. And it is certain their boundaries were set to their respective tribes; so that each one knew his own range. The poet speaks thus of Canonicus, in 1803:

> Almighty Prince, of venerable age,
> A fearless warrior, but of peace the friend;
> His breast a treasury of maxims sage,
> His arm a host, to punish or defend.[17]

It was said he was eighty-four years of age when he died, an able defender of his rights. Thus it does appear that Indians had rights, and those rights were near and dear to them, as your stores and farms and firesides are to the whites, and their wives and children also. And how the Pilgrims could rejoice at their distresses, I know not; what divinity men were made of in those days rather puzzles me now and then. Now, for example, we will lay before you the conduct of an Indian and the whites and leave you, dear sirs, to judge.

16. Mob violence, both in rural and urban areas, increased dramatically in the 1830s in the United States, reaching its peak in the summer of 1835. Anti-abolitionist mobs have been the most noticed but there were also nativist mobs attacking Catholics, anti-Mormon mobs, vigilantes lynching gamblers and others, and workingmen's mobs. Anti-abolition and anti-Negro mobs were particularly common and nowhere more so than in Massachusetts and Connecticut.

17. Canonicus was a sachem of the Narragansett who, with his nephew, Miantonomi, led the Narragansett so well that they were able to make tributary, without going to war, most of the Indian groups of the region from Narragansett Bay nearly to Boston.

History informs us that in Kennebunk there lived an Indian, remarkable for his good conduct, and who received a grant of land from the state and fixed himself in a new township, where a number of white families were settled. Though not ill treated, yet the common prejudices against Indians prevented any sympathy with him, though he himself did all that lay in his power to comfort his white neighbors, in case of sickness and death. But now let us see the scene reversed. This poor Indian, that had nourished and waited to aid the Pilgrims in their trouble, now vainly looks for help, when sickness and death comes into his family. Hear his own words. He speaks to the inhabitants thus: "When white man's child die, Indian man he sorry; he help bury him. When my child die, no one speak to me; I make his grave alone. I can no live here." He gave up his farm, dug up the body of his child, and carried it 200 miles, through the wilderness, to join the Canadian Indians. What dignity there was in this man; and we do not wonder that he felt so indignant at the proceedings of the then called Christians. But this was as they were taught by their haughty divines and orators of the day. But, nevertheless, the people were to blame, for they might have read for themselves; and they doubtless would have found that we were not made to be vessels of wrath, as they say we were. And had the whites found it out, perhaps they would not have rejoiced at a poor Indian's death or, when they were swept off, would not have called it the Lord killing the Indians to make room for them upon their lands. This is something like many people wishing for their friends to die, that they might get their property. I am astonished when I look at people's absurd blindness—when all are liable to die, and all subject to all kinds of diseases. For example, why is it that epidemics have raged so much among the more civilized? In London, 1660, the plague; and in 1830 and 1831, the cholera, in the Old and New World, when the inhabitants were lain in heaps by that epidemic. Should I hear of an Indian rejoicing over the inhabitants, I would no longer own him as a brother. But, dear friends, you know that no Indian knew by the Bible it was wrong to kill, because he knew not the Bible and its sacred laws. But it is certain the Pilgrims knew better than to break the commands of their Lord and Master; they knew that it was written, "Thou shalt not kill."

But having laid a mass of history and exposition before you, the purpose of which is to show that Philip and all the Indians generally felt indignantly toward whites, whereby they were more easily allied together by Philip, their king and emperor, we come to notice more particularly his history. As to His Majesty, King Philip, it was certain that his honor was put to the test, and it was certainly to be tried, even at the loss of his life and country. It is a matter of uncertainty about his age; but his birthplace was at Mount Hope, Rhode Island, where Massasoit, his father, lived till 1656, and died, as also his brother, Alexander, by the governor's ill-treating him (that is, Winthrop), which caused his death, as before mentioned, in 1662; after which, the kingdom fell into the hands of Philip, the greatest man that ever lived upon the American shores. Soon after his coming to the throne, it appears he began to be noticed, though, prior to this, it appears that he was not forward in the councils of war or peace. When he came into office it appears that he knew there was great responsibility resting upon himself and country, that it was likely to be ruined by those rude intruders around him, though he appears friendly and is willing to sell them lands for almost nothing, as we shall learn from dates of the Plymouth colony, which commence June 23, 1664. William Benton of Rhode Island, a merchant, buys Mattapoisett of Philip and wife, but no sum is set which he gave for it. To this deed, his counselors, and wife, and two of the Pilgrims were witnesses. In 1665 he sold New Bedford and Compton for forty dollars. In 1667 he sells to Constant Southworth and others all the meadowlands from Dartmouth to Mattapoisett, for which he received sixty dollars. The same year he sells to Thomas Willet a tract of land two miles in length and perhaps the same in width, for which he received forty dollars. In 1668 he sold a tract of some square miles, now called Swansea. The next year he sells five hundred acres in Swansea, for which he received eighty dollars. His counselors and interpreters, with the Pilgrims, were witnesses to these deeds.

Osamequan, for valuable considerations, in the year 1641 sold to John Brown and Edward Winslow a tract of land eight miles square, situated on both sides of Palmer's River. Philip, in 1668, was required to sign a quit claim of the same, which we understand he did in the presence of his counselors. In the same year Philip laid claim to a portion of land called New Meadows, alleging that it was not intended to be conveyed in a former deed, for which Mr. Brown paid him forty-four dollars, in goods; so it was settled without difficulty. Also, in 1669, for forty dollars, he sold to one John Cook a whole island called Nokatay, near Dartmouth. The same year Philip sells a tract of land in Middleborough for fifty-two dollars. In 1671 he sold to Hugh Cole a large tract of land lying near Swansea, for sixteen dollars. In 1672 he sold sixteen square miles to William Breton and others, of Taunton, for which he and his chief received five hundred and seventy-two dollars. This contract, signed by himself and chiefs, ends the sales of lands with Philip, for all which he received nine hundred and seventy-four dollars, as far as we can learn by the records.

Here Philip meets with a most bitter insult, in 1673, from one Peter Talmon of Rhode Island, who complained to the Plymouth court against Philip, of Mount Hope, predecessor, heir, and administrator of his brother Alexander, deceased, in an action on the case, to the damage of three thousand and two hundred dollars, for which the court gave verdict in favor of Talmon, the young Pilgrim; for which Philip had to make good to the said Talmon a large tract of land at Sapamet and other places adjacent. And for the want thereof, that is, more land that was not taken up, the complainant is greatly damnified. This is the language in the Pilgrims' court. Now let us review this a little. The man who bought this land made the contract, as he says, with Alexander, ten or twelve years before; then why did he not bring forward his contract before the court? It is easy to understand why he did not. Their object was to cheat, or get the whole back again in this way. Only look at the sum demanded, and it is enough to satisfy the critical observer. This course of proceedings caused the chief and his people to entertain strong jealousies of the whites.

In the year 1668 Philip made a complaint against one Weston, who had wronged one of his men of a gun and some swine; and we have no account that he got any justice for his injured brethren. And, indeed, it would be a strange thing for poor unfortunate Indians to find justice in those courts of the pretended pious in those days, or even since; and for a proof of my assertion I will refer the reader or hearer to the records of legislatures and courts throughout New England, and also to my book, *Indian Nullification*.

We would remark still further: Who stood up in those days, and since, to plead Indian rights? Was it the friend of the Indian? No, it was his enemies who rose—his enemies, to judge and pass sentence. And we know that such kind of characters as the Pilgrims were, in regard to the Indians' rights, who, as they say, had none, must certainly always give verdict against them, as, generally speaking, they always have. Prior to this insult, it appears that Philip had met with great difficulty with the Pilgrims, that they appeared to be suspicious of him in 1671; and the Pilgrims sent for him, but he did not appear to move as though he cared much for their messenger, which caused them to be still more suspicious. What grounds the Pilgrims had is not ascertained, unless it is attributed to a guilty conscience for wrongs done to Indians. It appears that Philip, when he got ready, goes near to them and sends messengers to Taunton, to invite the Pilgrims to come and treat with him; but the governor, being either too proud or afraid, sends messengers to him to come to their residence at Taunton, to which he complied. Among these messengers was the Honorable Roger Williams, a Christian and a patriot and a friend to the Indians, for which we rejoice. Philip, not liking to trust the Pilgrims, left some of the whites in his stead to warrant his safe return. When Philip and his men had come near the place, some of the Plymouth people were ready to attack him; this rashness was, however, prevented by the commissioner of Massachusetts, who met there with the governor to treat with Philip; and it was agreed upon to meet in the meetinghouse.

Philip's complaint was that the Pilgrims had injured the planting grounds of his people. The Pilgrims, acting as umpires, say the charges against them were not sustained; and because it was not, to their satisfaction, the whites wanted that Philip should order all his men to bring in his arms and ammunition; and the court was to dispose of them as they pleased. The next thing was that Philip must pay the cost of the treaty, which was four hundred dollars. The pious Dr. Mather says that Philip was appointed to pay a sum of money to defray the charges that his insolent clamors had put the colony to. We wonder if the Pilgrims were as ready to pay the Indians for the trouble they put them to. If they were, it was with the instruments of death. It appears that Philip did not wish to make war with them but compromised with them; and in order to appease the Pilgrims he actually did order his men, whom he could not trust, to deliver them up; but his own men withheld, with the exception of a very few.

Now, what an unrighteous act this was in the people who professed to be friendly and humane and peaceable to all men. It could not be that they were so devoid of sense as to think these illiberal acts would produce peace but, contrawise, continual broils. And, in fact, it does appear that they courted war instead of peace, as it appears from a second council that was held by order of the governor, at Plymouth, September 13, 1671. It appears that they sent again for Philip; but he did not attend but went himself and made complaint to the governor, which made him write to the council and ordered them to desist, to be more mild, and not to take such rash measures. But it appears that on the 24th the scene changed, that they held another council; and the disturbers of the peace, the intruders upon a peaceable people, say they find Philip guilty of the following charges:

1. That he had neglected to bring in his arms, although competent time had been given him.
2. That he had carried insolently and proudly toward us on several occasions, in refusing to come down to our courts (when sent for), to procure a right understanding betwixt us.

What an insult this was to His Majesty; an independent chief of a powerful nation should come at the beck and call of his neighbors whenever they pleased to have him do it. Besides, did not Philip do as he agreed, at Taunton? That is, in case there was more difficulty they were to leave it to Massachusetts, to be settled there in the high council, and both parties were to abide by their decision—but did the Pilgrims wait? No. But being infallible, of course they could not err.

The third charge was: harboring divers Indians, not his own men but the vagabond Indians.

Now, what a charge this was to bring against a king, calling his company vagabonds, because it did not happen to please them; and what right had they to find fault with his company? I do not believe that Philip ever troubled himself about the white people's company and prefer charges against them for keeping company with whom they pleased. Neither do I believe he called their company vagabonds, for he was more noble than that.

The fourth charge is that he went to Massachusetts with his council and complained against them and turned their brethren against them.

This was more a complaint against themselves than Philip, inasmuch as it represents that Philip's story was so correct that they were blamable.

5. That he had not been quite so civil as they wished him to be.

We presume that Philip felt himself much troubled by these intruders and of course put them off from time to time, or did not take much notice of their proposals. Now, such charges as those, we think, are to no credit of the Pilgrims. However, this council ended much as the other did, in regard to disarming the Indians, which they never were able to do. Thus ended the events of 1671.

But it appears that the Pilgrims could not be contented with what they had done, but they must send an Indian, and a traitor, to preach to Philip and his men, in order to convert him and his people to Christianity. The preacher's name was Sassamon. I would appeal to this audience: Is it not certain that the Plymouth people strove to pick a quarrel with Philip and his men? What could have been more insulting than to send a man to them who was false, and looked upon as such? For it is most certain that a traitor was, above all others, the more to be detested than any other. And not only so; it was the laws of the Indians that such a man must die, that he had forfeited his life; and when he made his appearance among them, Philip would have killed him upon the spot if his council had not persuaded him not to. But it appears that in March 1674 one of Philip's men killed him and placed him beneath the ice in a certain pond near Plymouth, doubtless by the order of Philip. After this, search was made for him, and they found there a certain Indian, by the name of Patuckson; Tobias, also, his son, were apprehended and tried. Tobias was one of Philip's counselors, as it appears from the records that the trial did not end here, that it was put over, and that two of the Indians entered into bonds for $400, for the appearance of Tobias at the June term, for which a mortgage of land was taken to that amount for his safe return. June having arrived, three instead of one are arraigned. There was no one but Tobias suspected at the previous court. Now two others are arraigned, tried, condemned, and executed (making three in all) in June the 8th, 1675, by hanging and shooting. It does not appear that any more than one was guilty, and it was said that he was known to acknowledge it; but the other two persisted in their innocence to the last.

This murder of the preacher brought on the war a year sooner than it was anticipated by Philip. But this so exasperated King Philip that from that day he studied to be revenged of the Pilgrims, judging that his white intruders had nothing to do in punishing his people for any crime and that it was in violation of treaties of ancient date. But when we look at this, how bold and how daring it was to Philip, as though they would bid defiance to him, and all his authority; we do not wonder at his exasperation. When the governor finds that His Majesty was displeased, he then sends messengers to him and wishes to know why he would make war upon him (as if he had done all right), and wished to enter into a new treaty with him. The king answered them thus: "Your governor is but a subject of King Charles of England; I shall not treat with a subject; I shall treat of peace only with a king, my brother; when he comes, I am ready."

This answer of Philip's to the messengers is worthy of note throughout the world. And never could a prince answer with more dignity in regard to his official authority than he did—disdaining the idea of placing himself upon a par of the minor subjects of a king; letting them know, at the same time, that he felt his independence more than they thought he did. And indeed it was time for him to wake up, for now the subjects of King Charles had taken one of his counselors and killed him, and he could no longer trust them. Until the execution of these three Indians, supposed to be the murderers of Sassamon, no hostility was committed by Philip or his warriors. About the time of their trial, he was said to be marching his men up and down the country in arms; but when it was known, he could no longer restrain his young men, who, upon the 24th of June [1675], provoked the people of Swansea by killing their cattle and other injuries, which was a signal to commence the war, and what they had desired, as a superstitious notion prevailed among the Indians that whoever fired the first gun of either party would be conquered, doubtless a notion they had received from the Pilgrims. It was upon a fast day, too, when the first gun was fired; and as the people were returning from church, they were fired upon by the Indians, when several of them were killed. It is not supposed that Philip directed this attack but was opposed to it. Though it is not doubted that he meant to be revenged upon his enemies; for during some time he had been cementing his countrymen together, as it appears that he had sent to all the disaffected tribes, who also had watched the movements of the comers from the New World[18] and were as dissatisfied as Philip himself was with their proceedings.

18. His "comers from the New World" may only be a slip of the pen, referring as he is to the Europeans, who are conventionally, of course, from the "Old" World, having "discovered" the

Now around the council fires they met,
    The young nobles for to greet;
Their tales of woe and sorrows to relate,
    About the Pilgrims, their wretched foes.

And while their fires were blazing high,
    Their king and Emperor to greet;
His voice like lightning fires their hearts,
    To stand the test or die.

See those Pilgrims from the world unknown,
    No love for Indians do know:
Although our fathers fed them well
    With venison rich, of precious kinds.

No gratitude to Indians now is shown,
    From people saved by them alone;
All gratitude that poor Indian do know,
    Is, we are robbed of all our rights.[19]

At this council it appears that Philip made the following speech to his chiefs, counselors, and warriors:

Brothers, you see this vast country before us, which the Great Spirit gave to our fathers and us; you see the buffalo and deer that now are our support. Brothers, you see these little ones, our wives and children, who are looking to us for food and raiment; and you now see the foe before you, that they have grown insolent and bold; that all our ancient customs are disregarded; the treaties made by our fathers and us are broken, and all of us insulted; our council fires disregarded, and all the ancient customs of our fathers; our brothers murdered before our eyes, and their spirits cry to us for revenge. Brothers, these people from the unknown world will cut down our groves, spoil our hunting and planting grounds, and drive us and our children from the graves of our fathers, and our council fires, and enslave our women and children.

This famous speech of Philip was calculated to arouse them to arms, to do the best they could in protecting and defending their rights. The blow had now been struck, the die was cast, and nothing but blood and carnage was

"New." This is, however, so like Apess's wit and his delight in inverting the conventions of language through which Europeans validated their presence and their dominance in the Americas that it may be entirely deliberate—for the Europeans were of course from a new world from the perspective of Native Americans.

19. I have not been able to identify this poem.

before them. And we find Philip as active as the wind, as dexterous as a giant, firm as the pillows of heaven, and fierce as a lion, a powerful foe to contend with indeed, and as swift as an eagle, gathering together his forces to prepare them for the battle. And as it would swell our address too full to mention all the tribes in Philip's train of warriors, suffice it to say that from six to seven were with him at different times. When he begins the war, he goes forward and musters about 500 of his men and arms them complete, and about 900 of the other, making in all about fourteen hundred warriors when he commenced. It must be recollected that this war was legally declared by Philip, so that the colonies had a fair warning. It was no savage war of surprise, as some suppose, but one sorely provoked by the Pilgrims themselves. But when Philip and his men fought as they were accustomed to do and according to their mode of war, it was more than what could be expected. But we hear no particular acts of cruelty committed by Philip during the siege. But we find more manly nobility in him than we do in all the head Pilgrims put together, as we shall see during this quarrel between them. Philip's young men were eager to do exploits and to lead captive their haughty lords. It does appear that every Indian heart had been lighted up at the council fires, at Philip's speech, and that the forest was literally alive with this injured race. And now town after town fell before them. The Pilgrims with their forces were marching ever in one direction, while Philip and his forces were marching in another, burning all before them, until Middleborough, Taunton, and Dartmouth were laid in ruins and forsaken by its inhabitants.

At the great fight at Pocasset,[20] Philip commanded in person, where he also was discovered with his host in a dismal swamp. He had retired here with his army to secure a safe retreat from the Pilgrims, who were in close pursuit of him, and their numbers were so powerful they thought the fate of Philip was sealed. They surrounded the swamp, in hopes to destroy him and his army. At the edge of the swamp Philip had secreted a few of his men to draw them into ambush, upon which the Pilgrims showed fight, Philip's men retreating and the whites pursuing them till they were surrounded by Philip and nearly all cut off. This was a sorry time to them; the Pilgrims, however, reinforced but ordered a retreat, supposing it impossible for Philip to escape; and knowing his forces to be great, it was conjectured by some to build a fort to starve him out, as he had lost but few men in the fight. The situation of Philip was rather peculiar, as there was but one outlet to the swamp and a river before him nearly seven miles to descend. The Pilgrims placed a guard around the swamp for 13 days, which gave Philip and his men time to prepare

20. The battle began July 18, 1675. It started when fifteen Englishmen were killed in ambush in woods so thick that there was fear the English would shoot one another.

canoes to make good his retreat, in which he did, to the Connecticut River, and in his retreat lost but fourteen men. We may look upon this move of Philip's to be equal, if not superior, to that of Washington crossing the Delaware. For while Washington was assisted by all the knowledge that art and science could give, together with all the instruments of defense and edged tools to prepare rafts and the like helps for safety across the river, Philip was naked as to any of these things, possessing only what nature, his mother, had bestowed upon him; and yet makes his escape with equal praise. But he would not even [have] lost a man had it not been for Indians who were hired to fight against Indians, with promise of their enjoying equal rights with their white brethren; but not one of those promises have as yet been fulfilled by the Pilgrims or their children, though they must acknowledge that without the aid of Indians and their guides they must inevitably been swept off. It was only, then, by deception that the Pilgrims gained the country, as their word has never been fulfilled in regard to Indian rights.

Philip having now taken possession of the back settlements of Massachusetts, one town after another was swept off. A garrison being established at Northfield by the Pilgrims, and while endeavoring to reinforce it with thirty-six armed, twenty out of their number was killed and one taken prisoner. At the same time Philip so managed it as to cut off their retreat and take their ammunition from them.

About the month of August, they took a young lad about fourteen years of age, whom they intended to make merry with the next day; but the Pilgrims said God touched the Indians' heart, and they let him go. About the same time, the whites took an old man of Philip's, whom they found alone; and because he would not turn traitor and inform them where Philip was, they pronounced him worthy of death and by them was executed, cutting off first his arms and then his head. We wonder why God did not touch the Pilgrims' heart and save them from cruelty, as well as the Indians.

We would now notice an act in King Philip that outweighs all the princes and emperors in the world. That is, when his men began to be in want of money, having a coat neatly wrought with mampampeag (i.e., Indian money), he cut it to pieces and distributed it among all his chiefs and warriors, it being better than the old continental money of the Revolution in Washington's day, as not one Indian soldier found fault with it, as we could ever learn; so that it cheered their hearts still to persevere to maintain their rights and expel their enemies.

On the 18th of September, the Pilgrims made a tour from Hadley to Deerfield, with about eighty men, to bring their valuable articles of clothing and provisions. Having loaded their teams and returning, Philip and his men attacked them, and nearly slew them all. The attack was made near Sugarloaf

Hill.[21] It was said that in this fight the Pilgrims lost their best men of Essex and all their goods—upon which there were many made widows and orphans in one day. Philip now having done what he could upon the western frontiers of Massachusetts and believing his presence was wanted among his allies, the Narragansetts, to keep them from being duped by the Pilgrims, he is next known to be in their country.

The Pilgrims determined to break down Philip's power, if possible, with the Narragansetts: Thus they raised an army of 1,500 strong, to go against them and destroy them if possible. In this, Massachusetts, Plymouth, and Connecticut all join in severally, to crush Philip. Accordingly, in December, in 1675, the Pilgrims set forward to destroy them. Preceding their march, Philip had made all arrangements for the winter and had fortified himself beyond what was common for his countrymen to do, upon a small island near South Kingston, R.I. Here he intended to pass the winter with his warriors and their wives and children. About 500 Indian houses was erected of a superior kind, in which was deposited all their stores, tubs of corn, and other things, piled up to a great height, which rendered it bulletproof. It was supposed that 3,000 persons had taken up their residence in it. (I would remark that Indians took better care of themselves in those days than they have been able to since.) Accordingly, on the 19th day of December, after the Pilgrims had been out in the extreme cold for nearly one month, lodging in tents, and their provision being short, and the air full of snow, they had no other alternative than to attack Philip in the fort. Treachery, however, hastened his ruin; one of his men, by hope of reward from the deceptive Pilgrims, betrayed his country into their hands. The traitor's name was Peter. No white man was acquainted with the way, and it would have been almost impossible for them to have found it, much less to have captured it. There was but one point where it could have been entered or assailed with any success, and this was fortified much like a blockhouse, directly in front of the entrance, and also flankers to cover a crossfire—besides high palisades, an immense hedge of fallen trees of nearly a rod in thickness. Thus surrounded by trees and water, there was but one place that the Pilgrims could pass. Nevertheless, they made the attempt. Philip now had directed his men to fire, and every platoon of the Indians swept every white man from the path one after another, until six captains, with a great many of the men, had fallen. In the meantime, one Captain Moseley with some of his men had somehow or other gotten into the fort in another way and surprised them, by which the Pilgrims were enabled to capture the fort, at the same time setting fire to it and hewing down men, women, and children indiscriminately. Philip, however, was enabled to escape

21. Opposite present-day Sunderland, Massachusetts.

with many of his warriors. It is said at this battle eighty whites were killed and one hundred and fifty wounded, many of whom died of their wounds afterward, not being able to dress them till they had marched 18 miles, also leaving many of their dead in the fort. It is said that 700 of the Narragansetts perished, the greater part of them being women and children.

It appears that God did not prosper them much, after all. It is believed that the sufferings of the Pilgrims were without a parallel in history; and it is supposed that the horrors and burning elements of Moscow will bear but a faint resemblance of that scene. The thousands and ten thousands assembled there with their well-disciplined forces bear but little comparison to that of modern Europe, when the inhabitants, science, manners, and customs are taken into consideration. We might as well admit the above fact and say the like was never known among any heathen nation in the world; for none but those worse than heathens would have suffered so much, for the sake of being revenged upon those of their enemies. Philip had repaired to his quarters to take care of his people and not to have them exposed. We should not have wondered quite so much if Philip had gone forward and acted thus. But when a people calling themselves Christians conduct in this manner, we think they are censurable, and no pity at all ought to be had for them.

It appears that one of the whites had married one of Philip's countrymen; and they, the Pilgrims, said he was a traitor, and therefore they said he must die. So they quartered him; and as history informs us, they said, he being a heathen, but a few tears were shed at his funeral. Here, then, because a man would not turn and fight against his own wife and family, or leave them, he was condemned as a heathen. We presume that no honest men will commend those ancient fathers for such absurd conduct. Soon after this, Philip and his men left that part of the country and retired farther back, near the Mohawks, where, in July 1676, some of his men were slain by the Mohawks. Notwithstanding this, he strove to get them to join him; and here it is said that Philip did not do that which was right, that he killed some of the Mohawks and laid it to the whites in order that he might get them to join him. If so, we cannot consistently believe he did right. But he was so exasperated that nothing but revenge would satisfy him. All this act was no worse than our political men do in our days, of their strife to wrong each other, who profess to be enlightened; and all for the sake of carrying their points. Heathenlike, either by the sword, calumny, or deception of every kind; and the late duels among the [so-] called high men of honor is sufficient to warrant my statements. But while we pursue our history in regard to Philip, we find that he made many successful attempts against the Pilgrims, in surprising and driving them from their posts, during the year 1676, in February and through till August, in which time many of the Christian Indians joined him. It is thought by many that all would have joined him, if they had been left to their choice, as it appears they did not like their white brethren very well. It appears that Philip treated his prisoners with a great deal more Christian-like spirit than the Pilgrims did; even Mrs. Rowlandson,[22] although speaking with bitterness sometimes of the Indians, yet in her journal she speaks not a word against him. Philip even hires her to work for him, and pays her for her work, and then invites her to dine with him and to smoke with him. And we have many testimonies that he was kind to his prisoners; and when the English wanted to redeem Philip's prisoners, they had the privilege.

Now, did Governor Winthrop or any of those ancient divines use any of his men so? No. Was it known that they received any of their female captives into their houses and fed them? No, it cannot be found upon history. Were not the females completely safe, and none of them were violated, as they acknowledge themselves? But was it so when the Indian women fell into the hands of the Pilgrims? No. Did the Indians get a chance to redeem their prisoners? No. But when they were taken they were either compelled to turn traitors and join their enemies or be butchered upon the spot. And this is the dishonest method that the famous Captain Church used in doing his great exploits; and in no other way could he ever gained one battle.[23] So, after all, Church only owes his exploits to the honesty of the Indians, who told the truth, and to his own deceptive heart in duping them. Here it is to be understood that the whites have always imposed upon the credulity of the Indians. It is with shame, I acknowledge, that I have to notice so much corruption of a people calling themselves Christians. If they were like my people, professing no purity at all, then their crimes would not appear to have such magnitude. But while they appear to be by profession more virtuous, their crimes still blacken. It makes them truly to appear to be like mountains filled with smoke, and thick darkness covering them all around.

But we have another dark and corrupt deed for the sons of Pilgrims to look at, and that is the fight and capture of Philip's son and wife and many of

22. Mary Rowlandson was captured, along with three of her children, by a group of Philip's allies in an attack that destroyed her home village of Lancaster, Massachusetts. She was ransomed after six months of living with Indian war parties. Her *Narrative* of her captivity, published in 1682, became almost instantly popular and inaugurated one of the most important genres in American literature. Apess has read the *Narrative* carefully because, despite speaking "with bitterness sometimes of the Indians," she does present a human and even fond portrait of Philip, one from which we can get a glimpse of the very considerable man to whom Apess pays tribute.

23. Benjamin Church was the most successful of the leaders of the forces of the United Colonies against Philip. His sympathy with the Indians, his close knowledge of them, and his careful wooing of groups who were either unfriendly to Philip or otherwise uncertain about the war enabled him, as Apess rightly argues, to succeed where most of the other English commanders failed—in part because of their disdain for the Indians and a refusal to consider their ways.

his warriors, in which Philip lost about 130 men killed and wounded; this was in August 1676. But the most horrid act was in taking Philip's son, about ten years of age, and selling him to be a slave away from his father and mother. While I am writing, I can hardly restrain my feelings, to think a people calling themselves Christians should conduct so scandalous, so outrageous, making themselves appear so despicable in the eyes of the Indians; and even now, in this audience, I doubt but there is men honorable enough to despise the conduct of those pretended Christians. And surely none but such as believe they did right will ever go and undertake to celebrate that day of their landing, the 22nd of December. Only look at it; then stop and pause: My fathers came here for liberty themselves, and then they must go and chain that mind, that image they professed to serve, not content to rob and cheat the poor ignorant Indians but must take one of the king's sons and make a slave of him. Gentlemen and ladies, I blush at these tales, if you do not, especially when they professed to be a free and humane people. Yes, they did; they took a part of my tribe and sold them to the Spaniards in Bermuda, and many others;[24] and then on the Sabbath day, these people would gather themselves together and say that God is no respecter of persons; while the divines would pour forth, "He says that he loves God and hates his brother is a liar, and the truth is not in him"—and at the same time they hating and selling their fellow men in bondage. And there is no manner of doubt but that all my countrymen would have been enslaved if they had tamely submitted. But no sooner would they butcher every white man that come in their way, and even put an end to their own wives and children, and that was all that prevented them from being slaves; yes, *all*. It was not the good will of those holy Pilgrims that prevented. No. But I would speak, and I could wish it might be like the voice of thunder, that it might be heard afar off, even to the ends of the earth. He that will advocate slavery is worse than a beast, is a being devoid of shame, and has gathered around him the most corrupt and debasing principles in the world; and I care not whether he be a minister or member of any church in the world—no, not excepting the head men of the nation. And he that will not set his face against its corrupt principles is a coward and not worthy of being numbered among men and Christians—and conduct, too, that libels the laws of the country, and the word of God, that men profess to believe in.

After Philip had his wife and son taken, sorrow filled his heart, but notwithstanding, as determined as ever to be revenged, though [he] was

24. At the end of the Pequot War of 1637 the English sold a number of Pequots, men, women, and children, into slavery in Bermuda as part of their determination to wipe out the culture so they would never again be at risk of being challenged by it. The Pequots on Bermuda, though long out of touch with their New England brethren, have maintained a somewhat distinctive cultural identity to the present.

pursued by the duped Indians and Church into a swamp, one of the men proposing to Philip that he had better make peace with the enemy, upon which he slew him upon the spot. And the Pilgrims, being also repulsed by Philip, were forced to retreat with the loss of one man in particular, whose name was Thomas Lucas, of Plymouth. We rather suspect that he was some related to Lucas and Hedge, who made their famous speeches against the poor Marshpees, in 1834, in the Legislature, in Boston, against freeing them from slavery that their fathers, the Pilgrims, had made of them for years.

Philip's forces had now become very small, so many having been duped away by the whites and killed that it was now easy surrounding him. There-fore, upon the 12th of August, Captain Church surrounded the swamp where Philip and his men had encamped, early in the morning, before they had risen, doubtless led on by an Indian who was either compelled or hired to turn traitor. Church had now placed his guard so that it was impossible for Philip to escape without being shot. It is doubtful, however, whether they would have taken him if he had not been surprised. Suffice it to say, however, this was the case. A sorrowful morning to the poor Indians, to lose such a valuable man. When coming out of the swamp, he was fired upon by an Indian and killed dead upon the spot.

I rejoice that it was even so, that the Pilgrims did not have the pleasure of tormenting him. The white man's gun, missing fire, lost the honor of killing the truly great man, Philip. The place where Philip fell was very muddy. Upon this news, the Pilgrims gave three cheers; then Church ordering his body to be pulled out of the mud, while one of those tenderhearted Christians exclaims, "What a dirty creature he looks like." And we have also Church's speech upon that subject, as follows: "For as much as he has caused many a Pilgrim to lie above ground unburied, to rot, not one of his bones shall be buried." With him fell five of his best and most trusty men, one the son of a chief, who fired the first gun in the war.

Captain Church now orders him to be cut up. Accordingly, he was quartered and hung up upon four trees, his head and one hand given to the Indian who shot him, to carry about to show, at which sight it so overjoyed the Pilgrims that they would give him money for it, and in this way obtained a considerable sum. After which his head was sent to Plymouth and exposed upon a gibbet for twenty years; and his hand to Boston, where it was exhibited in savage triumph; and his mangled body denied a resting place in the tomb, and thus adds the poet,

> Cold with the beast he slew, he sleeps,
> O'er him no filial spirit weeps.

I think that, as a matter of honor, that I can rejoice that no such evil conduct is

"King Philip Dying for His Country" [frontispiece for the 1836 edition of *Eulogy on King Philip*]. This visual depiction is at odds with Apess's own description of how Metacomet died. He went to some length to imply that no whites unaided would ever have captured Metacomet and that they were "doubtless led on by an Indian who was either compelled or hired to turn traitor." Equally important in Apess's reading is that Metacomet be killed not by a white man but by an Indian: "When coming out of the swamp, he was fired upon by an Indian, and killed dead upon the spot." The engraving might represent what Apess emphasized about the whites' role in the mutilation of the great man's corpse: "he was quartered and hung up upon four trees; his head and one hand given to the Indian who shot him, to carry about to show. . . . After which his head was sent to Plymouth, and exposed upon a gibbet for twenty years."

Benjamin Church, the most successful of the colonial officers in the prosecution of the war and the commander of the troops that surrounded Metacomet (one of whose Indian allies shot the fatal bullet), kept a diary, which was later published by his son. Apess's account follows it closely. Courtesy, American Antiquarian Society.

recorded of the Indians, that they never hung up any of the white warriors who were head men. And we add the famous speech of Dr. Increase Mather; he says, during the bloody contest the pious fathers wrestled hard and long with their God, in prayer, that he would prosper their arms and deliver their enemies into their hands. And when upon stated days of prayer the Indians got the advantage, it was considered as a rebuke of divine providence (we suppose the Indian prayed best then), which stimulated them to more ardor.

And on the contrary, when they prevailed they considered it as an immediate interposition in their favor. The Doctor closes thus: "Nor could they, the Pilgrims, cease crying to the Lord against Philip, until they had prayed the bullet through his heart." And in speaking of the slaughter of Philip's people at Narragansett, he says, "We have heard of two and twenty Indian captains slain, all of them, and brought down to hell in one day." Again, in speaking of a chief who had sneered at the Pilgrims' religion, and who had withal added a most hideous blasphemy, "Immediately upon which a bullet took him in the head, and dashed out his brains, sending his cursed soul in a moment among the devils and blasphemers in hell forever." It is true that this language is sickening and is as true as the sun is in the heavens that such language was made use of, and it was a common thing for all the Pilgrims to curse the Indians, according to the order of their priests. It is also wonderful how they prayed, that they should pray the bullet through the Indians' heart and their souls down into hell. If I had any faith in such prayers, I should begin to think that soon we should all be gone. However, if this is the way they pray, that is, bullets through people's hearts, I hope they will not pray for me; I should rather be excused. But to say the least, there is no excuse for their ignorance how to treat their enemies and pray for them. If the Doctor and his people had only turned to the 23rd of Luke, and the 34th verse,[25] and heard the words of their Master, whom they pretended to follow, they would see that their course did utterly condemn them; or the 7th of Acts, and the 60th verse,[26] and heard the language of the pious Stephen, we think it vastly different from the Pilgrims; he prayed: "Lord, lay not this sin to their charge." No curses were heard from these pious martyrs.

I do not hesitate to say that through the prayers, preaching, and examples of those pretended pious has been the foundation of all the slavery and degradation in the American colonies toward colored people. Experience has taught me that this has been a most sorry and wretched doctrine to us poor ignorant Indians. I will mention two or three things to amuse you a little; that is, as I was passing through Connecticut, about 15 years ago, where they are so pious that they kill the cats for killing rats, and whip the beer barrels for working upon the Sabbath, that in a severe cold night, when the face of the earth was one glare of ice, dark and stormy, I called at a man's house to know if I could not stay with him, it being about nine miles to the house where I then lived, and knowing him to be a rich man, and withal very pious, knowing if he had a mind he could do it comfortably, and withal we were both members of

---

25. "Then Jesus said, 'Father, forgive them; for they know not what they do.'"
26. "Then he fell to his knees and cried out in a loud voice, 'Lord, do not hold this sin against them'; and when he said this, he fell asleep."

one church. My reception, however, was almost as cold as the weather, only he did not turn me out-of-doors; if he had, I know not but I should have frozen to death. My situation was a little better than being out, for he allowed a little wood but no bed, because I was an Indian. Another Christian asked me to dine with him and put my dinner behind the door; I thought this a queer compliment indeed.

About two years ago, I called at an inn in Lexington; and a gentleman present, not spying me to be an Indian, began to say they ought to be exterminated. I took it up in our defense, though not boisterous but coolly; and when we came to retire, finding that I was an Indian, he was unwilling to sleep opposite my room for fear of being murdered before morning. We presume his conscience pled guilty. These things I mention to show that the doctrines of the Pilgrims has grown up with the people.

But not to forget Philip and his lady, and his prophecy: It is (that is, 1671), when Philip went to Boston, his clothing was worth nearly one hundred dollars. It is said by some of the writers in those days that their money being so curiously wrought, that neither Jew nor devil could counterfeit it—a high encomium upon Indian arts; and with it they used to adorn their sagamores in a curious manner. It was said that Philip's wife was neatly attired in the Indian style; some of the white females used to call her a proud woman because she would not bow down to them and was so particular in adorning herself. Perhaps, while these ladies were so careful to review the queen, they had forgot that she was truly one of the greatest women there was among them, although not quite so white. But while we censure others for their faults in spending so much time to view their fair and handsome features, whether colored or white, we would remind all the fair sex it is what they all love, that is, jewels and feathers. It was what the Indian women used to love, and still love—and customs, we presume, that the whites brought from their original savage fathers, 1,000 years ago. Every white that knows their own history knows there was not a whit of difference between them and the Indians of their days.

But who was Philip, that made all this display in the world, that put an enlightened nation to flight and won so many battles? It was a son of nature, with nature's talents alone. And who did he have to contend with? With all the combined arts of cultivated talents of the Old and New World. It was like putting one talent against a thousand. And yet Philip, with that, accomplished more than all of them. Yea, he outdid the well-disciplined forces of Greece, under the command of Philip, the Grecian emperor; for he never was enabled to lay such plans of allying the tribes of the earth together, as Philip of Mount Hope did. And even Napoleon patterned after him, in collecting his forces and surprising the enemy. Washington, too, pursued many of his plans in attacking the enemy and thereby enabled him to defeat his antagonists and conquer them. What, then, shall we say? Shall we not do right to say that Philip, with his one talent, outstrips them all with their ten thousand? No warrior, of any age, was ever known to pursue such plans as Philip did. And it is well known that Church and nobody else could have conquered, if his people had not used treachery, which was owing to their ignorance; and after all, it is a fact that it was not the Pilgrims that conquered him; it was Indians. And as to his benevolence, it was very great; no one in history can accuse Philip of being cruel to his conquered foes; that he used them with more hospitality than they, the Pilgrims, did cannot be denied; and that he had knowledge and forethought cannot be denied. As Mr. Gookin,[27] in speaking of Philip, says, that he was a man of good understanding and knowledge in the best things. Mr. Gookin, it appears, was a benevolent man and a friend to Indians.

How deep, then, was the thought of Philip, when he could look from Maine to Georgia, and from the ocean to the lakes, and view with one look all his brethren withering before the more enlightened to come; and how true his prophecy, that the white people would not only cut down their groves but would enslave them. Had the inspiration of Isaiah been there, he could not have been more correct. Our groves and hunting grounds are gone, our dead are dug up, our council fires are put out, and a foundation was laid in the first Legislature to enslave our people, by taking from them all rights, which has been strictly adhered to ever since. Look at the disgraceful laws, disfranchising us as citizens. Look at the treaties made by Congress, all broken. Look at the deep-rooted plans laid, when a territory becomes a state, that after so many years the laws shall be extended over the Indians that live within their boundaries. Yea, every charter that has been given was given with the view of driving the Indians out of the states, or dooming them to become chained under desperate laws, that would make them drag out a miserable life as one chained to the galley; and this is the course that has been pursued for nearly two hundred years. A fire, a canker, created by the Pilgrims from across the Atlantic, to burn and destroy my poor unfortunate brethren, and it cannot be denied. What, then, shall we do? Shall we cease crying and say it is all wrong, or shall we bury the hatchet and those unjust laws and Plymouth Rock together and become friends? And will the sons of the Pilgrims aid in putting out the fire and destroying the canker that will ruin all that their fathers left behind them to destroy? (By this we see how true Philip spoke.) If so, we hope

27. Daniel Gookin was an early attendant among the Indians and of their history. His *Historical Collections of the Indians in New England* was published in 1792.

we shall not hear it said from ministers and church members that we are so good no other people can live with us, as you know it is a common thing for them to say Indians cannot live among Christian people; no, even the president of the United States tells the Indians they cannot live among civilized people, and we want your lands and must have them and will have them. As if he had said to them, "We want your land for our use to speculate upon; it aids us in paying off our national debt and supporting us in Congress to drive you off.

"You see, my red children, that our fathers carried on this scheme of getting your lands for our use, and we have now become rich and powerful; and we have a right to do with you just as we please; we claim to be your fathers. And we think we shall do you a great favor, my dear sons and daughters, to drive you out, to get you away out of the reach of our civilized people, who are cheating you, for we have no law to reach them, we cannot protect you although you be our children. So it is no use, you need not cry, you must go, even if the lions devour you, for we promised the land you have to somebody else long ago, perhaps twenty or thirty years; and we did it without your consent, it is true. But this has been the way our fathers first brought us up, and it is hard to depart from it; therefore, you shall have no protection from us." Now, while we sum up this subject, does it not appear that the cause of all wars from beginning to end was and is for the want of good usage? That the whites have always been the aggressors, and the wars, cruelties, and bloodshed is a job of their own seeking, and not the Indians? Did you ever know of Indians hurting those who was kind to them? No. We have a thousand witnesses to the contrary. Yea, every male and female declare it to be the fact. We often hear of the wars breaking out upon the frontiers, and it is because the same spirit reigns there that reigned here in New England; and wherever there are any Indians, that spirit still reigns; and at present, there is no law to stop it. What, then, is to be done? Let every friend of the Indians now seize the mantle of Liberty and throw it over those burning elements that has spread with such fearful rapidity, and at once extinguish them forever. It is true that now and then a feeble voice has been raised in our favor. Yes, we might speak of distinguished men, but they fall so far short in the minority that it is heard but at a small distance. We want trumpets that sound like thunder, and men to act as though they were going at war with those corrupt and degrading principles that robs one of all rights, merely because he is ignorant and of a little different color. Let us have principles that will give everyone his due; and then shall wars cease, and the weary find rest. Give the Indian his rights, and you may be assured war will cease.

But by this time you have been enabled to see that Philip's prophecy has come to pass; therefore, as a man of natural abilities, I shall pronounce him the greatest man that was ever in America; and so it will stand, until he is proved to the contrary, to the everlasting disgrace of the Pilgrims' fathers.

We will now give you his language in the Lord's Prayer.

Noo-chun kes-uk-qut-tiam-at-am unch koo-we-su-onk, kuk-ket-as-soo-tam-oonk pey-au-moo-utch, keet-te-nan-tam-oo-onk ne nai; ne-ya-ne ke-suk-qutkah oh-ke-it; aos-sa-ma-i-in-ne-an ko-ko-ke-stik-o-da-e nut-as-e-suk-ok-ke fu-tuk-qun-neg; kah ah-quo-an-tam-a-i-in-ne-an num-match-e-se-ong-an-on-ash, ne-match-ene-na-mun wonk neet-ah-quo-antam-au-o-un-non-og nish-noh pasuk noo-na-mortuk-quoh-who-nan, kah chaque sag-kom-pa-ginne-an en qutch-e-het-tu-ong-a-nit, qut poh-qud-wus-sin-ne-an watch match-i-tut.

Having now given historical facts, and an exposition in relation to ancient times, by which we have been enabled to discover the foundation which destroyed our common fathers in their struggle together; it was indeed nothing more than the spirit of avarice and usurpation of power that has brought people in all ages to hate and devour each other. And I cannot, for one moment, look back upon what is past and call it religion. No, it has not the least appearance like it. Do not then wonder, my dear friends, at my bold and unpolished statements, though I do not believe that truth wants any polishing whatever. And I can assure you that I have no design to tell an untruth, but facts alone. Oft have I been surprised at the conduct of those who pretend to be Christians, to see how they were affected toward those who were of a different cast, professing one faith. Yes, the spirit of degradation has always been exercised toward us poor and untaught people. If we cannot read, we can see and feel; and we find no excuse in the Bible for Christians conducting toward us as they do.

It is said that in the Christian's guide, God is merciful, and they that are his followers are like him. How much mercy do you think has been shown toward Indians, their wives, and their children? Not much, we think. No. And ye fathers, I will appeal to you that are white. Have you any regard for your wives and children, for those delicate sons and daughters? Would you like to see them slain and lain in heaps, and their bodies devoured by the vultures and wild beasts of prey, and their bones bleaching in the sun and air, till they molder away or were covered by the falling leaves of the forest, and not resist? No. Your hearts would break with grief, and with all the religion and knowledge you have, it would not impede your force to take vengeance upon your foe that had so cruelly conducted thus, although God has forbid you in so doing. For he has said, "Vengeance is mine, and I will repay." What, then, my dear affectionate friends, can you think of those who have been so often betrayed, routed, and stripped of all they possess, of all their kindred in the flesh? Can or do you think we have no feeling? The speech of Logan,[28] the white man's friend, is no doubt fresh in your memory, that he intended to live and die the friend of the white man; that he always fed them and gave them the best his cabin afforded; and he appealed to them if they had not been well used, to which they never denied. After which they murdered all of his family in cool blood, which roused his passions to be revenged upon the whites. This circumstance is but one in a thousand.

Upon the banks of Ohio, a party of two hundred white warriors, in 1757 or about that time, came across a settlement of Christian Indians and falsely accused them of being warriors, to which they denied, but all to no purpose; they were determined to massacre them all. They, the Indians, then asked liberty to prepare for the fatal hour. The white savages then gave them one hour, as the historian said. They then prayed together; and in tears and cries, upon their knees, begged pardon of each other, of all they had done, after which they informed the white savages that they were now ready. One white man then begun with a mallet and knocked them down and continued his work until he had killed fifteen, with his own hand; then, saying it ached, he gave his commission to another. And thus they continued till they had massacred nearly ninety men, women, and children, all these innocent of any crime. What sad tales are these for us to look upon the massacre of our dear fathers, mothers, brothers, and sisters; and if we speak, we are then called savages for complaining. Our affections for each other are the same as yours; we think as much of ourselves as you do of yourselves. When our children are sick, we do all we can for them; they lie buried deep in our affections; if they die, we remember it long and mourn in after years. Children also cleave to their parents; they look to them for aid; they do the best they know how to do for each other; and when strangers come among us, we use them as well as we know how; we feel honest in whatever we do; we have no desire to offend anyone. But when we are so deceived, it spoils all our confidence in our

28. Logan's speech, made after having his home and family destroyed by the English in 1774, was often quoted in this period as follows: "I appeal to any white to say, if ever he entered Logan's cabin hungry, and he gave him not meat; if ever he came cold and naked, and he clothed him not. During the course of the last long bloody war, Logan remained idle in his cabin, an advocate for peace. Such was my love for the whites that my countrymen pointed as they passed and said, 'Logan is the friend of the white men.' I had even thought to have lived with you, but for the injuries of one man. Col. Cresap, the last spring, in cold blood, and unprovoked, murdered all the relations of Logan; not even sparing my women and children. There runs not a drop of my blood in the veins of any living creature. This called on me for revenge. I have sought it. I have killed many. I have fully glutted my vengeance. For my country, I rejoice at the beams of peace. But do not harbor a thought that mine is the joy of fear. Logan never felt fear. He will not turn on his heel to save his life. Who is there to mourn for Logan?—Not one!"

visitors. And although I can say that I have some dear, good friends among white people, yet I eye them with a jealous eye, for fear they will betray me. Having been deceived so much by them, how can I help it? Being brought up to look upon white people as being enemies and not friends, and by the whites treated as such, who can wonder? Yes, in vain have I looked for the Christian to take me by the hand and bid me welcome to his cabin, as my fathers did them, before we were born; and if they did, it was only to satisfy curiosity and not to look upon me as a man and a Christian. And so all of my people have been treated, whether Christians or not. I say, then, a different course must be pursued, and different laws must be enacted, and all men must operate under one general law. And while you ask yourselves, "What do they, the Indians, want?" you have only to look at the unjust laws made for them and say, "They want what I want," in order to make men of them, good and wholesome citizens. And this plan ought to be pursued by all missionaries or not pursued at all. That is not only to make Christians of us, but men, which plan as yet has never been pursued. And when it is, I will then throw my might upon the side of missions and do what I can to favor it. But this work must begin here first, in New England.

Having now closed, I would say that many thanks is due from me to you, though an unworthy speaker, for your kind attention; and I wish you to understand that we are thankful for every favor; and you and I have to rejoice that we have not to answer for our fathers' crimes; neither shall we do right to charge them one to another. We can only regret it, and flee from it; and from henceforth, let peace and righteousness be written upon our hearts and hands forever, is the wish of a poor Indian.

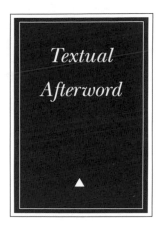

Textual Afterword

▲

In the interest of keeping as clean a reading text as possible, I have kept the editorial notes within each text to a minimum and sought, for the most part, to avoid a comparison therein of the several editions of Apess's books. The most substantial variations occur in the two editions of *A Son of the Forest,* which was considerably revised between the first edition (1829) and the second (1831). *The Experiences of Five Christian Indians* also had two editions, one in 1833, the other in 1837. There are some revisions in the 1837 edition, but the critical and unexplained change is the exclusion of "An Indian's Looking-Glass for the White Man" and the substitution of the brief and bland "An Indian's Thought." The *Eulogy on King Philip* had two editions (1836 and 1837). The second, much condensed from the first, seems intended to correspond to the shortened version of the eulogy that he delivered later the same January. *The Increase of the Kingdom of Christ* and *The Indians: The Ten Lost Tribes* (1831) and *Indian Nullification of the Unconstitutional Laws of Massachusetts Relative to the Marshpee Tribe* (1835) had only one edition each. *Indian Nullification* has its particular textual uncertainties because of the question of the nature of the collaboration between Apess and William G. Snelling and of who is responsible for what in the book.

Although I have done a line-by-line comparison between editions in each of those cases where there was more than one, I have not, regrettably, been able to compare more than a single copy of each. Those familiar with early nineteenth-century American publishing practices will recognize the problem. It is entirely possible that important variations occurred, for example, from copy to copy of the 1829 edition of *A Son of the Forest.* For the sake of textual scholars who might, in the future, find it important to compare copies of Apess's books, I should specify the source of each of the copytexts I used for this edition. The 1829 edition of *A Son of the Forest* is in Special Collections, Robert Frost Library, Amherst College, Amherst, Massachusetts. The 1831 edition is in the collection of the American Antiquarian Society, Worcester, Massachusetts. The 1833 edition of *The Experiences of Five Christian Indians* is at the Library of Congress, Washington, DC, and does not include the fuller title of some copies of the first edition: *The Experiences of Five Christian Indians of the Pequot Tribe; or, An Indian's Looking-Glass for the White Man;* the 1837 edition, under its slightly different title of *Experience of Five Christian Indians,* is at the Newberry Library, Chicago, Illinois. I was able to compare the 1829 and the 1831 editions of *A Son* held by the American Antiquarian Society, but I have not checked its 1829 edition against the Amherst College copy. I have also checked the 1833 (the title page of which also does not include *An Indian's Looking-Glass*) and 1837 editions of *The Experiences* at the American Antiquarian Society against each other but have not closely collated them with the copies I have used for this collection. *Indian Nullification* has been edited from the copy at the American Antiquarian Society, as has the *Eulogy on King Philip* (and there I checked the two editions against each other). *The Increase of the Kingdom of Christ* is at the State Historical Society of Wisconsin, Madison.

For those titles that appeared in more than one edition, I have made somewhat different editorial decisions as to which edition to use here. Only in one case, *A Son of the Forest,* have I chosen to use the later edition, partly because Apess chose both to revise it substantially and to advertise it as "revised and corrected," something he did not do with either of the later works that had second editions. I also think that his revisions may illustrate significant changes in his skills and tactics as a writer. And *A Son of the Forest* was more extensively and complexly revised than any of his other publications. For these reasons most of this afterword will be devoted to a review of those revisions, indexed by chapter, page, and paragraph (e.g., I: 3, #3) to the 1831 edition, so that anyone who is interested may see the variations I consider significant in the copies of the 1829 and 1831 editions that I have examined. These revisions are noteworthy, too, in that the 1829 *Son of the Forest,* though more roughly written, is often more direct, detailed, and even poignant in its awkwardnesses. At several places it also contains a fuller account of particular experiences than does the 1831 edition which, as I have mentioned in my notes, excises the entire account of Apess's bitter resignation from the Methodist Episcopal church and his joining the Protestant Methodists and being ordained by them in 1829. Reproduced in this afterword, keyed to the text of the 1831 edition, are all substantive excisions from the 1829 edition, along with summaries of other more subtle revisions, which I believe may indicate Apess's intentions as a writer. However, until I, or other scholars, can collate several copies of each of the editions, any conclusion about what the differences between editions indicate can only be tentative and speculative.

In the case of both *The Experiences of Five Christian Indians* and the *Eulogy on King Philip* I have chosen the first editions as copytexts because each is considerably fuller than the second. In the 1837 edition of *Experience*, not only is "An Indian's Looking-Glass for the White Man" cut in its entirety, but a paragraph is cut from the account of Aunt Sally George. There are also occasional alterations in word order and slight differences in punctuation.

The *Eulogy on King Philip* requires no annotation here, though I could note what was excised for the second edition. Since Apess's revisions were more in the nature of condensation than any alteration of meaning and tone, I do not think it essential to specify these changes. Lincoln Dexter's useful facsimile edition of the *Eulogy* remains in print, reasonably available from many libraries, and marks with sidebars what was cut from the second edition. Scholars who wish to examine the differences in the two editions of the *Eulogy* may thus do so with a minimum of inconvenience.

In each text I have silently corrected clear misspellings and typographical errors. Apess's punctuation has been modernized, which generally means greatly simplified, although I have occasionally added punctuation to help clarify his meaning; and I have changed the British spellings of words such as "neighbourhood," which were common enough in American writing of the period but which were consistently substituted in the 1831 edition for the American spelling used in the 1829 edition of *A Son of the Forest*. I have also altered the spelling of "Pequod," which Apess commonly used, to "Pequot," the spelling now agreed on by both scholars and contemporary Pequots. On the other hand, I have retained "Marshpee," instead of adopting the consistent modern usage for both the people and the place of "Mashpees" and "Mashpee." I have avoided the temptation to blend together elements of different editions in all cases but one, because to do so would be to create a text out of my fashioning of Apess. The institution of authorship in the early nineteenth century had its ample complexities and, though we may never discover all the collaborative forms it took in Apess's case, it seems best to leave the texts as close to their original printed state as possible. To do otherwise is to risk blurring whatever textual evidence might tell us of these practices.

The one exception is that in *The Experiences of Five Christian Indians* I have adopted Apess's careful correction in the 1837 edition of his name from "Apes" to "Apess," a change I have made throughout all his texts unless, as often in *Indian Nullification*, contemporary historical documents are quoted or excerpted, in which case I have left his name as spelled therein. I have also followed Apess's correction in the 1837 edition of *Experience* of the spelling of Anne Wampy's name (Wamply in the 1833 edition), because it is corroborated in all the documents in the Connecticut Historical Society on which her name appears and in John Avery's *History of the Town of Ledyard*.

The other textual differences between the two editions of *The Experiences*, being too few, I hope, to distract the reader, are recorded in my notes to the text.

SIGNIFICANT VARIATIONS BETWEEN THE TWO EDITIONS OF *A SON OF THE FOREST* (1829 AND 1831)

Preface

The preface to the 1829 edition reads entirely differently: "To the Reader. In offering to the public this little volume, containing the leading features in the eventful life of a Son of the Forest, the author would in the outset bespeak for the work a favorable reception. It was written under many disadvantages, and the bare acknowledgement of his entire want of a common education, will, he hopes, be a sufficient apology for any inaccuracies that may occur."

Apess's characterization of the changes in the 1831 edition is accurate. There are more chapter divisions, nine instead of the six of the 1829 edition; the writing is generally more grammatical and polished; altogether, there is evidence of thorough and deliberate revision in every part of the book.

Chapter I

I: 3–5. The opening is significantly changed from the 1829 edition by Apess's rearrangement of the order of exposition in the first three pages. In 1829 his birth is not announced until the third page of the chapter, whereas in 1831 he literally begins the autobiography with it. By beginning, in 1829, with "William Apes . . . is a native of the American soil, and a descendant of one of the principal chiefs of the Pequot Tribe" and continuing with a brief exposition of the history of the tribe, Apess emphasizes his membership in the collectivity of Native Americans and individuates himself only after establishing this context.

I: 4, #3. In the 1829 edition Apess included these interesting details: "My grandfather was a white and married a female attached to the royal family: she was fair and beautiful. How nearly she was connected with the king I cannot tell; but without doubt some degree of affinity subsisted between them. I have frequently heard my grandmother talk about it, and as nearly as I can tell, she was his grand or great-grand daughter." This is the only place in any of his autobiographical writings in which Apess indicates he had any relationship with his paternal grandparents. He makes no mention of where they lived or of what his grandmother's name was.

I: 4, #3. In the 1831 edition Apess adds, after "to which he was maternally connected," "He was well received . . ."

I: 5, #1. Instead of "Now my grandparents were not the best people in the world . . . ," the 1829 edition reads: "My grandfather and his companion were not the best people in the world . . ."

I: 5, #1. After "in a most cruel manner," the 1829 edition includes: "My two brothers and two sisters also lived with them, and we were always kept in continual dread or torment. My father and mother made baskets which they would sell to the whites, or exchange for those articles only, which were absolutely necessary to keep soul and body in a state of unity." The present conclusion to the paragraph is his addition of 1831 to replace this excised passage.

I: 5, #2. In 1831 but not in the 1829 edition, Apess adds, in reference to the cold potato, that "of this at times we were denied." The account of the white neighbors and the frozen milk is somewhat and interestingly amplified in the 1829 version: "Some of our white neighbors however taking pity on us, frequently brought us frozen milk, which my mother would make into porridge, and we would all lap it down like so many hungry dogs, and thought ourselves well off when the calls of hunger were thus satisfied." In general, the 1831 version of these incidents rearranges and edits the 1829 text so as to compress and focus it.

I: 5, #2. The 1829 edition reads: "my sister almost died of hunger," not "one of my sisters." The 1829 reference to a singular sister is compatible with the known birth records for the family in a way the 1831 reference is not. Also, in 1829 the apologia in this paragraph is more direct and appealing: "Think not dear reader that I have exaggerated—I assure you that I have not—I merely relate this circumstance to show you how intense our sufferings were."

I: 5, #3. Small details are changed in the account of the beating, but two seem especially important. In 1831 Apess adds that the beating occurred "shortly after my father left us," thus implying that his mother had left first. In 1829 he states baldly that on the day of the beating his grandmother "got too much rum from the whites."

I: 5, #3. The 1829 edition says simply: "I was only four years of age, and of course could not take care of himself." (Might the inadvertent "himself" suggest the hand of another in the manuscript, perhaps taking it down in dictation?) In the 1831 edition, this is interestingly revised to: "I was then only four years of age, and consequently could not take care of, or defend myself— and I was equally unable to seek safety in flight."

I: 6, #1. In the 1829 edition, there are additional details: "My uncle took and hid me away from them, and secreted me until the next day. When they found me, and discovered how dangerously I had been injured, they were compelled to have recourse to the whites." But in the 1831 edition, Mr. Furman is identified by name. Another significant excision is his reference to himself in the 1829 edition, as in "The Experience of the Missionary," as "a poor little Indian boy," a phrase that is removed throughout the 1831 edition.

I: 6. In many small details this whole page is much revised. Two important omissions: "I was then put among good Christian people, called the Close Order, who used me as tenderly as though I had been one of the elect, or one of their sons." And 6, #2. In the 1829 edition this long passage continues from where the paragraph ends in the 1831 edition: "Before, in order to satisfy the cravings of nature, I would frequently run away to the whites and beg food, who invariably supplied my wants in that respect, as they looked upon me with pity; considering me a poor helpless and neglected child.

"I recollect that on one occasion I had been out begging for food, and in returning home lost my way. After the darkness of night had closed upon me, I came to a large brook surround by woods, where I sat down and began to cry; at last some persons heard my lamentations, and came to my assistance. By them I was directed in the right way so that I reached home in safety, to catch a little more trouble, that is, to get a sound flagellation for begging for victuals, to keep me alive. Hence, I call my deliverance from such a scene of suffering, the Providence of God." Getting lost in the woods becomes established as a motif earlier in the 1829 edition than in the 1831. Another effect of this longer account is that his next paragraph, "In view of this treatment, I presume that the reader will exclaim, 'what savages your grandparents were . . . ,'" becomes all the more disarming in the 1829 edition because he appears to give the rhetorical question even more justification than in the 1831 edition.

I: 6, #3. The 1831 edition becomes much stronger by revising "I attribute it [his grandparents' behavior] in part to the whites" to "I attribute it in a great measure to the whites." At the end of the paragraph, in 1831, is added a more defensive comment, in what would seem evident response to someone's criticism of the 1829 version: "I do not make this statement [that whites are to blame] in order to justify those who had treated me so unkindly, but simply to show, that inasmuch as I was thus treated only when they were under the influence of spirituous liquor, that the whites were justly chargeable with at least some portion of my sufferings."

I: 7, #1. The tone and the greater fullness of the account in 1829 provide a considerably different sense of Apess's feeling for the Furmans than the revisions in the 1831 edition permit: "He [Mr. Furman] was a cooper by trade, and employed himself in his business when he was not engaged in working on his farm. They had become very fond of me, and as I could not be satisfied to leave them, as I loved them with the strength of filial love, he at last concluded to keep me until I was of age. According to the spirit of the indentures, if I mistake not, I was to have so much instruction as to be able to read and write, and at the expiration of my apprenticeship they were to furnish me with two suits of clothes. They used me with the utmost kindness—I had enough to eat and to wear—and everything in short to make me comfortable."

Chapter II

II: 8, #1 & 2. The opening two paragraphs are not in the 1829 edition, which begins, instead, with the question of infants' feelings.

II: 8, #5. The account of his conversation with Mrs. Furman and his first experience of a religious meeting is unchanged from the 1829 edition with one intriguing exception. In 1831, in his thanksgiving for being instructed on how to act in church, he says, "and to this very day I bless God for such wholesome and timely instruction," and the sentence ends. In the 1829 edition, it continues, "and the man who taught me these things," a change, like others in the 1831 edition, that eliminates or much diminishes signs of his intense emotional ties to the Furmans.

II: 10, #2. In the 1829 edition, unlike that of 1831, after Apess has run back to the Furmans to escape the berry-picking party, he says that "*we* sallied out in quest of the absent party, whom *we* found searching for me among the bushes." The substitution in 1831 of "he" for "we" heightens his sense of fear and alienation from his own people.

Chapter III

In the 1829 edition the break for chapter III comes much later in the narrative—at the place where, in the 1831 edition, chapter IV begins, after he has enrolled in the New York militia—so that in the 1829 edition chapter II includes his entire experience from the time he is taken from his grandparents through his running away from the William Williamses to New York and, shortly thereafter, being recruited in the militia bound for the Canadian front in the War of 1812.

III: 12, #2. The 1829 edition removes the ambiguity of who "They" were who "observed this change in my conduct" and "were filled with unbelief." "They" are "the people in the neighborhood."

III: 13, #1. In discussing the death of Mrs. Furman's mother there is this note of sympathy in the 1829 edition and not in that of 1831: "I was much concerned for the family and mourned with them." Its excision makes the passage seem much more self-centered.

III: 13, #2. After his comment that "neither had those about me ever witnessed any disorder of the kind," there is a further description in the 1829 edition of his strange malady: "Whenever I would try to lay down, it would seem as if something was choking me to death, and if I attempted to sit up, the wind would rise in my throat and nearly strangle me."

III: 19, #1. The people are turned from "bad" in 1829 to "wicked" in 1831.

Chapter IV

By making a new chapter where he does in the 1831 edition, after his conversion experience, Apess underscores both its significance and the role of the Williamses and other "respectables" in frustrating his growth in his newfound faith. They become, by analogy, simultaneously anti-Christian and anti-Indian. The "ladies and gentlemen" of southeastern Connecticut are associated with "the evil one," so clearly are they the agents who ridicule Apess's community of faithful and disbelieve his professions as well as disdaining his people and thus his identity.

IV: 22, #1. The first sentence of this paragraph begins thus in the 1829 edition: "The devil, I believe, was in the chamber maid . . ."

Chapter V

Chapter III in the 1829 edition begins where chapter V does in the 1831 edition.

Chapter VI

The chapter break is unchanged; only the chapter numbers differ between the two editions. Few revisions of any kind were made in chapters V through IX, a fact which may make those few of some importance.

VI: 32, #2. This paragraph ends in the 1829 edition with the additional phrase, "and they held all things in common." The whole presentation of this almost idyllic land of his brethren in Canada is complex, for Apess seems to want to damn all the effects of Euro-American culture, including that of the religion of the Christian missionaries. But then he pulls back to distinguish, as he does not always do in his later writing, between corrupt missionaries and those who might preach the Gospel in its true spirit. Removing the phrase "and they held all things in common" is to make them seem more assimilable and less alien to sympathetic white readers, a point that plays directly into the opening argument of the next chapter, in both editions, that those who claim that the Indians cannot be civilized, that the experiment has been tried and failed, have "sinister motives," that is, the taking of Native American lands.

Chapter VII

VII: 36, #1. In the midst of his account of again becoming a drunkard, Apess has the fascinating additional detail in the 1829 edition that when he went to New Haven "the first thing I knew I found myself in a dance house. This did not suit me." A "dance house" in a port city like New Haven in this period could have been a brothel.

This chapter ends with the incident with Mr. Geer in the 1831 edition. By breaking it at this point, Apess further emphasizes his determination not to be treated like a slave and "to have my rights this time, and forever after." This ending also enables him to focus the next chapter on his return to the ways of Christ. The 1829 edition simply continues at this point, so that the return to Connecticut and the return to Christian practice are both in the same chapter.

Chapter VIII

VIII: 38, #1. Chapter VI in the 1829 edition begins after the incident when Apess "swore a horrid oath." In the revision, by avoiding the break there, the whole chapter focuses on the decisive turn in his religious vocation when he returns, once and for all, to following in God's ways.

Chapter IX

The final chapter in the 1831 edition is devoted to Apess's coming to awareness of his call to preach the Gospel, his beginning as a prayer leader in Methodist class meetings, then exhorting, and finally preaching. The eventual outcome is his ordination as a minister in the Protestant Methodist church.

IX: 45, #3. After "why, he placed me under censure," Apess removes "Now his name was M———." This is the first of several substantial revisions in the 1831 edition that remove virtually all trace of his disputes with the Methodist Episcopal church. He seems to have been especially concerned to erase his nearly explicit naming of those who oppressed him. Although here he uses only the initial, presumably anyone among the Methodist Episcopal elders and bishops would know who this was.

IX: 45, #3. At the end of the paragraph he removes, after the present last sentence, "my candid reader can place a proper estimate on such procedures." The implication is that any true evangelical will recognize such respect for the power of bishops as a regrettable remnant of papist practices in the Protestant church.

IX: 46, #1. In 1829 Apess continued, after "had nearly proved the ruin of my soul," "and I have no doubt but that many souls are lost by having the s[hackles] placed on them by t[yrannical] ministers." I regret that I have been unable to fill in the ellipses definitively.

IX: 50, #1. At the end of this paragraph begin the major cuts from the 1829 edition: "But before I proceed to narrate the doings of the conference, I will inform the reader what the Lord did for me in the mean time." This excision signals the entire omission of Apess's experience with the Conference in Albany, New York, in April 1829.

IX: 51, #1. After the paragraph about his success in Watervliet in awakening sinners and reclaiming backsliders, the following has been removed: "My wife and my little son had taken board with one of the brethren. About this time I left the circuit for a spell, as I had some business at Hudson which I had to transact in person, and I felt no uneasiness about my family, presuming that they would be made comfortable as I paid for their board. On my return, I found my wife quite unwell—and I pretty soon learned that the treatment she received was very unkind, if not cruel—not fit for a dog, and what surprised me was that the woman of the house where my poor wife boarded, and who treated her so bad, *professed* to be a Methodist. She was even so cruel as to refuse a light in her room, and when medicines were ordered, she had to take them without sweetening, or anything whatsoever to make them palatable. No wonder, therefore, that on my return, I found my wife dissatisfied with her situation and anxious for a change. But she was unwell, and I endeavored to pacify her, believing it improper to remove her at that season, on account of the deep snow and intense cold. So we concluded to stay a little longer and I purchased some few necessaries for my wife. However we soon moved to Troy, in order to get out of such an unlucky dilemma; my wife was extremely rejoiced to get out of their fangs."

IX: 51, #3. After this paragraph in the 1829 edition comes the entire account of what happened at the April Conference and after. There is no trace of it in the 1831 edition; indeed, there is no mention that he left the Methodist Episcopal church to join the newly forming Protestant Methodist church, which would and did ordain him sometime later in 1829 or early in 1830: "At the time appointed the meeting was held. A preparatory sermon was preached by the presiding elder—the conference was called, and the business of the circuit was attended to. My case came up in course, and the president (the P[residing] E[lder]) asked me if I thought the Lord had called me to preach, to which I answered in the affirmative. I was then questioned as to my faith in the doctrine and discipline of the church, and whether I would conform to the same, to which I assented. An opportunity was now given to the brethren to ask me any questions they thought proper; one only was asked, and that was, how long I had been converted. I then withdrew from the room to give them an opportunity to decide on my application. My mind was perfectly easy. After I was out about half an hour, Brother Strong came out to inform me that the conference would rather that I should take an exhorter's license again, as they knew nothing of my character, but all the while they knew nothing against me. Now let it be observed that I had not only presented a certificate of my good standing, but also a number of recommendations of character and usefulness, from several well-known itinerant ministers of the connection, and as they could find nothing against me, it appeared singular to me, that men who had thrown open their doors to the poor Indian, and had often sat with apparent profit under his ministry, could thus oppose me, and cry out 'We do not know you.' I told the brother who gave me this information that if they did not comply, that they would hinder my doing that work which the Lord required of me. He then returned, and after deliberating about fifteen minutes, I was called in, when the presiding elder (Stratton) said. 'This conference do not see fit to grant your request—are you willing to receive an exhorter's license again?' To which I hastily replied in the negative. After considering the subject a little, I spoke to Brother Covel, the preacher in charge, and he advised me to take an exhorter's relation: *a license was readily granted me to exhort*. Now, one single question which I will leave with the reader to answer, viz: As this conference refused me a license to preach on the ground that its members did not know enough of my character, had they any right to grant a license to exhort, at the *same time* that they refused one to preach?

"Shortly after, I met Brother Covel and his colleague in Albany and informed them that it was my intention not to present the papers I had received to the *Episcopal Methodists*, as it was my intention to join the *Methodist Society*. They appeared somewhat surprised and endeavored to persuade me to remain where I was, that is, not to leave the church. I told them that my mind was fully made up—there was too much oppression for me in the old church, and that a disposition prevailed to keep the local preachers down. They then asked me why I had said that I believed in the doctrine and discipline.—I replied that I did fully believe in the *doctrine*, but that I had taken exceptions to the *discipline;* that while I was with them and they did not stretch the chords of government too tight, I was contented, but I could not go the whole, and pin my faith and hope, as many of them did, entirely upon their government. They appeared to think that I had done wrong in saying that I would be governed by the discipline—but I could not see in the same glass, for as long as I continued in *that* church I conformed to *its* rules; and as this law was not continuous in its nature, whenever I ceased to be a member of that church, its binding and distinctive law, touching my *person* and my conduct became *dead*—it had no farther of future jurisdiction over me. I cannot think that I violated any holy law, by promising obedience to the rules of the Methodist Episcopal Church, and redeeming that pledge so long as I continued in the jurisdiction of its law. But I will tell the reader that in the judgment of charity, I think they (the members of the conference) broke the commandments of God; Brother Covel said, 'As it has come to this, I will tell you that it was mentioned (much to your prejudice in the conference) that your wife in a *hasty way*, or unguarded moment, had said that she would expose you.' Now this had a bad appearance—the term of itself is bad enough, as it implies guilt, or offense of some kind—and this slang was retailed and descanted on in the conference, and what do you think they did with it?—It was raised as a barrier between me and a license from *men* professedly religious to preach the Gospel; and I should never have known the cause if I had not left the church!!! I told Brother Covel that I could not believe that my wife had ever said it, and on asking her she had no recollection of saying any such thing, and I believe her. I ascertained that the report came from the woman who was so cruel to my wife, while I was absent at Hudson, as related before, she was angry with us, and sought, I think, to do us evil. Should not the members of the conference have informed me of this circumstance, and by neglecting to do so, did they not violate the commandment of God, which says explicitly, 'If thou hast ought against thy brother, go and be reconciled to thy brother!' I presume that every candid reader will say, if they credit my statement, that they violated this sacred and imperative obligation.

"I will not charge this to the members of the church at large, and condemn *all* for the unkind and improper conduct of a *few*. Far be such a course from me. If their life corresponds with the Gospel, I can take them by the hand, and I hope they may all contend for that faith which *was once delivered to the saints;* and wherever I see the image of Christ, there I can [find] fellowship—and where my lot is now cast I think I can be more useful in promoting the glory of God. It is a great trial for me to be [a] *mouth for God*—to stand up before my fellow men, and warn them to flee the wrath to come. I do it to please God and not man, from a settled conviction that it is my duty, and that I cannot remain in the enjoyment of religion if I neglect it.

"I pray God to banish all prejudice from my mind—that it may die forever should be the prayer of every person; but I suspect that this will not be the case with many of my brethren in the Methodist Episcopal Church—they do not like this separation which is contrary to their former sayings, for when I joined them, it was on the express condition that I should stay with them as long as I liked them—and I did so. I have frequently heard them say, when a member was dissatisfied, or could enjoy himself better elsewhere, that they would hold up both hands for him to go—but let him go and join another church, and what a storm they will raise; and in fact, they had rather that those who leave them should remain without the pales of any church rather than join the Methodist Society. It is greatly to be lamented that a spirit like this is felt, and exhibited. I feel a great deal happier in the *new* than I did in the *old* church—the government of the first is founded on *republican,* while that of the latter is founded on *monarchial* principles—and surely in this land where the tree of liberty has been nourished by the blood of thousands, we have good cause to contend for *mutual rights,* more especially as the Lord himself *died to make us free!* I rejoice sincerely in the spread of the principles of civil and religious liberty—may they ever be found 'hand in hand' accomplishing the designs of God, in promoting the welfare of mankind. If these blessed principles prevail, sectarianism will lose its influence, and the image of God in his members will be a sufficient passport to all Christian privileges; and all the followers of the most high will unite together in singing the song of praise, 'Glory to God in the highest,' etc."

The issues at play here can only seem obscure to most readers in the twentieth century. The American Methodists, in 1784, earlier than all other denominations, organized themselves into a national entity. The spread of revivalism, especially its great stirring up on the western frontier in 1797 with the Second Great Awakening, fostered within all the established churches great impatience with any form of hierarchical authority. Many wished to approximate what they believed was the egalitarian organization of the early Christian communities. As a result, schisms and splits of every kind occurred within every denomination. To these the Methodists were perhaps no more vulnerable than others, but from early in the nineteenth century many of its members chafed against the rule of bishops and the authority of the Conference. These agitations were at their height at exactly the time Apess found his vocation as a preacher. A number of Methodist preachers were expelled from the church in the 1820s, a large enough number to begin to form new and, initially, entirely locally based Methodist societies. The Methodist Episcopals were, then, especially sensitive about preachers who showed signs of disregarding the settled forms of authority. A number of times before he requested a license to preach, Apess had simply ignored the rules, and it was, I suspect, for this reason that the Conference refused his request and asked him to wait longer. His account suggests his awareness that this was probably the cause; however, his story about the abuse of the woman in the lodging house and his reminders to the reader of his status as an Indian also indicate that he suspected, or wanted his readers to do so, that the denial of his request for a license to preach might have been simply one more expression of white racism. The various Methodist societies that had formed in opposition to the Methodist Episcopal hierarchy united in 1830 under the name of the Protestant Methodists, and it was to this new denomination that Apess joined himself.

Bibliographic Essay

▲

WORKS BY WILLIAM APESS

Apess first published *A Son of the Forest: The Experience of William Apes, a Native of the Forest, Comprising a Notice of the Pequot Tribe of Indians* (New York: By the author, 1829). His revised edition of it appeared in 1831 as *A Son of the Forest: The Experience of William Apes, a Native of the Forest*, 2nd ed., rev. and corr. (New York: By the author; G. F. Bunce, Printer). *The Increase of the Kingdom of Christ: A Sermon* (New York: By the author; G. F. Bunce, Printer, 1831) was his next publication. It also includes *The Indians: The Ten Lost Tribes*, though this does not appear on the title page. *The Experiences of Five Christian Indians of the Pequot Tribe* (Boston: By the author; James B. Dow, Printer, 1833), appears in the two copies I have examined with just this title, though other copies of the first edition have the title (*The Experiences of Five Christian Indians of the Pequot Tribe; or, An Indian's Looking-Glass for the White Man.* "The Experience of the Missionary," on the basis of internal evidence, seems to have been the first piece of Apess's writing that has survived. For the 1833 edition have the title *The Experiences of Five Christian Indians of the Pequot Tribe; or, An Indian's 1827–29*, when he seems first to have composed it. It is also possible that others of the lives in the *Experiences*, as well as "An Indian's Looking-Glass" were written considerably before 1833. Somewhat revised and edited and without "An Indian's Looking-Glass," the book was republished in 1837 as *Experience of Five Christian Indians of the Pequot Tribe* (Boston, 1837). It is with this edition that Apess alters the spelling of his name on the title page and throughout the text. His *Indian Nullification of the Unconstitutional Laws of Massachusetts Relative to the Marshpee Tribe; or, The Pretended Riot Explained* (Boston: Jonathan Howe, 1835) has "William Apes, an Indian and Preacher of the Gospel" on its title page. The *Eulogy on King Philip, as Pronounced at the Odeon, in Federal Street, Boston* (Boston: By the author, 1836) provides the full text of the address he delivered on January 8, 1836. The second edition of the *Eulogy on King Philip* has the same title but changes the spelling of his name to Apess. It appeared in 1837. Considerably shorter than the first edition, it seems to be the shortened version of the original speech, which he gave on request on January 26, 1836. Both editions have the following on the title page: "Who shall stand in after years in this famous temple, and declare that Indians are not men? If men, then heirs to the same inheritance."

None of Apess's writing was reprinted in book form until the late twentieth century. I have not done a systematic search of nineteenth-century periodicals and anthologies to see if he was ever noticed or reprinted in those venues. In this century, "An Indian's Looking-Glass for the White Man" has twice been reprinted, first in Bernd Peyer, ed., *The Elders Wrote: An Anthology of Early Prose by North American Indians, 1768–1931* (Berlin: Dietrich Reimer, 1982), and most recently in Paul Lauter et al., eds., *The Heath Anthology of American Literature*, vol. 1 (Lexington, MA: Heath,

1990). The headnote by A. LaVonne Brown Ruoff, a scholar of Native American literature, is reliable and reasonably comprehensive. It was in Peyer's anthology that I first encountered and became interested in Apess. Two facsimile editions have also appeared: The first was *Indian Nullification* (Stansfordville, NY: Coleman, 1979), with a foreword by Jack Campisi. The second, which remains in print, though somewhat hard to find, is the *Eulogy on King Philip* (Brookfield, MA: Dexter, 1985). For this edition Dexter provides a short and somewhat inaccurate biographical sketch of the Apesses, some annotation of the text, a bibliography, and very helpfully marks with sidebars those passages excised in the 1837 edition.

Works on Apess

So far very little has been written about Apess. Ernest Sutherland Bates wrote a knowledgeable and comprehensive entry for the *Dictionary of American Biography* (1928), 1:323, but despite his appreciation of Apess's writing few scholars seem to have noticed. James D. Hart, *The Oxford Companion to American Literature*, 5th ed. (New York: Oxford University Press, 1983), also has a short history. Robert E. Spiller et al., eds., *Literary History of the United States*, 3rd ed. rev. (New York: Macmillan, 1963), until recently the standard history, has no mention of Apess. Roy Harvey Pearce, *Savagism and Civilization: A Study of the Indian and the American Mind* (1953; rev. ed., Berkeley: University of California Press, 1988), mentions *A Son of the Forest* in two footnotes. Kim McQuaid, "William Apes, A Pequot: An Indian Reformer in the Jackson Era," *New England Quarterly* 50 (1977): 605–25, is the first substantial examination of Apess's life and work. In many ways it is a remarkable essay for its range and its appreciation of Apess as a reformer, writer, and thinker, but most of all McQuaid deserves notice for being the first to see (and when he was only a graduate student) that this neglected man was important. There are a few mistakes: Apess was left in the care not of his "paternal grandparents" but of his maternal ones; he was beaten not by his "white grandfather" but by his Indian grandmother; but McQuaid's basic research stands. All who have since worked on Apess are deeply in his debt. Beginning in the early 1980s, perhaps because of McQuaid's essay, Apess gradually received more mention and, eventually, some extended critical discussion. Two scholars, H. David Brumble III and Arnold Krupat, both students of Native American literature with a particular interest in autobiography, have, in different ways, opened out the conversation. Brumble's *An Annotated Bibliography of American Indian and Eskimo Autobiographies* (Lincoln: University of Nebraska Press, 1981) is a crucial research tool for anyone interested in this field. But it is Krupat's *For Those Who Come After: A Study of Native American Autobiography* (Berkeley: University of California Press, 1985) that brings to Native American autobiography the theoretical sophistication and critical intelligence it deserves. Though that book does not discuss Apess, Krupat devotes considerable attention to him in *The Voice in the Margin: Native American Literature and the Canon* (Berkeley: University of California Press, 1989), esp. 143–49 and 171–82, and in an essay, "Native American Autobiography and the Synecdochic Self," in Paul John Eakin, ed., *American Autobiography: Retrospect and Prospect* (Madison: University of Wisconsin Press, 1991). H. David Brumble III, *American Indian Autobiography* (Berkeley: University of California Press, 1988), though it only occasionally mentions Apess, is, nonetheless, an important study for anyone interested in Apess and in Native American literature. David Murray, *Forked Tongues: Speech, Writing and Representation in North American Indian Texts* (Bloomington: Indiana University Press, 1991), did not, regrettably, become available until after I had finished this book. Murray writes extensively on Apess and, to my pleasure, his readings and mine echo and reinforce each other. The entire book adds substantially to the scant critical literature on Native American writing and should be regarded as indispensable. A. LaVonne Brown Ruoff should also be mentioned for her interest in and work on Apess, which has been gathered together in her long-awaited essay "Three Nineteenth-Century American-Indian Autobiographers," in Ruoff and Jerry W. Ward, Jr., eds., *Redefining American Literary History* (New York: MLA, 1990). Her contributions to the field, and to my work, also include several extensive bibliographies, the latest of which is *American Indian Literatures: An Introduction, Bibliographic Review, and Selected Bibliography* (New York: MLA, 1990). Donald M. Nielsen, "The Mashpee Indian Revolt of 1833," *New England Quarterly* 58 (1985): 400–20, is thus far the definitive historical account and contains invaluable information on Apess.

Donald B. Smith, *Sacred Feathers: The Reverend Peter Jones (Kahkewaquonaby) & the Mississauga Indians* (Lincoln: University of Nebraska Press, 1987), while it has no direct reference to Apess, is a model study of his Native American contemporary and, as such, illuminates the conditions both men struggled with to become ministers, writers, and defenders of their people.

Apess has also recently been noticed in an unexpected place, which encourages the hope that knowledge of him may spread beyond a few scholars: A short essay, "The Real Savages?" in *Scholastic Search* 19, no. 1 (1990): 18–19, focuses on Apess's *Eulogy on King Philip*. The publication is one of many from the Scholastic Magazine Company, which supplies elementary and high schools all over the country with its weekly and monthly magazines.

Although the scholarly literature on the Mashpees is neither abundant nor dependably focused on Apess, much of it is of interest to anyone studying Apess. Apart from Nielsen's essay, Francis G. Hutchins, *Mashpee: The Story of Cape Cod's Indian Town* (West Franklin, NH: Amarta Press, 1979), though not a very astute history, has valuable information that appears nowhere else. Although Rona Sue Mazer, "Town and Tribe in Conflict: A Study of Local-Level Politics in Mashpee, Massachusetts" (Ph.D. diss., Columbia University, 1980); Paul Brodeur, *Restitution: The Land Claims of the Mashpee, Passamaquoddy, and Penobscot Indians of New England* (Boston: Northeastern University Press, 1985); and James Clifford, "Identity in Mashpee," in *The Predicament of Culture: Twentieth-Century Ethnography, Literature, and Art* (Cambridge, MA: Harvard University Press, 1988), 277–346, all focus on contemporary Mashpee, each has material on Apess and, perhaps more importantly, illustrates the unbroken continuity of New England Native Americans' struggles to maintain their cultures and their rights.

THE HISTORY AND CULTURE OF THE PEQUOTS AND OTHER NEW ENGLAND NATIVE AMERICANS

Much remains unstudied and unknown, but there are a number of books with which to begin, all of which are particularly valuable. For most purposes, one might best start with *Handbook of North American Indians*, vol. 15, *Northeast*, ed. Bruce G. Trigger (Washington, DC: Smithsonian Institution, 1978), a model for reference books. Howard S. Russell, *Indian New England Before the Mayflower* (Hanover, NH: University Press of New England, 1980), is an interesting and useful book for a newcomer to the field. William S. Simmons, *Spirit of the New England Tribes: Indian History and Folklore, 1620–1984* (Hanover, NH: University Press of New England, 1986), is more scholarly, no less readable, and a book indispensable for any serious student of the subject. Neal Salisbury, *Manitou and Providence: Indians, Europeans, and the Making of New England, 1500–1643* (New York: Oxford University Press, 1982), and *The Indians of New England: A Critical Bibliography* (Bloomington: Indiana University Press, 1982), are equally essential. So, too, is the older and more polemical, but important, Francis Jennings, *The Invasion of America: Indians, Colonialism, and the Cant of Conquest* (Chapel Hill: University of North Carolina Press, 1975). Anything James Axtell writes is thought-provoking and interesting. No serious student of the Northeast would be without, especially, *The European and the Indian: Essays in the Ethnohistory of Colonial North America* (New York: Oxford University Press, 1981), and *The Invasion Within: The Contest of Cultures in*

Colonial North America (New York: Oxford University Press, 1985), although *After Columbus: Essays in the Ethnohistory of Colonial North America* (New York: Oxford University Press, 1988) also has some valuable essays. His *Indian Peoples of Eastern America: A Documentary History of the Sexes* (New York: Oxford University Press, 1981) is a superb example of the art of anthologizing historical documents, and on a subject that has so far received very little scholarly attention. Laurel Ulrich, *Good Wives: Image and Reality in the Lives of Women in Northern New England, 1650–1750* (New York: Oxford University Press, 1983), is a valuable exception and, additionally, is unusual among American historians for attending the lives of the Euro-American and the Native American as though each was integral to American history. William Cronon, *Changes in the Land: Indians, Colonists, and the Ecology of New England* (New York: Hill and Wang, 1983), is not only fascinating, page after page, but evidence that some historians can still write like angels. Colin G. Calloway has recently published two fine books that greatly advance the study of Native Americans in northern New England: *The Western Abenakis of Vermont, 1600–1800: War, Migration, and the Survival of an Indian People* (Norman: University of Oklahoma Press, 1990), and an excellent collection of documents: *Dawnland Encounters: Indians and Europeans in Northern New England* (Hanover, NH: University Press of New England, 1991). The best single source for the Pequots is now Laurence M. Hauptman and James D. Wherry, eds., *The Pequots in Southern New England: The Fall and Rise of an American Indian Nation* (Norman: University of Oklahoma Press, 1990). Ann McMullen and Russell G. Handsman, eds., *A Key into the Language of Woodsplint Baskets* (Washington, CT: American Indian Archaeological Institute, 1987), offers many rich insights into a set of vital and persisting cultural practices among Native Americans in southern and northern New England. Among older scholarly writers on southern New England, Frank G. Speck remains important: *Decorative Arts of the Indian Tribes of Connecticut*, Anthropological Series 10, Memoirs of the Canadian Geological Survey, no. 75 (Ottawa: Canadian Department of Mines, 1915); *The Functions of Wampum among the Eastern Algonkian*, Memoirs of the American Anthropology Association, no. 6 (1919); "Native Tribes and Dialects of Connecticut: A Mohegan–Pequot Diary," in *Forty-third Annual Report of the Bureau of American Ethnology, 1925–1926* (Washington, DC: Government Printing Office, 1928); and *Territorial Subdivisions and Boundaries of the Wampanoag, Massachusett, and Nauset Indians*, Indian Notes and Monographs 44 (New York: Museum of the American Indian, Heye Foundation, 1928).

Autobiographical and Literary Studies

For a general introduction to the study of Native American literature, Andrew Wiget's *Native American Literature* (Boston: Twayne, 1985) is well-written and concise. Kenneth Lincoln's *Native American Renaissance* (Berkeley: University of California Press, 1983) is perceptive and focuses, for the most part, on contemporary Native American writing. Three critical anthologies, however, collect much of the most sophisticated and interesting work recently done on this large subject: Brian Swann, ed., *Smoothing the Ground: Essays on Native American Oral Literature* (Berkeley: University of California Press, 1983); Brian Swann and Arnold Krupat, eds., *Recovering the Word: Essays on Native American Literature* (Berkeley: University of California Press, 1987); and Gerald Vizenor, ed., *Narrative Chance: Postmodern Discourse on Native American Indian Literatures* (Albuquerque: University of New Mexico Press, 1989). Another resource for the interested reader might well be, as it is for so many aspects of Native American written and oral expression, Paula Gunn Allen, ed., *Studies in American Indian Literature: Critical Essays and Course Designs* (New York: MLA, 1983).

For Native American autobiographies, I have already mentioned Brumble, *An Annotated Bibliography* and his *American Indian Autobiography*, and Krupat, *For Those Who Come After*. Krupat distinguishes between American Indian autobiographies, by which he means the large genre of autobiographies as told by Indians to, mostly, Euro-American editors, anthropologists, and writers, and those autobiographies actually written by American Indians. Apess's is the first autobiography written by an Indian, whereas the other genre has a longer history, beginning at least as early as the conversion accounts set down in the seventeenth century by Puritan missionaries. Gretchen M. Bataille and Kathleen Mullen Sands, *American Indian Women: Telling Their Lives* (Lincoln: University of Nebraska Press, 1984), is also important. Brian Swann and Arnold Krupat, eds., *I Tell You Now: Autobiographical Essays by Native American Writers* (Lincoln: University of Nebraska Press, 1987), has material fascinating in its own right but of special interest for Native Americans' own ideas about the anomalies of the autobiographical act within the "Native" part of their cultural heritage.

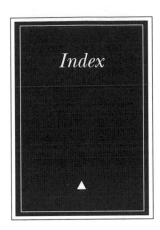

Index